Other Kaplan Books Related to Law School Admissions:

LSAT

LSAT with CD-ROM

Law School Admissions Adviser

LSAT* 180

by Eric Goodman
and the Staff of Kaplan, Inc.

Simon & Schuster

NEW YORK · LONDON · SINGAPORE · SYDNEY · TORONTO

*LSAT is a registered trademark of Law School Admission Council, which is not affiliated with this product.

Kaplan Publishing
Published by Simon & Schuster
1230 Avenue of the Americas
New York, NY 10020
Copyright © 2001, by Kaplan, Inc.

From "Symbiotic Stars," by Minas Kafatos and Andrew G. Michalistisianos. Copyright © 1984 by *SCIENTIFIC AMERICAN, Inc.* All rights reserved.

"Must Virtue Be Taught?" by Thomas D. Eisele, *Journal of Legal Education*, vol. 37, December 1987. Copyright © 1987. Reprinted by permission of the author and *Journal of Legal Education*.

From "Mitochondrial DNA" by Leslie A. Grivell. Copyright © 1983 by *SCIENTIFIC AMERICAN, Inc.* All rights reserved.

"The Evolutionary Tradition in Jurisprudence," by E. Donald Elliott. Copyright © 1985 by the Directors of the Columbia Law Review Association, Inc. All right reserved. This article originally appeared in 85 Column. L. Rev. 39 (1985). Reprinted by permission.

Project Editor: Megan Duffy
Contributing Editors: Trent Anderson and Albert Chen
Cover Design: Cheung Tai
Interior Page Design and Production: Laurel Douglas
Production Editor: Maude Spekes
Production Manager: Michael Shevlin
Executive Editor: Del Franz
Editorial Coordinator: Déa Alessandro

Special thanks to Ben Paris

Manufactured in the United States of America
Published simultaneously in Canada

March 2002
10 9 8 7 6 5 4 3 2 1
ISBN: 0-7432-2435-3

Table of Contents

Dear Student:

For more than 60 years, Kaplan has been helping students meet their academic and admissions goals. More than three million students have passed through our doors, and as their evaluations of our courses have repeatedly shown, one thing stands out that sets Kaplan apart from the rest: our teachers.

We have long known that our outstanding teaching staff is Kaplan's most important asset. Throughout the years we have committed ourselves to finding expert, enthusiastic, and engaging teachers for every Kaplan course. That's why we interview only those candidates who scored high on the test they are to teach and from this pool select only the most promising candidates: individuals who are enthusiastic about helping students reach their goals. All prospective teachers complete an intensive Kaplan training, and from ongoing observations, evaluations, and reviews of student feedback, they get even better as they teach.

The knowledge and experience that our teachers have acquired from working with students like you—about standardized tests, study habits, test panic, and more—is something we'd like to share outside of the classroom. We're pleased to incorporate the wisdom, tips, and inspiration of Kaplan's teachers in this test-prep guide so that you may benefit from the best we have to offer. I hope you find their expertise useful in your quest for academic success. If you decide you'd also like to work with our first-rate instructors in person, give us a call at (800) KAP-TEST.

Sincerely,

Jonathan Grayer
President and CEO, Kaplan, Inc.

About the Author

Eric Goodman began teaching and writing for Kaplan two years after graduating from Cornell University. For over 12 years Eric has written courses, software, and books that have helped thousands of test takers master the LSAT, GMAT, and GRE. As an instructional designer, he has also authored online courses and computer-based simulations in the fields of economics, corporate training, and e-commerce. Eric lives in New York City with his wife Cathy and daughters Memphis and Dasha.

The Perfect Score

Ah, *perfection* . . .

We humans are a demanding bunch. We don't bound out of bed in the morning aspiring to mediocrity, but rather striving for *perfection*. The *perfect* mate. The *perfect* job. The *perfect* shoes to go with the *perfect* outfit. We head to the beach on a *perfect* summer day to find the *perfect* spot to get the *perfect* tan.

Webster's defines perfection as "the quality or state of being complete and correct in every way, conforming to a standard or ideal with no omissions, errors, flaws or extraneous elements."

The LSAT test makers define perfection as a score of 180.

If LSAT perfection is what you're after, then you've come to the right place. We at Kaplan have been training test takers to ace the LSAT for over 30 years. We understand your desire for the highest possible score. For those of you shooting for the moon, we salute your quest for perfection. The *perfect* LSAT score. The *perfect* law school. The *perfect* career. Do we have the *perfect* book for you? You bet we do. You're holding it in your hands.

WHO SHOULD USE THIS BOOK

We should warn you up front: This book is not for the faint at heart. It is comprised exclusively of examples of the toughest material you're likely to see on the LSAT. No easy stuff, no run-of-the-mill strategies—just killer games, passages, and questions, complete with Kaplan's proven techniques to help you transcend "above average" and enter the rarefied arena of LSAT elite. If you're entertaining the notion of pulling off the perfect 180, then you're going to have to face down the most brutal material the LSAT test makers have to offer, and we've compiled an entire book of such questions to help you do just that. Even if a perfect score is not your immediate goal, diligent practice with the difficult material in this book can help develop your skills and raise your score. If you're looking for a more fundamental introduction to the LSAT, or practice with questions ranging from easy to difficult, then we recommend working through the traditional Kaplan LSAT book as a prerequisite for the highly challenging material contained in this volume.

HOW TO USE THIS BOOK

This book is divided into three sections corresponding to the three scored question types contained on the LSAT: Logic Games, Logical Reasoning, and Reading Comprehension. (The Writing Sample is not included in this book because it doesn't contribute to your 120–180 score, and no Writing Sample prompt is written to be any more difficult than any other.) Each section of the book provides detailed guidelines on how to make the most of the material. Jump right to the section that gives you the most trouble, or work through the sections in the order presented— it's up to you. You'll notice that the habits and thought processes of top test takers are highlighted throughout the book. Study these thoroughly, and look to make these effective techniques your own. No matter what you do, try not to overload; remember, this is dense, complicated material, and not representative of the range of difficulty you'll see on test day. One thing's for sure: If you can ace this stuff, the real thing will be a breeze.

Good luck, and enjoy!

section one

LOGIC GAMES

CHAPTER ONE

The Logic Games Challenge

Exactly five guests—August, Dasha, Henry, Memphis, and Nicholas—arrive at a Super Bowl party. No guest arrives at the same time as any other guest. Each guest brings exactly one of the following items to the party: beer, chicken wings, ice cream, pizza, or soda. Each guest brings a different item. Exactly two guests arrive between Henry's arrival and the arrival of the guest who brings chicken wings. The guest who brings the ice cream arrives fourth. Nicholas arrives after Dasha. Memphis is the only guest to arrive between the arrival of the guest who brings chicken wings and the arrival of the guest who brings beer.

If Memphis brings ice cream to the party, then the order of guest arrivals and the item each brings would be precisely determined if it were also known that . . .

Huh? What the . . . ?!

Who knows? Who cares?

Well, for starters, the admission board at most accredited law schools does—and if you're reading these words, chances are you're someone who's looking to impress that particular crowd. To most law school admission officers, the LSAT Logic Games section is not some arbitrary exercise in tortured logic (as it no doubt may seem to some test takers), but rather a realistic test of the kinds of reasoning skills necessary to think through complex legal issues and situations. Many test takers, understandably so, find Logic Games to be the most challenging section on the LSAT. If we round up examples of the most difficult games the LSAT has to offer, as we've done for you in this book, then arguably we'd have a collection of some of the most demanding material in all of standardized testing. How's that for motivation!

Above-average difficulty games appear often on the LSAT. Unfortunately, the advice to "just skip the tough ones and do the best you can on the others" simply won't cut it for those aspiring to enter 180 territory. If that's your quest, then you have no choice but to muster all your skill, speed, and stamina to face these killers head-on. For those of you simply interested in improving your gaming techniques, cutting your teeth on the hardest games will certainly help you to hone your skills and raise your score.

It is in this spirit, and with these objectives in mind, that we present the Logic Games in this book for both your edification and enjoyment.

USING THE LOGIC GAMES IN THIS BOOK

The Logic Games in this book are broken up into four categories:

Super-Charged Standards

Time Warps

Volatile Mixtures

What the . . . ?

Together, these represent the full range of the types of difficult games you may encounter on your test. You'll find descriptions of these categories at the beginning of each chapter. You're probably best off working your way up to the games in the final chapter, which, as the name implies, are particularly nasty. You can do the games one at a time before reviewing the explanations, or plow through a bunch before coming up for air—really, it's up to you. A few suggestions, however:

Observe timing guidelines. You'll surely get the right answers eventually if you take an hour to do each game. The point, however, is how well you can handle the tough stuff under true LSAT conditions. You don't have to go so far as to hiring a proctor to stand over you with a timepiece (although that probably couldn't hurt), but make sure you spend no more than nine and one-half minutes per game. Four games in 35 minutes allows for roughly eight and one-half minutes per game, but considering the difficulty level of these, it's reasonable to allow a little extra time.

Read the explanations. Review the keys to each game, comparing your own approach to the insights provided. Notice whether you are consistently coming up with the same deductions as us, and recognizing the same factors that cut these killers down to size. Take special note of the thought processes and habits of 180 test takers highlighted throughout the explanations.

Have fun. Remember, these are games. Games are meant to be fun.

A 180 test taker approaches the Logic Games section with good humor, a positive attitude, and enthusiasm for the challenge of facing the toughest material the test makers have to offer.

Oh, by the way: Regarding the Super Bowl feast, one way the arrival order and items brought by the guests would be fully known is if August shows up with the pizza.

But you already figured that out . . . right?

CHAPTER TWO

Supercharged Standards

What makes a Logic Game hard? Certainly games that contain very unusual game actions are difficult to manage. Games that consist of a mixture of multiple game actions can also be cumbersome and trying. Have no fear: You'll see plenty of examples of these later on. But some standard, textbook-style Logic Games that seem fairly straightforward at first glance, by virtue of complicating elements, must be counted among the killer elite as well.

Each of the games in this first Logic Games chapter involves one of three single standard game actions. Each is structured around a single task, what we at Kaplan call sequencing, grouping, or matching. For this reason, they may not seem as nasty as what's to come later, but beware: while these games represent standard LSAT fare, they are nonetheless deceptively difficult. Miss one key deduction or interpretation, and you're in for a long haul.

Keep your guard up. Don't let yourself be blindsided by a slick, unassuming, supercharged standard.

LOGIC GAME 1

A committee is scheduling the events for a town's Summer Festival. The festival lasts three days, from Friday to Sunday. The eight events to be scheduled are a bake sale, a craft show, a dance contest, a fireworks display, an obstacle course, a parade, a relay race, and a softball game. Each event will be held during a single time period—morning, afternoon, or evening—on a single day, and no two events will be held during the same time period. The following conditions must also be met:

The softball game must be held after the parade.

The relay race must be held in the morning.

The fireworks display must be held on Saturday evening.

The bake sale must be held in the evening and before the parade.

The dance contest must not be held on Friday.

The craft show is the first event held.

1. Which one of the following is a complete and accurate list of the events that could be held on Saturday morning?

   (A) dance contest, obstacle course, parade
   (B) dance contest, parade, softball game
   (C) dance contest, obstacle course, parade, relay race
   (D) dance contest, obstacle course, parade, relay race, softball game
   (E) obstacle course, parade, relay race

2. If no event is held on Sunday morning, then which one of the following events must be held on Friday afternoon?

   (A) the bake sale
   (B) the dance contest
   (C) the obstacle course
   (D) the relay race
   (E) the softball game

3. If the relay race is held on the same day as the softball game, each of the following could be true EXCEPT:

   (A) Exactly three events are held between the craft show and the dance contest.
   (B) Exactly two events are held between the dance contest and the relay race.
   (C) Exactly one event is held between the obstacle course and the parade.
   (D) Exactly one event is held between the fireworks display and the relay race.
   (E) Exactly three events are held between the parade and the softball game.

4. If the softball game is held on a day before the dance contest and at the same time of day, then how many different schedules of events are possible?

   (A) 2
   (B) 3
   (C) 4
   (D) 5
   (E) 6

5. If exactly two events are held between the craft show and the softball game, then the scheduling of how many events can be precisely determined?

   (A) 3
   (B) 4
   (C) 5
   (D) 6
   (E) 7

6. Each of the following is an acceptable schedule of events held on Sunday EXCEPT:

	Morning	Afternoon	Evening
(A)	no event	softball game	obstacle course
(B)	parade	softball game	no event
(C)	relay race	no event	dance contest
(D)	relay race	softball game	dance contest
(E)	softball game	obstacle course	dance contest

Logic Game 1: Summer Festival

What Makes It Difficult

We're asked to schedule a set of events into a standard calendar sequence: three consecutive days, three time slots per day. On the face of it, this is not an uncommon or particularly unusual request from the LSAT test makers. But there are lots of events to juggle (no, juggling is not one of them)—eight to be precise—and nine possible time slots for them. That means that one time slot must be empty, which surely complicates matters. Even the names of the events are cumbersome; all but the parade contain two words instead of the usual one word used to denote entities.

On top of that, the rules are no picnic (or should we say, "day at a summer festival"?). There are six total, which is a bit on the high side. Only one of the six rules, Rule 3, is concrete: The fireworks are definitely held on Saturday night. (Well, that actually makes sense—who'd want to watch fireworks in the morning or afternoon?) Rule 6 can be especially misleading. Usually, the first event in a sequence falls automatically into the first time slot, but here, the existence of an empty slot (designated in the questions as "no event") foils any attempt to definitively schedule the craft show for Friday morning.

As if that's not enough, the questions themselves are somewhat complex. Question 3's "could be true EXCEPT," a complex task to begin with, is made more difficult by the numerical nature of its choices. And placing a "how many schedules are possible" question immediately before a "how many events can be precisely determined" question (questions 4 and 5) can lead to confusion as well.

All in all, there's no doubt that we'd rather be at the festival playing softball, dancing, and stuffing ourselves at the bake sale than puzzling over how to schedule the events.

> The 180 test taker finds ways to make even the most difficult games manageable.

Perhaps you noticed the following points that cut this one down to size.

Keys to the Game

B must be on Friday evening. Rule 4 states that B is in the evening, and before P. So B can't possibly be on Sunday evening, since that would leave no room for P. And given that F is on Saturday evening, the only available evening for B is Friday evening.

B . . . P . . . S must obtain at all times. That's simply a combination of Rules 1 and 4.

R is on either Saturday morning or Sunday morning. That's because R must be in the morning (Rule 2), but cannot be the first event (Rule 6).

If the empty slot is not on Friday, then Friday's schedule is C, O, B, in that order. That's because every remaining event other than O is on Saturday or Sunday.

If the empty slot is on Friday, then C can be on Friday morning or afternoon. Those who automatically place C on Friday morning are in for a rude awakening.

Answers and Explanations

1. C   2. C   3. D   4. B   5. C   6. A

1. C

This question is surely worth postponing, since we're likely to find possible scenarios in other questions that will help us eliminate wrong choices. In the scenario for question 2, R must be on Saturday morning, so (A) and (B), which don't include R, must be wrong. In question 3, D could be on Saturday morning, so (E), which doesn't include D, can't be right. That leaves (C) and (D), and the only thing that distinguishes them is that (D) includes S. Could S be on Saturday morning? No way: With B always on Friday evening, placing S on Saturday morning would violate the required B . . . P . . . S ordering. So (C) is correct.

> A 180 test taker postpones working on "complete and accurate" questions that appear early in the question set until helpful information is generated from later questions.

2. C

As we already deduced, if the empty slot is on Saturday or Sunday, then C, O, and B must be the events scheduled for Friday. So C is in the morning (Rule 6), B is in the evening (our earlier deduction), and O is in the afternoon. There you have it.

> A 180 test taker knows that almost every Logic Game battle is won or lost before the first question is answered, and that spending time up front making deductions and recognizing restrictions on the entities' behavior translates into quick and easy points later on.

3. D

If R and S are on the same day, which day could that be? Neither one can go on Friday, but how about Saturday? Nope: If R and S join F on Saturday, there will be no room for P. So R and S must be on Sunday, with R in the morning (Rule 2). That's all we know for sure going into the choices. "Each could be true EXCEPT" means that the right answer must be false. Let's find the violator:

(A), (C) If C is on Friday morning and D is on Saturday afternoon, O, B, and P can come between them, so (A) could be true and we can cross it off. This schedule proves also that (C) could be true, with B serving as the one event between O and P.

(B), (E) Switch D and P in the ordering described in (A) and you'll see that (B) is possible. Furthermore, if we move O to Sunday and round out the schedule with a Sunday consisting of R, O, and S, in that order, then we see that that (E) could be true as well.

(D) This is the one we want: We deduced that in this scenario, R must be held on Sunday morning, and with F always on Saturday night, no events can be held between them.

4. B

Here's an abstract question stem that requires translation. If S is on the day before D, and we know that S is on either Saturday or Sunday, then S must be on Saturday and D must be on Sunday. Next we're told that S and D are at the same time of day. Well, it can't be evening, since F is on Saturday evening. It can't be morning either, since R must be on either Saturday or Sunday morning. So S and D must be on Saturday and Sunday afternoons, respectively. Now the only place for P is Saturday morning, and the only place for R is on Sunday morning. So here's what we're sure of so far:

	Fri	Sat	Sun
Morn		P	R
Aft		S	D
Eve	B	F	

Now, in order to figure out the number of possible schedules based on this state of affairs, we'll have to consider the remaining entities: C, O, and the empty slot. Let's look at C's situation: C can be on Friday morning or afternoon. If it's on Friday morning, then there are two possibilities: O on Friday afternoon and no event Sunday evening, or vice versa. If, however, C is on Friday afternoon, then there will be no event on Friday morning and O will have to be on Sunday evening. So that's one more possibility, giving us a total of three, choice (B). Note that we could have done the same analysis for O or the empty slot and come up with the same result.

5. C

Here's another toughie. Two events are between C and S. Well, P must be before S (Rule 1) and so if S were on Sunday, then at least three events would come between C and S—B, P, and F. So P and S must both be on Saturday, P in the morning and S in the afternoon. The empty time slot must be on Friday, since C must be the first event and we can't have anything breaking up our C-B-P-S combination, lest we violate the mandate in the stem. P on Saturday morning places R on Sunday morning, leaving O and D to float between the afternoon and evening slots on Sunday. Here's how that looks:

	Fri	Sat	Sun
Morn	C/empty	P	R
Aft	C/empty	S	O/D
Eve	B	F	O/D

So what *don't* we know?

A 180 test taker is crystal clear on the difference between what's known in a particular situation and what's left undetermined.

O and D split the last two slots, but we can't tell their order. We also can't place C definitively. C could be either first or second, depending on where the empty slot goes. So five events can be precisely determined, choice (C).

6. A

We have not much choice here but to test out the choices. The correct answer will be the choice that cannot be the list of events on Sunday. We shouldn't expect, nor do we find, an obvious rule violation concerning the events listed in the choices, so the correct answer will force a violation on another day. Ugh. Luckily, (A) is the winner: Placing the empty slot, S, and O on Sunday forces R, P, and D onto Saturday, but F is already on Saturday, so there isn't room for all of them. On test day, you would simply mark (A) and move on.

A 180 test taker never wastes time on remaining answer choices in Logic Games once she has found a choice that works.

Just for the record:

(B) The only available morning slot for R is on Saturday, the only available post-Friday slot for D is Saturday afternoon, and C and O occupy the first two slots. That's okay, so (B) is wrong.

(C) would force P and S into the first two slots on Saturday, with C and O in the first two slots on Friday. No problem there.

(D) leaves us more acceptable options. P and O can split the first two slots on Saturday, and C goes on Friday with the empty slot, in either order. There are a few more acceptable arrangements here, but you need to find only one to disprove (D).

(E) Again, the only available morning slot for R is on Saturday, the only available post-Friday slot for P is Saturday afternoon, and C and the empty time period occupy the first two slots. That's fine, so (E) is wrong.

What's Next?

Pure sequencing games (that is, those that don't involve other game actions) are generally the most straightforward games on the Logic Games section. This one is quite possibly as difficult a straight sequencing game as you're likely to see on the LSAT. Let's move on to see what kinds of challenges are presented in another standard Logic Game type, grouping games of distribution.

Break out your homemaking skills. It's time for a little interior design.

LOGIC GAME 2

An interior designer is hired to decorate the bedroom, den, and living room of a client's house. The designer has exactly eight items with which to work: a lamp, mirror, painting, rug, sofa, table, vase, and wardrobe. Each item is placed in one of the three rooms, in accordance with the following conditions:

At least one item is placed in each room.

The mirror and the wardrobe are placed in the same room.

The painting and the vase are placed in different rooms.

The sofa is placed in the living room.

A different number of items is placed in each of the three rooms.

1. Which one of the following could represent the complete contents of the bedroom and the den, respectively?

    (A) *bedroom*: lamp; *den*: mirror, rug, table, wardrobe
    (B) *bedroom*: lamp, rug; *den*: vase
    (C) *bedroom*: lamp, painting, rug, table; *den*: mirror, wardrobe
    (D) *bedroom*: mirror, painting, wardrobe; *den*: lamp, rug, sofa, table
    (E) *bedroom*: painting; *den*: lamp, mirror, rug, table, vase

2. Which one of the following must be true?

    (A) Exactly one item is placed in one of the rooms.
    (B) Exactly two items are placed in one of the rooms.
    (C) Exactly three items are placed in one of the rooms.
    (D) Exactly four items are placed in one of the rooms.
    (E) Exactly five items are placed in one of the rooms.

3. If the mirror and the wardrobe are the only items placed in the bedroom, then each of the following must be true EXCEPT:

    (A) The lamp is placed in the living room.
    (B) Exactly one item is placed in the den.
    (C) The rug is placed in the same room as the table.
    (D) Exactly five items are placed in the living room.
    (E) The vase is placed in the den.

4. If more items are placed in the den than in the living room, and if the mirror is placed in the same room as the sofa, then which one of the following is impossible?

    (A) The vase is placed in the bedroom.
    (B) The painting is placed in the bedroom.
    (C) The table is placed in the den.
    (D) The rug is placed in the bedroom.
    (E) The vase is placed in the den.

5. If the living room contains fewer items than each of the other rooms, then which one of the following CANNOT be the complete contents of the den?

    (A) lamp, vase
    (B) mirror, rug, table, vase, wardrobe
    (C) mirror, table, wardrobe
    (D) painting, rug, table
    (E) table, vase

6. If the lamp, the painting, and the mirror are each placed in a different room, and if the wardrobe, the lamp, and the sofa are each placed in a different room, then all of the following pairs of items could be placed in the same room EXCEPT:

    (A) the lamp and the vase
    (B) the mirror and the rug
    (C) the painting and the rug
    (D) the rug and the table
    (E) the sofa and the table

Logic Game 2: House Decoration

What Makes It Difficult

The task in this one is to distribute furniture items among three rooms of a house. Again, the action of this LSAT standard is quite straightforward, so the difficulty must lie elsewhere. Like the Summer Festival game, there are eight entities, but one, the sofa, is safely tucked away in the living room, and the mirror and wardrobe are a constant pair. So keeping track of the items is not as tough as it may appear at first glance.

The real complexity lies with the numbers that govern the game—specifically, as given in Rules 1 and 5. Each room gets at least one item, but the three rooms each contain a different number of items. That sounds simple enough, but those who failed to deduce the implication of these rules were in for a lot of trouble.

On top of that, the questions themselves are long and complex. Question 1, the "acceptability" question, presents the items of only two rooms, the bedroom and den, which, on the face of it, may seem easier than if it included the living room items as well. Not so—leaving off the living room forces us to figure out what's in there in order to eliminate some choices. Furthermore, two questions contain multiple hypotheticals (new information posited in the form of an "if-then" statement), and the last four questions in the set are presented in the negative: two "EXCEPT" questions, one "which is impossible?" question, and one "which CANNOT be true?" challenge.

Makes us wonder why the bloody client didn't just buy the house already decorated. As always, there are ways into the game that top test takers find to ease their burden:

Keys to the Game

There are only two possible numerical breakdowns of items in rooms—groups of 1, 2, and 5 or groups of 1, 3, and 4. This is derived from a combination of Rules 1 and 5. There's simply no other way for three different numbers to add up to eight.

> A 180 test taker mercilessly interrogates numerical information to determine what must, could, or cannot be true.

P and V must always be split up, but they are functionally identical. This may not occur to many people, but realizing that there are many situations in which either P or V could suffice (as long as they're split up) allows one to simply throw them into rooms instead of agonizing over the next step. This is especially helpful in rounding out various groupings and, as we'll see, eliminating wrong answer choices.

L, R, and T are not governed by any rules. These are the entities that need to be accounted for after the rules are enacted. Understanding their function as "floaters" (or "free agents," if you prefer) helps us to manage the large pool of entities.

> A 180 test taker takes note of a game's "floaters" and has them close at hand when fleshing out possible groupings.

Answers and Explanations

1. B   2. A   3. E   4. D   5. C   6. A

1. B

Checking the rules directly against the choices works up to a point: Rule 2 eliminates (E), which has the mirror flying solo in the den without the wardrobe, and Rule 4 eliminates (D), which attempts to place the sofa in the den. The other wrong choices, as alluded to above, require consideration of the room not listed on the page in order to disqualify them. The grouping listed in (A) would leave the painting and vase together in the living room, in violation of Rule 4. As for (C), placing four items in the bedroom and two in the den would leave two in the living room, in violation of Rule 5. The problem with these two choices is not what's on the page, but what's left over for the living room, which makes this Acceptability question a bit more difficult than the norm. (B) works fine, living room and all.

2. A

A direct and welcome payoff of our numbers deduction. No matter which number scenario is exhibited (1, 2, 5 or 1, 3, 4), one of the rooms must get exactly one item, choice (A). The possible 1,2,5 breakdown kills (C) and (D); the possibility of 1, 3, 4 kills (B) and (E).

> A 180 test taker recognizes that the existence of a "must be true" question with no new information suggests that something may be deducible from the setup. If he made a key deduction up front, he scans the choices for his deduction or a direct implication of it. If he didn't make a deduction up front, he uses such a "must be true" question to help him find it, and then uses the deduction for the rest of the game.

3. E

Since only (and therefore exactly) two items, M and W, are in the bedroom, we know we must be dealing with the 1, 2, 5 grouping. Since the painting and the vase must be separate, one of them (we don't know which) will go in the den, while the other will join the sofa in the living room. But now that there are two items in both the bedroom and the living room, the den must be the room with only one. Floaters L, R, and T must therefore go in the living room, making that the room with five items. Everything is definitively placed except for P and V. (E) is the answer: The vase *could be* in the den, but it could also be in the living room while the painting is in the den.

> A 180 test taker understands that the answer to a "must be true EXCEPT" question will often be a statement that is only possibly true, and therefore gravitates instinctually toward choices containing entities whose status is uncertain.

4. D

There are two new pieces of information, and the second one is more concrete: The mirror goes with the sofa, which means it, as well as its perennial partner, the wardrobe, must go in the living room.

A 180 test taker deals with the most concrete pieces of information first, realizing that building a foundation makes it easier to handle the more abstract *if*-clauses.

Now the numerical information: Since there must be more items in the den than in the living room, the living room, with three items already, is now maxed out. This also tells us that we must be dealing with the 1, 3, 4 breakdown, so we know there must be four items in the den, leaving one item in the bedroom. Again, we must break up the painting and vase, so one will be the single item in the bedroom while the other will join "free agents" L, R, and T in the den. Here's what we have:

Bedroom	Den	Living Rm
(P or V)	(P or V) L R T	S M W

(A) and (B) are two sides of the same coin; both the vase and painting could be in the bedroom, but neither need be. As we pointed out above, there's no functional difference between them.

A 180 test taker recognizes interchangeable entities, and uses that knowledge to both flesh out arrangements and eliminate wrong answer choices.

(C) must be true. (D) cannot be true, so it's the correct answer. (E) could be true.

5. C

The major keys to the game can be applied here in rapid succession to wrestle this one down to the ground. Due to the 1, 2, 5 or 1, 3, 4 breakdown, any room containing the fewest items must contain exactly one. So the stem really tells us that the living room has one item, and we know what it is—the sofa. As always, we now need to consider the P/V split-up, which, as in the previous question, forces us to place one in the bedroom and one in the den. Now here's the clever part: The choice containing a list of items that cannot be in the den can simply be a choice that doesn't include either P or V. And that's (C).

A 180 test taker gives thought as to what right and wrong answers must look like. That is, she characterizes the choices in order to prephrase answers to Logic Games questions whenever possible.

---

6. A

Which hypothetical are you going to handle first? Adhering to the first test-taker point in question 4, we'd have to go with the second on account of the fact that the sofa is placed, thus providing a starting point. This is another tricky question, but here's the key: We're not asked where the items go, but only which can go with which.

> A 180 test taker zeroes in on the relevant issue in each Logic Games question.

The direct consequence of this is that for this question, there's no functional difference between the bedroom and the den. So while many test takers stare at this question searching in vain for a way in, the 180 test taker gets to work breaking up the entities as mandated in the stem. When we're told in the second hypothetical that W, L, and S must be separated, we have free reign to assign W and L to the bedroom or den (since S always occupies the living room), in either order. How about like this, taking Rule 2 into account, as usual:

Bedroom	Den	Living Rm
(MW)	L	S

Now it's not so tough to accommodate the first condition in the stem, splitting up L, P, and M. With L and M already situated (again, it doesn't matter where they are, only who they're with), P must join S in the living room. Did you see the final deduction? Since two rooms now have two definite items, L's room must be the single-item room. Since V can't ever be with P, and can't in this case be with L, V must be in a room with M and W. Keeping in mind that the contents of the bedroom and den can be switched without altering the answer at all, this gives us:

Bedroom	Den	Living Rm
MWV	L	SP

R and T are left to be distributed in some fashion between the bedroom and living room. It's not worth working out all the permutations; we have enough to work with to go to the choices. As we saw in our final deduction above, L must be alone in either the bedroom or den, and therefore can't be paired up with V. (A) gets the point. Each of the remaining pairings is possible.

So how did you do on this house decoration grouping game? As noted above, there's really nothing unusual about the game action, but the 1, 2, 5–1, 3, 4 breakdown deduction and a full understanding of the mechanics and implications of the P-V split-up are absolutely essential to getting through it in one piece. That's what gives this otherwise standard game its killer edge.

What's Next?

Now try your hand at another type of grouping game. Instead of distributing items into subgroups, you'll have to select a group of items from a larger group. Sounds simple, right? Well, by now you know that if it was, it wouldn't be here. Pack a lunch, grab the camera—we're off to the zoo.

LOGIC GAME 3

A zoo curator is selecting animals to import for the zoo's annual summer exhibit. Exactly one male and one female of each of the following types of animal are available: hippo, llama, monkey, ostrich, panther. The following restrictions apply:

If no panthers are selected, then both ostriches must be selected.

A male panther cannot be selected unless a female llama is selected.

If a male monkey is selected, then neither a female ostrich nor a female panther may be selected.

At least one hippo must be selected.

1. Which one of the following is an acceptable selection of animals for the exhibit?

    (A) female hippo, female monkey, male monkey, male ostrich, male panther
    (B) female hippo, male llama, female monkey, female ostrich, male ostrich
    (C) male hippo, female llama, male llama, female monkey, female ostrich
    (D) male hippo, female llama, male monkey, female panther, male panther
    (E) female llama, male llama, male monkey, female ostrich, male panther

2. Which one of the following must be false?

    (A) Both a female hippo and male panther are selected.
    (B) Both a male monkey and a female llama are selected.
    (C) Both a female ostrich and a male hippo are selected.
    (D) All of the animals selected are female.
    (E) All of the animals selected are male.

3. If a male monkey is selected, then which one of the following animals must also be selected?

    (A) female hippo
    (B) male hippo
    (C) female llama
    (D) female monkey
    (E) male ostrich

4. If the smallest number of animals is selected, then which one of the following animals must be selected?

    (A) male hippo
    (B) female llama
    (C) male monkey
    (D) female panther
    (E) male panther

5. All of the following could be true EXCEPT:

    (A) A female llama is the only female animal selected.
    (B) A female monkey is the only female animal selected.
    (C) A female ostrich is the only female animal selected.
    (D) A male ostrich is the only male animal selected.
    (E) A male panther is the only male animal selected.

6. If a female llama is not selected, then which one of the following is a pair of animals at least one of which must be selected?

    (A) female hippo, female monkey
    (B) male hippo, male llama
    (C) female ostrich, male ostrich
    (D) male ostrich, female panther
    (E) female panther, male panther

Logic Game 3: Zoo Animals

What Makes It Difficult

Our mandate in this game is to select animals for an exhibit. Difficulties abound. For one thing, there are 10 entities to manage—one male and one female of five different kinds of animals. That alone makes the choices fairly cumbersome, and forces us to come up with a convention to keep the animals straight. The ambiguity is heightened by what we're not told, namely: How many of these critters are we to take? It's always easier when we have an exact number to shoot for.

The rules offer an impressive array of formal logic. Rule 1 is an if-then statement presented in the negative, telling us what happens when no panthers are taken. Not fun. Surely it would be easier if they told us what happens if one were selected. Rule 2 is presented in a "cannot-unless" format, which requires a bit of translation, while Rule 3 is another if-then with negative shadings (although easier to handle than Rule 2). Rule 4 is the easiest of the bunch, but even that one doesn't give us anything definite—which hippo is it? Or maybe both? Can't tell. In a nutshell: heavy-duty formal logic, lots of entities with a troublesome male/female distinction, and nothing settled for sure.

What about the questions? Not much relief there: With all that's up in the air, we'd expect some comforting hypotheticals to set us on our way, but only two of the six question stems deals with specific animals, and one of them does so only in the negative, citing an animal that's not selected. That question, question 6, requires a fairly complex test of the choices. Even the Acceptability question, question 1, is made more difficult by the male/female distinction, which makes it hard to scan the choices as we prefer for this type. After all this trouble, this better be a darn good summer zoo exhibit. If not, we can always boycott it in favor of the summer festival from two games back. How did you do recognizing the keys to the game?

Keys to the Game

Settle on a convention for representing the entities. One way is to use a small letter "f" or "m" to signify gender followed by a capital letter representing animal type. That would give us a roster of fH, mH, fL, mL, fM, mM, fO, mO, fP, mP.

> A 180 test taker quickly and confidently decides how to represent even a complicated set of entities.

If both ostriches are not selected, then at least one panther must be selected. This is the proper interpretation of Rule 1. This can in turn be combined with Rule 3, as follows:

If a male monkey is selected, both a male panther and a female llama must also be selected. Rule 3 says that selecting a male monkey means not taking a female ostrich, but without both ostriches we're forced to choose a panther, as noted just above. But the other part of Rule 3 forbids a female panther with a male monkey. Therefore, the requisite panther under these circumstances must be male. Rule 2 further forces us to take the female llama.

> A 180 test taker can draw the correct interpretations from formal logic statements and then combine those interpretations with other rules to form larger deductions.

Answers and Explanations

1. B   2. E   3. C   4. D   5. B   6. D

1. B

We can use the standard method for Acceptability questions, checking the rules against the choices, crossing off those that don't conform, until only one choice is left standing. Rule 4 is the easiest to check—(E) is the only one without a hippo, so get rid of that one to start. Rule 3 provides a lot to go on: (D) violates Rule 3, attempting to pair a male monkey and female panther. (Choice (E) violates Rule 3 too, but we already eliminated that one using Rule 4.) (A) violates Rule 2, by including a male panther without also including a female llama, which leaves only Rule 1 left to check. Neither (B) nor (C) contains a panther, and according to Rule 1, that means that both ostriches must be selected. Only (B) meets this requirement; (C) falls one male ostrich short.

> A 180 test taker breezes through Acceptability questions, examining the easier rules first in order to eliminate choices before handling the more abstract rules.

2. E

No new information, so we have no recourse but to test the choices. However, we need not test them in order. We're looking for a statement that cannot be true. Choices (A) through (C) each contain a single pairing of animals, which doesn't seem too restrictive; whereas (D) and (E) seem to be much more inclusive: all males, all females. Moreover, (A) and (C) involve hippos, which are fairly unrestricted. (Sure, we need one of them, but which one we don't know.) All in all, the sharp test taker would probably find (D) and (E) more likely to lead to a violation, and would check those first.

> A 180 test taker looks to zero in on the most likely candidates when forced to test out choices.

(D) It is possible to select only females: The twosome fH and fP readily attests to this, so (D) is not the answer we seek.

(E) It is impossible to select only males. If we tried, then we'd have to leave out the female ostrich, but we know from our analysis of Rule 1 what happens then: Without both ostriches, we'll need at least one panther. Sticking to the all-male mandate of the choice means we'd have to select the male panther, not the female one, but that would lead us down a dead end, as the male panther requires the female llama. No simple matter, but either way we slice it, we can't get away with a strictly male roster, so (E) is correct. As for the others:

(A) It's eminently possible to include a female hippo and male panther—just be sure to add a female llama (Rule 2). Rule 4 is taken care of by the selection of fH, and Rules 1 and 3 don't even apply.

(B) In this one we're looking to pair a male monkey and female llama in the same selection. First thing we need to add is a hippo—got to have one of those according to Rule 4, and either one is fine for now. We know that a male monkey precludes the selection of a female ostrich and female panther, and we deduced above that any selection including a male monkey must include a male panther. There you have it; this rounds out an acceptable list: mM, fL, mP, and either hippo will do just fine, so it is possible to select the pair in (B), which is why (B) is wrong.

(C) A female ostrich and male hippo can be chosen together, although we'll need either to select the male ostrich, allowing us to leave out the panthers, or else leave out the male ostrich, in which case we'll have to take one of the panthers. Either way, (C) is possible.

3. C

Our key deduction from above: A male monkey means no female ostrich. Without both ostriches, we're forced by Rule 1 to choose a panther. But Rule 3 forbids a female panther with a male monkey, so the panther we select must be male. A hop, skip, and a jump to Rule 2 forces us to select the female llama to go with the male panther; thus, choice (C).

(A), (D), (E) The acceptable group mM, mP, fL, and mH demonstrates that if a male monkey is selected, we can do without the animals in all three of these choices.

(B) Substitute the female hippo for the male hippo in the group listed above and we see that the male hippo is expendable as well.

4. D

We're looking for the smallest group possible, and we know that at least one hippo must be selected, so let's start there. Either a male one or female one will do. Can that be an entire acceptable group? Well, no; Rule 1 won't allow it. If only a single hippo were selected, then certainly both ostriches wouldn't be taken, and Rule 1 would therefore force us to take at least one panther. We can avoid a panther altogether by selecting both ostriches, but that would give us three animals. Can we do better? Yup—we can leave out the pair of ostriches and take a single panther. But which one? Not the male panther, because then we'd have to take the female llama as well, and remember, we're looking to take the minimum number of animals. The female panther comes with no additional baggage, so taking her, along with either hippo, results in the smallest group possible, a group of two.

Notice that we've seen this group before: In question 2, we eliminated choice (D) by choosing a twosome of females: the female hippo and the female panther. The work you did in that question could have helped you in this question as well.

> A 180 test taker puts work on previous questions (even the thinking that goes into eliminating wrong choices) to use while proceeding through the game.

(A), (B), (C), (E) No need to belabor these choices once we've seen that the smallest group possible is the female panther and either one of the hippos.

5. B

Again, no new information in the stem, so we need to work efficiently through the choices, eliminating the ones that could be true and choosing the one that proves to be impossible. Notice that the choices all involve the selection of a single animal in a particular gender. Since we're looking for the case where this can't be true, it makes sense to gravitate toward the animals with more restrictions; that is, the ones who rely on other animals to be selected. In fact, the only dependent animal in the list is the male panther in (E), and as it turns out, a group consisting of mP, fL, fH proves that (E) is possible. This type of proactive thinking is still strongly encouraged, even though it didn't pan out here.

A 180 test taker doesn't sour on strategies that are generally effective when they don't yield benefits in a particular case.

We'll simply test the other choices.

(A) A group consisting of the female llama, the male panther, and the male hippo works just fine, proving that the female llama can be the only female animal selected, so we can cross off (A).

(B) Nope; can't do it. It all comes back to Rule 1 again: We can't take the female ostrich, because we're testing to see if the female monkey can be the only female selected. Therefore, according to the implication of Rule 1, we must take a panther. But again, we are trying not to select the female in this choice, so we have to take the male, which ultimately brings us back to selecting a female after all: the female llama mandated by Rule 2. In the end (B) is impossible, and is therefore the choice we seek.

The following acceptable selections show how the remaining choices are possible:
(C) fO, mO, mH
(D) mO, fO, fH

6. D

No female llama means no male panther (Rule 2). Any situation involving panthers always brings us back to Rule 1: With the male panther out of the picture, there's a choice: take the female panther, and then we can do anything we want about the ostriches. But if we leave out the female panther, then Rule 1 kicks in and we have to select both ostriches. This is why (D) is correct: Of the pair "male ostrich"/"female panther," it is necessary to take at least one. Female ostrich could substitute for male ostrich and the choice would still be correct. As for the others:

(A), (C) The acceptable group made up of the male hippo and female panther that we've seen a number of times throughout the game proves that both members of the pairs listed in (A) and (C) can be left out without a problem.

(B) Female hippo/female panther is but one acceptable group that demonstrates that both members of this pair are expendable under these circumstances.

(E) We can do without the female panther if we take both ostriches (remember, the male panther is already out of commission thanks to the stem), and throw in a male or female hippo and we're good to go.

What's Next?

Had enough of hippos, panthers, monkeys, and the rest? Or are you sorry this game is over, just getting the hang of manipulating these complex entities and daunting formal logic rules? Then rejoice! Next up is another grouping game of selection that presents similar challenges, although we have to trade in the open air of the zoo for the stodgy confines of a banking seminar.

LOGIC GAME 4

A bank manager selects at least four, and no more than six, new employees to attend a regional training event. Each new employee is either a loan officer or a teller, and each works either part time or full time. Of the eight new employees, three are part-time loan officers, two are full-time loan officers, two are part-time tellers, and one is a full-time teller. The manager selects the attendees according to the following conditions:

No other employees are eligible to attend the event.
At least three loan officers are selected.
At least two full-time employees are selected.
If the full-time teller is selected, then at least one part-time teller is also selected.

1. Which one of the following is an acceptable group of employees that can attend the event?

    (A) two full-time loan officers, one full-time teller, two part-time tellers
    (B) one full-time loan officer, one full-time teller, two part-time loan officers, one part-time teller
    (C) one full-time loan officer, two part-time loan officers, two part-time tellers
    (D) two full-time loan officers, one full-time teller, three part-time loan officers, one part-time teller
    (E) one full-time loan officer, one full-time teller, three part-time loan officers

2. If not all of the new full-time loan officers are selected, then which one of the following must be true?

    (A) At least one part-time teller is selected.
    (B) Exactly one part-time teller is selected.
    (C) No full-time tellers are selected.
    (D) Exactly two part-time loan officers are selected.
    (E) Exactly three part-time loan officers are selected.

3. If the maximum number of loan officers is selected, then which one of the following must be true?

    (A) Exactly five employees are selected.
    (B) Exactly six employees are selected.
    (C) No part-time tellers are selected.
    (D) At least one part-time teller is selected.
    (E) No full-time tellers are selected.

4. Which one of the following CANNOT be true?

    (A) More full-time loan officers than part-time loan officers are selected.
    (B) More part-time tellers than full-time loan officers are selected.
    (C) More full-time tellers than part-time loan officers are selected.
    (D) An equal number of part-time tellers and full-time tellers are selected.
    (E) An equal number of part-time loan officers and full-time loan officers are selected.

5. If an equal number of part-time loan officers and full-time tellers is selected, then which one of the following must be false?

    (A) More part-time employees than full-time employees are selected.
    (B) More full-time employees than part-time employees are selected.
    (C) Exactly five employees are selected.
    (D) An equal number of part-time tellers and full-time tellers are selected.
    (E) Exactly six employees are selected.

6. If the minimum number of employees is selected, then each of the following must be true EXCEPT:

    (A) No more than two part-time loan officers are selected.
    (B) Exactly two full-time loan officers are selected.
    (C) No full-time tellers are selected.
    (D) No part-time tellers are selected.
    (E) No more than one part-time teller is selected.

Logic Game 4: Bank Employees

What Makes It Difficult

We said in the previous game that in grouping games of selection it's easier when we have an exact number to shoot for. On that count, we're better off in Bank Employees than in Zoo Animals, as the limitation of 4–6 entities selected is set from the start. But as the test makers giveth, they also taketh away: The entities are even more difficult to distinguish, falling into four very similar-sounding categories; and a strict number element pervades the entire game which complicates matters even further.

The rules aren't so bad: The first is what we at Kaplan call a "loophole closer," which is a rule that ties up a possible loose end but offers no real additional information. So there are functionally only three rules to deal with in the game. Rules 2 and 3 deal with number considerations, and may be slightly confusing to some because one concerns employee type (loan officer) while the other speaks of employee status (full time). Rule 4 offers a fairly straightforward formal logic if-then statement—mild, in fact, in comparison to those offered in the previous game.

The questions pose the same kind of wording difficulty posed in Zoo Animals, only worse: the eye simply has trouble distinguishing "part-time loan officers," "full-time loan officers," "part-time tellers," and "full-time tellers" on the page. It's fairly easy to confuse them. Finally, the test makers play up the numbers element to the hilt: "more of these than those, an equal number of these and those, exactly this many of these and that many of those . . . ." Ugh! Combine that with trying to keep the employee types straight, and it gets mind-numbing after a while.

In the real world, a bank manager, presumably trained in numerical operations, might be the perfect person to sort through all of this nonsense. Unfortunately, on the LSAT it's your job to stand in for the manager and make the selections. Here are some points that significantly simplify your task. Did you see them yourself?

Keys to the Game

Settle on a convention for representing the entities. Same advice as in the previous game. You absolutely need a way to represent the entities that's both clear and easily accessible. How's about using uppercase for full time, and lowercase for part time? That way the entities will be lll / LL / tt / T. Then you can simply circle or cross off employees as need be.

A 180 test taker doesn't balk at recopying an initial setup for the questions when necessary.

At least one part-time loan officer will always be selected. This is due to Rule 2's mandate for at least three loan officers, combined with the fact that there are only two full-time loan officers. Circle one l.

At least one full-time loan officer will always be selected. That's because we need at least two full-time employees according to Rule 3, but there's only one full-time teller. Circle one L. These two deductions in effect simplify the game down to a selection of two to four employees from the remaining six.

A 180 test taker drives numerical information to concrete conclusions.

If no part-time teller is selected, then the full-time teller is not selected, and both full-time loan officers are selected. This is the implication of Rule 4, and this implication combined with Rule 3.

Answers and Explanations

1. B   2. A   3. E   4. C   5. A   6. D

1. B

A standard Acceptability question, but one made more difficult by the wordy entities. The usual strategy for these applies; use the rules to eliminate choices. (D), which lists seven employees selected for training, directly contradicts the condition in the first sentence of the game requiring four to six employees for the event. Rule 2 kills (A), which has only two loan officers. Rule 3 eliminates (C), which has just one full-time employee, and Rule 4 gets rid of (E), which has a full-time teller, but no part-time teller. (B) is the only one left, so it's correct.

A 180 test taker does not lose sight of rules that are buried in the scenario.

---

2. A

If not all of the full-time loan officers are selected, then exactly one full-time loan officer is (the one we deduced above). Then we have to add another part-time loan officer to the one we already deduced above, in order to satisfy Rule 2, not to mention the full-time teller to take care of Rule 3. Since the full-time teller is selected, Rule 4 requires a part-time teller to be selected. (A) is thus the winner: At least one part-time teller must be selected. (C) is impossible, while the other choices are possible only.

3. E

Next we're instructed to select the maximum number of loan officers. Might as well shoot for the moon: Since no rule specifically prevents us from choosing all five loan officers, let's see what follows if we do.

A 180 test taker knows how to test for maximums and minimums. When looking for a maximum, she'll choose the largest number possible to test and work her way down. That way, when a scenario works out, she has her answer.

Selecting all five loan officers violates no rules, but we have to examine what else is possible in order to test the choices. One more employee can join them to give us six total, but need not. However, selecting the full-time teller would mess things up, since that would force us to add a part-time teller, giving us a grand total of seven—no good. So (E) must be true. Since we could add one part-time teller to the mix, but don't have to, (A), (B), (C), and (D) all could be true, but need not be.

4. C

No new information, and we're looking for an impossibility. As it turns out, our deduction regarding the necessity for at least one part-time teller helps us cut right to the chase: Since there is only one full-time teller and at least one part-time teller is always selected, there's no way for full-time tellers to outnumber part-time tellers. At best, they're even. (C) is the impossibility we seek.

A 180 test taker uses the deductions he makes up front to scan the choices in questions containing no new information.

(A) is wrong because we can select two full-time loan officers, one part-time loan officer, and one part-time teller.

(B) is out because we can select two part-time tellers, one full-time teller, one part-time loan officer, and one full-time loan officer.

(D) The correct choice for question 1 demonstrates that it's quite possible for the number of part-time tellers selected to equal the number of full-time tellers selected.

A 180 test taker uses the right answer to Acceptability questions to test choices in later questions whenever possible.

(E) is no good because we can choose two full-time loan officers and two part-time loan officers.

5. A

Selecting an equal number of part-time loan officers and full-time tellers means one of each. Selecting the full-time teller means that at least one part-time teller is selected as well. Additionally, since at least three loan officers must be selected, both full-time loan officers will be selected. The only variable is the second part-time teller; maybe she's in, maybe she's out—no way to tell. Testing the choices against this nearly completed arrangement, we don't have to look far: (A) must be false. With all three full-time employees selected and only one part-time loan officer eligible, the best that can happen is that the part-timers tie the score with variable part-time teller. But there's no way to get more part-timers than full-timers under these circumstances.

(B), (C), and (D) are all possible. All we'd have to do is leave out that final part-time teller.

(E) Put that second part-time teller in, however, and there will be exactly six employees selected.

6. D

The minimum number of employees is four. To satisfy Rules 2 and 3, three of them must be loan officers and two must be full-time employees. We can do this in two ways: We can select one part-time loan officer, two full-time loan officers, and one part-time teller; or we can take two part-time loan officers and two full-time loan officers. Any other scenario will force us to choose at least five employees. (A), (B), (C) and (E) all conform to both scenarios, and are therefore wrong. (D) need not be true because the first scenario includes the selection of a part-time teller.

What's Next?

Well, enough of selection chores for now. Don't worry—we'll see more of this game action coupled with others later on in the more complex mixture game types. For now, let's move on to the final type of standard single game action that may just cause you trouble all by itself. We call these "matching" games, and as the name implies, they require you to match up different elements with one another according to strict conditions. We return to the household motif we last saw in "House Decoration" to help our new friend Leah dry her clothes.

LOGIC GAME 5

Leah has a pile of wet clothes that consists only of shirts and jeans. She places some of the clothes into exactly three dryers, labeled dryer 1, dryer 2, and dryer 3. Each article of clothing is made of all cotton or all rayon. She does not mix jeans and shirts in any dryer, and she does not mix cotton articles and rayon articles in any dryer. The control setting on each dryer is set to either permanent press or delicates. The clothes were placed into dryers according to the following conditions:

If there is rayon clothing in a dryer, then at least dryer 2 must contain rayon clothing.

Dryer 1 is set to delicates.

No dryer set to permanent press contains rayon clothing.

If any dryer contains jeans, then all jeans must be made of cotton.

1. If dryer 2 contains cotton clothing, then which one of the following must be true?

   (A) Dryer 1 contains cotton clothing.
   (B) Dryer 1 contains shirts.
   (C) Dryer 1 contains jeans.
   (D) Dryer 2 is set to permanent press.
   (E) Dryer 3 contains rayon clothing.

2. If at least one dryer contains rayon clothing, then all of the following must be true EXCEPT:

   (A) Dryer 2 contains rayon clothing.
   (B) All of the rayon clothing in the dryers are shirts.
   (C) At least one dryer contains jeans.
   (D) Dryer 2 is set to delicates.
   (E) At least one dryer contains shirts.

3. If more dryers contain jeans than contain shirts, then which one of the following must be true?

   (A) Dryer 2 contains cotton clothing.
   (B) Dryer 2 contains rayon clothing.
   (C) Dryer 3 contains cotton clothing.
   (D) Dryer 2 is set to delicates.
   (E) Dryer 3 is set to delicates.

4. If dryer 1 contains rayon clothing and dryer 3 is set to permanent press, then which one of the following could be false?

   (A) More dryers contain shirts than contain jeans.
   (B) More dryers contain rayon clothing than contain cotton clothing.
   (C) More dryers are set to delicates than are set to permanent press.
   (D) A dryer set to permanent press contains jeans.
   (E) Two dryers contain rayon shirts.

5. If no dryer set to delicates contains cotton clothing, then how many different combinations of dryer contents and settings are possible?

   (A) 1
   (B) 2
   (C) 3
   (D) 4
   (E) 5

6. Which one of the following CANNOT be true?

   (A) Dryer 1 contains cotton clothing.
   (B) Dryer 2 contains jeans.
   (C) Dryer 3 is the only dryer containing shirts.
   (D) Dryer 1 contains shirts, and dryer 2 is set to permanent press.
   (E) Dryer 3 contains rayon clothing, and dryer 2 is set to permanent press.

Logic Game 5: Leah's Clothes

What Makes It Difficult

Much like the rest of the games in this Supercharged Standards chapter, this one doesn't pose any sort of conceptual problem—it's just laundry, after all. The difficulty lies in the number of attributes we're given to work with. As alluded to earlier, in matching games we have to link up elements, and here there are four distinct aspects to consider. We have to match each dryer (1, 2, and 3) to the type of clothes in it (shirts or jeans) to the material of the clothes (cotton or rayon) to the dryer setting (delicates or permanent press). The whole game is really won or lost in the interpretation of the rules and the deductions drawn from them, so let's jump right to the keys to the game to sort all of that out.

Keys to the Game

The dryers can contain shirts only or jeans only. Notice that the game intro never stipulates that there actually are any shirts or any jeans placed into a dryer—it says only that there are wet shirts and jeans, and that some of them are placed into dryers. That doesn't preclude the possibility that all of the clothes in the dryers are jeans, or that all of the clothes are shirts. Rule 4, by its very wording ("if any dryer contains jeans . . ."), suggests that this is the case. The same, incidentally, holds for cotton and rayon.

Each dryer contains exactly one kind of clothes made of exactly one kind of material, and is set to exactly one setting. That's what all the "does not mix" wording amounts to, and it makes our lives easier if we understand it as such.

If dryer 2 does not contain rayon clothes, then no dryer can contain rayon clothes. This is the proper interpretation of Rule 1.

Any dryer set to permanent press must contain cotton clothing. Any dryer containing rayon clothing must be set to delicates. That's Rule 3 stated in the positive.

> A 180 test taker turns negative statements into positive ones.

Any dryer containing rayon clothing must contain shirts and be set to delicates. That's a proper extension of Rule 4 combined with our interpretation of Rule 3. Rayon turns out to be a major key to the game, since any R that appears must be followed by S and D, and if R shows up in dryers 1 or 3, then dryer 2 must be R, S, D as well.

> A 180 test taker deduces as much up front as possible.

It makes one wonder how Leah conducts the rest of her life if she's this particular about her laundry. In any case, the questions fall much more readily with these keys at our disposal. Let's see.

Answers and Explanations

1. A   2. C   3. C   4. D   5. E   6. E

1. A

If there is cotton clothing in dryer 2, then there must be cotton clothing in dryers 1 and 3 as well. Having rayon clothing in 1 or 3 and cotton in 2 would be a clear violation of Rule 1. (A) echoes this sentiment—cotton clothing in dryer 1—and is therefore correct. (E) is false, as dryer 3 must contain cotton. There can be shirts or jeans in both dryers 1 and 2, so (B) and (C) could be true, but need not be. The same goes for (D); dryer 2 could be set on permanent press, but could just as easily be set on delicates.

2. C

We deduced above what happens when rayon clothing appears on the scene: the clothing must be shirts, and must be in a dryer set on delicates. According to Rule 1, if any dryer contains rayon clothing, then at least dryer 2 contains rayon clothing. That means that in this question, dryer 2 is set to delicates and contains rayon shirts. And that alone confirms that choices (A), (B), (D), and (E) must be true. However, there need not be a dryer containing jeans, because nothing prohibits all of the dryers from containing shirts. (C) is correct.

> A 180 test taker gets the most out of deductions made up front, using them to pick up quick and easy points even in tough games.

3. C

Jeans, when they appear, are made of cotton, and here they make an appearance; in fact, they're in the majority. That means that dryers with cotton must outnumber dryers with rayon (Rule 4).

> A 180 test taker never accepts any statement in the Logic Games section at face value; she always looks for its implications in the context of the game.

By now we're familiar with the rayon requirement: If there is rayon clothing in dryers 1 or 3, then there must be rayon in 2 as well, in which case there would be more rayon than cotton, and by extension, more shirts than jeans. No good—the stem won't allow that. So there can't be rayon in 1 or 3, which means 1 and 3 must contain cotton clothing. (C) has it right. Since dryer 2 could contain cotton or rayon clothing, neither (A) nor (B) must be true. As for (D) and (E), if there are jeans in dryer 2, then that dryer could be set to permanent press, and dryer 3 can also be set to either delicates or permanent press.

4. D

Now that we know so much about rayon, the question stem in this one is a gift. (The question itself—"which could be false"—and the choices are no picnic, of course). If there's rayon clothing in dryer 1, then dryer 1 contains rayon shirts and is set to delicates. Thanks to Rule 1 the S/R/D combo also obtains in dryer 2. Furthermore, we're told that dryer 3 is set to permanent press, which thanks to Rule 3 means that the clothes in that dryer are made of cotton:

	Dryer 1	Dryer 2	Dryer 3
S or J	S	S	
R or C	R	R	C
D or P	D	D	P

So of the nine possible dryer attributes, eight are determined. The only thing we don't know is whether dryer 3 contains shirts or jeans, so let's hit the choices. Remember, we're looking for the one that could be false, so anything that must be true can be chopped.

(A) Even if there are jeans in 3, dryers 1 and 2 still have shirts, so there will still be more dryers with shirts than jeans. (A), therefore, must be true and can be eliminated.

(B) and (C) are true statements also—rayon outnumbers cotton two to one, and delicates are one better than permanent press.

(D) is the winner: Dryer 3 (a dryer set to permanent press) could contain shirts, which would make (D) a false statement.

(E) must be true—there are exactly two dryers with rayon shirts. Dryer 3 could contain cotton shirts, but dryers with rayon shirts number exactly two.

5. E

This question bears a resemblance to the previous one. The difference is that in question 4, we were explicitly told that there was rayon in dryer 1. Here we're given enough information to deduce the same thing. If no dryer set to delicates contains cotton, then dryer 1 (which is set to delicates according to Rule 2) must contain rayon. The chain of deduction then proceeds as it did in many of the previous questions. We end up with rayon shirts set to delicates in dryer 1, and rayon shirts set to delicates in dryer 2.

No problem so far, but the question itself is a bit intimidating. Essentially it's asking how many different match-ups are possible.

A 180 test taker has a knack for decoding wordy and complex question stems.

This may appear daunting at first until we realize that dryers 1 and 2 are totally set, so we really need only concern ourselves with the number of possible permutations in dryer 3—still, no easy task. We need to be methodical, and it doesn't hurt to start with our old standby, rayon, since that entity gives us the most bang for the buck. If there's rayon in 3, then our trusty S/R/D combo emerges, which is one possibility. If, however, cotton clothing is in dryer 3, then those can be jeans or shirts. If jeans, then the dryer could be set to delicates or permanent press, so there are two more possibilities. Same for shirts, resulting in two more possibilities, giving us a grand total of 5, choice (E).

	Dryer 3	Dryer 3	Dryer 3
S or J	S	J	S
R or C	R	C	C
D or P	D (1 way)	D or P (2 ways)	D or P (2 ways)

5 total possibilities

6. E

If you resorted to testing out the choices (there's a better way, as you'll see below), you could still have saved time by using previous work to help you along. Remember, anything that could have or must have been true in a previous question could be true generally (unless it was based on a rule change, but we haven't had any of those). Choice (A) asks whether dryer 1 can contain cotton clothing. In question 1, dryer 1 did contain cotton clothing (in fact, that was the correct answer), so we know that (A) is possible. (B) asks whether dryer 2 can contain jeans. In question 3, all three dryers could have contained jeans, so it must be possible for dryer 2 to contain jeans. So we can cross off (B).

A 180 test taker keeps his work neat and accessible for use in later questions.

(C) requires some new work. If dryer 3 is the only dryer containing shirts, then the other two contain jeans. According to Rule 4, all jeans are made of cotton, and so dryer 1 and dryer 2 contain cotton jeans. Since there is no rayon clothing in dryer 2, no dryer contains rayon clothing (Rule 1), and so dryer 3 contains cotton clothing. That's the last deduction we can make (since dryer 2 and dryer 3 could each be set to either delicates or permanent press). Since this scenario doesn't violate any rules, (C) is possible, and we can cross it off.

(D) asks whether dryer 1 could contain shirts while dryer 2 is set to permanent press. If dryer 1 contains shirts, then . . . nothing! Be careful. Just because all rayon clothing are shirts doesn't mean that all shirts are made of rayon. They could also be made of cotton. Since dryer 2 is set to permanent press, we know dryer 2 must contain cotton clothing, but that's all. This scenario is possible, and so (D) can be eliminated.

(E) On test day, we would just select (E) and move on, but for the record, here's why (E) is impossible. If dryer 3 contains rayon clothing, then dryer 2 must as well (Rule 1). If dryer 2 contains rayon clothing, then it must be set to delicates. It cannot be set to permanent press, as (E) claims, and so (E) is impossible.

We alluded above to a better way. Believe it or not, the 180 test taker may very well have cut right to the chase and avoided trying out all of these choices. How, you say? Thanks to the following habit of top Logic Games practitioners:

> A 180 test taker milks the game's most influential entity for all it's worth. When he gets stuck, or is forced to try out choices given no new information, he turns to his "bread and butter" rule or entity.

Here, when asked for something that cannot be true, why not focus on the entity that presents the most restrictions? If there's one thing we know by now, it's that R means S/R/D. Only one choice in question 6 contains R, and lo and behold it's the one containing the impossibility.

Will this strategy work every time? No, probably not. But it doesn't waste any time trying it—you'd be stuck testing out choices anyway, so testing (E) first, even if it doesn't pan out, wouldn't set you back.

> A 180 test taker knows that clever proactive approaches do work out often enough to set those who employ them apart from the rest of the LSAT crowd.

What's Next?

If you're in the top tier of test takers, then you no doubt already have many clever strategies under your belt. If, however, you're still making that climb to join the elite, you'll need to start employing a few tricks of your own. And what better opportunity to work your magic than another game? See what you can make of this next matching game, "Show Riders."

LOGIC GAME 6

Three show riders—Art, Brenda, and Chaz—perform in all three of the Rosstown Rodeo's daily performances. Each rider rides one of the rodeo's horses—Nutmeg, Oz, and Paint—for the duration of an entire show, one rider per horse. The daily shows consist of a morning show, an afternoon show, and an evening show. The following is known about the riders and their mounts:

Brenda does not ride Oz in any of the shows.

Chaz rides Paint in at least one of the three shows, but not in the afternoon show.

Art rides the same horse in the afternoon and evening shows.

Chaz does not ride Oz in the morning show.

1. Which one of the following must be true?

    (A) Art rides Oz in the morning show.
    (B) Brenda rides Nutmeg in the morning show.
    (C) Chaz rides Oz in the afternoon show.
    (D) Art rides Paint in the evening show.
    (E) Chaz rides Nutmeg in the evening show.

2. If Art rides Oz in the evening show, then which one of the following must be true of Brenda?

    (A) She rides Nutmeg in the morning show.
    (B) She rides Paint in the morning show.
    (C) She rides Nutmeg in the afternoon show.
    (D) She rides Paint in the afternoon show.
    (E) She rides Paint in the evening show.

3. If Brenda rides Paint in the afternoon show, then which one of the following must be false?

    (A) Art rides Oz in the morning show and Brenda rides Paint in the evening show.
    (B) Art rides Nutmeg in the afternoon show and Chaz rides Paint in the morning show.
    (C) Art rides Nutmeg in the evening show and Brenda rides Paint in the evening show.
    (D) Brenda rides Paint in the morning show and Brenda rides Nutmeg in the evening show.
    (E) Brenda rides Nutmeg in the evening show and Chaz rides Oz in the evening show.

4. If Chaz rides the same horse in the morning and afternoon shows, then all of the following must be true EXCEPT:

    (A) Art rides Oz in all three shows.
    (B) Brenda rides Paint in exactly two of the shows.
    (C) Brenda rides Nutmeg in the afternoon show.
    (D) Chaz rides Nutmeg in the morning show.
    (E) Chaz rides Paint in the evening show.

5. Which one of the following must be true?

    (A) If Art rides Paint in the afternoon show, then Chaz rides Paint in the evening show.
    (B) If Chaz rides Nutmeg in the morning show, then Chaz rides Oz in the afternoon show.
    (C) If Brenda rides Paint in the evening show, then Art rides Nutmeg in the afternoon show.
    (D) If Brenda rides Nutmeg in the afternoon show, then Chaz rides Paint in the morning show.
    (E) If Chaz rides Paint in the evening show, then Brenda rides Nutmeg in the morning show.

6. If Chaz rides Nutmeg in the afternoon show only, then which one of the following must be true?

    (A) Art rides Oz in as many shows as he rides Paint.
    (B) Brenda rides Nutmeg in as many shows as she rides Paint.
    (C) Chaz rides Nutmeg in as many shows as he rides Oz.
    (D) Art rides Nutmeg in as many shows as he rides Paint.
    (E) Brenda rides Oz in as many shows as she rides Paint.

Logic Game 6: Show Riders

What Makes It Difficult

The intro paragraph of this matching game is a bit cumbersome, but cutting through the wordiness reveals a fairly straightforward game action: pairing up three riders to three horses in three time slots—morning, afternoon, and evening. The game involves a great deal of process of elimination, since once a rider is pegged for a horse, no one else can ride that horse during that show. Sounds easy enough, but lose sight of this fact (and we're called upon to remember it in pretty much every question) and the questions are simply unworkable.

The rules are not very forthcoming. No definite match-up is stated; mostly what we get is information on pairings that can't exist. And the last four questions of the set are downright unfriendly, most requiring numerous steps. Question 3 has a lot of nerve following up a "must be false" question stem with choices containing two match-ups each. That's possibly a lot of testing to do for each choice. Question 5 contains hypotheticals (if-then statements) in the choices themselves—never a sunny prospect. And question 6 introduces a numerical element into the pairing scenarios, requiring us to compare the number of times a rider rides one horse with the number he or she rides another.

As usual, there are a few things to do and/or notice that help turn this potential killer into a manageable experience.

Keys to the Game

Settle on a convention to represent the action. Matching games are usually amenable to lists and grids; some prefer one, some the other. If you sketch a 3×3 table, and put the time slots across the top (morn, aft, and eve) and the riders down the side (A, B, and C), then you can simply fill in the horses in the nine boxes as needed.

Brenda rides Nutmeg or Paint in all three shows. Chaz rides Nutmeg or Oz in the afternoon, and rides Nutmeg or Paint in the morning. These are Rules 1, 2, and 4 stated positively. Get that info into your sketch.

A 180 test taker turns negative statements into positive ones.

Art rides Oz in the morning. Our big deduction, derived from the fact that both Brenda and Chaz must ride Nutmeg or Paint in the morning show. The only rider eligible for Oz in the morning show is therefore Art, so we can build that right into the sketch.

Yee-ha! Saddle 'em up—we're ready to ride.

Answers and Explanations

1. A   2. D   3. E   4. C   5. D   6. D

Putting all of our insights together into one grid, here's what we have going into the questions:

	morn	aft	eve
A	O		
B	N or P	N or P	N or P
C	N or P	N or O	

1. A

Just as we deduced. The other four choices are possibilities only.

2. D

The if-clause plus Rule 3 tells us that Art rides Oz in the afternoon and evening. Looking over our afternoon list, we see that Chaz can ride only Nutmeg or Oz, and since Oz is taken, Chaz must ride Nutmeg in the afternoon, leaving Paint for Brenda, choice (D). This is a taste of the process of elimination element that we're faced with in most questions. (C) is flat-out false, while the other choices are possibilities only. Not so bad so far, right? Well, the honeymoon's pretty much over, as the next four take a turn for the worse.

3. E

This question begins where we ended in the last question, with Brenda riding Paint in the afternoon; but that doesn't mean that everything has to fall out the same way. With Brenda taking Paint in the afternoon, all we know for sure is that Art and Chaz between them will ride Nutmeg and Oz in that show. We're looking for something that can't be true. There's no real way to avoid testing out some choices here, but perhaps you prephrased something concrete to look for?

A 180 test taker takes matters into her own hands. Rather than simply let the choices in an open-ended question wash over her, she gives some thought as to what the right answer might look like or do.

With Paint taken by Brenda in the afternoon, Paint can't be ridden by Art or Chaz during that show. Either of those things would make for a fine answer choice, but of course that would be too simple, right? Well, what about a scenario that forces one of those things to happen? It's a bit more roundabout, but that's exactly what we get in (E). If Nutmeg and Oz are ridden in the evening show by Brenda and Chaz, Art must ride Paint in the evening. But Rule 3 would then force Art to ride Paint in the afternoon as well . . . and there you have it—a conflict with the mandate in the stem. (E) must be false. The rest could be true.

4. C

If Chaz rides the same horse in the first two shows, what horse would that be? A quick glance at our sketch reveals that only Nutmeg qualifies. That assignment makes everything else fall into place. To wit: Brenda needs to ride Paint in the morning and afternoon (Rule 1); Art is left with Oz in the afternoon and (Rule 3) the evening; and Chaz has to ride Paint (Rule 2) in the evening, leaving Nutmeg for Brenda in the evening. There are lots of steps here, but ultimately every slot is filled:

	morn	aft	eve
A	O	O	O
B	P	P	N
C	N	N	P

The only choice that doesn't correspond to the correct assignments is (C): Brenda rides Paint, not Nutmeg, in the afternoon.

5. D

Yipes! If-then statements in the choices give us little alternative but to try out each choice. However, as usual there's a shortcut, and it involves using previous work.

(A) is flat-out false. Art riding Paint in the afternoon means he rides Paint in the evening as well, so can't have that horse in the evening show.

(B), (E) If Chaz gets Nutmeg in the morning, must Chaz ride Oz in the afternoon? Let's try giving him a horse other than Oz—for example, his other possibility for that time slot, Nutmeg. Can that work? Well, it just did work above in question 4, as the diagram above indicates, so (B) need not be true. And wait a minute: The same scenario proves that (E) need not be true, either.

A 180 test taker always looks for shortcuts. When given no new information to work with, and forced to simply test out choices, she asks herself: "Have I seen this situation somewhere before?"

A 180 test taker is adept at eliminating answer choices containing hypotheticals by "proving the exception." If the choice reads "if X, then Y," the 180 test taker attempts to prove that X need not lead to Y. For the correct choice, no exception will be possible.

(C) If Brenda rides Paint in the evening, does that require Art to ride Nutmeg in the afternoon? Try the "proving the exception" strategy just discussed—see if Art can ride some other horse instead. The following arrangement shows that this is possible, allowing us to kill (C):

	morn	aft	eve
A	O	O	O
B	N	P	P
C	P	N	N

(D) must be correct, since we've eliminated all the others, but for the record: If Brenda rides Nutmeg in the afternoon, then Chaz rides Oz in the afternoon. Consequently, Art has to ride Paint in the afternoon show and (Rule 3) in the evening as well. And with Paint ridden by Art in the evening, Chaz's required ride on Paint (Rule 2) will have to take place in the morning. No exceptions possible here, so (D) gets the point.

6. D

If you miss the "only" here, it's fairly hopeless. Otherwise, it's not so tough: If Chaz's one and only ride on Nutmeg is in the afternoon, then he'll have to ride Paint in the morning, leaving Nutmeg as Brenda's morning horse. Meanwhile, Brenda will have to ride Paint in the afternoon, leaving Oz for Art in the afternoon and (Rule 3) the evening as well. Remaining are Brenda and Chaz's evening assignments; and because of the question stem's "only," it'll be Nutmeg for Brenda and Paint for Chaz in the evening. The entire roster is complete, and only (D) has it right: For Art, zero Nutmeg rides does equal zero Paint rides.

A 180 test taker does not miss key words in a Logic Games question stem, or, for that matter, anywhere else on the LSAT.

What's Next?

Without further ado, let's move on to another matching game and the last of our Supercharged Standards, "Class Pictures."

LOGIC GAME 7

A teacher instructs her class to create four separate pictures to be used as scenery for a school play. There are to be one dog picture, one house picture, and two tree pictures. Each picture is done in one of two media: paint or crayon. Each picture is done in one of three colors: blue, red, or yellow.

There is exactly one blue and one yellow picture.

The two tree pictures are done in different colors but in the same medium.

The blue and yellow pictures are not done in the same medium.

The dog picture is done in crayon.

One tree picture is done in red.

1. Which one of the following is an acceptable group of four pictures?

    (A) blue crayon dog, red painted house, red painted tree, yellow crayon tree
    (B) yellow crayon dog, red painted house, blue painted tree, red crayon tree
    (C) blue crayon dog, red painted house, red painted tree, yellow painted tree
    (D) yellow crayon dog, blue painted house, red crayon tree, red crayon tree
    (E) yellow painted dog, red painted house, blue crayon tree, red crayon tree

2. If the maximum number of pictures is done in crayon, which one of the following must be true?

    (A) A tree is done in blue.
    (B) A tree is done in yellow.
    (C) The dog is done in red.
    (D) The house is done in blue.
    (E) The house is done in yellow.

3. If the dog picture is done in blue, which one of the following must be false?

    (A) The number of pictures done in red paint equals the number of pictures done in red crayon.
    (B) The number of pictures done in red paint does not equal the number of pictures done in red crayon.
    (C) The number of pictures done in yellow paint equals the number of pictures done in blue crayon.
    (D) There are more crayon pictures than painted pictures.
    (E) There are more painted pictures than crayon pictures.

4. If the house is done in yellow, which one of the following CANNOT be true?

    (A) The trees are done in paint.
    (B) The trees are done in crayon.
    (C) There are an equal number of pictures done in crayon and in paint.
    (D) Both red pictures are done in paint.
    (E) The yellow picture is done in crayon.

5. If neither of the tree pictures is done in yellow, and if there are more painted pictures than those done in crayon, then which one of the following must be true?

    (A) The dog picture must be done in blue paint.
    (B) The house picture could be done in red crayon.
    (C) The house picture could be done in yellow paint.
    (D) The dog picture must be done in red crayon.
    (E) The house picture must be done in red paint.

6. Which one of the following pieces of additional information would make it certain that the dog picture is done in blue or yellow?

    (A) There are more crayon pictures than painted pictures.
    (B) There are more painted pictures than crayon pictures.
    (C) The house is done in blue.
    (D) A tree is done in blue.
    (E) A tree is done in yellow.

Logic Game 7: Class Pictures

What Makes It Difficult

One dog, one house, and two trees, each done in either paint or crayon, each either red, blue, or yellow—again, lots to keep track of. And the rules don't make it particularly easy, especially Rule 2, which deals with both color and media. The trees have to be different in one respect, but alike in the other, and it's certainly easy to mix these up. Rule 3 is fairly abstract, since we don't know off hand which picture is blue and which is yellow, but whichever they turn out to be, one must be painted and one must be crayoned. It's the kind of rule we can't apply until more information is known.

The other rules are fairly straightforward and concrete, but the questions are tough. There's a strong numerical aspect to the questions. While some of the choices are stated simply, as in "such and such painting is done in this color" or "such and such painting is done in this medium," many others are stated in terms of comparisons: "There are more of these than those," or "there are an equal number of these and those," etc. Question 6 is a generally tough type: the kind that asks what additional information would make a specific result certain. Even the "acceptability" question, question 1—usually the easiest of the game—is made more difficult by the wordiness of the choices; that is, the fact that each entity in each choice is comprised of the three elements present in the game.

All in all, not as pleasant an experience for us as for the budding artists. And unfortunately, no key deductions are present to blow the game open. That's not to say, of course, that there aren't a few helpful things to notice:

Keys to the Game

Begin with Rules 4 and 5. Incorporating the most concrete rules up front can help lay a solid foundation for your attack on the game.

The nonred tree must be done in blue or yellow. A combination of Rules 2 and 5.

Of the dog and the house, one must done in red, and the other done in blue or yellow, whichever color the second tree is not.

Not much to go on, actually—which means we'll simply have to crank through the questions as more information becomes available.

> A 180 test taker recognizes when there are no major deductions to be made, and anticipates that the questions will generally supply a lot of information to get the ball rolling.

Answers and Explanations

1. C   2. C   3. E   4. D   5. E   6. B

1. C

As mentioned earlier, the Acceptability question here is a bit annoying, thanks to the complex nature of the choices, but it works just the same as any other of this type: We simply check the rules against the choices and eliminate the ones that don't conform.

> A 180 test taker is not intimidated by complex or wordy choices; he keeps his focus and confidently marches ahead.

All of the choices satisfy Rule 1; blue, yellow, red, and red are indeed the colors represented in each choice. Rule 2, however, helps in a big way: In (B), the two tree pictures are done in different media, and (D) also violates Rule 2, which requires the tree pictures to be of different colors. (A) can be eliminated because in that one both the blue and yellow pictures are drawn in the same medium (crayon), in violation of Rule 3. Finally, (E) can be knocked thanks to Rule 4, which explicitly specifies that the dog be crayoned, not painted. (C) remains and is correct.

2. C

Next we're looking for the greatest number of pictures that can be done in crayon, so how about all four?

> A 180 test taker starts at the top when seeking maximums and at the bottom when seeking minimums.

Well, as it turns out all four pictures can't be done in crayon, because the blue and the yellow pictures must be in different media. What about three pictures in crayon? Sure, that's possible: The dog is always crayon (Rule 4), and since the two tree pictures must be in the same medium, let's make those two crayon as well. The house must therefore be done in paint. Does this new info correspond to any of the choices?

> A 180 test taker intuitively knows when it's worth scanning the choices. In a "must be true" question, any new deduction can theoretically answer the question, so she takes a quick peek at the choices as soon as anything new has been determined.

Unfortunately, none of this appears as a choice, so we must press on and consider the color aspect. We already know that one tree will be red and that the other tree must be blue or yellow. Since the latter is in crayon, we know that the other picture done in blue or yellow must be painted (Rule 3), which in this case is the house. Since the second red is all that's left, we can mark the dog as red and the answer as (C). The house and one of the trees will be the blue and yellow pictures, although we don't know which is which. The other four choices, therefore, all could be true, but need not be.

3. E

If the dog is blue, the second tree must be yellow, which leaves red for the house. In an easier question in an easier game, this may be enough information already to allow us to figure out what's impossible. Here, however, the choices all deal in some way with the crayon-paint issue, so we must press forward. Rule 3 comes into play: The blue dog and the yellow tree must be done in different media, and since the dog is always done in crayon, the yellow tree (and the red tree, for that matter, thanks to Rule 2) must be done in paint. The only information we're missing is whether the red house is in paint or crayon, so now we know all that we possibly can know, and there's not a question in the world we can't answer. What must be false? (E)'s the impossibility we seek: At best, the house is crayon and there's an equal number of paint and crayon pictures, but in this situation there can't be more crayon pictures than painted ones. (A), (B), and (D) all could be true, while (C) is a statement that must be true.

4. D

If the house is yellow, then the nonred tree must be blue, which makes the dog red. This time that is enough information to allow us to answer the question. Since the dog is always done in crayon, and in this case the dog is red, (D) is impossible: Both red pictures can't be painted.

A 180 test taker remains true to his strategies, even when they don't pan out in a particular case.

Scanning the choices early on didn't save any time in question 2, but it certainly saves time here. As for the rest (not that you would bother to check the others on test day):

(A) and (B) could be true, as the trees could be done in paint or crayon. Likewise, (C) and (E) could be true if the house was done in crayon and the trees in paint.

5. E

The implication of the first if-clause is that the second tree will be done in blue.

A 180 test taker looks beyond what the stem says to what it means in the context of her understanding of the game.

The second hypothetical is a roundabout way of telling us that there will be three pictures done in paint and one in crayon—and we know which one that is: the dog. So the trees and the house must be done in paint. The blue picture, in this case a painted tree, must be done in a different medium than the yellow picture, so the yellow picture must be the crayon dog, once again leaving the house as the second red picture. This supports correct choice (E).

(A) and (D) bite the dust because the dog is done in yellow crayon. The house, on the other hand, must be done in red paint, killing both (B) and (C).

A 180 test taker is not intimidated by question stems that contain lots of information. He knows that the more he gets to work with, the more he can figure out.

---

6. B

Here's a somewhat unusual question: We are asked to figure out how to force the dog to be blue or yellow. We know from our earlier analysis that one of the trees must be blue or yellow. So the easiest way to force the dog to be blue or yellow would be to make the house red. However, we're not so lucky to find this easy solution in the choices (no surprise there). So let's search the choices for the one that brings about the desired result.

(A) More crayon masterpieces than paint, says (A). Will that do it? Well, that's a fancy way of saying that three pictures are done in crayon and one in paint, since a 4–0 breakdown isn't allowed by Rule 3. But under these conditions the house could still be the other blue/yellow picture, instead of the dog.

(B) What about the opposite, more paint than crayon? That would mean three paint pictures. Since the dog is in crayon, this means that the house and both trees must be paint. Could the house still be the other blue/yellow picture? No; this would violate Rule 3, because both blue and yellow pictures would be done in paint. So (B), in fact, does force the dog to be done in blue or yellow, so you can mark that choice at this point and move on.

A 180 test taker knows that Logic Games answers are objectively correct. When she finds the correct answer, she has the confidence to move on without double-checking the remaining choices to "make sure." This is a big part of the reason why a 180 test taker can get through the entire Logic Games section while others run out of time.

(C), (D), and (E) all result in situations where the house and one tree could make up the blue/yellow pictures.

What's Next?

So, you with us so far? This concludes our Logic Games warm-up, as we move on to more challenging material. "Warm-up?!", you say? "*More* challenging material?" Perhaps you found these to be pretty tough already. Tough, maybe. But not quite brutal. Despite some complexities, all the games in this chapter revolve around a single game action, which is almost always easier than handling multiple tasks at once. Furthermore, all are amenable to a few key deductions and a little cleverness employed during the questions.

But perhaps you breezed through the games in this chapter, wondering to yourself, "I thought these were going to be difficult? What gives?" Have no fear. It gets worse. Much worse.

The final question here in "Class Pictures" serves nicely as a preview to the games you're about to battle in the next chapter. In question 6 above, you had to employ a form of backward reasoning to determine what would force a desired result. And that's exactly the essence of the games contained in chapter 3—games that ask you to put a designated process into action while looking forward and backward in time. We affectionately dub these monstrosities "Time Warps."

CHAPTER THREE

Time Warps

Once upon a time the LSAT test makers (perhaps out of boredom, who knows?) decided to stray from the usual game types and introduced aspiring law students to the wonderful world of what we at Kaplan call "process" games. A process game is one in which your task is to fit behavior to a prearranged plan or pattern. Since a key skill tested in this game type is your ability to think forward and backward in time, we also call them "Time Warps."

Games fitting this definition appeared regularly from LSAT PrepTest X through LSAT PrepTest XVI (1994–1995). They've been pretty much absent since then, but there are a few good reasons why wracking your brain on this game type will benefit your preparation. First, there's no guarantee that they won't appear again; in fact, one *did* appear on an undisclosed test in 1998. Secondly, there's always a chance that you'll see a game on your test that doesn't fit into the standard categories—what we at Kaplan call an "oddball" game—so pitting your wits against games that are, well, *unusual*, can't hurt, and will almost certainly help prepare you for any type of oddball that you may encounter.

Before you begin, here are some useful questions to think through when faced with a Time Warp game containing a process element:

- What is the situation at the start?
- How often do changes occur?
- What specifically happens during a change?
- How is the situation different after the change?
- Hypothesize: What could happen? Go through some "what ifs" about the game to get a feel for how the process works.

Besides the unusual game action, the games in this chapter contain a colorful cast of characters: a botanist, astronauts, professors, and a general. Immerse yourself in their worlds to help them all do what they need to do.

LOGIC GAME 8

A botanist is testing the effects of sunlight on four plants. At the beginning of the first month of the experiment, the plants—F, G, H, and I—are in front of the north window, the east window, the south window, and the west window, respectively. The botanist will rotate the plants exactly once a month, at the end of each month, in one of the following two ways:

Rotation 1: The plant in front of the north window will be moved to the east window. The plant in front of the east window will be moved to the south window. The plant in front of the south window will be moved to the west window. The plant in front of the west window will be moved to the north window.

Rotation 2: Plant F will be moved to the window that H was in front of during the previous month. Plant H will be moved to the window that Plant I was in front of during the previous month. Plant I will be moved to the window that G was in front of during the previous month. Plant G will be moved to the window that F was in front of during the previous month.

1. Which one of the following could be the window locations for the four plants at the beginning of the second month?

	north	east	south	west
(A)	F	G	H	I
(B)	F	I	H	G
(C)	G	F	I	H
(D)	I	F	G	H
(E)	I	G	F	H

2. If G is in front of the north window at the beginning of the second month, which one of the following must be true?

   (A) F is in front of the east window.
   (B) F is in front of the west window.
   (C) H is in front of the east window.
   (D) I is in front of the east window.
   (E) I is in front of the west window.

3. If F is in front of the east window at the beginning of the second month, which one of the following is a complete and accurate list of the windows that F could be in front of at the beginning of the third month?

   (A) north
   (B) west
   (C) south, west
   (D) east, south
   (E) north, east, south, west

4. Which one of the following CANNOT be true at the beginning of the third month?

   (A) Plant F is in front of the west window.
   (B) Plant G is in front of the east window.
   (C) Plant H is in front of the east window.
   (D) Plant I is in front of the east window.
   (E) Plant I is in front of the west window.

5. If, at the beginning of the third month, G is in front of the south window, which one of the following must be true?

   (A) Plant F was in front of the east window at the beginning of the second month.
   (B) Plant G was in front of the east window at the beginning of the second month.
   (C) Plant I was in front of the east window at the beginning of the second month.
   (D) The botanist used Rotation 1 to rotate the plants at the end of the first month.
   (E) The botanist used Rotation 1 to rotate the plants at the end of the second month.

6. If, at the beginning of the second month, I is in front of the north window, which one of the following could be true at the beginning of the third month?

   (A) Plant F is in front of the east window.
   (B) Plant F is in front of the north window.
   (C) Plant G is in front of the north window.
   (D) Plant H is in front of the west window.
   (E) Plant I is in front of the south window.

7. Which one of the following CANNOT be true at the beginning of the third month if the botanist rotated the plants according to Rotation 1 at least once during the first two months?

   (A) F is in front of the south window.
   (B) G is in front of the east window.
   (C) H is in front of the east window.
   (D) I is in front of the east window.
   (E) I is in front of the south window.

Logic Game 8: Plant Rotations

What Makes It Difficult

The presentation of an initial situation, followed by a description of how things change over time, are the sure giveaways that we have a Time Warp, or "process" game on our hands. The rules are long and intimidating. However, once you get past the initial shock, you'll find that they simply describe the mechanics of two possible rotation methods. You're best served spending a bit of extra time to make sure you get them right and find a reasonable way to represent the action.

The questions pose the usual difficulties found in these kinds of games. Some questions ask you to look forward in the process and follow the steps through to a result, while others—generally the tougher ones—tell you what the result of the process was, and ask you to work backward to reconstruct the situation that made this result possible. Another difficulty is that there are no big deductions to make up front. We simply have to bang out the questions one by one (seven, no less), following the rotations wherever they may lead.

There really isn't much to draw for this kind of game, but you have to compensate for this lack of pencil work with extra brainwork. As always, there are still a few key things you can do that should ease your brain's burden a bit.

Keys to the Game

Anticipate the relevant issues that will be tested. Namely, what can, cannot, or must be the plants' locations after one, two, or more rotations? What window can each plant be rotated to from their previous month's position? Based on the plants' locations after a certain number of rotations, what locations were possible in the previous months?

Simplify Rotation 1: Think of it simply as each plant moving one space clockwise. You may wish to indicate this visually on the page. Unfortunately, there's no analogous method to make Rotation 2 easier to handle. You simply have to note those switches on the page and refer to them when necessary.

Use your work on previous questions to help you with later ones. This is always a good strategy, but turns out to be especially helpful here.

Answers and Explanations

1. D   2. D   3. C   4. E   5. C   6. E   7. C

1. D

What does "at the beginning of the second month" mean? Since the plants are rotated exactly once a month, at the end of each month, this means that at the beginning of the second month the plants have gone through one rotation from their initial placements. So pick a rotation and set 'em in motion. Enacting Rotation 1 sends each plant one space clockwise, giving us:

north	east	south	west
I	F	G	H

Is that a choice? Yup, (D). Easy enough. But then again, we're just getting started, and the test makers often throw us a "gimme" early on in a tough game just to test if we understand the game's basic concept.

> A 180 test taker use Acceptability questions as tools to help cement the game's workings.

2. D

The plants have undergone one rotation, and G is at the north window. G starts at the east. If Rotation 1 was used, G would go south, so Rotation 2 must have been used. Using Rotation 2 on the initial setup, we see that G goes to the north (F's previous location), F goes to the south (H's old home), H goes to the west (I's last spot), and I goes to the east (G's old location). I at the east window is choice (D), the answer.

3. C

After one rotation F is at the east window. F starts up north. The only way for F to get to the east after one move is by way of Rotation 1, which puts F east, G south, H west, and I north. Where could F go next? Under Rotation 1, the east plant goes to the south. Under Rotation 2, F goes to H's previous location, so F would go to the west. South and west are the only two possibilities, choice (C).

> A 180 test taker stays active. He keeps asking himself the relevant questions, in this case: "How could this happen?" and "Where can or must the other entities be?"

4. E

Now we're entering pretty abstract territory: We're given no new information, and are asked about what can't be true at the beginning of month 3. First we have to translate what "the beginning of the third month" means: it means after two rotations.

> A 180 test taker cuts past abstraction by translating statements into a form that she can use.

So we need to take the entities through two rotations. From the initial setup, the plants could move to the following positions:

Rotation 1

north	east	south	west
I	F	G	H

Rotation 2

north	east	south	west
G	I	F	H

Now, begin with each of these new positionings and see where the plants could go next. After Rotation 1, if Rotation 1 is used again, I would go east, F would go south, G would go west, and H would go north, giving us:

north	east	south	west
H	I	F	G

Checking this against the choices, we see that I could be at the east window after two rotations, so we can cross off choice (D) since we're looking for something that *cannot* be true.

After Rotation 1, if Rotation 2 is used, F would go west, G would go east, H would go north, and I would go south, yielding:

north	east	south	west
H	G	I	F

We see from this that F could be at the west window and G could be at the east window after two rotations, which allows us to axe both (A) and (B).

After Rotation 2, if Rotation 1 is used, F would go to the west, G would go to the east, I would go to the south, and H would go to the north, giving us the same arrangement as the previous one. It therefore doesn't allow us to eliminate any of the remaining choices, so we press on.

After Rotation 2, if Rotation 2 is used, again F would go to the west, G would go to the south, H would go to the east, and I would go to the north.

north	east	south	west
I	H	G	F

This arrangement proves that H could be at the east window after two rotations, so axe choice (C). We're left with (E), the answer.

Takes a bit of work, doesn't it? But as you'll see, it turns out to be well worth the effort.

A 180 test taker often finds clever ways to cut questions down to size, but can force his way through a tough question when need be, too.

---

5. C

This potentially nightmarish question can be discarded quickly and painlessly if you handled question 4 in the manner described above, and you remembered to make use of that previous work here. We just went through the process of plotting out all the possibilities leading up to the month 3 arrangement, so we can just check the question stem against those. From them, we see that the only way for G to land at the south window at the beginning of month 3 is if Rotation 2 is performed consecutively. 1-1 puts G in the west, while 1-2 and 2-1 lands G in the east. Now it's simply a matter of scanning the choices for the one that accords with a double shot of Rotation 2.

(A) No, Rotation 2 sends F from north to south for the beginning of the second month.

(B) No, Rotation 2 sends G from east to north for the beginning of the second month.

(C) Yup: Rotation 2 sends I from west to east. (C) must be true and is the answer we seek.

(D), (E) No. We already decided that Rotation 2 must be used at the end of the first and second months in order for G to face south at the beginning of month 3.

A 180 test taker knows that long and difficult games must be written in such a way as to make at least a few shortcuts possible, and looks for such shortcuts at every turn.

---

6. E

If I is at the north window after one rotation, Rotation 1 must have been used on the initial arrangement. You've seen this before; this places F at the east, G at the south, H at the west, and I at the north. Where could the plants go from there? Again, use your previous work in question 4. Starting with the ordering just listed for the beginning of the second month, the plants could go to the following positions based on which rotation method is used next:

Rotation 1

north	east	south	west
H	I	F	G

Rotation 2

north	east	south	west
H	G	I	F

From there it's a simple matter of checking the choices against these two possibilities. I could be in front of the south window; choice (E) could be true and is the answer.

7. C

Now we're looking for what can't be true after two rotations if Rotation 1 was used for at least one of those rotations. This leads to three possibilities: Rotation 1 then Rotation 1; Rotation 1 then Rotation 2; and Rotation 2 then Rotation 1. Once again, we worked through each of these possibilities back in question 4:

Rotation 1 followed by Rotation 1

north	east	south	west
H	I	F	G

Rotation 1 followed by Rotation 2 and Rotation 2 followed by Rotation 1

north	east	south	west
H	G	I	F

Once again, all we have to do to find the choice that can't be true is match the choices against these possibilities. H is never at the east window, so (C) can't be true and is therefore the correct answer.

What's Next?

How'd you do? Not a bad game to cut your teeth on this Time Warp business. Notice how question 4 was the turning point of the game. Fighting your way through the hardest question of the set in fact made the following three questions much easier to handle. Here's a case in which what seemed to be a curse (you *were* cursing during that question, admit it) turned out to be a blessing in disguise. But don't expect such kind treatment from every process game. The next one, in fact, takes place in outer space, which seems to be where some of the questions originate. Onward!

LOGIC GAME 9

Four astronauts aboard a space shuttle—Dalton, Ellis, Ford, and Gunther—are assigned the following responsibilities on the first day of a three-day space mission: monitoring communications, walking in space, taking photos, and making repairs, respectively. At the beginning of each subsequent day of the mission, the astronauts' responsibilities are rotated, in accordance with exactly one of the following scenarios:

Scenario 1: Ford and Gunther are assigned to switch responsibilities.

Scenario 2: The astronaut last assigned the responsibility of walking in space is assigned the responsibility of making repairs, and the astronaut last assigned the responsibility of making repairs is assigned the responsibility of walking in space.

Scenario 3: Dalton and Gunther are assigned to switch responsibilities, and Ellis and Ford are assigned to switch responsibilities.

1. Each one of the following could be the assignment of astronaut to responsibility on the second day of the mission EXCEPT:

    (A) Dalton; monitoring communications
    (B) Ford; making repairs
    (C) Dalton; making repairs
    (D) Ellis; monitoring communications
    (E) Gunther; walking in space

2. Which one of the following is a complete and accurate list of astronauts whose responsibility on the second day of the mission could be the same as their responsibility on the first day of the mission?

    (A) Dalton, Ellis, Ford
    (B) Dalton, Ford, Gunther
    (C) Dalton, Ellis, Ford, Gunther
    (D) Dalton, Ellis
    (E) Ellis, Ford

3. If Ford's responsibilities remain constant throughout the mission, all of the following must be true EXCEPT:

    (A) Dalton's responsibilities remain constant throughout the mission.
    (B) Gunther is assigned to walk in space on the second day of the mission.
    (C) Ellis is assigned to walk in space on the third day of the mission.
    (D) The responsibilities are not rotated according to scenario 3 on the second day of the mission.
    (E) Ellis's responsibilities remain constant throughout the mission.

4. If no scenario is repeated and if responsibilities are rotated according to scenario 3 on the second day of the mission, then which one of the following could be true on the third day of the mission?

    (A) Ellis is assigned to monitor communications.
    (B) Ford is assigned to make repairs.
    (C) Dalton is assigned to take photos.
    (D) Ellis is assigned to walk in space.
    (E) Gunther is assigned to take photos.

5. If Ellis is assigned to make repairs on the third day of the mission, which one of the following CANNOT be true?

    (A) The responsibilities are rotated according to scenario 1 on the second day of the mission.
    (B) The responsibilities are rotated according to scenario 1 on the third day of the mission.
    (C) The responsibilities are rotated according to scenario 2 on the second day of the mission.
    (D) The responsibilities are rotated according to scenario 3 on the second day of the mission.
    (E) The responsibilities are rotated according to scenario 3 on the third day of the mission.

6. If at some point during the mission Dalton is assigned to take photos, which one of the following must be true on the second day of the mission?

    (A) Ellis is assigned to walk in space.
    (B) The responsibilities were rotated according to scenario 2.
    (C) Gunther is assigned to walk in space.
    (D) The responsibilities were rotated according to scenario 3.
    (E) Ford is assigned to monitor communications.

Logic Game 9: Space Mission

What Makes It Difficult

Dalton, Ford, Ellis, and Gunther have a pretty cool mission. Your mission, however—should you choose to accept it (and on test day, of course, you'd have no choice, especially if you're shooting for the big 1-8-0)—is pretty mundane: figuring out who does what on each day.

We're up against the same basic thing as in the previous game. It's hard because it's unfamiliar and a bit unusual, and the switches described are fairly wordy. "Scenarios" labeled 1, 2, and 3 may jut up against "days" one, two, and three in your head. As always, thinking backward in time requires mental agility, and what complicates things further is the fact that the switches take place on both the astronaut level (as per scenarios 1 and 3) and on the responsibility level (scenario 2). Not a big deal, but something we have to keep track of.

There are no deductions to blow the game wide open, which is par for the course in these process types. But that doesn't mean there's nothing that can help you get through in one piece. Here are the keys:

Keys to the Game

Anticipate the relevant issues that will be tested. Same as before. Here, we need to focus on who's doing what on each of the three days, and what assignments on one day make it possible for specific assignments to arise on other days.

Responsibilities are changed exactly twice. This is a helpful thing to notice. Day one is set, and the mission is only three days total. It's good to have an upward limit in place.

In scenarios 1 and 2, two astronauts switch tasks, and two stay the same. In scenario 3, all four switch. Not a major revelation, but again, anything that we can latch onto that places some restrictions on the action should help us in the long run.

A 180 test taker sees a Logic Game from all possible angles, noticing everything from big deductions down to small observations.

Don't assume anything that you're not explicitly told. Do the intro or the rules specify that each person must do a different job each day? No. Do they specify that no scenario can be repeated? No. Unless we're told otherwise, jobs can be repeated and any scenario can be executed twice.

A 180 test taker remains open to all possible game actions that are not explicitly forbidden.

Answers and Explanations

1. D   2. A   3. E   4. B   5. D   6. A

1. D

If the four wrong choices are possible assignments for the second day, then simply thinking through what could happen on day two—that is, after the enactment of exactly one scenario—should allow us to throw out those choices in fairly short order.

A 180 test taker is not thrown by a variation on an Acceptability question. She still uses it to think through, in advance of the remaining questions, the ways in which the game action works.

If scenario 1 is enacted on day two, Ford takes Gunther's repair job (B) while Gunther becomes the photographer (not a choice). Meanwhile, Dalton (A) and Ellis retain their previous jobs.

If scenario 2 is enacted, then Ellis and Gunther switch; Ellis does repairs (not a choice) while Gunther walks in space (E). Finally, scenario 3 sees Dalton take over Gunther's repair job (C), while Gunther monitors communications, Ellis takes over the photos, and Ford walks in space. Ellis must be the noncommunicative one of the bunch; we'll never see him monitoring communications, choice (D).

2. A

We got something of a head start on this question during question 1, where we saw (using scenario 1) that both Dalton and Ellis could retain their previous jobs on day two. Only choices (A), (C), and (D) mention both of those astronauts, so the other two must be tossed out. Under scenario 2, Dalton and Ford retain the same jobs while Ellis (the initial walker) and Gunther (the initial repairperson) switch. So Ford has to be included in the right answer too. But that's the lot: Everyone changes with scenario 3, so no matter what happens on day two, Gunther will have to change jobs. Dalton, Ellis, and Ford represent the "complete and accurate list" sought here.

3. E

If, as we're told, Ford never switches jobs over the entire three-day mission, then it has to be true that neither scenario 1 (where Ford switches with Gunther) nor scenario 3 (where everyone switches) can be executed. Which in turn means that scenario 2 must take place on both the second and third day. On day 2, Ellis the walker and Gunther the repairperson must switch, and on day three, they must switch back. Choices (A) through (D) all point to specific elements of the process just described. (E), however, is false: Ellis does a stint as repairperson on day two before resuming his space walk on the final day of the mission.

4. B

According to this if-clause, what just happened in question 3 cannot happen here; no scenario can be repeated. Then we're told to apply scenario 3 on day two, so during that day the assignments become:

D	E	F	G
repairs	photos	walking	comm

Given the prohibition against repetition, scenario 1 or 2 must be enacted on day three. If scenario 1 happens, Dalton and Ellis retain their jobs while Ford and Gunther switch. Since we're looking for something that could be true, it makes sense to take a quick peek at the choices to see if we can stop here.

A 180 test taker avails himself of every opportunity to make his work faster. In a "could be true" question, this means checking the choices as soon as something new is deduced.

Unfortunately, none of the choices corresponds to that state of affairs, so we'll have to press on. The only remaining possibility is that day three sees scenario 2 take place, in which case Ellis and Gunther retain their jobs while Dalton and Ford (currently repairperson and walker, respectively) switch. At the end of that process, Ford is the repairperson, as (B) has it.

5. D

Ouch. This question ups the ante even higher, taking us further into "backward reasoning" than we've gone up to now. Think about our ultimate goal: Ellis making repairs on day three. So Ellis, who starts day one walking in space, has to end up in repairs, the job that Gunther starts out with. Now scan the scenarios, and notice that scenario 2 seems to do what we need: switching Ellis the walker with Gunther the repairperson. Clearly we cannot execute scenario 2 twice, because Ellis and Gunther would begin day three in the same jobs they began with. But if scenario 2 were executed (giving Ellis the repair job), and another scenario could then take place that would *leave Ellis in that job* . . . well, that would be what we'd need. And, of course, scenario 1 is available for that very purpose. If scenario 2 is executed on day two and scenario 1 on day three, then Ellis ends up as repairperson and we see that (B) and (C) are true. Since we're looking for something that cannot be true, we can cross those off and move on.

Meanwhile, scenario 1 has another use, in tandem with scenario 3. Scenario 1 gives Gunther's job to Ford, while scenario 3 sees Ford exchange jobs with Ellis. Executed in that order, the repair job will go from Gunther on day one, to Ford on day two, to Ellis on day 3. And that demonstrates the possibility of (A) and (E) being true. What cannot happen is scenario 3 on day two, for that would bestow Gunther's repair job on Dalton, and there'd be no way for Ellis to inherit the repairs from Dalton on day three—no scenario allows for that.

6. A

This one has the vaguest opening of any question on this game ("If at some point . . ."), but it does give us a definite starting point: Dalton, who begins day one monitoring communications, must at some point take photos, the job Ford begins with. (And notice that the question leads to some kind of definition: The right answer is something that must be true on day two.) No scenario sees Dalton and Ford switch directly, so the "some point" must be day three. Our job therefore is to get Dalton in position to snag the photo gig, and one glance at the scenarios tells us that scenario 3 must be involved. Why? Because that's the only one in which Dalton makes a direct switch, and scenario 2 won't help because although Dalton may be involved there, it deals with walking and repairs only, while the stem is trying to get a camera into Dalton's hands.

It takes a little forward vision, but perhaps you noticed that if scenarios 1 and 3 were executed in that order, then Ford's initial photo job would go to Gunther on day two, and finally to Dalton on day three. In the process, as (A) has it, Ellis would indeed continue to walk in space on day two as he did on day one. As it happens, and as trial and error (if nothing else) might reveal, the process described is the *only* way to get the photo job to Dalton, so only (A) is true; the other choices either describe something that happens on day three (D) or that never happens at all: (B), (C), and (E).

What's Next?

These Time Warps are surely heating up, no? The next one introduces a new element not seen in these first two. See what you can make of "University Promotions."

LOGIC GAME 10

Promotions within a university's physics department are determined by a system involving an annual vote of the department's Promotions Committee. In January of the first year of the system, the faculty members of the department are as follows:

Full Professors: Kraft, Leon, Marko
Associate Professor: Norman
Assistant Professors: Oscar, Powell, Quinn
Lecturers: Rose, Stuart, Tower

Under the system, in June of each year at least one lecturer must be promoted to assistant professor, at least one assistant professor must be promoted to associate professor, and at least one associate professor must be promoted to full professor. The Promotions Committee consists of only the current full professors, and no one abstains on any promotion vote.

Everyone below the rank of full professor is voted on by each member of the Promotions Committee.
A faculty member is promoted upon receiving three or more Yes votes from the Promotions Committee.
Leon always votes No to Rose.
Kraft always votes No to Rose and Yes to Powell.
Marko always votes Yes to Powell.
During the first three years of the system, no faculty members leave the department and no new members are hired.

1. Which one of the following must be true?

   (A)   Powell is promoted to associate professor in the second year of the system.
   (B)   Norman is promoted to full professor in the first year of the system.
   (C)   Rose is promoted to full professor in the third year of the system.
   (D)   Quinn is promoted to associate professor in the first year of the system.
   (E)   Tower is promoted to assistant professor in the second year of the system.

2. Which one of the following must be false?

   (A)   Stuart and Tower are promoted to assistant professor in the first year of the system.
   (B)   Oscar, Powell, and Quinn are promoted to associate professor in the first year of the system.
   (C)   Neither Rose nor Quinn is promoted in the second year of the system.
   (D)   Neither Tower nor Oscar is promoted in the first year of the system.
   (E)   Either Stuart or Tower is promoted to assistant professor in the second year of the system.

3. Which one of the following must be true about the third year of the system?

   (A)   Powell is promoted to full professor.
   (B)   Stuart is promoted to associate professor.
   (C)   Tower is promoted to assistant professor.
   (D)   Oscar is promoted to full professor.
   (E)   Rose is promoted to assistant professor.

4. If Leon and Kraft always cast exactly the same votes, then which one of the following must be true?

   (A)   Rose is promoted to assistant professor in the second year of the system.
   (B)   Powell is promoted to full professor in the second year of the system.
   (C)   Oscar is promoted to associate professor in the second year of the system.
   (D)   Norman is promoted to full professor in the second year of the system.
   (E)   Tower is promoted to assistant professor in the second year of the system.

5. What is the maximum possible number of full professors following the vote in the second year of the system?

   (A)   4
   (B)   5
   (C)   6
   (D)   7
   (E)   8

6. If Powell is an associate professor for the entire second year of the system, then all of the following must be true EXCEPT:

   (A)   Leon voted Yes to Powell in the first year of the system.
   (B)   Leon voted No to Powell in the second year of the system.
   (C)   Leon voted Yes to Quinn in the second year of the system.
   (D)   At least two assistant professors are promoted in the first year of the system.
   (E)   Oscar or Quinn or both are promoted to full professor in the second year of the system.

Logic Game 10: University Promotions

What Makes It Difficult

The process element is of course a complexity to reckon with in this one, much as it was in the previous two games. We have to think flexibly, applying much mental dexterity working out the usual situations, continually asking ourselves such things as: "If this happens, what will be the case later on?" Or "if this is the case later on, what must have happened earlier?" But this one has a few added complications. The game is long and intimidating on the page. We begin with a given hierarchy, and then have changes determined by votes. Three positive votes result in a promotion; anything less and the faculty member in question stays where he or she is for another year. So we have to count votes, but that's not all: The people casting the votes changes over time also, as more people attain the rank of full professor each year.

And speaking of years, the time element is a bit confusing, what with the program beginning in January of Year 1, but the first vote taking place in June of that year, and in June of each subsequent year. Your understanding of this is certainly put to the test in the confusing question 6.

It's a good thing these people are in academia, considering that a Ph.D. may be needed to figure out this promotion scheme. Let's see how we can make this thing more manageable. In fact, there are many deductions to be made, which is actually suggested by the open-ended structure of the first three questions.

A 180 test taker notices when the question set includes "must be true" and "must be false" questions with no new information, and uses that information to infer that at least some things can be deduced up front.

Keys to the Game

Streamline the action. Condense it in your mind to "at least one person in each category gets bumped up each year."

Norman is promoted to full professor in Year 1's vote. He's the only eligible associate that year, and the requirement is clear: " . . . at least one associate professor must be promoted to full professor." Take it one step further:

Kraft, Leon, and Marko all voted for Norman in Year 1. Three votes are needed for promotion, and they're the only ones voting that year.

Rose is not promoted to assistant professor in Years 1 or 2. Two of the three original full professors are anti-Rose, so there's no way she's going anywhere until new blood joins the rank of full professor. The real clever among you probably sniffed out the further consequence of this:

Rose must be promoted to assistant professor in Year 3. The instructions are clear: Someone gets bumped from lecturer to assistant each year, and if Rose can't go in Years 1 or 2, then she'll be the only one left to go in Year 3. Wait, there's more:

Stuart and Tower must be promoted in Years 1 and 2, one in Year 1, the other in Year 2. If they both got bumped up in the first year, then no lecturer would be available for promotion in Year 2, as we've seen that Rose ain't moving on that soon.

Answers and Explanations

1. B   2. A   3. E   4. B   5. D   6. C

Well, it seems like we've answered a number of questions already, and in fact, we have. That's the whole point of thinking through the initial setup, looking for things that can be determined in advance. As far as process games are concerned, this was heavily stocked with possible deductions. If you didn't notice these things up front, that's okay, but you'd still be called upon to notice them in the course of answering the questions.

A 180 test taker looks to nail down all that she can during the setup stage in order to ease the burden of working through the question set.

---

1. B

Even in hard games we should anticipate a "gimme" or two—questions that reward us directly for our deductive work (or for simply hanging in there). We've just seen that (B) must be true: Norman must be promoted in Year 1.

(A) could be true but need not be: Powell could easily move from assistant to associate in Year 1.

(C) is impossible: Rose is simply not rising that high that fast, with Leon and Kraft's thumbs down.

(D) and (E) are also possible only, and easiest to spot since we know so little about Quinn and Tower.

2. A

Another of our deductions above: Once we noticed that Rose was mired in Lecturer Land for the first two years, we saw that one of Stuart and Tower must make the jump in each of the first two years. If *both* Stuart and Tower move up in Year 1, then they leave Rose behind; but Rose (as we've seen) cannot possibly move up in Year 2, because two of the four full professors voting that year, Leon and Kraft, will vote her down. And even if Rose *could* move up in Year 2, no lecturers would be left to be promoted in Year 3. No way around it: (A) is impossible.

A 180 test taker uses deductions made up front to knock off questions quickly and confidently.

(B) No problem. It's "at least one," remember. All three assistants can move up, because either Stuart or Tower (not, as we've just seen, both) will move up to take their place.

(C) Certainly Rose is going nowhere in Year 2, and Quinn could stay put as well.

(D) If true, then Stuart would move up to Assistant, and either Powell or Quinn to associate. Eminently possible.

(E) must be true. Some lecturer has to be promoted to assistant in Year 2; Rose is staying put, so of Stuart and Tower, whichever stays back in Year 1 will go forward in Year 2.

If you didn't make the deductions discussed above, then this is a good question to come back to after learning more about the game and seeing possible promotions in action.

A 180 test taker is armed with many strategies. Failing to notice a deduction in a Logic Game need not be disastrous because he finds other ways to streamline his work and get through the question set.

---

3. E

Perhaps a tough question to figure out on the fly, thinking three years into the future. But if you interrogated the situation as we did above, then this thinking is already done. As we've seen, Rose cannot move up until at least three full profs are willing to vote for her and outvote perennial naysayers Leon and Kraft. That cannot happen before the Year 3 vote; and since in Year 3 Rose will be the only lecturer left, she will have to move up after that vote. As for the others:

(A) and (D) could happen as early as Year 2; on the other hand, either Oscar or Powell could get no higher than associate.

(B) could happen as early as Year 2, but need not happen at all.

(C) could happen as early as Year 1, and *must* happen by Year 2. So (C) would be a perfectly good answer to the question of what *cannot* be true in the third year of the system.

4. B

What does it mean that Kraft and Leon always vote in lockstep? It means that Leon must always vote for Powell, which in turn means that Powell is always assured of three yes votes and hence will advance until achieving full professorship in Year 2. (B) is correct.

A 180 test taker transforms abstract "if" statements into concrete realities whenever possible.

(A) The stem doesn't change Rose's situation; she still cannot do any better than reach the assistant level in Year 3.

(C) and (E) are only possibly true, while (D) we've known to be false all along—Norman's on the Year 1 promotion plan.

5. D

Here's one that scratchwork can help with, since the movement of a maximum number of entities is concrete; we can plot it. Let's try to get as many as possible up to full status following Year 2's vote, which also means putting as many as possible in position Year 1 to get promoted to full professor in Year 2. At best, Year 1's vote could see N moving to full professor, all three assistants (O, P, and Q) becoming associates, and either Stuart or Tower becoming an assistant. Then, in Year 2's vote, O, P, and Q could all become full professors, while of S and T, one moves to associate and the other moves up to assistant. Those movements are all copacetic, so seven can be on the top rung of the academic ladder after Year 2's vote.

6. C

Here's the one that harps on the time element, as mentioned above. It's strangely worded, and difficult to decipher. At least we have only a single faculty member to deal with: Powell. So let's track her plight starting at the beginning of the system so that we can work in this "entire second year" business.

In January of Year 1, Powell was an assistant professor. If she became an associate professor by Year 2, then she must have won promotion in the vote in June of Year 1, getting three thumbs-ups from Kraft, Leon, and Marko. (A) is proven true right there, so we can cross if off. During the entire length of Year 2, however, Powell remained in that same job, which means that she must have been voted down in Year 2. If she were promoted, then she would be an associate for only half of Year 2. Powell always gets solid votes from Kraft and Marko, so Norman and Leon—choice (B)—must have voted thumbs-down; a yes from either would turn Powell into a full professor in June of Year 2. The kicker is that in Year 1, someone else besides Powell must have been promoted from assistant to associate—that's because *somebody* has to be promoted to full professor in Year 2, and we've just seen that it isn't Powell. Therefore (D) and (E) must be true: Powell and at least one other (O or Q, maybe both) must be promoted to associate in Year 1, and O or Q or both must have made it to Full Prof in Year 2. (C) is only possibly true, and hence correct.

What's Next?

Eek. Things sure took a turn for the worse there at the end, huh? This game is generally pretty nasty, deductions or no deductions. And speaking of generals, we have one coming up next in our final Time Warp challenge. This one harks back to "Plant Rotations," involving a similar north, south, east, west configuration. Of course, "Regiments and Areas" will pose its own unique difficulties, although thankfully we can leave this university-voting thing behind. There's only one decision maker in "Regiments and Areas": a general directing troops in the defense of a city. Let's see how you would fare as a military tactician.

LOGIC GAME 11

Four regiments—A, B, C, and D—are positioned to defend the areas to the north, south, east, and west of a city, respectively. At their general's command, exactly two of the regiments will join forces to form one large regiment, in accordance with the following conditions:

No regiment will be commanded to join forces with any other regiment more than once.

No regiment will defend two areas simultaneously.

If Regiment A joins forces with Regiments B or C, the resulting regiment will defend the west.

If Regiment B joins forces with Regiment D, the resulting regiment will defend the south.

If Regiment C joins forces with Regiments B or D, the resulting regiment will defend the north.

If Regiment D joins forces with Regiment A, the resulting regiment will defend the east.

1. If the only areas defended are the south and east, then which one of the following pairs of regiments must have joined forces?

    (A) A and B
    (B) B and D
    (C) C and D
    (D) A and D
    (E) B and C

2. If the general issues exactly one command, then which one of the following CANNOT be the areas defended by regiments?

    (A) east, west
    (B) north, south
    (C) north, south, east
    (D) north, south, east, west
    (E) south, west

3. If exactly one area is not defended by a regiment, then each of the following must be true EXCEPT:

    (A) Regiment A did not join forces with another regiment.
    (B) The west is not defended by a regiment.
    (C) Regiment B did not join forces with another regiment.
    (D) The general issued exactly one command.
    (E) Regiment D joined forces with another regiment.

4. If none of the original regiments is defending its original area, then which one of the following must be true?

    (A) Regiment A joined forces with another regiment to defend the west.
    (B) Regiment B joined forces with another regiment to defend the west.
    (C) Regiment C joined forces with another regiment to defend the north.
    (D) Regiment D joined forces with another regiment to defend the east.
    (E) Regiment A joined forces with another regiment to defend the east.

5. If the general's second command results in two regiments joining forces to defend the north, then which one of the following must be false?

    (A) The east is not defended after the general's first command.
    (B) The west is not defended after the general's first command.
    (C) The east is defended after the general's first command.
    (D) The west is defended after the general's first command.
    (E) The south is not defended after the general's first command.

6. If at some point exactly three regiments are defending their original areas, and the general issues the maximum number of commands, which one of the following must be true?

    (A) Regiment A joined forces with another regiment to defend the east.
    (B) Regiment B joined forces with another regiment to defend the north.
    (C) Regiment B joined forces with another regiment to defend the west.
    (D) Regiment C joined forces with another regiment to defend the north.
    (E) Regiment C joined forces with another regiment to defend the west.

Logic Game 11: Regiments and Areas

What Makes It Difficult

How'd you do? Are you rushing to the phone to call West Point? Or did you find that the city would be overrun and burnt to the ground if you were in charge?

The action is a bit more straightforward than that of the previous game (as if that's any consolation!), and may remind you a bit of the Plant Rotations game, although there's a new wrinkle we need to consider—this business of *combining* the regiments. How does that happen? It's left kind of vague in the introductory paragraph, and we need the first two indented rules to fully understand the game's action. The last four rules set out the consequences of the various combinations, and we have no choice but to get them down on the page, while of course noting the regiments' initial positions. There's nothing more to sketch.

Unlike in the previous game, there's also not much in the way of deductions, so you simply have to rely on your ability to power through the questions. And those are no picnic, either. There's the usual amount of backward thinking involved in these process games, and a number of questions contain multiple possibilities that simply need to be plotted out before an answer can be determined.

Here are a few things that you may have noticed that make the game a bit easier to handle.

Keys to the Game

When two regiments combine, they go where the rules take them, and then they're done. Also, regiments never split up. These are the correct interpretations of Rules 1 and 2.

After an initial command, one or two areas will be left undefended. A second command is possible after the first switch—the two regiments not involved in the first command can combine, leaving two definite areas undefended.

The general issues a maximum of two commands. After two commands, all four regiments will have been involved in a combination, meaning that nothing further is possible.

A 180 test taker looks to establish numerical parameters in games that don't explicitly set them out.

The scenario set out in Rule 4 is unique—it's the only case in which a regiment (B, to be precise) combines with another regiment but stays to defend its original area. Noticing this is the key to a few of the more difficult questions.

Answers and Explanations

1. D   2. D   3. C   4. C   5. A   6. E

1. D

For the south and east to be the only defended areas, regiments must disappear from the north and west. Regiments A and D are in those areas initially, and if they join forces, the combined new regiment would join C in the east, which fits perfectly with the stem. In fact, that's the only way to satisfy the stem: If the general issues two commands, then somehow the four regiments would have to form two pairs that would end up in the south and east only. But the only combo that ends up in the south is B + D, and the only one that ends up in the east is A + D. So that doesn't work. A + D heading east must be the command here, so (D) is correct.

> A 180 test taker uses the first few questions of a difficult game to confirm that he fully understands the game action and rules. If he encounters any unexpected problems, he looks back at the game intro for something he may have missed.

2. D

Not so difficult for those who keep the big picture in mind. Recall the earlier observations regarding the consequences of commands. After one command either one area (if Rule 4 is enacted) or two areas (if Rules 3, 5, or 6 are enacted) will be undefended, so the clever test taker speeds down to and marks off choice (D) without much ado, or much time spent, for that matter. The following actions prove that the other choices are all possible:

(A) A + B → west

(B) C + D → north

(C) B + D → south

(E) A + C → west

> A 180 test taker looks for shortcuts to rack up as many 10-second points as possible, and resorts to brute force techniques only when necessary.

3. C

Here's the first place where our analysis of Rule 4 comes in handy. There's only one way for exactly one area to be left undefended, and that's if B joins with D to defend the south. As we saw, B begins in the south, so the result looks like this:

north	south	east	west
A	B	C	
	D		

All other combinations entail both regiments traveling to new territory, which would immediately leave two areas undefended. But maybe a second command could remedy that situation, enabling the defense of three areas so that only one would be undefended? No way. No matter what successive combos the general picks, two commands would mean two conglomerate regiments defending two areas, leaving two open for attack. So in order to satisfy the stem, we need exactly one command sending Regiment D to join B in the south, leaving the west as the single undefended area. Every choice accords precisely with this scenario except for (C), which in fact must be false under these circumstances.

4. C

Every regiment moves in this one, which should immediately suggest two things: First, having just dealt with a B + D → south scenario in the previous question, we know that this command is verboten, since B would stay at home in the south, in violation of the stem. Secondly, the general must have issued two commands; if only one command is issued, at least some regiments will remain where they are. Now perhaps this is a simple question buried within a difficult question set, in which case one of those deductions would be listed as a choice. No such luck. Based on the nature of the choices, we're forced to examine the more complicated question—where do they go? Let's power through the choices:

(A) Must Regiment A head west? Let's try to send A somewhere else in order to prove that choice (A) need not be true. The only other option for A is joining up with D (which starts out west) to defend the east. So far so good. Then B and C can merge and head north, new territory for both of those regiments. Since we've shown that Regiment A need not go east, choice (A) need not be true. Applying the same method to the other choices:

(B) B + C → north, A + D → east proves (B) need not be true.

(C) Regiment C's only other possible destination besides north is west, which it defends in conjunction with A. That leaves B and D, and the problem discussed above: When these two hook up, B stays put in the south, and that violates the stem. Regiment C therefore must, as this choice maintains, hook up and head north.

(D) C + D → north, A + B → west proves (D) need not be true.

(E) A + B → west, C + D → north proves (E) need not be true.

A 180 test taker is adept at eliminating choices in "must be true" questions by proving exceptions to the assertions in the wrong choices.

---

5. A

Question 5 takes us to a predictable place in process games—beyond the first step to a later stage in the process. We're told that the second command results in forces combining to march north, so we need to work backward to infer what might have or must have happened before that. Only a limited number of commands send regiments north: C + B and C + D. If C and B join to head north after command 2, then A + D → east would be the necessary combination in command 1. Here's what that would look like. Let's call it Option 1:

after one command

north	south	east	west
	B	C	
		A/D	

after two commands

north	south	east	west
B/C		A/D	

If, however, C and D join to head north after command 2, then A + B → west would be the necessary combination in command 1. Option 2 would therefore look like this:

after one command

north	south	east	west
		C	D
			A/B

after two commands

north	south	east	west
C/D			A/B

Now that we've covered all possibilities, we can check our scenarios against the choices, looking for the one that must be false. And we don't have to look far: The east is defended after command 1 in both options, so (A) must be false and (C) must be true. (A) is therefore the correct answer. As for the others, Option 1 shows that (B) could be true, while Option 2 shows that both (D) and (E) are possible.

A 180 test taker is not afraid to plot out multiple options when necessary, and does so quickly and confidently.

---

6. E

This one is the flip side of question 3, and in fact we can use the same reasoning to speed us on our way. We saw in the earlier question that in order for exactly one area to be undefended, D must have joined with B to defend the south as a result of the general's first command. That way, B stays in the south, leaving the west as the only undefended area. If any other command is issued first, then two regiments will head to new territory, and there will never be a point at which three regiments are defending their original areas, as required by the stem. "Exactly three regiments defending their original areas" here in question 6 is functionally identical to question 3's "exactly one area is not defended," so as in the earlier question, B + D → south must be the general's first command here.

A 180 test taker recognizes when questions that employ different wording in actuality mean the same thing or hinge on the same concept.

That takes care of the "at some point" part of the question stem, but wait, there's more: The general issues the maximum number of commands, which we know to be two. So after B and D combine, A and C must get together and head west.

after one command

north	south	east	west
A	B/D	C	

after two commands

north	south	east	west
	B/D		A/C

Now it's a simple matter of scoping out the truism. (E) has it right for this final question of the game.

What's Next?

You've now seen examples of sequencing, grouping, matching, and process game actions playing out individually in various games. Now let's turn to chapter 4 and see what happens when these actions are combined *within* single games.

CHAPTER FOUR

Volatile Mixtures

The plot thickens, as we move now from single-action games to multiple-action games. What does that mean, exactly? Well, remember "House Decoration" in chapter 2, the game in which we had to help a designer distribute eight furniture items into three different rooms? Not a simple task, was it? Well, now imagine that we also had to determine, for example, which pieces of furniture were new and which were used. That certainly complicates matters, doesn't it? Or how about chapter 2's "Show Riders"? Instead of Art, Brenda, and Chaz magically appearing as the stars of the show, what if we had to first select the three lucky showpeople from a pool of seven eligible riders? That would, annoyingly, add a grouping element to the game's basic matching action.

And that's essentially what these "mixture"—or as we at Kaplan often call them, "hybrid"—games do: add one game action on top of another. They're complicated because they require us to handle many things at once. As the games in previous chapters aptly illustrate, managing a single game action can be daunting enough; now we have to become jugglers.

So, what can you do? A few pointers:

- Keep your focus as you scope out the various challenges presented by hybrid games. It's easy to get distracted when there's a lot going on, but you must be clear on exactly what it is you're asked to do. And one way to do that . . .

- Think in terms of active verbs when decoding the game introductions. For example, say to yourself: "My job is to *select*; to *match*; to *order*"; and so on.

- Determine which, if any, action is the primary driver of each game. Not all game actions are created equal. In one game, sequencing may dominate, while a grouping element may be secondary. In another game, these may be reversed. Understanding which action dominates will help you relate to the essence of the game, and that will ultimately translate into points.

- When answering individual questions, focus on the action that's tested. Even when multiple game actions are present, some questions focus on only one, and recognizing that will enable you to home in on the relevant issue.

Enough said—let's get at 'em, beginning with everyone's favorite messenger, Wendell.

LOGIC GAME 12

Wendell, a messenger, makes exactly six deliveries during the course of a five-day work week, from Monday to Friday. He makes no more than two deliveries on any given day. Each delivery consists of exactly one item, either a single package or a single document. The six items delivered are selected from the following items: packages A, B, C, D, and E, and documents F, G, H, J, and K.

> If Wendell delivers C, then he delivers K the very next day.
> If Wendell delivers B, then he does not deliver E.
> If Wendell delivers F, then he delivers G.
> If Wendell delivers G, then he delivers F.
> If Wendell delivers K, then he delivers A on a later day of the week than K.
> Wendell delivers D on Thursday.
> The number of packages and the number of documents Wendell delivers during the week are not equal.

1. Which one of the following is impossible?

    (A) Wendell makes one delivery on each of exactly two days during the week.
    (B) Wendell makes one delivery on each of exactly three days during the week.
    (C) Wendell makes two deliveries on exactly one day during the week.
    (D) Wendell makes two deliveries on each of exactly two days during the week.
    (E) Wendell makes two deliveries on each of exactly three days during the week.

2. Wendell CANNOT deliver which one of the following pairs of items on the same day?

    (A) A and H
    (B) C and D
    (C) D and E
    (D) F and J
    (E) G and K

3. The delivery of which one of the following items would make it impossible for Wendell to deliver G?

    (A) A
    (B) C
    (C) E
    (D) H
    (E) K

4. If Wendell delivers E exactly two days before he delivers C, then all of the following could be true EXCEPT:

    (A) Wendell delivers C the day after H and the day before D.
    (B) Wendell delivers D the day after C and the day before H.
    (C) Wendell de livers H the day after E and the day before C.
    (D) Wendell delivers J the day after C and the day before A.
    (E) Wendell delivers K the day after J and the day before A.

5. Which one of the following could be true?

    (A) A and E are the only packages Wendell delivers.
    (B) C and D are the only packages Wendell delivers.
    (C) F and G are the only documents Wendell delivers.
    (D) H and J are the only documents Wendell delivers.
    (E) J and K are the only documents Wendell delivers.

6. If Wendell delivers more documents than packages, then Wendell CANNOT deliver which one of the following pairs of items?

    (A) A and D
    (B) B and D
    (C) E and K
    (D) F and H
    (E) H and J

7. If Wendell makes deliveries on the fewest number of days possible, and if he delivers C on Monday, then which one of the following must be false?

    (A) Wendell delivers C on an earlier day of the week than J.
    (B) Wendell delivers E on the same day of the week as K.
    (C) Wendell delivers H on a later day of the week than E.
    (D) Wendell delivers K on an earlier day of the week than B.
    (E) Wendell delivers C on the same day of the week as H.

Logic Game 12: Wendell's Deliveries

What Makes It Difficult

Our first game is a fairly common hybrid variety: a mixture of sequencing and grouping. As for the grouping aspect, six items need to be selected for delivery from a group of 10 items total. Complicating this grouping feature is the fact that the available items themselves are broken up into two categories: packages and documents. The sequence element involves a straightforward calendar schedule; once the items for delivery are selected, Wendell delivers them in some order during the five days of a single week. So we not only need to worry about which items are in play, but also standard sequencing concerns such as which items are delivered before and after which others.

There are as many rules as questions—a high number of each—and only one concrete piece of information among them. Rule 7 is particularly troublesome, compounding the numbers element introduced in the introductory paragraph. There are exactly six deliveries, with no more than two on any given day, but now we have to also make sure that Wendell deliver an unequal number of packages and documents.

The question set is fairly difficult, containing a large number of abstract stems with no new information as well as an unusually large number of questions phrased in the negative; that is, looking for things that *cannot* be true, are *impossible*, and must be *false*. The choices in question 1 take a certain amount of deciphering. The questions involving sequencing all contain shades of the grouping element, since there's no way to order the deliveries without first knowing which items are delivered. All in all, a very complex treatment of a fairly straightforward scenario. Luckily there are a few key deductions that simplify things for us. Did you notice them?

Keys to the Game

Wendell delivers either four packages and two documents or two packages and four documents. There are only two ways to get to six without selecting an equal number of each type: one and five or two and four. But Rule 2 forbids us to select all five packages, and taking all five documents doesn't work either: Since K requires A, and D is always selected, that would be seven items selected. So a 4/2 breakdown it is. And we can be more specific . . . .

If four packages and two documents are delivered, A and C must be delivered. D is always taken, and only one of B and E is eligible (Rule 2). **K must also be delivered (Rule 1), which means F and G cannot be,** since choosing one means choosing the other and in this 4/2 breakdown only two documents can be delivered.

If two packages and four documents are delivered, F and G must be selected. That's because leaving out one means leaving out the other, and there would be no way to select four documents. **And in this scenario, C cannot be delivered,** since choosing C means choosing K, and by extension, choosing A, which, including the omnipresent D, would put us over the top on the package front.

A 180 test taker scopes out all of the number breakdown possibilities in games that are heavily invested in numerical restrictions.

These deductions don't blow the game wide open, but they do give the clever test taker a way in to each question that others may not have at their disposal. And any advantage is significant on the difficult, time-pressured Logic Games section.

Answers and Explanations

1. B   2. B   3. B   4. D   5. E   6. C   7. D

1. B

We're looking for an impossibility, given no new information, and perhaps you noticed that each choice deals with the number of deliveries on different number of days during the week. That means that the test makers are simply interested in seeing if we understand how six entities can be distributed among five days when the maximum per day is two.

A 180 test taker uses the nature of the answer choices in abstract questions to help direct her attack on the question.

Here are the possibilities:

2, 1, 1, 1, 1

2, 2, 1, 1, 0

2, 2, 2, 0, 0

Checking these against the choices, (A) and (D) conform to the second option, (C) matches the first scenario, and (E) pegs the third possible breakdown of items per day. (B) is the impossibility: Having exactly one delivery on each of exactly three days would require scheduling a three-delivery day, which isn't allowed, so (B) is correct.

2. B

Since the correct answer is a pair that *cannot* be chosen together on the same day, the four wrong choices will be pairs that *can* (or must) be. This question might be profitably postponed until later in the game, since in the course of the questions, we're bound to see lots of pairs of items chosen together on the same day; in other words, more than one wrong answer for question 2 is likely to emerge as we go along. If you answered it right off, however, you'd see it's not very difficult. Rule 6 tells us a fact (our one single concrete fact at this point) about a day late in the week, and Rules 1 and 5 deal with entities later in the week than other entities, so chances are a combination of these rules will lead to the impossible pair of items we seek.

A 180 test taker zeros in on what appear to be the heaviest restrictions when faced with a "CANNOT be true" type of question.

If, as (B) has it, C and D are delivered on the same day, that day would of course be Thursday; K would have to be delivered on Friday (Rule 1), but then there would be no place to put A as mandated by Rule 5. All of the other choices are perfectly possible—no need to run through them.

3. B

Which item is incompatible with G? All we know about G from the rules is that the delivery of document G requires the delivery of document F, but a combination of two of our deductions above tells us right off the bat that G and C can never be a part of an acceptable group. If there are four packages and two documents delivered, A and C must be delivered, because D is always taken, and only one of B and E is allowed. Since C is taken, K must also be delivered, which means F and G cannot be, because this 4/2 breakdown allows for only two documents. So the only way that Wendell can deliver F and G is if he delivers four documents and two packages, in which case choosing C would lead to a violation since C requires K which in turn requires A. That's too many packages. Definitely not an easy question, and another which may have benefited from your skipping and returning to after more acceptable orderings were in the books.

A 180 test taker senses when postponing a question may be the optimal way to go.

---

4. D

The relevant question to work our way into this one is: "Where could C be?" Well, begin with where C *can't* be—Thursday or Friday—since if C is delivered, K must be delivered on a later day and A on an even later day than K. So the latest C can be delivered is Wednesday, lest we run out of room for K and A. Taking into account the requirement in the stem, it turns out C in fact *must* be delivered on Wednesday, resulting in the arrangement:

Mon	Tues	Wed	Thurs	Fri
E		C	D/K	A

With A, C, D, and E already present, we know we're in the four packages, two documents world, which means the final item must be document H or J, since the FG pair would put us over the limit. With that in mind, we can test the choices, in search of the one that can't be true:

(A), (C) Pop H into Tuesday and we can cross off (A) and (C) as eminently possible.

(B) However, maybe H is on Friday, in which case (B) would work.

(D) would require putting J on Thursday, which would result in three items delivered on Thursday, a definite no-no according to the "two max per day" numbers rule in the intro. (D) is what we want.

For the record, (E) works just fine as long as J joins C on Wednesday.

5. E

Another vague question offering no new information, so we have two choices: We can try the choices out one by one, or we can look to see if any of the choices conform to an arrangement already seen. Well, the previous question resulted in a nearly full ordering, and lo and behold, in the 4/2 packages-to-documents breakdown depicted, J and K could be the only documents delivered, as choice (E) maintains. We can see this as well from our earlier deduction that in the four packages, two documents scenario, one of the documents selected must be K, with the other being H or J. This, incidentally, eliminates (C) and (D) from consideration.

(A) is easy to kill on account of Rule 6: D is an omnipresent package in this game.

(B) C requires K, and K requires package A, so C and D can't be the only two packages taken.

6. C

"More documents than packages" may not mean a lot to someone who didn't put any effort into forming deductions, but for those who saw the kinds of keys discussed above, and especially the numbers breakdown, know this immediately puts us into the four documents, two packages world. And we also know exactly what that entails: F and G are delivered, but C cannot be. With that in mind, let's find our illegal pairing:

(A) AD / FGHK works fine, so (A) is out.

(B), (D), (E) BD / FGHJ works fine, so we can kill (B), (D), and (E) from that delivery roster alone.

A 180 test taker is adept at using a single valid scenario to eliminate a number of different choices. Her goal is to not do any more work than necessary.

(C) K requires the delivery of A, and D is always delivered, so throwing E in as well would give us three packages right there. But then there would be no way for more documents than packages to be delivered, so the pair in (C) is the one that doesn't work.

7. D

Sequencing makes a reappearance after a brief hiatus over the last two questions; we can tell by the stem's requirement that C must be dropped off on Monday, and also by the "earlier, later, same day" wording of the choices. But grouping is never far behind in this game, and, in fact, we can hark all the way back to our work in question 1 to get a leg up here. There, we decided that the only possible number distributions of items to days of the week are:

$$2, 1, 1, 1, 1$$
$$2, 2, 1, 1, 0$$
$$2, 2, 2, 0, 0$$

The fewest number of possible delivery days is therefore three, as long as two packages are delivered on each of the three days. Back to the sequencing element: C on Monday means K on Tuesday and A sometime after that. But to keep with the three-delivery-days requirement, we'll have to pair A up with D on Thursday, giving us:

Mon	Tues	Wed	Thurs	Fri
C	K		D/A	

Furthermore, with three packages already, there must be one more package and one more document added to the roster. B or E must be the other package, and H or J will do it for the documents. We don't know which of these will be delivered, but we do know that one will have to be delivered on Monday and the other on Tuesday to give us the 2/2/2 breakdown. And that's what allows us to single out (D) as the choice that must be false: For K to be delivered on an earlier day of the week than B, B will have to either be delivered on Thursday, which already has two deliveries, or Wednesday or Friday, in violation of the mandate in the stem. Various ways of inserting B or E and H or J into the first two days of the week show the remaining choices to be possible.

What's Next?

As you can see, there's a lot going on in these mixture games, but the upside is that they usually provide fertile ground for deductions. So keep your eyes open for opportunities to combine the rules. "Wendell's Deliveries" combines a time sequence with a grouping aspect. The following game, "Wax Statues," combines a basic linear sequencing arrangement with a matching element. Don't get spooked out by the combination of tasks, or, for that matter, by the realistically lifelike wax gangster, inventor, and athletes haunting the corridors of the wax museum. See what you can do with them.

LOGIC GAME 13

Exactly four statues stand in line on the floor of a wax museum, numbered 1 through 4 from left to right. Two of the statues are male figures and the other two are female figures. Two of the statues represent athletes, one represents a gangster, and the other represents an inventor. Exactly one of the four statues glows in the dark.

> The statue that glows in the dark is either statue 1 or statue 4.
> Statue 2 represents an athlete.
> At least one male figure stands in line between the two female figures.
> One of the statues representing an athlete glows in the dark.

1. Which one of the following must be true of statue 3?

    (A) It represents either the gangster or an athlete.
    (B) It is either a male figure or it represents the inventor.
    (C) It stands in line immediately adjacent to a statue that glows in the dark.
    (D) It is either a male figure or it stands in line immediately adjacent to a female figure.
    (E) It stands in line immediately adjacent to two statues representing athletes or immediately adjacent to two statues that do not glow in the dark.

2. If statue 4 is a male figure that glows in the dark, then all of the following must be true EXCEPT:

    (A) Statue 1 is a female figure.
    (B) Statue 2 is a male figure.
    (C) Statue 3 represents the gangster.
    (D) Statue 4 represents an athlete.
    (E) Exactly one statue stands in line between the two statues representing athletes.

3. If the two male figures stand in line immediately adjacent to each other, then which one of the following must be false?

    (A) A female figure glows in the dark.
    (B) The statue representing the inventor is a female figure.
    (C) Statue 3 is a male figure.
    (D) Both statues representing athletes are male figures.
    (E) The statue representing the gangster is a female figure.

4. If the two statues representing athletes stand in line immediately adjacent to each other, then which one of the following would make it possible to precisely determine every characteristic of the four statues in line?

    (A) A statue representing a female inventor stands in line immediately adjacent to a statue representing the gangster.
    (B) A statue representing a male gangster stands in line immediately adjacent to a statue representing an athlete.
    (C) A statue representing a male athlete stands in line immediately adjacent to a statue representing the other athlete.
    (D) A statue representing a female gangster stands in line immediately adjacent to a statue representing an athlete.
    (E) A statue representing a male inventor stands in line immediately adjacent to a statue representing an athlete.

5. If statue 3 represents a female gangster, then all of the following must be true EXCEPT:

    (A) If statue 1 represents the inventor, then statue 4 glows in the dark.
    (B) If the statue that glows in the dark is a female figure, then the statue representing the inventor is a male figure.
    (C) If statue 1 glows in the dark, then only one statue representing an athlete is a male figure.
    (D) If the statue representing the inventor is a female figure, then both male figures represent athletes.
    (E) If statue 2 is a male figure, then statue 4 glows in the dark.

6. If the statue representing the inventor is a male figure, and if it stands at some distance to the left of the statue representing the gangster, then which one of the following must be true?

    (A) Statue 1 is a male figure.
    (B) Statue 1 glows in the dark.
    (C) Statue 2 is a female figure.
    (D) Statue 3 represents the inventor.
    (E) Statue 3 is a male figure.

Logic Game 13: Wax Statues

What Makes It Difficult

The sequencing element isn't so bad here—only four statues standing in a row. But the matching part is a little involved, what with three types of statues of various genders, one glowing in the dark. We have to keep tabs on three things about four statues, and combining all that with the 1–4 sequencing element makes for a somewhat complicated mixture. There is a heavy number dimension to incorporate as well: exactly two males, two females, two athletes, one gangster, and one inventor grace the floor of the museum. Rule 3 is less definite, requiring at least one male standing between two females.

Despite these complexities, the setup is really not so bad. The questions, however, make up for that, containing a usual mix of difficulties: "EXCEPT" questions that require you to weed out things that cannot or need not be true; a question with hypotheticals (if-statements) in the answer choices; and long-winded questions containing wordy answer choices that require extra concentration to keep the entities and match-ups straight.

As usual, a little insight up front goes a long way toward making your task much more manageable. How did you do pinpointing the keys to the game?

Keys to the Game

Either statue 1 or 4 must be a glowing athlete. This deduction results from combining Rule 1, Rule 4, and the last line of the intro.

> A 180 test taker knows that not every rule is indented—that often, important rules (especially ones regarding the numbers that govern the game) appear in the opening paragraph.

> A 180 test taker looks to combine rules containing the same entity, understanding that these present the best opportunities for deductions.

Statue 3 must be the gangster or the inventor. Since Rule 2 locates an athlete in space 2, and we've narrowed the second athlete's position to 1 or 4, statue 3 must be G or I.

The two female statues cannot stand next to one another. This is the simplest and most efficient understanding of Rule 3. As long as we never order adjacent females, this rule will be satisfied.

> A 180 test taker looks past the wording of rules to figure out what they mean in the simplest terms possible; that is, in terms that will be easy to apply in the context of the game.

Answers and Explanations

1. E   2. C   3. D   4. D   5. E   6. E

1. E

We deduced that statue 3 must be the gangster or inventor, and it pays to scan for that. Unfortunately, the test makers will have none of making things that easy for us. We have here examples of the complex and wordy choices alluded to above. Let's simply go about eliminating the ones that need not be true.

(A) At least our deduction above allows us to kill this one quickly: Statue 3 could be the inventor.

(B) What's wrong with female gangster for statue 3? Nothing, as the following arrangement clearly shows.

1	2	3	4
female inventor	male athlete	female gangster	male athlete (glow)

This scenario eliminates choice (D) as well.

(C) need not be true. The glowing athlete could line up in spot 1.

That leaves (E), which you could (and should!) circle with no further fanfare.

A 180 test taker has the utmost confidence in his work. When he has confidently eliminated all but one choice, he marks down the remaining one without bothering to check it.

For the sake of completeness, we'll treat choice (E) here, even though the advice above should prompt you not to do so on test day. If the second glowing athlete takes spot 4 in line, as indicated in the sequence above, then the first part of (E) is true. If, however, the second glowing athlete stands in space 1, then the second part of (E) is true as well. Either way you slice it, (E) must be true.

2. C

We can use the arrangement created in choice (B) above as our base. The figure that glows in the dark is an athlete, so the male glower in spot 4 must be an athlete, and the females must alternate in 1 and 3 in order to satisfy Rule 3. The only thing left unresolved is whether the gangster is first and the inventor third, or the other way around. All of the choices conform to this state of affairs except for (C): Statue 3 could be the inventor.

3. D

There's only one way for the male statues to stand next to each other and still maintain the integrity of Rule 3, and that's if the male statues are 2 and 3, leaving the female statues as 1 and 4.

(A) and (C) are therefore statements that must be true—a male is third in line; and the glowing statue, whether it's first or fourth, must be female. The statement that must be false is (D). The athlete that's second in line must be male, but the other athlete, the glowing one, is either statue 1 or 4, and in this situation those statues are female. As for the others: If the male in the third space is a gangster, then (B) would be true, but if the male in the third space is an inventor, then (E) would be true. The only statement that cannot be true, and therefore must be false, is (D).

4. D

First off, we have to deal with the sequencing concern in the stem and get those athletes next to each other. It turns out there's only one way to do that: Since one of the athletes is in space 2, the other one must be standing in 1 or 3. But one of those athletes must glow, and of 1 and 3 only space 1 allows for this, so the glowing athlete must be first in line, next to the other athlete in spot 2. In a simpler game, this realization might be enough to answer the question. As if! Here, the question itself is complex, and the choices no picnic, either. We're looking for a piece of information that would solidify the entire ordering; that is, one that make it possible to know every attribute of every statue in line. That means that the wrong choices all leave at least one thing up for grabs. Let's see what effect each one has on the situation.

(A) If the athletes are in spaces 1 and 2, the inventor and the gangster must take 3 and 4, in some order. Can we tell which statue is in which spot? Nope. Either way works fine, so this isn't the choice that squares everything away.

(B) What if a male gangster stands next to an athlete? Well, that tells us something helpful. With athletes in 1 and 2, the only open space adjacent to an athlete is space 3, so we can fill that slot with a male gangster, resulting in:

1	2	3	4
athlete (glow)	athlete	male gangster	inventor

The inventor must be in the last slot, but now we have the male/female aspect to deal with. Can we settle that issue as well? Well, we can't place a male statue in spot 4, because then the females would be adjacent in 1 and 2, in violation of Rule 3. So 4 must be female. But what about 1 and 2? Male in 1 and female in 2 would satisfy Rule 3 as well as the other way around, so we can't say that everything is precisely determined.

(B) must be axed, but it got us so close that it in fact points the way toward correct choice (D), which is identical to (B) except for making the gangster in 3 female, which *does* fully determine the sex of each statue. A female in 3 means a female in 1 and males in 2 and 4. And that's the whole shebang.

A 180 test taker is able to use the learning gained in eliminating certain choices to zero in on the right choice, or at least narrow the field in searching for the correct choice.

(C) tells us the least of all: We already know the two athletes are next to each other. Knowing that one is male doesn't tell us *which* one, nor does it solidify the gangster/inventor placements in spots 3 and 4.

(E) Since the gangster and inventor are functionally identical in this game, this choice has the same exact consequences as choice (B)—we'd still be up in the air regarding the sex of statues 1 and 2.

A 180 test taker takes note of entities whose functions and restrictions are exactly the same, and uses that information to quickly eliminate wrong choices.

---

5. E

With all those if-statements in the answer choices, this one looks to be a horror show, but it's manageable if you use your pencil and your head, in either order. If statue 3 is a female gangster, then the other female statue must be statue 1, in order to satisfy Rule 3. That means statues 2 (which we know is an athlete) and 4 are male. All that's up for grabs is which of the second athlete and the inventor is in 1 and which is in 4. If the athlete takes spot 1, then we'd have:

1	2	3	4
female athlete (glow)	male athlete	female gangster	male inventor

Choices (B) and (C) pertain to this state of affairs, and indeed, in this ordering the inventor is male (B) and only one athlete is male (C). So these two can be crossed off.

However, if the inventor takes spot 1, then the ordering would look like this:

1	2	3	4
female inventor	male athlete	female gangster	male athlete (glow)

(A) and (D) conform to this arrangement, and yes, statue 4 is glowing (A) and both males are athletes (D). But (E)—well, (E)'s if-clause is true in *both* options (we deduced that from the get-go), but only in the latter arrangement does statue 4 glow. (E) is therefore only possibly true, so it's correct here.

A 180 test taker is not afraid to quickly plot out a few possible arrangements when necessary, especially when faced with the prospect of testing out complex choices.

---

6. E

Next we get multiple pieces of hypothetical information in the stem. We're told that the inventor is male and is also ahead of the gangster in line. We deduced up front that the third statue has to be a gangster or an inventor, so let's try out each scenario.

If statue 3 is the gangster, then the male inventor would have to be statue 1; statue 4 would therefore be an athlete, and a glowing one at that. As for gender, given that statue 1 is male, statue 3 would have to be male as well, or else the females would be adjacent in violation of Rule 3. Here's this possibility:

1	2	3	4
male	female	male	female
inventor	athlete	gangster	athlete
			(glow)

We can see from this arrangement that (B) and (D) need not be true. As for the other possibility, the inventor can be statue 3 and still satisfy the mandate in the stem. That would result in this arrangement:

1	2	3	4
		male	female
athleter	athlete	inventor	gangster
(glow)			

In this scenario, statue 4 would have to be female, and 3 is male due to the stem, but we cannot be sure about the gender of 1 and 2. One of them is male and the other female, but Rule 3 will stand no matter which way we assign them. The upshot is that in both scenarios above, statue 3 is male, making (E) the correct answer. We can see from this latter ordering that (A) and (C), the remaining two choices, are only possibly true.

What's Next?

Are you getting the hang of these mixture types? As involved as this game is, the sequencing element—ordering four statues in a line—is still fairly straightforward. The following game, "Locker Room," illustrates what happens when a more complicated spatial sequence is combined with a matching task.

LOGIC GAME 14

One wall of a locker room contains exactly eight lockers, arranged in two rows of four lockers each. The top row of lockers is numbered 1, 3, 5, and 7, from left to right, and the bottom row is numbered 2, 4, 6, and 8, from left to right. The lockers are arranged such that locker 1 is positioned directly above locker 2, locker 3 directly above locker 4, locker 5 directly above locker 6, and locker 7 directly above locker 8. Each locker is either small, medium, or large, and each locker is either empty or full.

No large locker can be arranged directly above another large locker.

Each medium locker must be arranged either directly above or directly below another medium locker.

All medium lockers are empty.

The top row contains exactly two empty lockers.

Locker 5 is small.

Locker 4 is large and empty.

No more than four lockers are empty.

In the bottom row, exactly one large locker is adjacent to a medium locker.

1. Which one of the following must be true?

   (A) Locker 3 is small.
   (B) Locker 2 is empty.
   (C) Locker 7 is medium.
   (D) Locker 5 is empty.
   (E) Locker 8 is large.

2. Which one of the following is impossible?

   (A) a large, empty locker in the top row
   (B) a small, full locker in the bottom row
   (C) a medium, empty locker in the top row
   (D) a small, empty locker in the bottom row
   (E) a large, full locker in the top row

3. All of the following could be true EXCEPT:

   (A) Locker 1 is large.
   (B) Locker 2 is small.
   (C) Locker 3 is empty.
   (D) Locker 6 is empty.
   (E) Locker 7 is full.

4. If locker 2 is large, then all of the following must be true EXCEPT:

   (A) Locker 2 is full.
   (B) Locker 8 is medium.
   (C) Locker 5 is empty.
   (D) Locker 6 is large.
   (E) Locker 7 is empty.

5. The maximum number of small, medium, and large lockers, respectively, is which one of the following?

   (A) 5, 4, 4
   (B) 5, 2, 3
   (C) 4, 3, 4
   (D) 4, 2, 3
   (E) 5, 3, 3

6. If as few of the lockers as possible are large, which one of the following could be false?

   (A) Exactly one of the empty lockers is small.
   (B) The bottom row contains more large lockers than the top row.
   (C) The top row contains more small lockers than the bottom row.
   (D) The bottom row contains adjacent empty lockers.
   (E) The top row contains adjacent empty lockers.

Logic Game 14: Locker Room

What Makes It Difficult

This one's a sequencing/matching mixture, but the sequencing element is spatial as opposed to the usual linear variety, an example of which being the statues standing in a row in the previous game. Sure, there's a row of entities here, but then there's *another* row as well. We need to be cognizant of which lockers are next to which others, as well as which ones are *on top of* which others. This requires a bit of visualization, and a sketch that accurately reflects the sequencing action while allowing you to incorporate the matching element too.

A 180 test taker intuitively comes up with the sketch that works best for her.

The description of the lockers is fairly wordy, and there's a decent amount to keep track of: the location and size of each locker, and the status of each one's contents (empty or full). There are a ton of rules (eight), and they take all different forms. Some deal with the physical layout of the lockers (Rules 1, 2, 4, and 8) while Rule 3 involves the more abstract matching aspect. Three rules set out the number specs for the game (Rules 4, 7, and 8), while two are thankfully concrete (Rules 5 and 6).

At first glance it may seem as if the large number of rules adds to the game's complexity, and perhaps it does until you wrestle them to the ground. But once you do, you'll see that deductions abound which greatly simplify your work with the questions.

Keys to the Game

Start with the information in Rules 5 and 6 and build from there.

A 180 test taker seeks out the most concrete information and gets that down first in an attempt to make the more abstract rules easier to handle.

Locker 3 must be small. Since locker 4 is large, locker 3 cannot be large (Rule 1), and cannot be medium either, since it isn't above another medium locker (Rule 2). Since locker 3 cannot be large or medium, it must be small.

There will be exactly one more empty locker in the bottom row, besides locker 4, making exactly four empties altogether. That's because there must be no more than four empty lockers, and there are exactly two in the top row and one so far in the bottom row (locker 4). So at most there can be one more empty locker, but Rules 3 and 8, taken together, tell us that there must be exactly one more, since there must be at least one medium locker in the bottom row (Rule 8), and all medium lockers are empty. This realization, finally, enables one more deduction:

There must be exactly two medium lockers total—either 1 and 2, or 7 and 8. We definitely need at least one medium locker in the bottom row to satisfy Rule 8, but more than one would violate Rule 7. So there must be one medium empty locker in the bottom row, and it must be directly under a medium empty locker in the top row. 3 and 5 are both small, so 1 and 2 or 7 and 8 it is for the mediums.

A 180 test taker looks to see how number rules restrict the action and the entities, and pushes such information forward until solid deductions emerge.

Answers and Explanations

1. A   2. D   3. D   4. C   5. B   6. E

1. A

A "must be true" question with no new information is normally testing for a key deduction. We deduced above that locker 3 must be small, and there it is as choice (A).

2. D

With no new information, you have to tackle this question choice-by-choice, but this task is significantly easier with all of the information above at our disposal. Could we have a large empty locker in the top row, as in (A)? Sure, either locker 1 or locker 7 could be large and empty. Either locker 2, locker 6, or locker 8 could be small and full, which kills (B). As for (C), we deduced that either locker 1 or locker 7 must be medium and empty, so there must be a medium empty locker in the top row. (D) asks if we can have a small, empty locker in the bottom row. Since there can be no more than four empty lockers (Rule 7), and exactly two of them are in the top row (Rule 4), the bottom row can contain no more than two empty lockers. One of those is locker 4 (Rule 6), which is large, and we deduced that one empty locker in the bottom row will be medium. Therefore, we cannot have a small, empty locker in the bottom row, so (D) is impossible. On test day, you wouldn't even check choice (E). For the record, however, either locker 1 or locker 7 could be large and full.

> A 180 test taker circles a choice and moves on as soon as he finds a Logic Games answer that works. That's one of the reasons why he can finish the section, and often have some time left over to double-check his work.

3. D

Again, you have to tackle this question choice-by-choice, but we can use our previous work to speed things up a bit. In the last question, we saw that locker 1 can be large, which knocks off (A). As for (B), locker 2 could be small as long as locker 7 and locker 8 are medium and locker 6 is large, to satisfy Rule 8. Locker 3 could be empty without causing any problems, so (C) is wrong. Next, we have to see whether locker 6 could be empty, and our work on the previous question comes into play again. We know that there are no more than two empty lockers in the bottom row, that locker 4 will be one of the empties, and that either locker 2 or 8 will be both medium and empty. Therefore, if locker 6 is empty, then there would be three empty lockers in the bottom row, which is impossible. So, (D) cannot be true. Again, you wouldn't need to check (E), but locker 7 could be full as long as both locker 1 and locker 2 are medium and empty.

4. C

Locker 2 is large (and full, because we'd have too many empties otherwise). We still need a medium locker adjacent to a large one in the bottom row, so locker 8 must be medium (and therefore empty), locker 6 must be large (Rule 8), and locker 7 must be medium and empty. The only choice that need not be true is (C): Locker 5 can be empty or full.

5. B

We deduced above that there must be exactly two medium lockers in the game at all times, which immediately narrows our search to choices (B) and (D).

A 180 test taker doesn't simply make deductions; she uses them in the course of answering questions, either directly, to get a point, or indirectly, by eliminating choices that conflict with the deduction.

Both choices indicate three large lockers max, so we'll take that for granted and simply check out the small situation.

A 180 test taker uses good answer-choice elimination strategy, always looking for the quick and easy ways to chop or test out choices when necessary.

It's possible for lockers 3, 5, 6, 7, and 8 to all be small, so (B) with five small lockers is correct.

6. E

The fewest number of large lockers occurs if lockers 1 and 2 are medium and 3, 5, 6, 7, and 8 are small (if the mediums were 7 and 8, then 6 would need to be large to satisfy Rule 8). In fact, we employed this arrangement when maximizing the number of small lockers. Notice how maximizing the number of one set of entities minimizes the number of another set—this is often the case. So much is determined, but there's still the matter of answering the question, which is of the tricky "could be false" variety. Let's discard the choices that must be true.

(A) must be true because the top lockers consist of one medium and three small, and exactly two of them must be empty—the medium and one of the small lockers.

(B) is true; the bottom row has one large locker, the top row zero.

(C) is true, by a count of three to two.

(D) is true: 2 is a medium (and therefore empty), and 4 is always empty from Rule 6.

(E) That leaves (E): Locker 1 is empty (medium), but locker 3 need not be the other empty one. Either locker 5 or locker 7 could do the honors.

What's Next?

As you've seen here and before, mixture games are often amenable to some big deductions that effectively cut them down to size. Without the kinds of realizations discussed above, this game takes on a nightmarish tinge. With them, it's just another game, "ripe for the pickings."

Our next offering, "Dogs on Podiums," presents another opportunity for you to practice with hybrids. If you'll pardon the reference, we think you'll find this one to be quite a *Doozi*.

LOGIC GAME 15

A dog groomer displays dogs on two different podiums, Podium 1 and Podium 2. Each podium contains exactly three dogs: one on the left, one in the middle, and one on the right. Only dogs displayed in adjacent spaces are considered "next to" each other. The dogs available for display are BJ, Doozi, Ivory, Nutley, Pepper, Quest, and Shamash. The dogs are displayed according to the following conditions:

Nutley and Pepper cannot be displayed on the left side of either podium.

BJ and Ivory cannot be displayed in the middle of either podium.

Nutley and Quest cannot be displayed on the right side of either podium.

If Shamash is displayed on Podium 1, then Doozi is displayed on Podium 1.

If Quest is displayed on Podium 2, then BJ is displayed on Podium 2.

If BJ is displayed on Podium 1, then Nutley is displayed on Podium 2.

Doozi and Pepper cannot be displayed on the same podium.

1. If BJ is displayed on Podium 1, which one of the following must be true?

   (A)   Quest is displayed on Podium 1.
   (B)   Quest is not displayed next to Doozi.
   (C)   Quest is displayed on one of the two podiums.
   (D)   Quest is not displayed on Podium 2.
   (E)   Quest is displayed next to Pepper.

2. If Pepper is displayed in the middle of Podium 1, and Ivory is not displayed on either podium, then all of the following must be true EXCEPT:

   (A)   Quest is displayed on the left side of Podium 1.
   (B)   Shamash is displayed on the left side of Podium 2.
   (C)   Pepper is displayed next to BJ.
   (D)   Doozi is displayed next to Nutley.
   (E)   BJ is displayed on the right side of Podium 1.

3. If BJ and Shamash are displayed on Podium 1, which one of the following must be false?

   (A)   Pepper is displayed on the right side of Podium 2.
   (B)   BJ is displayed next to Doozi.
   (C)   Quest is displayed next to Nutley.
   (D)   Doozi is displayed next to Shamash.
   (E)   Ivory is displayed on the left side of Podium 2.

4. If Pepper is displayed next to Shamash, which one of the following could be true?

   (A)   BJ is displayed on Podium 1.
   (B)   Nutley is displayed on Podium 2.
   (C)   Shamash is displayed on Podium 1.
   (D)   Quest is displayed on Podium 2.
   (E)   Ivory is displayed on Podium 1.

5. If Nutley is not displayed on either podium, and Doozi and Shamash are displayed on different podiums, then how many different displays of dogs are possible for Podium 2?

   (A)   1
   (B)   2
   (C)   3
   (D)   4
   (E)   5

6. Which one of the following is impossible?

   (A)   Quest is displayed next to both Ivory and Shamash.
   (B)   Nutley is displayed next to both Doozi and Shamash.
   (C)   Doozi is displayed next to both Ivory and Quest.
   (D)   Shamash is displayed next to both BJ and Pepper.
   (E)   Pepper is displayed next to both BJ and Quest.

Logic Game 15: Dogs on Podiums

What Makes It Difficult

The phrase "next to" in quotes in the introduction suggests the sequencing element here: a mini left-middle-right exercise to perform for each podium. So first we have to figure out which dogs are on which podiums, and then have to determine *where* on the podium each is displayed. Not too tough on the face of it, but the rules are many and involved. The first three are stated in the negative, telling us what parts of the podiums certain dogs *can't* be; while the rest have to do with the grouping element, dealing with the podiums on which the dogs can appear.

There's a subtle complexity that involves the numbers that govern the game: There are six spots, but seven dogs, and you have to figure out just how to handle that wrinkle. The kicker is that the kinds of deductions we can usually make from the type of if-then statements in this game are thwarted by the fact that one dog will not be chosen. That makes it hard to combine the rules. Finally, many of the questions require multiple steps. The game's involved enough; the questions are simply tough. A "Doozi," indeed. But a few key interpretations speed us on our way.

Keys to the Game

Make use of the fact that one dog must be left off the podiums. While appearing to make the game more difficult, this wrinkle actually gives the clever test taker an additional way into the questions. In order to figure out who's where, one can begin by asking "which dog is left out?"

A 180 test taker turns even the game's complexities to her advantage.

Nutley, if displayed, must be in the center of one of the podiums. That's the upshot of Rules 1 and 3.

Pepper, if displayed, must be middle or right. BJ and Ivory, if displayed, must be left or right. Q, if displayed, must be middle or left. Not great revelations, perhaps, but it's always easier to think in terms of where entities could be than where they cannot be.

A 180 test taker turns negatives to positives at every opportunity.

Work out and be crystal clear about the implications of if-then Rules 4–6:

Rule 4: If D2, then if S is displayed, S2. The implication is tricky here, since we also have to account for the possibility that D is not displayed at all. Since only one dog will not be displayed, we also know that if D is not displayed, S must be displayed, and cannot be displayed on Podium 1 (or else D would have to be there as well). Therefore, if D is not displayed, then S2.

Rule 5: If B1, then if Q is displayed Q1; and, as with rule 4, if B is not displayed, then Q1.

Rule 6: If N1, then if B is displayed, B2; and, as above, if N is not displayed, then B2.

Answers and Explanations

1. D   2. B   3. C   4. E   5. C   6. A

1. D

Rule 6 says that if B is on 1, N must be on 2. That's not a choice, so we have to keep looking. Rule 5 involves BJ as well, and thinking through its implication: If B is on Podium 1, then Q, if displayed, must be on 1. Either way, that means that Quest is not on 2, so (D) is correct.

> A 180 test taker knows that even hard games usually have some easy questions, and looks to knock these off as quickly as possible to gain extra time for the tougher ones.

2. B

Once we know which dog sits out, we also know the six dogs that must be displayed, and that, of course, is powerful information. If I isn't displayed, and P is in the middle of Podium 1, then N must be displayed in the middle of 2. D must be on 2 (Rule 7), which means S must be on 2 as well (the implication of Rule 4). That leaves B and Q for Podium 1, with Q on the left (Rule 3), and B on the right. The choice that need not be true is (B); Shamash could be displayed on the left *or* right side of Podium 2.

Lots of steps, huh? Some involve the rules directly, some the *implications* of the rules we discussed above. Either way, this is what we're in for in this game: much step-by-step deductive work requiring a fair amount of concentration and precision.

3. C

What happens if B and S are on 1? D must be on 1 (Rule 4). N must be displayed on Podium 2 (Rule 6), and in the middle of that podium, thanks to our combination of Rules 1 and 3. The implication of Rule 5 dictates that if B is on 1, then Q, if displayed, must be on 1 also. Since that's impossible here (Podium 1 is already full), Quest must sit this one out, and (C) must be false. (A), (D), and (E) must be true, while (B) could be true but need not be.

4. E

P next to S can't happen on Podium 1; D would have to be there also (Rule 4), but that would violate Rule 7. So we should place P and S on 2, which eliminates choice (C). If they're to be next to one another, then N can't be on that podium because N, as we've seen, must always be in the middle, which would separate P and S and violate the question stem. So N can't be on 2, which means that B can't be on 1 due to the implication of Rule 6. That kills choices (A) and (B). (D) is no good—Q on 2 means B on 2, which would give us four dogs on Podium 2, so (E) turns out to be the only statement that could be true under these circumstances. Whew! Not fun, but doable.

> A 180 test taker is skilled at ferreting out the rules that are relevant to each new situation. When given no recourse, she sets to finding and applying the relevant rules with speed and accuracy.

5. C

S must be on 2 and D on 1 in order for S and D to be on different podiums (if S were on 1, then D would have to be there too, according to Rule 4). Without N, every other dog must be placed somewhere. Rule 7 forces P onto Podium 2, while the implication of Rule 6 places B on 2 as well. That leaves I and Q for Podium 1, but those who took in the rest of the question stem can dismiss Podium 1 altogether now, since the question centers on Podium 2 and all the dogs for that podium have been determined.

> A 180 test taker always keeps one eye on the question that's asked. That way, he can zero in on the relevant entities or groups and avoid wasting time on determinations that yield no reward.

Now that we know *which* dogs are on 2, we can figure out how many arrangements are possible for that podium by taking Rules 1 and 2 into account: BSP, BPS, and SPB are the only possible orderings, from left to right, which gives us three possible Podium 2 displays, choice (C).

6. A

With no new information to go on, there's no real way to go about this one other than to try out each choice. In this case, we luck out because the answer happens to be (A). QIS can't be displayed on Podium 1, because then D would have to join them according to Rule 4, and QIS can't go on Podium 2 because then B would have to join them, thanks to Rule 5. But even if the answer wasn't located so conveniently in (A), trying out these choices turns out to be not nearly as difficult as it seems—in fact, not difficult at all, considering that each one corresponds to a situation we've already seen. (B) and (E) describe the exact podiums we formulated back in question 2, while (C) and (D) represent two of the possible orderings we just uncovered in question 5.

> A 180 test taker uses previous work to quickly eliminate choices whenever possible and necessary.

What's Next?

That does it for the dog show. Let's move on to the final hybrid game of this chapter, and a deceptively hybrid game at that.

LOGIC GAME 16

A car dealer orders seven new cars. Each car consists of a single model and a single color. The models that the dealer can choose from are the Puma, the Radon, the Swan, the Tutu, and the Universe. The colors that the dealer can choose from are black, green, maroon, and yellow. The dealer orders in accordance with the following guidelines:

At least three black cars are ordered.

If one or more black Tutus are ordered, then any and all Radons ordered will be green.

If one or more maroon Pumas are ordered, then any and all Universes ordered will be black.

If a maroon Tutu is ordered, then exactly six of the cars ordered will be black.

If no yellow Universes are ordered, then any and all Radons ordered will be yellow.

1. Which one of the following is an acceptable list of cars ordered by the car dealer?

    (A)   three black Radons, one maroon Tutu, three black Swans
    (B)   three black Pumas, three yellow Universes, one green Radon
    (C)   four black Tutus, two maroon Swans, one yellow Radon
    (D)   three yellow Radons, two maroon Pumas, two black Swans
    (E)   five black Pumas, one maroon Tutu, one green Universe

2. What is the maximum number of black cars the dealer can order?

    (A)   3
    (B)   4
    (C)   5
    (D)   6
    (E)   7

3. If the dealer orders four green Swans, which one of the following must be true?

    (A)   At least one maroon Puma is ordered.
    (B)   At least one yellow Radon is ordered.
    (C)   At least one black Swan is ordered.
    (D)   No Pumas are ordered.
    (E)   No Radons are ordered.

4. If the dealer orders a green Radon, which one of the following CANNOT be included in the order?

    (A)   a yellow Universe
    (B)   a green Swan
    (C)   a maroon Puma
    (D)   a black Tutu
    (E)   a yellow Swan

5. If the dealer orders at least one car of each model, and the Radon is the only yellow car ordered, which one of the following must be included in the order?

    (A)   a green Tutu
    (B)   a maroon Puma
    (C)   a black Swan
    (D)   a black Puma
    (E)   a black Universe

Logic Game 16: Seven Cars on Order

What Makes It Difficult

The Radon? The Tutu? What kind of cars are these? A better question is: What kind of *rules* are these? Nasty formal logic ones, to be sure. As we indicated at the end of "Dogs on Podiums," this game is a hybrid game, but a deceptive one. After all, the matching aspect seems clear—we have to link up cars and colors—but what's the other game action? In a standard matching game, the entities to be matched are given; in this one, however, we have to *select* the models and colors from a list of possibilities, so there's a grouping element present as well.

The rules, simply put, are the real killers here. The "any and all" formulation found in three of the five rules is ripe for misinterpretation, and the negatively stated Rule 5 has been known to give people fits. Other than suggesting that you find a convenient way to distinguish the models from the colors (e.g., capital and lowercase abbreviations), the major key to the game is nothing more complicated than understanding the rules and their implications, so let's spell those out here.

Keys to the Game

Rule 1: There are at least three black cars. This is the only simple rule of the bunch.

Rule 2: If bT, then all R's are g. Get this "any and all" business straight from the outset: If a black Tutu is ordered, that doesn't necessarily mean that a green Radon must be ordered—there could be NO Radons ordered at all. The correct interpretation is that IF a Radon is ordered along with a black Tutu, then it must be green. Once you understand this correctly, you can and should think through its implication, namely: If R not g, then no bT. In other words, if a Radon is ordered in any color besides green, then no black Tutus can be ordered. Applying this line of thinking to the rest of the rules:

Rule 3: If mP, then all U's are b. Implication: If U not b, then no mP.

Rule 4: If mT, then six b. Implication: If there are not six b, then no mT. Take a moment to think through the further implications of this rule. Since seven cars are ordered, this means that at most one maroon Tutu may be ordered. If another Tutu is in the order, it (along with all of the other cars) must be black.

Rule 5: If no yU, then all R's are y. Implication: If R not y, then there must be a yU. If a Radon's ordered that's not yellow, then a yellow Universe must be ordered.

If a maroon Tutu is ordered, then no Radons can be ordered. This can be deduced from combining Rules 4 and 5. It's not crucial, but if you can pick up on subtle and tricky deductions like this, then you're definitely on the right track.

These rules and their implications are quite complex and easily confused, but you should have no problem, right?

A 180 test taker can think through, combine, and apply the toughest Formal Logic rules that appear on the LSAT.

Answers and Explanations

1. B   2. E   3. E   4. C   5. A

1. B

There are only five questions in the set—a minor blessing—and the first two simply test your basic understanding of the game. The normal technique for Acceptability questions works fine here: testing each rule against each choice. Rule 1 kills (D), which doesn't have the requisite three black cars. Rule 2 axes (C), which contains black Tutus but a Radon that's not green. Rule 4 eliminates (E): a maroon Tutu can't be part of an order containing a green car. Finally, Rule 5 takes care of (A), which has no yellow Universe and non-yellow Radons. (B) remains as the acceptable list.

> A 180 test taker uses the first few questions of a tough game to get "the lay of the land"; that is, to shore up her conception of the game and to get practice applying the rules.

2. E

In questions seeking maximums, the best strategy is to shoot for the moon; in other words, to try out the highest number and work your way down from there. We know there must be at least three black cars, but can all seven be black? Why not? There are no rules restricting Swans, so the dealer could easily order seven black Swans. There's no need to find other possible groups of seven black cars to conclude that seven works, so (E) is the answer.

> A 180 test taker recognizes the "floaters" or "free agents" in a game, and gravitates toward those in situations calling for the least restrictions.

3. E

What does four green Swans mean? Well, Swans are our floaters, so no rules directly come into play based on their inclusion. But what about the numbers game? We have to have three black cars, and in this question four of the seven are green Swans, so the other three remaining must be black. Therefore, there can't be any yellow Universes ordered, which triggers Rule 5: any Radons ordered will have to be yellow. But that's impossible: Since the other cars ordered are all black, we know that no Radons can be included in the order, choice (E).

> A 180 test taker asks himself the relevant questions in the process of seeking answers, and understands that such questions usually revolve around the issue of which rules are put into play by the question stem's hypothetical information.

4. C

Inclusion of a green Radon leads us to Rules 2, 4, and 5. It meets the requirements of Rule 2, so a black Tutu could be ordered, eliminating (D). According to Rule 4, a maroon Tutu cannot be ordered when a green car is included, but unfortunately, that's not a choice. But Rule 5 tells us that a yellow Universe *must* be included in the order, since leaving one out forces all Radons to be yellow, and here we have a green one. This is seemingly no help, since we're trying to *eliminate* a choice. But all that means is that we have to go one step further to see where this new information leads. A yellow Universe leads us to Rule 3, the implication of which gives us our answer, (C). Since the order must include a yellow Universe, then there's no way for all Universes ordered to be black, which means that a maroon Puma cannot be included in the order.

Lots of steps are required, much like the more involved questions in "Dogs on Podiums." What makes these questions difficult is not necessarily the difficulty level of each step, but simply the number of steps required and therefore the number of possible places to slip up. Note that if you were running out of time, and had to guess on a question like this, you could still narrow down the choices at a glance by eliminating (B) and (E). Why? Because these involve Swans, our floater model, which means that unless Rule 4 is invoked, we can probably slip any color Swan into the order.

A 180 test taker is not often forced to guess on a question, but when she absolutely has to, she takes an educated guess based on her overall knowledge of the game and its entities.

---

5. A

One complex question to go, and this one offers two pieces of information. And it's a particularly tough question because in order to figure out what car must be included, we have to eliminate color options for a certain model until only one color remains. Unfortunately, there's nothing to suggest that this is the way to go, so either you saw this intuitively, or had enough time to work out enough possibilities until this "process of elimination" idea struck you. In any event, the reasoning goes like this: The fact that a Radon is the only yellow car leads us to Rule 2, and tells us that a black Tutu can't be ordered. It also points to Rule 4—a maroon Tutu is out of the question as well. And guess what? Since the Radon is the *only* yellow car, any Tutus ordered can't be yellow, and we just saw that they can't be black or maroon. Since, according to the stem, at least one car of each model is ordered, at least one Tutu must be included, and since it can't be yellow, black, or maroon, a green Tutu (or Tutus) must be ordered. That's choice (A).

A 180 test taker understands that sometimes the only way into a difficult matching question is to work out what can't be matched up with what.

What's Next?

All right then—we're four-fifths of the way through this Logic Games section, and if you've gotten this far you're probably ready for the final four killer games. "*It gets worse?*" you ask? Oh, *yeah* . . .

Those who dare, turn to chapter 5.

CHAPTER FIVE

What the…?

.The title of this chapter reflects the response most test takers have upon encountering the kind of games you're about to see. We also like to call them "Games That Make You Reconsider Your Decision to Go to Law School."

So far, in chapters 2–4, you've done battle with individual sequencing, grouping, matching, and process games, as well as mixture games that combine these game actions in various ways. What more is there, you ask? What can possibly be even harder than these first 16 games?

Well, the games in this chapter all involve and combine these same types of game actions, but they do so in particularly novel (read: "brutal") ways. As usual, we'll touch on the specific difficulties of each in the individual game explanations. For now, suffice it to say that these final four games represent the toughest of the tough, the scariest of the scary—to put it bluntly, the nastiest possible material you may encounter on the LSAT Logic Games section. Be advised that these are NOT for the faint at heart.

Let it not be said that you have not been warned . . .

Hey, wait a minute—that last bit itself kind of sounds like a Logic Games rule, doesn't it? Analyzing it in typical LSAT manner, we find a formal logic construction consisting of a double negative. Implication:

You *have been* warned.

Good luck.

LOGIC GAME 17

Five chests are numbered 1 through 5 from left to right, and a monarch is filling each with treasure. Each chest will contain at least one, but not more than two of the following types of treasure: gold, opals, platinum, rubies, silver, and topaz. Each type of treasure will be placed in at least one chest. Each chest will be secured by exactly one mechanism—bolt, chain, or lock. The monarch fills the chests according to the following conditions:

At least two chests must contain rubies.

Exactly two chests must contain opals, and these chests cannot be adjacent to each other.

Both chests that contain opals must be to the left of any chests that contain gold.

Chests 2, 3, and 4 cannot contain silver.

Any chest that contains rubies must be secured by a chain.

Any chest that contains opals must be secured by a bolt.

Chest 2 is secured by a chain.

1. Which one of the following CANNOT be true?

   (A) Chest 1 is secured by a lock.
   (B) Chest 2 contains topaz.
   (C) Chest 3 is secured by a lock.
   (D) Chest 4 contains opals.
   (E) Chest 5 is secured by a chain.

2. If a chest containing treasure and secured by a lock is not adjacent to a chest secured by a bolt, then which one of the following must be true?

   (A) Chest 1 contains platinum.
   (B) Chest 4 contains opals.
   (C) Chest 4 contains rubies.
   (D) Chest 5 contains gold.
   (E) Chest 5 contains silver.

3. If rubies are contained in the maximum number of chests, which one of the following must be true?

   (A) Chest 3 is secured by a bolt.
   (B) Chest 4 is secured by a bolt.
   (C) A chest containing silver is secured by a bolt.
   (D) A chest containing gold is secured by a chain.
   (E) A chest containing platinum is secured by a lock.

4. Which one of the following must be true?

   (A) At least one chest containing gold is adjacent to a chest containing opals.
   (B) At least one chest containing platinum is adjacent to a chest containing silver.
   (C) At least one chest containing rubies is adjacent to a chest containing topaz.
   (D) At least one chest containing gold is adjacent to a chest containing topaz.
   (E) At least one chest containing opals is adjacent to a chest containing rubies.

5. If chest 4 contains platinum and topaz, which one of the following pairs of treasures must be contained in the same chest as each other?

   (A) opals and silver
   (B) gold and platinum
   (C) rubies and topaz
   (D) gold and silver
   (E) opals and platinum

6. If chest 3 is secured by a lock, which one of the following could be false?

   (A) Chest 1 contains silver.
   (B) Chest 2 contains rubies.
   (C) Chest 3 contains topaz.
   (D) Chest 4 is secured by a bolt.
   (E) Chest 5 is secured by a chain.

Logic Game 17: Treasure Chests

What Makes It Difficult

Well, at least there's one thing in our favor: the action of this game is not too difficult to understand (something we emphatically *won't* be able to say about at least a few of the games that follow). A greedy monarch filling up treasure chests with loot—nothing fancy about that. Each chest secured by a single mechanism? Sure, makes sense. After all, we don't expect the king to just let his treasures stand around unguarded. Essentially we have a hybrid game on our hands. "Numbered 1 through 5 from left to right" is a big hint that sequencing is involved, and in fact, we later find that the issues of adjacency and order are relevant. The fact that each chest will contain *at least one, but not more than two* types of treasure also suggests a distribution element; each chest can be thought of as a "group" containing up to two different treasure types. But wait, there's more: A whole different set of entities must also be doled out to the chests; namely, the type of fastening mechanism—bolt, chain, or lock. So there's a matching element as well: We have to match the chests to the treasures contained inside to the mechanism that secures it. Surely a lot to keep track of.

The number conditions stated in the intro are also a bit wordy. "At least one, but not more than two types of treasure" in each chest that each chest must contain exactly one or two treasure types.

A 180 test taker drives numerical information to its most definite conclusion.

Moreover, "each type will be placed in at least one chest" means we can't leave out any of the five types entirely; every type must appear somewhere.

All that to assimilate and we haven't even gotten to the rules yet. There are a lot of them to work with, although there's no rule that's particularly hard to understand. However, if you don't put them together and nail down a few important things up front, the game is nearly impossible (at least in the time you're allotted on the test). The keys to the game are therefore a few major deductions. Did you see them?

Keys to the Game

Any chest not secured by a chain cannot contain rubies. Likewise, any chest not secured by a bolt cannot contain opals. These are the correct, and very important, implications of Rules 5 and 6.

Rubies and opals cannot be contained in the same chest, since one must be contained in chain-secured chests, the other in bolt-secured chests. These chests are mutually exclusive, since each chest is secured by exactly one kind of mechanism.

Opals cannot be contained in chest 2, because chest 2 is secured by a chain, and opals must go in chests secured by a bolt. **Opals also can't be in chest 5**, because there would be no room for the required gold chest (Rule 3). With those two chests off limits to opals, there's only one way to place the two opals chests nonconsecutively: **Chest 1 must contain opals, and the other chest containing opals must be either chest 3 or chest 4.** Furthermore, since chest 1 contains opals, **chest 1 must be secured by a bolt.**

That's a lot of ammunition, huh? And we certainly need it to get through the questions. It's even helpful to check out a few possibilities based on this state of affairs. If the second opals chest is chest 3, then gold can be in chest 4 or 5, or both. If the second opals chest is chest 4, gold can be only in chest 5.

A 180 test taker not only formulates key deductions, but also works through a few implications of those deductions when possible to solidify her overall grasp of the game.

Answers and Explanations

1. A   2. C   3. D   4. E   5. A   6. C

1. A

We're given no new information and asked to find the statement that cannot be true. Normally, we may think of holding off on such a question until various scenarios are revealed in the later questions, but having made so many deductions up front, it's worth at least scanning the choices to see if there's an easy point to be had. And indeed, correct choice (A) is simply an extension of one of our deductions. We saw that chest 1 must contain opals; this was because chest 2, secured by a chain, can't have opals, and there's no way to fit both nonconsecutive opals chests between 3 and 5 while still leaving room for the chest containing gold. That means that opals is a definite for chest 1, which further means that chest 1 must be secured by a bolt, not a lock as stated in (A).

2. C

Without the deductions above, there's virtually no way into a question like this; if everything's wide open, then the information in the stem barely tells us anything. But knowing what we know, it tells us plenty. A locked chest can't be chest 1, which we deduced is bolted, or chest 2, which we're told is chained. Furthermore, we deduced that opals must be in chest 3 or chest 4, secured by a bolt. If the opals are in 4, then the locked chest required by the stem must be in 3 or 5, which would make it adjacent to bolted chest 4. So the bolted opals chest in this case must be chest 3, and the locked chest must therefore be far away in chest 5:

1	2	3	4	5
bolt		bolt		lock
opals		opals		

We can kill choice (B) at this point, but that's all, so we need to press on. What about the rubies?

A 180 test taker gravitates toward the game's most "influential" entities when the next step is unclear, which are the ones that take up the most space in the arrangement, or the ones that we know the most about.

Those who overlook the implication of Rules 5 and 6 are stuck at this point, but for the rest it's a simple matter to recognize that chests 1, 3, and 5 are not secured by chains, and therefore aren't suitable for the rubies. The two rubies chests must therefore be 2 and 4, which means that (C) is correct. (B), as we saw, must be false, while the rest could be true, but need not be.

3. D

In this one we need to place rubies in as many chests as possible. Chest 1 is off limits, since we know by now that opals are for sure contained there, and no chest with opals can also contain rubies. Chest 2 is wide open for rubies; it's even secured by a chain, the requisite mechanism for a rubies chest, so we can place R in 2. Now we have a choice: As we saw earlier in the keys to the game, the second opals chest will be either chest 3 or 4, and depending on which it is, we can then figure out how to place the maximum number of R's. No sense trying to psychically intuit the whole thing; work out on paper what happens in each case, remembering that you want to maximize the occurrence of rubies.

A 180 test taker is not afraid to use his pencil when necessary to chart out multiple possibilities.

If opals (with a bolt) are in chest 3, then rubies (with chains) can be placed into chests 4 and 5:

1	2	3	4	5
bolt	chain	bolt	chain	chain
opals		opals	rubies	rubies

In this scenario, gold, always to the right of opals, must be in chest 4 or 5 or both. On the other hand, if the opals are placed in chest 4, then rubies can be placed in chests 3 and 5:

1	2	3	4	5
bolt	chain	chain	bolt	chain
opals		rubies	opals	rubies

In this scenario, gold would have to be in chest 5. Either way, it will share a chest with rubies. And since rubies are always in a chest with a chain, (D) is correct. One way or another, gold will be in a chain-secured chest. Now that's a long chain of deduction—even using our key deductions as a starting point.

(A) is true only in scenario one above; in scenario two, chest 3 contains rubies and is therefore secured by a chain.

(B) is the opposite of (A): It's true for scenario two above, but not for scenario one.

(C) is true only in scenario two, when silver (always restricted by Rule 4 to chests 1 and 5) would have to be forced into bolted chest 1, since chest 5 would be filled up with rubies and gold. However, in scenario 1, silver could end up only in chest 5 along with rubies, nicely secured by a chain.

(E) Platinum is a total free agent here; in either scenario we could place platinum in chest 2 with rubies, secured by a chain, which is enough to kill choice (E).

4. E

Another non-if question testing our basic understanding of the game. All of the choices are in the same format, each dealing with the notion of adjacency. In other words, the correct answer pairs up two chests that must be right next to one another. We have no other option but to work through the choices, eliminating the bad ones by coming up with exceptions to them. However, a little cleverness is in order. It stands to reason that the treasures that must be next to one another will likely be the ones that with the severest restrictions. Platinum and topaz, for example, our "free agents" here, don't really *need* to go anywhere in particular; they just need to be included somewhere. So while (B), (C), or (D) could theoretically be the right answer, they aren't the best candidates, and we're better off trying the other two first.

A 180 test taker looks for the optimal order in which to test choices when faced with the necessity of trying them out.

A 180 test taker pays attention to "free agents," which are the entities least restricted by the rules.

(A) No, we can place opals in chests 1 and 3 and gold only in 5, filling in the other treasures around them.

(E) must be true: No matter how we slice it, at least one opals chest must be next to a rubies chest. Again we begin from our big deductions: Chest 1 contains opals, while the other opals chest is either chest 3 or chest 4. But we need at least two rubies chests. If opals are in 1 and 3, then rubies must be in chests 2 and 4, 2 and 5, or 3 and 5 (or all three—2, 3, and 5). If, however, opals are in 1 and 4, then rubies must be in chests 2 and 3, 2 and 5, 3 and 5, or 2, 3, and 5. No matter what, at least one opals chest must be next to a rubies chest, and (E) is therefore correct. And notice how, true to the strategy cited above, the right answer involves the two most influential, that is, the two most restricted entities in the game.

(B), (C), (D) There are many ways to split up the treasures in these choices. As we mentioned above, platinum and topaz are restricted so little in this game that it's not a problem separating each from just about any other treasure type. If you noticed that these choices all try to place severe restrictions on entities that are essentially "free agents," then the right thing to do is look elsewhere.

5. A

And speaking of our "free agents," they're highlighted in this question. A simple case of one thing leading to another: If P and T occupy chest 4, then the second opals chest must be chest 3 (and of course we deduced earlier that chest 1 *always* contains opals). Gold must therefore be contained in chest 5 (Rule 3). Now we need to include at least two rubies chests, but two is actually all we have room for: Rubies can't go in the chests containing opals (because these treasures must be in chests secured by different mechanisms), and chest 4 is maxed out, so rubies must therefore be placed in chests 2 and 5. Now chest 5 is maxed out also, since it contains both rubies and gold; so silver, which we haven't used yet and which can be placed only in chests 1 or 5, must be placed in chest 1, joining the opals that are always there. This lengthy chain of deduction explains why "opals and silver," choice (A), must be together under these circumstances.

(B), (D) Neither of these choices can be true. The only chest containing gold in this question is chest 5, which also contains rubies. Silver, as we saw while deriving the correct answer, can only be in chest 1, along with opals.

(C) and (E) both could be true, but need not be: We *could* place topaz in chest 2 along with rubies, but we need not do so, because topaz is already assigned to chest 4. Similarly, platinum could join opals in chest 3, but the platinum requirement is also taken care of by the question stem.

6. C

If chest 3 is secured by a lock, then clearly chest 3 can contain neither rubies (Rule 5) nor opals (Rule 6). We deduced that opals are always in chest 1, and in either 3 or 4, so now we know that the second opals chest—always secured by a bolt—must be chest 4. This, in turn, means that gold must be contained in chest 5 and *only* in chest 5 (Rule 3). Now for the rubies: Chests 1, 3, and 4 are off limits to rubies because they're all secured by mechanisms other than chains; thus we can satisfy Rule 1 only by placing rubies in chests 2 and 5. Of course, that means chest 5 gets a chain. Finally, just like in question 5, chest 5 is now full, which forces silver into chest 1.

1	2	3	4	5
bolt	chain	lock	bolt	chain
opals	rubies		opals	gold
silver				rubies

In a question looking for what "could be false," the wrong choices all *cannot* be false, which means they must be true.

> A 180 test taker is comfortable with every question type, and is able to characterize in every case what the right answer and the wrong choices will be like. When nearly everything is determined, knowing what the wrong answers will do makes eliminating them a breeze.

(A), (B), (D), and (E) all conform perfectly to this arrangement, so we can cross those off.

(C) must therefore be the choice that could be false. We know that locked chest 3 doesn't have opals or rubies, and it *never* contains silver or gold, so it must contain platinum and/or topaz. Chest 3 could contain just platinum instead of the topaz listed in the choice, so (C) is indeed what the test makers are after here.

What's Next?

Did this one drive you nuts? If so, you must not have made the deductions discussed above, because, as you can see from the explanations above, these deductions really make the questions much more manageable. The game is very difficult—nearly impossible for some—to handle without them.

Big deductions, however, won't save you in the following game. In "Children's Questions," you'll revisit the Time Warp, or "process" game type that you saw in chapter 3. (You probably thought you saw the last of those . . . surprise!) But this time, it's mixed with a definite sequencing element, making it all the more annoying. Rev up your forward and backward thinking skills and see what you can make of this game within a game.

LOGIC GAME 18

A teacher is organizing a game of "Questions" to be played by the five children in her class. The game begins with the children standing in five adjacent spaces, numbered 1 to 5 from front to back. As the game begins, the children are standing in the following order, from front to back: Kim, Ho, Mal, Quincy, Fahroud.

In each round of the game, the teacher calls out one of two colors, either red or blue.

If red is called, then exactly two questions will be asked: The child in space 3 will ask a question of the child in space 2, and the child in space 5 will ask a question of the child in space 4.

If blue is called, then exactly two questions will be asked: The child in space 2 will ask a question of the child in space 1, and the child in space 4 will ask a question of the child in space 3.

When a child who has been asked a question does not answer correctly, he or she changes places in line with the asker. When a child who has been asked a question answers correctly, he or she does not change places with the asker.

The teacher never calls the same color in two consecutive rounds of the game.

1. Which one of the following could be the order of children, listed from front to back, after exactly one round of the game in which the teacher called red?

   (A) Quincy, Ho, Mal, Kim, Fahroud
   (B) Ho, Kim, Mal, Fahroud, Quincy
   (C) Kim, Mal, Ho, Quincy, Fahroud
   (D) Ho, Kim, Mal, Quincy, Fahroud
   (E) Kim, Mal Quincy, Fahroud, Ho

2. Which one of the following could be the order of children, listed from front to back, after exactly one round of the game in which the teacher called blue?

   (A) Ho, Mal, Kim, Quincy, Fahroud
   (B) Kim, Mal, Ho, Fahroud, Quincy
   (C) Ho, Kim, Mal, Fahroud, Quincy
   (D) Ho, Kim, Quincy, Fahroud, Mal
   (E) Kim, Ho, Mal, Quincy, Fahroud

3. Which one of the following could be true after the first two rounds of the game?

   (A) Fahroud has answered one question.
   (B) Ho has asked two questions.
   (C) Kim has asked one question.
   (D) Mal has answered two questions.
   (E) Quincy has answered two questions.

4. If after three rounds of the game Ho and Fahroud have advanced as far to the front of the line as possible, then all of the following pairs of children could be standing in adjacent spaces after the third round of the game EXCEPT:

   (A) Fahroud and Ho
   (B) Fahroud and Mal
   (C) Kim and Mal
   (D) Kim and Quincy
   (E) Mal and Quincy

5. If, after three rounds of the game, Quincy has advanced as far to the front of the line as possible, and if the other four children are still in the same positions relative to each other, then which one of the following must be true?

   (A) After three rounds of the game, Fahroud stands in the space in which Mal was standing after two rounds of the game.
   (B) After two rounds of the game, Ho stands in the space in which Quincy was standing after one round of the game.
   (C) After two rounds of the game, Kim stands in the space in which Ho was standing after one round of the game.
   (D) After three rounds of the game, Kim stands in the space in which Mal was standing at the beginning of the game.
   (E) After two rounds of the game, Mal stands in the space in which Quincy was standing after one round of the game.

6. If, after four rounds of the game, the order of children from front to back is Fahroud, Ho, Quincy, Kim, Mal, then which one of the following must be false?

   (A) Ho answered a question correctly in round 1.
   (B) Ho answered a question incorrectly in round 4.
   (C) Kim answered a question correctly in round 2.
   (D) Mal answered a question incorrectly in round 2.
   (E) Mal answered a question incorrectly in round 3.

Logic Game 18: Children's Questions

What Makes It Difficult

A quick scan of the game—with its references to things like "if blue is called" and "if after three rounds"—suggests that this is a process game, but it also contains a strong sequencing element: five students lined up from front to back, 1 through 5. Our main job—keeping track of the changes in position that result from questions being answered correctly or incorrectly—doesn't become fully clear until the fourth indented rule, and that's disconcerting to some.

A 180 test taker perseveres and doesn't get flustered if the full dimensions of the game aren't revealed immediately.

So we're faced with a process/sequencing hybrid—surely no walk in the park. As mentioned earlier, process games are generally not very ripe for big deductions, and this one is no exception. The rules speak to the question-answer and switching mechanisms in general, but you need to wait for the questions to provide concrete information that put the rules into action. That means that you simply have to find a reasonable way to represent the action in a manner that's accessible to you, and then power through the questions. And there are some truly nasty ones in this set. For example, in this game type we expect the test makers to ask us to think forward and backward in time—but four rounds out (question 6)?! That's just mean. And in question 5, the choices are almost as long as the wordy stem, requiring us to perform mental gymnastics to work through the question *and* to decipher the choices. No punches pulled in this one, that's for sure.

There's not much you can do up front other than understand the general situation, work through each rule, and settle on a means of sketching the action that will help you through the questions. From there, it's simply a matter of execution, although as always there are a few points that will aid you in your attack on the game.

Keys to the Game

Red and blue rounds must alternate (Rule 5), and it's crucial that you keep track of the colors of each round. Some early questions explicitly indicate which colors are called out; others will strongly suggest it by implication; and the hardest questions force you to figure out in what order the colors are called out based on the ordering of the children in later rounds.

Stay focused on the key issues governing the game, namely: What happens when a color is called out? What happens when a question is answered correctly? What happens when a question is answered incorrectly? And most importantly: What must have happened in earlier rounds to put the children into position to end up where we find them later on?

Hypothesize: What *could* happen? Go through some "what ifs" about the game to get a feel for how the process works. There's no need to go crazy working out scenarios to get your feet wet, since the first question or two in process games usually tests your basic understanding of the game. But it's still good to do a quick warm-up for those.

Answers and Explanations

1. C   2. E   3. D   4. B   5. B   6. C

1. C

The first question, as is often the case in process games, tests nothing more than a most rudimentary understanding of the game action and rules. We're asked to project just one round out, and we're told explicitly that it's a red round. When red is called, child 3 asks child 2 a question, 5 asks 4, and 1 is uninvolved. This last bit means that after this round the original child 1, Kim, will remain in her original place. So the best way to begin is by immediately rejecting (A), (B), and (D), the choices that shift Kim's position.

> A 180 test taker relies on effective answer choice strategies to eliminate choices in bulk whenever possible.

Of the remaining choices, (C) reflects the outcome if Quincy in space 4 answers correctly but Ho in space 2 does not: Fahroud and Quincy would stay put, while Ho and Mal would exchange spaces 2 and 3.

2. E

In the same vein, and even easier. In a "blue" round, child 5 (Fahroud, to begin with) is inactive, so the three choices that displace Fahroud, (B), (C), and (D), bite the dust immediately. If answerers 1 (Kim) and 3 (Mal) are both correct, then no one will move from the opening position, which just happens to be the scenario reflected in choice (E). The only possible difficulty here is if you assumed that the order must change. But then this question would in fact be a blessing in disguise, since it would eventually force you to abandon that notion. For the record, Kim can't possibly move back two places in line after only one round, so (A) can't possibly be the acceptable ordering we seek.

It was very generous of the test makers to begin the game with two basic questions testing the fundamentals. Things, however, get a bit more difficult from here.

3. D

We're given no new information, and need to find something that could be true after two rounds of the game. There's really no other option but to test the choices.

(A) Fahroud is all the way down in space 5 to begin with. If the game starts out with a blue round, Fahroud sits out round 1, and then asks a question in round 2. If red begins the game, then Fahroud asks Quincy a question in round 1. If Quincy answers correctly, Fahroud stays in space 5 and sits out blue round 2. If, however, Quincy answers Fahroud's question incorrectly in red round 1, they swap, and then Fahroud will have to ask the child in space 3 a question in blue round 2. No matter how we slice it, there's no way for Fahroud to have answered a question after the first two rounds, so (A) is incorrect.

(B) Can Ho ask two questions in the first two rounds? Well, we better start with a blue round, so that Ho in space 2 can present a question to Kim in space 1 (if we started with red, Ho would begin by answering a question, which isn't what we want). Again, there are two choices. If Kim answers Ho's question correctly, then Ho stays in space 2 and would be forced to answer a question in red round 2. If Kim botches the question, then Ho moves up to space 1, and then neither asks nor answers a question in red round 2. No good.

(C) If red-blue is the order of the first two rounds, then Kim is idle in round 1 and answers a question in round 2. If blue-red is the order, then Kim would answer a question in round 1 and could possibly move down to space 2, but then would have to answer another question in red round 2. The bottom line is that Kim can't ask a single question in the first two rounds, so we have to press on.

(D) If we start off with a blue round, Mal in space 3 would answer a question addressed by Quincy in space 4. If Mal fumbles it, he would drop down to space 4, and then would answer a question from Fahroud in red round 2. (D) is therefore possible, and correct. For the record:

(E) Quincy can answer a question in round 1 if red is called out first, but cannot answer a second question in round 2. That's because if he answers correctly, he stays in space 4 and then must ask a question in blue round 2. And if he answers incorrectly, then he drops down to space 5 where he'd have to sit out blue round 2.

Notice that there's really nothing to draw here; you simply need to run through the first two rounds in your head to see whether each choice is possible.

A 180 test taker can mentally process many "what if?" scenarios quickly and accurately.

---

4. B

A complex challenge, considering that we must deduce the colors called out, and the switches that must occur, to get Ho and Fahroud as far to the front as possible by the end of the third round. Then we need to evaluate the ordering at the end. Now Ho, beginning in space 2, is pretty close to the front as is. Three rounds is plenty of time to get him up to the front of the line, and that could happen whether red-blue-red is called or blue-red-blue. Fahroud, however, begins way down in the cellar, so the operative question concerns what must happen to enable him to cover the most distance.

A 180 test taker focuses on the operative questions; that is, the ones that immediately help him drive the action forward.

In order for Fahroud to get as far as possible, the order of the rounds must be red-blue-red; if blue was first, then Fahroud would sit out the entire first round, contrary to our cause. Meanwhile, as long as Ho answers Mal's opening question correctly and stumps Kim in blue round 2, he could get to No.1 and keep that position after round 3. So here's what must be the case following red round 1:

intial order	after round 1
K	K
H	H
M	M
Q	F
F	Q

In blue round 2, Fahroud continues his advance, while Ho captures the No. 1 space:

intial order	after round 1	after round 2
K	K	H
H	H	K
M	M	F
Q	F	M
F	Q	Q

In red round 3, Fahroud must advance yet again by stumping Kim, as the stem requires, and Quincy in 5 poses a question to Mal in 4. The mandate in the stem, however, says nothing about this interaction, so Mal may get it right, and stay put, or may bobble it, and slip into last place:

intial order	after round 1	after round 2	after round 3
K	K	H	H
H	H	K	F
M	M	F	K
Q	F	M	M or Q
F	Q	Q	M or Q

Finally we're in a position to answer the question: After round 3, Fahroud and Mal can't be next to each other in line, which makes (B) correct. (A) and (E) list children that must be adjacent (notice that no matter what happens between Mal and Quincy in the last round, they'll still be adjacent), while (C) and (D) contain kids that merely could be neighbors, depending on Mal's answer in round 3.

5. B

This time it's Quincy who moves "as far to the front of the line as possible," but the investigation works the same way: How far can he get in three rounds? Given a "blue" round 1, which of course is possible, he can stump Mal, move to position No. 3, stump the No. 2 kid, take over position No. 2, and then stump the No. 1 kid and move into first place. This is the only way Quincy can move that far front, so blue-red-blue must be the order of the rounds. But wait—there's another piece of hypothetical info: At the end of the third round, the other four kids must still be "in the same positions relative to each other." So with Quincy in space 1 after round 3, Kim, Ho, Mal, and Fahroud must bring up the rear in that order.

intial order	after round 3
K	Q
H	K
M	H
Q	M
F	F

So figuring out the shape of things after three rounds isn't so difficult, but the choices pose new problems, comparing, as they do, the positions after round 3 with positions earlier in the game. We can dispose of (D) quickly: We know that Kim is in second place after round 3, while Mal started the game in third. The rest, however, deal with interim rounds 1 and 2, which are a bit hard to visualize without officially plotting them out. If you can handle all that in your head, fantastic, but if not, it's not unreasonable to quickly fill in the gaps between the beginning and round 3.

In blue round 1, we know Quincy must begin his ascent by switching with Mal, but what happens between Kim and Ho? A little analysis reveals that Kim must answer correctly, because if she doesn't, she'll slip into space 2, which will make her Quincy's next victim in round 2. That's too much space lost for Kim; she'll never be able to get back to space 2 by the end of round 3. So here's what we now know:

intial order	after round 1	after round 2	after round 3
K	K		Q
H	H		K
M	Q		H
Q	M		M
F	F		F

All of the remaining choices involve round 2, so we'll have to press on and fill in the final empty column. Start with the obvious: Quincy continues to climb, stumping Ho, so switch those. In this red round, Fahroud in 5 interrogates Mal in 4, but knowing that after round 3 they remain in that order, it's impossible for them to switch and then immediately switch back a round later. So Mal will have to get it right, keeping those two where they are:

intial order	after round 1	after round 2	after round 3
K	K	K	Q
H	H	Q	K
M	Q	H	H
Q	M	M	M
F	F	F	F

This is the only way the children can be in a position to produce the ordering that we know results from round 3. In round 3, Quincy completes his journey to the top, satisfying one condition in the stem, while Ho in 3 holds off Mal in 4, satisfying the other requirement. Now we can see for sure that (B) has it right while the others are off base.

Sheesh! That's a decent amount of work, but still, it's feasible if you maintain your focus and follow through the necessary steps in an efficient and orderly manner.

A 180 test taker creates the time needed for working out the toughest questions by employing effective time-management strategies during the rest of the section.

---

6. C

One final question, and there's no relief in sight—in fact, this one's even worse, if possible, since it appears we have to go out four rounds in search of something that must be false. How can we possibly know what happens between the initial ordering and the one we're told is in effect after round 4? A little cleverness is required here. Does anything in particular strike you about the ordering given in the stem? Fahroud's performance should stand out; he started the game in the basement, and is now proudly standing in first place. How could that have happened? There's only one way: red-blue-red-blue must be the four rounds, since starting with blue wouldn't give Fahroud enough time to capture first place. So once again, we know the colors of each round, and thanks to our work in the previous questions it might now be obvious that Fahroud must advance through a string of stumpers that allow him to move ahead one space at a time. The difficulty, again, will be to figure out what happens in the other question asked in each round in order to make the ordering listed in the stem possible. We'll just have to plot out the rounds.

We know the initial ordering, of course; we know that red is called in round 1; and we know that F and Q must switch places. The issue is the other question, in this case, Mal asking Ho. If Ho gets it wrong, then Mal will take over second place; but since Mal needs to end up in the cellar after round 4, this can't be—it would put Mal too far up after round 1 to get down to space 5 by the end of round 4. So Ho must have met the challenge.

intial order	after round 1	after round 2	after round 3	after round 4
K	K			F
H	H			H
M	M			Q
Q	F			K
F	Q			M

You can (or perhaps you already did) fill in the remaining two rounds in similar fashion, keeping in mind Fahroud's steady and relentless advance, and the other correct or incorrect answers that must be given in order for round 4 to turn out as it does. Here's the complete picture:

intial order	after round 1	after round 2	after round 3	after round 4
K	K	H	H	F
H	H	K	F	H
M	M	F	K	Q
Q	F	M	Q	K
F	Q	Q	M	M

Now we can determine that (C) must be false: Kim must have fumbled her question in round 2, or else she wouldn't be able to get down to fourth place by the end of round 4.

What's Next?

The good news is that this game is finally over. The bad news is that there are two left that are just as bad, maybe worse. (But you *are* enjoying these, right?) In our next offering, "Plane Passengers," we continue the flying theme introduced way back in "Space Mission." In this case, however, we don't expect the characters to leave the vehicle until it's safely on the ground—Earth, that is.

LOGIC GAME 19

Exactly six passengers occupy four adjacent rows on a landing commuter plane. The rows are numbered 1 through 4 from front to back. Three of the passengers are businesspeople, and three are tourists. Two of the passengers are connecting to another flight, and four are arriving home. The rows are occupied by passengers in accordance with the following conditions:

If a row is occupied by a tourist, it is not also occupied by a businessperson.

No arriving tourist occupies a row immediately adjacent to a row occupied by a connecting businessperson.

Each row is occupied by fewer than three passengers.

1. Which one of the following is an acceptable assignment of passengers to rows?

   (A) 1: one arriving tourist, one connecting tourist; 2: empty; 3: three arriving businesspeople; 4: one connecting tourist

   (B) 1: one arriving businessperson; 2: one arriving tourist; 3: one arriving tourist, one connecting tourist; 4: one arriving businessperson, one connecting businessperson

   (C) 1: one arriving businessperson, one connecting businessperson; 2: one connecting tourist; 3: two arriving tourists; 4: one arriving businessperson

   (D) 1: one connecting tourist; 2: two arriving businesspeople; 3: one connecting tourist, one arriving businessperson; 4: one arriving tourist

   (E) 1: two connecting businesspeople; 2: one arriving tourist; 3: two arriving tourists; 4: one arriving businessperson

2. Which one of the following must be true?

   (A) No row is occupied by exactly one passenger.
   (B) No row is occupied by exactly two passengers.
   (C) No row is empty.
   (D) Row 1 is occupied by the same number of passengers as is row 3.
   (E) Row 4 is occupied by twice as many passengers as is row 2.

3. If a tourist is seated alone in row 4, and no two adjacent rows are occupied by businesspeople, then which one of the following must be true?

   (A) Row 1 is occupied by exactly one businessperson.
   (B) Row 2 is occupied by exactly two tourists.
   (C) Row 3 is occupied by exactly two businesspeople.
   (D) Row 1 is occupied by a connecting passenger.
   (E) Row 4 is occupied by an arriving passenger.

4. If a connecting businessperson occupies row 3, and exactly two of the six passengers are arriving businesspeople, then which one of the following must be true?

   (A) An arriving tourist sits alone in one of the rows.
   (B) Two arriving businesspeople sit together in one of the rows.
   (C) A connecting businessperson sits alone in one of the rows.
   (D) An arriving businessperson and a connecting businessperson sit together in one of the rows.
   (E) A connecting tourist sits alone in one of the rows.

5. Each of the following could be a complete and accurate list of the passengers in row 2 EXCEPT:

   (A) one arriving businessperson
   (B) two connecting businesspeople
   (C) one arriving businessperson, one connecting businessperson
   (D) one connecting tourist
   (E) two arriving businesspeople

6. If all of the businesspeople are arriving home, which one of the following is impossible?

   (A) Both connecting passengers are seated alone in different rows.
   (B) Exactly one arriving passenger is seated alone in a row.
   (C) Exactly two of the arriving passengers are seated alone in different rows.
   (D) Both connecting passengers are seated together in a row.
   (E) Exactly two of the arriving passengers are seated together in a row.

Logic Game 19: Plane Passengers

What Makes It Difficult

The major difficulty in this one is keeping track of all that's going on. First of all, we're faced with a triple hybrid game action: Four adjacent rows implies a sequencing element. Distributing six passengers into four rows means that some of the rows will have more than one passenger, which suggests a grouping element at work here as well. Finally, we have a Matching element to consider: passengers are either businesspeople or tourists, and either arriving home or connecting.

On top of these general difficulties, some questions (like questions 4 and 5, for example) force us to extrapolate from the given information who's left for the *other* seats—always a challenging task. And even the "acceptability" question, question 1, is difficult due to the complicated nature of the entities. Remember the entities in chapter 2's "Class Pictures"—"blue crayon dog, red painted house," etc.? One glance at the choices in question 1 tells us that the sheer wordiness of the four-seat arrangement is at least as bad, maybe even worse. Luckily, there are some major deductions to make and helpful strategies to employ.

Keys to the Game

When in doubt, start with the most familiar element. A simple row of four will help us keep track of the four rows, and the entities listed above the sketch will remind us what we need to fill into those rows.

Be clear on the task: Our task is to match up the travelers' two characteristics (arriving-connecting with business travel) and to fill these different types of travelers into the rows where appropriate, given the grouping and sequencing restrictions noted in the rules.

One row will have two tourists, and one row will have one. Similarly, one row will have two businesspeople, and one row will have one. This is the only breakdown possible, considering that we can't mix businesspeople and tourists, and we can't have more than two passengers per row.

A 180 test taker ruthlessly interrogates the numbers that govern the game.

At least one businessperson and at least one tourist must be arriving home. This is due to the fact that four passengers are arriving home. Even if all three businesspeople were arriving passengers, there would still be one arriving passenger left, and the same would be true if all three tourists were arriving home. Hence, at least one arrival for each passenger type.

A 180 test taker attempts to define the entities as clearly as possible before launching into the question set.

Answers and Explanations

1. C   2. C   3. B   4. E   5. B   6. A

1. C

As mentioned above, the choices may be hard on the eye, but the usual method for Acceptability questions prevails: using the rules to knock off the choices. Rule 1 kills (D), which mixes tourists and businesspeople. Rule 2 kills (B) and (E), which have arriving tourists next to connecting businesspeople. Rule 3 kills (A), which has three people in one of the rows, and we're done. (C) remains.

> A 180 test taker knows that even hard games have manageable questions. If he's low on time, he looks to bag these first before attempting the more complicated and time-consuming questions.

2. C

This flows directly from the key numbers deduction cited above. No row could be empty, since that would place six people in the remaining three rows, and we can't do that without mixing businesspeople and tourists. So (C) is correct.

(A) and (B) are impossible. We always need two singles and two doubles, so it can't be true that no row is occupied by exactly one passenger, (A), or that no row is occupied by exactly two passengers, (B).

(D) and (E) are possible only.

> A 180 test taker suspects that the answer to a "must be true" question with no new information will stem from one of the game's big deductions.

3. B

If a tourist is alone in 4 and the businesspeople rows aren't adjacent, then the businesspeople must be in rows 1 and 3. So the other two tourists go in 2. That's (B). Notice that this is not so difficult, once armed with our deductions above. It's another matter altogether if we approach the questions cold, with little or no thought up front.

(A) and (C) could be true, but we could have two passengers in 1 and only one passenger in 3.

(D) is impossible. If one of the businesspeople in 1 were connecting, then he or she would be next to two tourists in 2, at least one of whom would have to be arriving.

(E) is possible only.

4. E

The stem tells us that one businessperson is connecting and two businesspeople are arriving. That means that one tourist is connecting and two tourists are arriving.

> A 180 test taker carries information to its logical, and relevant, conclusions. She knows that in a difficult hybrid game with a matching element, any information that helps to determine who the entities are in a particular question is golden.

The arriving tourists can't be adjacent to the connecting businessperson in 3, so those two arriving tourists are in seat 1. The other tourist, the connecting one, will be alone in either row 2 or row 4. So (E) is correct.

(A) is impossible. The arriving tourists are together in row 1.

(B), (C), (D) Careful! The stem says that a connecting businessperson occupies row 3, but it doesn't say that *only* a connecting businessperson occupies row 3. We don't know how the two arriving businesspeople are distributed. They could go together, or one of them could join the connecting businessperson in row 3. So these choices are possible only.

5. B

From here, you could have tested each choice one by one, or tried to apply your previous work. As it happens, (A), (D), and (E) could have been true in the previous question, so we can cross those right off.

> A 180 test taker always looks for shortcuts, and often that means using previous work to eliminate choices in the question at hand.

(C) is fine if we place an arriving businessperson in 1, a connecting tourist in 3, and two arriving tourists in 4. (B), however, is impossible. If we have two connecting businesspeople in 2, then all of the tourists must be arriving.

> A 180 test taker always looks to ascertain the impact the behavior of one entity or group has on the other entities in the game.

And no matter how we arrange these arriving tourists, we'll always have at least one adjacent to row 2, in violation of Rule 2. So (B) is correct for this difficult, open-ended question.

6. A

If all the businesspeople are arriving home, then we don't have to worry about connecting businesspeople sitting next to arriving tourists. So Rule 2 is off the table for this one. Who's left? The three tourists, and we know which ones they are: two connecting, and one arriving. Of the three arriving businesspeople, two must be together in a row while the other sits alone. As for the tourists, there are two ways to break them up: Either the arriving tourist sits alone with the connecting tourists paired up; or the arriving tourist sits with one of the connecting tourists while the other connecting tourist sits alone. Notice that while we don't know what rows these pairs and solo folks occupy, it doesn't matter—the choices don't mention specific row numbers, so we needn't worry about that.

A 180 test taker uses the choices as clues to what the test makers are concerned with in a particular question.

On to the choices:

(A) We don't have to look far for our violator: As we saw, either the two connecting tourists sit together, or one sits alone while the other hangs with the arriving tourist. There's no way for both connecting passengers (tourists in this case) to fly solo. For the record:

(B) could be true: If we pair the arriving tourist with one of the connecting tourists, then the arriving businessperson sitting alone is the only arriving passenger sitting alone.

(C), (D) However, (C) could be true also: If we place the arriving tourist in her own row, then exactly two arriving passengers (that one and the solo arriving businessperson) would be alone in a row. That, of course, would require the two connecting tourists to share a row, so this scenario also eliminates (D).

(E) must be true: Our arriving tourist is either by herself, or paired with a connecting tourist. Either way, we're still left with the pair of arriving businesspeople mentioned above who must share a row while the other arriving businessperson flies solo.

What's Next?

Things got a bit nasty at the end there, big deductions and all. But that is, after all, what we'd expect from the toughest of the tough. Next up is our final Logic Game, and of course it wouldn't be right if we didn't end with another real killer. It's the story of a small town as submitted by town residents and compiled into a documentary by a video editor. We call it: "The Story of a Small Town as Submitted by Town Residents and Compiled into a Documentary by a Video Editor."

Enjoy . . .

LOGIC GAME 20

A video editor is assembling a single documentary of a small town from five reels of footage submitted by town residents. Exactly three reels—R, S, and T—contain town events, and exactly two reels—M and N—contain landscapes. Each reel arrives at the editor's studio separately. Immediately upon receipt, each reel is used in exactly one of two ways:

Either the reel, by itself, forms a single scene of the documentary, or the reel is combined with one or more reels to form a single scene of the documentary.

The documentary is assembled according to the following restrictions:

Any reel that is not combined with another reel forms a single scene bearing the name of that reel.

If either landscape reel is received immediately before or immediately after reel R, then the footage on that landscape reel will be combined with the footage on reel R to form a single scene R.

If either landscape reel is received immediately before or immediately after reel S, then the footage on that landscape reel will be combined with the footage on reel S to form a single scene S.

Reel N is received before reel R.

Scenes will appear in the completed documentary in the order in which they are formed.

1. Which one of the following could be the ordering of scenes, from first to last, contained in the completed documentary after all of the reels have been received?

    (A)   N, R, S, T, M
    (B)   R, S, T, M, N
    (C)   N, T, M, S, R
    (D)   N, M, T, S, R
    (E)   M, T, S, T, N

2. What is the minimum number of scenes that the documentary must contain after all of the reels have been received?

    (A)   1
    (B)   2
    (C)   3
    (D)   4
    (E)   5

3. If the unfinished documentary consists of exactly two scenes, and reel S is the only reel yet to be received, then all of the following could be true EXCEPT:

    (A)   Reel T was received second.
    (B)   Reel N was received second.
    (C)   Reel T was received first.
    (D)   Reel M was received third.
    (E)   Reel R was received third.

4. Which one of the following must be true of a completed documentary that consists of exactly five scenes?

    (A)   Reel M was received second.
    (B)   Reel N was received first.
    (C)   Reel R was received third.
    (D)   Reel S was received fifth.
    (E)   Reel T was received third.

5. If the completed documentary consists of exactly four scenes, then the first four reels can have been received in which one of the following orders?

    (A)   N, S, T, R
    (B)   N, M, T, S
    (C)   S, M, R, T
    (D)   M, T, N, R
    (E)   T, N, S, M

6. If the completed documentary consists of scenes R, T, and S, in order from first to last, then which one of the following must be true?

    (A)   Reel N was received first.
    (B)   Reel R was received third.
    (C)   Reel T was received third.
    (D)   Reel T was received fourth.
    (E)   Reel S was received fifth.

7. If, after all the reels are received, no two reels have been combined to form a scene, then which one of the following CANNOT be true?

    (A)   Reel N was received before reel T.
    (B)   Reel S was received before reel M.
    (C)   Reel S was received before reel R.
    (D)   Reel M was received before reel N.
    (E)   Reel T was received before reel S.

Logic Game 20: The Story of a Small Town as Submitted by Town Residents and Compiled into a Documentary by a Video Editor

Hey, it's a complicated game—why not have a complicated title? This is, after all, the final Logic Game in the book, so it deserves special status on that count alone.

What Makes It Difficult

What makes it difficult? What *doesn't* make it difficult? We trust that you found enough to give you a real headache in this one to safely skip this formality and move right to the keys to the game.

Keys to the Game

Get a grasp of the unusual game action. As unusual as the game is, it's comprised of game actions you've seen before. Footage reels are received in order, no two reels at the same time, which suggests sequencing. And the reels and scenes change over time, which suggests a process element. A tough combo, no doubt, but if you rely on your skills in each individual area, you should be okay.

A 180 test taker breaks down even an unusual "oddball" type of games into its most familiar elements.

Get a grasp of the key issues that govern the game, namely: In what order are the reels received? What happens when a reel arrives? Based on the order of reels received, what scenes, in what order, will make up the documentary?

Distinguish between the different types of reels to keep them straight. Using uppercase for town events (R, S, T) and lowercase for landscapes (m, n) works fine.

Perform a few run-throughs to make sure you understand how the rules work. It pays to even use an extreme example to illustrate. If the first three scenes to arrive are m, R, and n, in that order, then both m and n will be consumed by R, resulting in one scene entitled R, containing the footage from m, n, and R combined.

A 180 test taker does not hesitate to work out complicated rules to make sure she understands how they work before wading into the questions.

Each town events reel (R, S, and T) will end up in the completed documentary as a scene bearing its name; that's because no rules allow for the renaming of R, S, and T. The only question is whether m and n, the landscape reels, will make it unscathed into the big show, or if (depending on the order in which the reels are received) they'll get eaten and incorporated into R and/or S. This leads to a numbers deduction:

The completed documentary will consist of a minimum of three scenes (if both m and n disappear) or a maximum of five scenes (if both m and n survive).

The only entity that has no part in the combination rules is town events reel T. As the free agent in this game, T has the ability to get between R and S and the vulnerable landscape reels, and will therefore most likely play a large role in determining the fate of m and n.

A 180 test taker keeps track of the game's floaters and in some cases may even note possible roles they play in the game.

Answers and Explanations

1. D   2. C   3. A   4. E   5. D   6. A   7. B

1. D

This Acceptability question provides a welcome chance to test your understanding of the game. Rule 4 is the easiest to check, and it clearly eliminates (B), which has reel n received way after reel R. Choice (A) is no good because it features n next to R; but R would swallow up n and n would disappear, according to Rule 2. Similarly, (C) is out thanks to Rule 3: S would modify scene m to create a new scene S. (E) is out of the question: As we saw above, scenes R, S, and T must be part of the completed documentary, but in (E), R has inexplicably disappeared and T has been used twice. No good; only one appearance per reel, and only m and n can disappear. That leaves (D), and it's okay: If the reels came in in that order, none would be eaten by any of the others and no rules would be violated.

A 180 test taker avails himself of every opportunity to test his understanding of the game and the rules. He knows that if he has immediate trouble with an Acceptability question, then it's a sure sign that he has misunderstood the workings of the game and should revisit the intro.

2. C

We already considered this issue in our dissection of the game above, so this question is a breeze. We saw that the completed documentary must consist of a minimum of three scenes, if both m and n disappear, or a maximum of five scenes if both m and n survive.

A 180 test taker expects even a bear of a game to yield some easy points; specifically, in the form of questions that demand she demonstrate a basic understanding of the game.

3. A

The second part of the if-clause is a good place to start: S is the only reel not yet received, meaning that R, T, m, and n have been received.

A 180 test taker always strives to turn negative statements into positive ones.

But wait: Even having received all four of these reels, the unfinished documentary, we're told, contains only two scenes so far. That can only mean that m and n have been eaten up; that they've disappeared. Well, who could have done such a thing? It's pretty clear by now: The only reels that swallow up other reels in this game are R and S, but S hasn't showed up yet, so we're forced to conclude that the reels must have been received in such a way as to allow R to swallow up both m and n. R, therefore, must have been received right in between m and n.

The only choice not consistent with this state of affairs is choice (A): If reel T were received second, then there'd be no way for R to be in position to eat both m and n. Receiving reels m-T-n-R, in that order, would lead to an unfinished piece with three scenes: m, T, and R. Similarly, n-T-m-R or n-T-R-m would also give us three scenes. R can't be received before n, so these are the only possibilities under (A)'s circumstances; and since none of them result in only two scenes, (A) cannot be true and is therefore the correct answer.

(B), (C), and (E) are all shown to be possible by this ordering of received reels: T-n-R-m. In this case, reel n is received immediately before R, and reel m is received immediately after R, which means both would be combined with R and would therefore disappear, leaving exactly two scenes (T and R) awaiting S's arrival.

(D) If the first four reels are received in the order n-R-m-T, then n and m will again disappear into R, and only R and T will be left, so it is possible for m to have been received third in this situation.

4. E

"Completed documentary" means that all five reels have been received, and " . . . consisting of five scenes" means that no reel got swallowed up by another; in other words, both m and n must have survived.

A 180 test taker has the ability to see past the wording the test makers give him, and recognize the more specific and helpful implications of that wording.

How can this be? Well, m and n can survive only if they both keep plenty of distance from the landscape-reel eaters, R and S. In fact, the only way that m and n aren't received at some point consecutively with R and S is if neutral reel T breaks the two groups up. If T is received third, then it's possible to place the two landscape reels m and n on one side of T, and the other two events reels R and S on the other side of T. Thanks to Rule 4, we can't have n coming after R, so this situation further breaks down to this: Reels m and n, in either order, are received first and second; T is received third; R and S, in either order, come in fourth and fifth. There's no other way to protect m and n from being consumed by R or S. T must be received right in the middle in order to allow the documentary to have the full five scenes, so (E) is the correct answer here.

(A), (B), and (D) are all possible based on the ordering discussed above—there's flexibility as to the order of m in relation to n in the first two slots, and R in relation to S in the last two. But none of these must be true.

(C) No way: T is received third, as discussed above.

5. D

Don't be fooled—the answer choices list only the first four reels received, but the question is about the *completed* documentary, which means that we have to take into consideration the fifth reel received as well. (That might not be a bad way to start—add the missing reel to each of the choices:

(A) m; (B) R; (C) n; (D) S; (E) R.) We're trying to find the ordering of received reels (including the fifth reel that we just indicated) that will result in a *four*-scene documentary. Let's see what happens.

(A) Follow the action from the beginning: n forms a scene, S swallows up the n scene to form a single S scene, T and R follow with their own scenes . . . but then m, as the fifth reel received, will be combined with scene R, leaving only three scenes in the final documentary: S, T, and R.

(B) We just saw in the previous question that if T is third, no reels get combined and the completed documentary will contain five scenes, not the four we're going for here.

A 180 test taker picks up ideas as he goes along to exploit later on.

(C) Rule 4 kills this one immediately—n can't be the last reel received, since it can never be received after R.

(D) does the trick: If the first four reels received are m, T, n, and R, in that order, then up to that point, reel m will stay intact but reel n will be absorbed by reel R, and the documentary scenes will look like this: m, T, R. The scene yet to be received in this scenario is S, and after receipt it will form its own scene after R, giving us the requisite four-scene documentary (m, T, R, S).

(E) Same logic here as in (A) above: S would swallow up both n and m, even before reel R was received, again resulting in a three-scene documentary (T, S, and R).

6. A

The stem, once translated, tells us that both reels m and n have been swallowed up—the only question is *when*. Rule 4 specifies that n must be received before R. Beginning then with n—R—T—S as the partial order of reels received, our only task is to fit m into this order in such a way as to result in a completed documentary made up of scenes R, T, and S. Under these circumstances m can't come right before n, because if that happened, m would survive, and the completed piece would consist of scenes m, R, T, and S. And that's enough to get us to the right answer: No matter where we end up working m into the ordering, n must be the first reel received, choice (A). Note that m cannot be received second, immediately after n, because then n would not combine with R and scene n would be the first scene of the documentary.

(B) is impossible: If R is received third, and T and S come after it in the finished documentary, then both m and n must have been received before R, in which case one of those reels would have been converted into its own scene.

(C) is possible, but not necessary; the order of reels received could have been n-R-m-T-S, in which case m, rather than T, would be received third.

(D) and (E) are both invalidated by this ordering of reels received: n-R-T-S-m. Both m and n would drop out as scheduled, leaving us with the completed documentary listed in the stem.

A 180 test taker gets stronger as she progresses through a game thanks to her increased familiarity with it, which makes questions late in the set a bit more manageable.

KAPLAN

7. B

If this sounds familiar, there's a good reason: it's just question 4 all over again. " . . . no two reels were combined to form a scene . . . " is the same thing as " . . . completed documentary consisting of five scenes."

> A 180 test taker is expert at translating statements, including question stems, and immediately recognizes when a new question relates back to work he has already done.

And we saw in question 4 how this must come about: m and n, in either order, are received first and second; T is received third; R and S, in either order, must come in fourth and fifth. Simplified: m/n-T-R/S. From this it's simple to see that S cannot be received before m, and that choice (B) is correct.

(A) and (E) both must be true, according to the ordering listed above.

(C) and (D) both could be true, as the acceptable ordering m-n-T-S-R shows.

> A 180 test taker employs effective time management strategies, and is often rewarded with a "gimme" simply for making it to the end of a difficult game.

section two

LOGICAL REASONING

CHAPTER SIX

The Logical Reasoning Challenge

Do you like to point out the assumptions in others' arguments?
Do you like to home in on logical flaws like a detective, and
analyze precisely how arguments could be made better, or
worse? Then LSAT Logical Reasoning, which accounts for not
one, but two of the four scored sections of the LSAT, is for you.
So start dissecting op-ed pieces, and cutting the contestants on
television debates down to size. When you see your LSAT
score, you'll be glad you did!

1. If all of the statements in the passage are true, each of the
    following must also be true EXCEPT:

    (A) Op-ed pieces and television debates contain content that
         is related in some way to material tested in the Logical
         Reasoning sections of the LSAT.
    (B) No question type contained on the LSAT is represented
         in more sections of the LSAT than is Logical
         Reasoning.
    (C) Mastering the Logical Reasoning question type will
         ensure an excellent LSAT score.
    (D) Logical flaws and assumptions are among the topics
         tested on the LSAT.
    (E) Thinking like a detective can favorably improve one's
         LSAT score.

Choice (C) is correct. Mastering Logical Reasoning is *necessary* to achieve a top LSAT score, but is not *sufficient;* one must ace the other two sections on the test as well. You'll be hearing more about this distinction between necessary and sufficient conditions later on. (A) is valid: The instructor strongly implies that dissecting op-eds and debates will lead to a higher score, which, in fact, it certainly can. (B) plays off the numbers in the text. Since two of the four sections on the LSAT consist of Logical Reasoning questions, you don't have to know anything else about the test to deduce that no other question type could possibly take up more than two sections of the test. (D) legitimately ties the first two sentences to the first part of the third, and (E) is strongly suggested by the fact that the proclivity for playing detective is relevant to (hence, inferably bodes well for) one's LR performance.

So win arguments! Prove people wrong! Amaze your friends! Be the life of the party! Get a score of 180 on the LSAT! . . . Just a few of the many and varied uses of the ability to master the subtle art of Logical Reasoning.

Disclaimer: Hacking through the bogus arguments of others and/or demonstrating superior logical acumen in everyday conversation will NOT make you the most popular person in town.

However, the ability to do so *will* do wonders for your LSAT score. The purpose of this chapter is to help you hone your critical thinking skills through practice on some of the toughest Logical Reasoning material around. The following offers some guidelines on how to get the most out of the Logical Reasoning material in this book.

USING THE LOGICAL REASONING QUESTIONS IN THIS BOOK

This section is broken up into a number of chapters each detailing various difficulties commonly encountered in LSAT Logical Reasoning. It is designed to allow you to learn as you go and to apply your learning to subsequent questions as you progress through the section.

- First, we introduce you to the five major categories of difficult Logical Reasoning questions.
- Then we offer in-depth practice with each of these five major categories of tough questions.
- After that, nine other common but often difficult Logical Reasoning features or structural elements are presented, each highlighted by an example.
- Finally, 38 additional questions representative of all the elements and forms discussed are served up for your practicing pleasure.

Instructions are provided throughout intended to lead you through the various sections. Here are a few general pointers to keep in mind when tackling all Logical Reasoning questions, but especially challenge questions like the ones you're about to see:

Keep your eye out for the author's evidence, conclusion, and any assumptions relied upon in the argument. The wordiness and logical subtlety of the questions that follow often cause test takers to lose sight of what's actually being said, and it's nearly impossible to answer questions like these correctly when one is foggy about the specifics. The conclusion is the "what" of the matter; the evidence is the reasons "why" the author feels entitled to make that particular claim; and assumptions are any missing premises that are nonetheless needed in order for the conclusion to stand.

Paraphrase the text. We include the same advice later on for the longer Reading Comprehension passages. You can get a leg up on tough text by simplifying the passage's ideas and translating them into your own words.

Observe timing guidelines. On the real test, 24–26 questions in 35 minutes works out roughly to a minute and a quarter per question. Try to answer the questions in this section in about that time, but you can certainly cut yourself a little slack considering the high level of difficulty of the questions in this section.

Familiarize yourself with the common LR concepts tested. Review the logical elements and structures discussed throughout the chapter, and look to recognize which of them are present in each Logical Reasoning question you encounter in this book as well as in any other questions you practice with during your LSAT preparation. While the specific subject matter (names, places, scenarios, etc.) changes from question to question and test to test, the underlying logical patterns remain incredibly consistent. Get to know them.

What's Next?

The Logical Reasoning questions begin in the next chapter. Work through the questions, one at a time, and see if you can spot the logical element at work in each.

CHAPTER SEVEN

Types of Challenging Logical Reasoning Questions

In this chapter, we'll take a brief look at five categories of difficult Logical Reasoning questions: Formal Logic, Parallel Reasoning, Numbers and Statistics, Surveys and Studies, and Just Plain Tough. Chapter 8 will provide you with additional, in-depth practice with these categories, but first you need to familiarize yourself with the types of tough Logical Reasoning questions you're likely to see on test day.

FORMAL LOGIC

Formal logic is characterized by the use of words and phrases such as *if/then, only if, all, some, none, no, unless, most, every, always,* and *never*. When a stimulus contains these words, translations and deductions are often possible, which in a way brings us into Logic Games territory. For some, this is good news. For others, the appearance of such Logic Games elements on the Logical Reasoning sections is an unmitigated disaster.

A 180 test taker recognizes and can interpret formal logic statements no matter where on the LSAT they appear.

Let's try a Formal Logic example.

1. Kurtis wants to repair his vintage guitar. Only an experienced craftsperson can repair a vintage guitar, but no craftsperson has a chance of becoming a virtuoso guitar player.

   Which one of the following can be properly inferred from the passage?

   (A) Kurtis will be able to repair his vintage guitar.
   (B) Kurtis is not an experienced craftsperson.
   (C) Kurtis has no chance of becoming a virtuoso guitar player.
   (D) If Reed is an experienced craftsperson, then he will be able to repair Kurtis's vintage guitar.
   (E) If Reed has a chance to become a virtuoso guitar player, then Reed cannot repair Kurtis's vintage guitar.

Explanation: Kurtis's Guitar

Poor Kurtis is in a jam. His vintage guitar is on the blink and he needs to have it repaired. The "only" statement can be translated into a simple "if/then" statement: If someone can repair a vintage guitar, then that person is an experienced craftsperson. But (and here's the proper translation of the next clause) if someone has a chance at becoming a virtuoso, then that person is not a craftsperson. (Evidently, life's too short to master both.) Putting those together—which is essentially what we need to do in all Formal Logic questions—we see that repairing a vintage guitar and being a virtuoso are mutually exclusive, since the first requires a craftsperson and the second excludes all craftspeople.

Not terrible tricky, but we're not out of the woods yet; the test makers have one last curve to throw us. Reed in choices (D) and (E) appears to pop out of nowhere, and normally in such cases we say that such characters are outside the scope. But Reed, while not mentioned in the stimulus, is actually *within* the scope since (D) and (E) contain hypotheticals. And (E) is simply an extension of what we just deduced: If Reed has a chance to become a virtuoso, then he can't be a craftsperson. And since only a craftsperson can repair a vintage guitar, noncraftsperson Reed can't help Kurtis out.

(A), (B), (C) All we know about Kurtis is what he *wants* to do: repair his guitar. And none of the statements tells us what that want leads to, so we can deduce nothing from it. We don't know whether Kurtis is an experienced craftsperson, or has a shot at virtuosity, so none of these can be inferred here.

(D) Did you get tricked by this one? The second clause translates to "If one can repair a vintage guitar, then one is an experienced craftsperson." That doesn't mean that any old experienced craftsperson can make the repairs—other skills might be needed that Reed doesn't possess. Stated another way: Being an experienced craftsperson is a *necessary,* but not *sufficient* trait of anyone who can repair a vintage guitar. (Remember those words—you'll be seeing them again.) In (D), Reed makes the cut on that account, but may fail in other ways.

PARALLEL REASONING

Parallel Reasoning is a perennial LSAT question type. Since time immemorial (well, at least since the early '90s) there have been two Parallel Reasoning questions on every LSAT Logical Reasoning section (occasionally just one, but almost always two per section). So on test day you can just about count on seeing four questions that ask you to find the choice that mirrors the logic of a stimulus. Test takers generally find these difficult because they're usually fairly lengthy and involved, and each choice tells a different story, making it hard to focus on the underlying logic of the original.

A 180 test taker understands that in a Parallel Reasoning question, the stimulus and the right answer both use the same kind of evidence to draw the same kind of conclusion. She's not distracted by the subject matter of the stimulus and five choices, which usually varies considerably.

Question 2 is a Parallel Reasoning question.

2. The only vehicles that have come across the bridge since dusk have been tanks. All of the tanks that came across the bridge since dusk were light tanks. Thus, all of the vehicles that have come across the bridge since dusk have been light.

   Which one of the following exhibits faulty reasoning most similar to the faulty reasoning exhibited in the passage above?

   (A) The only flowers in the garden are roses, and all of the roses in the garden are red. Therefore, all of the flowers in the garden are red flowers.

   (B) All of the bears in the zoo are carnivores. All of the bears in the zoo are also large. So all carnivores are large.

   (C) The only objects on the showroom floor are kitchen appliances. All of the kitchen appliances on the showroom floor come with two-year warranties. Therefore, all of the objects on the showroom floor come with two-year warranties.

   (D) All of the objects that spilled out upon the counter were rocks from Professor Wainright's collection. Professor Wainright's collection is exclusively made up of soft rocks. Thus, all of the objects that spilled out upon the counter were soft.

   (E) All of the paintings hanging in the gallery are oil paintings. The only paintings in the gallery are still-lifes and portraits. So all of the portraits hanging in the gallery are oil paintings.

Explanation: *Light* Tanks?

The flaw in the logic of the stimulus argument is suggested in its title: Can a tank be considered a *light* vehicle? A tank can certainly be light relative to other tanks; those are the kind we find here crossing the bridge since dusk. But a tank, by its very definition, cannot be considered a light *vehicle*; in fact, common sense would dictate otherwise. A tank is, by definition, a big, heavy, armor-plated vehicle, and so even the lightest tank is a heavy vehicle. The qualifier "light" is thus a relative term, and can't be automatically transferred from one class of objects to another class. A light elephant, for instance, is not a light animal. Which one of the choices makes the same mistake of misapplying a relative qualifier? (D), the correct choice, copies the flaw exactly; the objects in Professor Wainright's collection may have been soft rocks (say shale or sandstone), but that doesn't mean they can be described as soft *objects*. Even a soft rock is a hard object, just as even a light tank is a heavy vehicle. And indeed, the chance of coming upon a light tank is just about as good as the chance of finding a soft rock. Note how the flaw here is based on a misunderstanding of sets. We'll be seeing that again later on.

(A) does not use a relative qualifier: red is red. Thus, (A) is perfectly right in saying that if all the flowers are red roses, then they all must be red flowers.

(B) makes a different kind of mistake: All X is Y, all X is Z; therefore, all Y is Z. Basically, (B) says that because the property of being a carnivore happens to coincide with the property of being large in this particular collection of zoo bears, therefore the property of being a carnivore must always be accompanied by the property of being large. There's no parallel to the misuse of a relative term in this one.

(C), like (A), does not use a relative qualifier. A "two-year warranty" means the same thing when applied to a "kitchen appliance" as it does when applied to "object" in general. So (C)'s argument is sound.

(E) follows suit; if all the paintings in the gallery are oil paintings, then any subset of the paintings in the gallery, such as the portraits in the gallery, must also be oil paintings. The term "oil painting" doesn't change its meaning when applied to "portrait" and to "painting."

NUMBERS AND STATISTICS

The LSAT test makers just *love* their statistics. Perhaps that's because statistics are used these days—often fallaciously—to supposedly "prove" or justify just about anything. That makes numbers and statistics a particularly fertile ground for Logical Flaw and Weaken the Argument questions, or, as in the case of question 3 below, a plain old inference question that requires us to simply interpret the stats.

3. The paintings of French painter Trianne Dejere sold best in the period following the production of *La Triumph*, now Dejere's most famous piece. In the twelve-month period preceding the unveiling of this piece, Dejere sold 57% of the works she produced in this period, a far greater percentage than in previous years. In the twelve-month period following a glowing review of *La Triumph* in a popular magazine, however, Dejere sold 85% of the paintings she produced. Interestingly, Dejere's revenue from painting sales was roughly the same in both periods, since she sold the same number of paintings in the twelve months before presenting *La Triumph* as she did in the twelve months following the favorable review.

    Which one of the following statements can be properly concluded from the passage, if the information above is true?

    (A) Due to the positive review, Dejere was able to charge substantially more for the works produced after *La Triumph* than the works produced before it.
    (B) Dejere was more concerned with positive reviews than with increasing the prices of her paintings.
    (C) The positive review of *La Triumph* brought Dejere's work to the attention of more art collectors than were previously aware of her work.
    (D) Dejere painted fewer works in the twelve-month period following the review of *La Triumph* than she had in the twelve month period preceding its unveiling.
    (E) Dejere paid more attention to marketing her paintings after *La Triumph* received such a positive reception.

Explanation: The Paintings of Trianne Dejere

Trianne Dejere's paintings sold best after she revealed her most famous piece. In the twelve months before that unveiling, she sold 57% of her works. In the twelve months following the unveiling, she sold 85% of her works. Nevertheless, in both periods, she sold the same number of paintings.

A 180 test taker zeros in on percents and ratios, knowing that often the test makers are testing his ability to distinguish between rates and raw numbers.

We need to consider what conclusion this evidence would support. If 57% equals the same number of paintings before the unveiling as 85% equals after the unveiling, then Dejere must have produced more paintings in the period before the unveiling—that's the only way that the numbers could work out. (D) states this from the other angle: Dejere must have painted fewer paintings after the unveiling. So, (D) is our correct answer choice.

(A) The author tells us that revenue from both periods is equal since Dejere sells the same number of paintings in both. Therefore, if she had charged more in the second period, she would have made more money than she had in the first, which would contradict the stimulus. Because this is inconsistent with the passage, it certainly can't be inferred from it.

(B) The information given pertains solely to the hard facts of the matter: the number sold and revenues gained during different time periods. (B) is therefore outside of the scope of the argument, since the author never mentions Dejere's motivations for painting. We can't reasonably conclude anything about her "concerns" here.

(C), if anything, might suggest that Dejere sold more paintings in the second period, which the stimulus explicitly contradicts. Further, the stimulus provides no information about how art collectors might have responded to the review, giving us no basis to form a conclusion about those collectors.

(E) might also suggest that sales would be higher in the second period, but we know that the sales were the same. However, there's really no reason to look this deeply into it. The main reason for chopping (E) is because marketing is never discussed.

A 180 test taker does not read more into a stimulus than what's given.

SURVEYS AND STUDIES

This category is intimately related to the previous one. More often than not, the surveys, studies, and occasional experiments that show up in Logical Reasoning questions are backed by numbers and percentages, and we can almost consider these two types as one big category. However, it's worth breaking them up because 1) surveys and studies have their own predictable patterns on the LSAT, and 2) they don't always involve numbers or percentages, and sometimes, when they do, as is the case in question 4 below, the numerical info is secondary to the mechanisms of the study itself. You'll be seeing quite a few surveys and studies in this book.

> A 180 test taker approaches with skepticism any survey, study, or experiment described in a LR stimulus, knowing full well that very often what's tested is an understanding of how these surveys go awry.

Here is an example of a question that falls into the Surveys and Studies category.

4. Attention Deficit Disorder (ADD) is a condition characterized by an inability to focus on any topic for a prolonged period of time, and is especially common among children five to ten years old. A recent study has shown that 85 percent of seven-year-old children with ADD watch, on average, more than five hours of television a day. It is therefore very likely that Ed, age seven, has ADD, since he watches roughly six hours of television a day.

The argument above is flawed because it

(A) cites as a direct causal mechanism a factor that may only be a partial cause of the condition in question

(B) fails to indicate the chances of having ADD among seven-year-old children who watch more than five hours of television a day

(C) limits the description of the symptoms of ADD to an inability to focus for a prolonged period of time

(D) fails to consider the possibility that Ed may be among the 15 percent of children who do not watch more than five hours of television a day

(E) does not allow for other causes of ADD besides television watching

Explanation: Attention Deficit Disorder

The author's conclusion pops up at the end, where she states that Ed is likely to have ADD because he watches television a lot and is seven. The key piece of evidence is a recent study that the author cites which states that 85% of seven-year-olds with ADD watch more than five hours of television per day. The study thus only discusses the television-watching habits of seven-year-olds *who have ADD*. The author's conclusion is flawed because it makes a conclusion about a seven-year-old television watcher based on a study about seven-year-old television watchers *with ADD*. In other words, there's a scope shift (another notion to keep in mind for later on) between the evidence and the conclusion. The author errs in accepting the survey as relevant to Ed. (B) expresses this flaw most clearly: In order to make conclusions about Ed and whether he might have ADD, the author must come up with evidence that pertains to Ed, since the original evidence does not. She needs a statistic that states the likelihood that a seven-year-old who watches more than five hours of TV a day would have ADD. The evidence provided *sounds* like that, but isn't, and (B) captures the gist of the author's mistake, making it our winner.

(A) is confusing, but the argument isn't really about degrees of causation. The author doesn't suggest that age and television watching *cause* a child to contract ADD, but that those factors generally appear with the disorder. (A) distorts the author's conclusion by suggesting that it says that Ed's television watching has caused him to contract ADD, but the author never suggests this.

(C) Yes it does, but that's not a problem. Perhaps some doctors might disagree with the author's definition, but its validity is not the issue at the heart of this argument. Rather, the argument is concerned with Ed's chances of having ADD based on a particular study.

(D) is easiest to remove for the fact that it contradicts the stimulus, where we learn that Ed *does* actually watch more than five hours of television per day. (You may have also noticed that the 15% figure is bogus; it's derived from the 85% figure in the stimulus, but that figure refers to the percentage of children with ADD who watch more than five hours of TV a day. Inferably, we can therefore say that 15% of children with ADD do not watch more than five hours of TV a day, but we can't turn this into 15% of children *in general* who don't watch more than five hours, as (D) attempts to do.)

(E) again distorts the argument, which never suggests that television watching causes ADD. Since no causality is mentioned, we can only assume that the data represents a correlation.

JUST PLAIN TOUGH

Not every difficult Logical Reasoning question is distinguished by a common logical feature—some are "just plain tough." These are akin to the Super-Charged Standards of the Logic Games section, and foreshadow the "Just Plain Tough" Reading Comprehension passages you'll see later on. These general killers come in all varieties: standard question types like Assumption, Inference, and Strengthen/Weaken the Argument, as well as less common types such as Paradox questions like the example below. If you're shooting for that elusive 180, you simply have to be prepared to face down the tough stuff no matter what form it takes.

Give this tough question a shot:

5. Before the advent of writing, each of the isolated clans of the Comaquogue tribe contained master storytellers whose function was to orally transmit the tradition of each clan from one generation to the next. When writing was developed within certain clans of the tribe, the master storytellers of these clans disappeared within a few generations. This stands to reason, considering that the availability of written records obviated the need for masterful oral communicators to keep the tradition of literate clans alive. What has puzzled anthropologists, however, is the total lack of masterful storytellers in modern illiterate Comaquogue clans.

    Which one of the following, if true, best helps to explain the puzzling situation mentioned above?

    (A)   Modern illiterate Comaquogue clan members display personality characteristics that resemble their ancestors more closely than they resemble the characteristics of modern literate Comaquogue clan members.

    (B)   Modern illiterate Comaquogue clans participate in more ritual gatherings than most modern literate Comaquogue clans do, but they participate in fewer ritual gatherings than did their common ancestors.

    (C)   Modern illiterate Comaquogue clans are recently descended from long-time literate clans that failed to pass on the skills of reading and writing due to a devastating 75-year war.

    (D)   The celebrations of modern illiterate Comaquogue clans involve a great deal of singing and dancing, and children are taught clan songs and dances from a very young age.

    (E)   The traditions of modern illiterate Comaquogue clans are an amalgamation of the cumulative experiences of previous generations plus innovations to the heritage added by the current generation of clan members.

Explanation: Comaquogue Storytellers

The author clearly identifies the source of the confusion when he mentions what puzzles anthropologists. They're perplexed by two facts that seem inconsistent with each other. First, the advent of writing in certain Comaquogue clans seems to have caused the disappearance of the master storytellers within those tribes. Nevertheless, the second fact is that modern illiterate Comaquogue clans also lack master storytellers. The basic question is: Why do these modern illiterate clans lack storytellers when earlier clans lost their storytellers only after they learned how to read? Let's look to the answer choices and find one that specifically answers this question.

A 180 test taker rephrases the paradox as a question and proceeds through the answer choices in an attempt to answer it.

(A) does nothing to explain why the modern illiterate clans lack storytellers. Personality similarities don't have any clear relationship to literacy and storytellers.

(B) A comparison of the frequency of clan gatherings also does not in any way explain why the current illiterate tribes lack storytellers.

(C) would explain the discrepancy and is therefore the correct answer. If it were true, then the storytellers did disappear when the clans became literate, but they subsequently lost that literacy. Thus the modern tribes could both be illiterate and lack storytellers, as is the case in the stimulus, and they could have lost their storytellers during an earlier literate period. The inconsistency is no longer an inconsistency—all of the pieces of the puzzle find a home in this explanation.

(D) again touches on the issue of modern Comaquogue rituals without referring to literacy and storytelling, the central elements of the argument's paradox.

(E) is too broad to resolve this discrepancy. It might give you the room to start making assumptions, but it doesn't specifically address the issues of literacy and storytelling. Regardless of the sentiments in (E), the fact remains that the modern illiterate clans have no master storytellers when the evidence suggests that they should.

A 180 test taker doesn't read too much into a choice in order to try to make it work.

NOW TRY THESE . . .

Next, try your hand at the following five questions. Each question represents one of the categories just discussed. See if you can pick out the logical element operating in each.

6. Choi: All other factors being equal, children whose parents earned doctorates are more likely to earn a doctorate than children whose parents did not earn doctorates.

   Hart: But consider this: Over 70 percent of all doctorate holders do not have a parent that also holds a doctorate.

   Which one of the following is the most accurate evaluation of Hart's reply?

   (A) It establishes that Choi's claim is an exaggeration.
   (B) If true, it effectively demonstrates that Choi's claim cannot be accurate.
   (C) It is consistent with Choi's claim.
   (D) It provides alternative reasons for accepting Choi's claim.
   (E) It mistakes what is necessary for an event with what is sufficient to determine that the event will occur.

7. An economic or political crisis in a poor country can lead to a lack of faith in the country's leaders, which is often followed by violent behavior, dissent, and even revolt among specific segments of the population. In many cases, propaganda is immediately issued from media outlets that quells such reactions by downplaying the extent of the recent crisis, thereby helping to restore belief in the efficacy of the government. However, the habitual violence exhibited by certain groups of disaffected youths in such countries generally has nothing to do with a lack of faith in their leaders, but rather is the consequence of an endemic boredom and lack of any vision of a positive future for themselves.

   Which one of the following statements follows most logically from the statements in the passage above?

   (A) It is easier to quell periodic revolts in poor countries than it is to solve the habitual problem of youth violence.
   (B) In all poor countries, propaganda alone cannot entirely diffuse dissent stemming from an economic or political crisis.
   (C) Economic and political crises do not lead to any instances of youth violence in poor countries.
   (D) The effect that propaganda has in putting down revolts in poor countries is primarily related to its ability to alter people's fundamental beliefs.
   (E) To the extent that propaganda may help to decrease youth violence in a poor country, it is probably not the result of restoring the youths' faith in their country's leadership.

8. A computer crash has occurred when a computer's central processing unit "freezes up" and cannot respond to further commands or perform additional functions. In the split second during a computer crash, however, certain functions are still possible. When Cindy's Micron 401 computer crashed, she suspected it was due to an electrical power surge to the computer. The Micron 401 processor usually does not work fast enough during a crash to produce an error message on the screen before the computer "freezes." However, an error message can be triggered by an electrical power surge to the computer. Whenever a Micron 401 computer crashes without producing an error message on the screen, the computer's hard drive is damaged. Upon restarting her computer, Cindy determined that its hard drive was not damaged.

   Which one of the following must be true on the basis of the information above?

   (A) If the Micron 401's processor worked faster during the crash, the computer's hard drive would have been damaged.

   (B) The Micron 401's hard drive is specially suited to withstand computer crashes.

   (C) If the Micron 401's crash was not due to an electrical power surge, the computer's processor worked unusually fast during the crash.

   (D) The Micron 401 computer is built to withstand electrical power surges.

   (E) If an error message appeared on the screen of the Micron 401, it did so only after the computer crashed.

9. A social worker surveyed 200 women who recently had given birth to their first child. Half of these women had chosen to have their children in a hospital or obstetric clinic; the other half had chosen to give birth at home under the care of certified midwives. Of the 100 births that occurred at home, only five had presented any substantial complications, whereas 17 of the hospital births had required extra attention because of complications during delivery. The social worker concluded from this survey that the home is actually a safer environment in which to give birth than is a hospital or clinic.

   Which one of the following, if true, most seriously calls the social worker's conclusion above into question?

   (A) All of the women in the study who were diagnosed as having a high possibility of delivery complications elected to give birth in a hospital.

   (B) Many obstetricians discourage their patients from giving birth in their own homes.

   (C) Women who give birth in their own homes tend to experience less stress during labor and delivery than do those who deliver in hospitals.

   (D) Women who give birth in hospitals and clinics often have shorter periods of labor than do those who give birth at home.

   (E) Pregnant doctors prefer giving birth in a hospital.

10. Mitchell will play basketball tomorrow only if Allyson takes the day off. Allyson will not take the day off unless Lisa borrows a car. Since Lisa has not borrowed a car, Mitchell will not play basketball tomorrow.

The pattern of reasoning displayed above is most closely paralleled in which one of the following?

(A)   Jeannie will not go out to dinner unless Sheila also goes out to dinner. Kurt will travel upstate tomorrow only if Jeannie goes out to dinner. However, since Sheila cannot go out to dinner, Kurt will not travel upstate tomorrow.

(B)   Ashley will run the race this weekend only if Jon or Randi also runs. Jon will not run the race, but Randi will. So Ashley will run the race this weekend.

(C)   Matthew will go to the amusement park next weekend only if Jack agrees to go. Jack will not go to the amusement park unless the admission fee is inexpensive. Since the admission fee is expensive, Jack will not go to the amusement park next weekend.

(D)   Sean will go bowling tonight if he finishes his work and there is no league play scheduled at his local bowling alley. Although he has confirmed that no league play is scheduled, Sean has not finished his work, and therefore will not go bowling tonight.

(E)   If Karen gets baseball tickets, Ira will not wash the car tomorrow. Karen will not get baseball tickets unless Jimmy goes out of town. However, since Jimmy has gone out of town, Karen will get baseball tickets.

ANSWERS AND EXPLANATIONS

Explanation: Doctorate Children

6. C

Hart's 70 percent figure pretty much tells us that Numbers and Statistics is the name of the game here. We're asked to evaluate Hart's response to Choi, so let's see what Choi has in mind. Choi's statement is a comparison among individuals: If my parents have earned doctorates and yours didn't, then Choi says that the odds are better that I will earn a doctorate than that you will. Choi's claim goes no further. He doesn't claim that children of doctors are *guaranteed* to earn doctorates, and he doesn't even claim that they are *likely* to earn doctorates. He merely claims that these children are *more likely* to earn doctorates than their counterparts who do not have a parent that earned a doctorate. So even if only 5 percent of doctors' children earn doctorates themselves, Choi's claim is still correct as long as fewer than 5 percent of children whose parents didn't earn a doctorate went on to earn a doctorate themselves.

Thus the irrelevancy of Hart's 70 percent figure, which gives us information on a different group—*those who already earned their doctoral degree*. So the data Hart presents can be true and yet have no bearing on Choi's claim. An example: Suppose that there are 10 people in the world with doctorates. Choi merely claims that children of these people are more likely to get doctorates than children of other people. Hart comes along and says that of the 10 people, say, 8 of them (over 70%) come from doctorate-less parents. Does that alter Choi's claim in any way? No. All other factors being equal, the children of those doctors could still be more likely to earn doctorates, even if most doctorate holders don't have that particular heritage. Because of this, Hart's consideration doesn't contradict Choi's claim in any way, and we can therefore say that Hart's is consistent with it (C).

A 180 test taker can spot inconsistencies, but can also recognizes statements that are consistent; that is, those that do NOT contradict one another.

(A), (B), and (D) are all off the mark in that they require a connection between Hart and Choi that simply isn't there. Because the speakers' target groups are different, no positive or negative connection can be made between the two claims, and so we therefore cannot say that one shows the other to be exaggerated (A) or false (B), or that one helps the other (D).

(E) The concept of necessity vs. sufficiency cannot be invoked against Hart because Hart's statement is merely the presentation of a statistic. As such, in this case there is no "event" to which this common type of LSAT mistake could apply. (More about necessary and sufficient conditions later.)

Explanation: Teen Angst

7. E

This is the one that's just plain tough, although there is an element of causation present, an issue we'll be taking up later. The argument begins with a chain of causality: A crisis (step 1) can lead to a decrease in people's faith in their country's leaders (step 2), which can in turn lead to violence in unspecified segments of the population (step 3). Propaganda limits the perception of the crisis, thereby keeping the first domino from falling, and therefore favorably impacting at least the second step in the chain. This is the author's first explanation for violence, and the propaganda solution refers only to it. The author then gives an entirely different explanation for violence, this time more specifically explaining *youth* violence. Accordingly, youth violence is caused by boredom and lack of vision regarding a promising future. We have two paths explaining violence, and the answer to this inference question will certainly test our ability to distinguish between them. Let's evaluate the answer choices keeping the distinctions in mind.

(A) While the author offers us one potential antidote to the first type of violence without making any such reference in regards to the second, that doesn't mean that there is no solution for the second type. Because something isn't mentioned, that doesn't mean it doesn't exist, so we have no way of inferring which type of violence is easier to quell.

(B) For all we know, propaganda alone may be enough to entirely diffuse dissent in some poor countries, possibly those without disaffected youth, or even those with disaffected youth who are not driven to dissent by such crises.

(C) is too extreme and distorts the argument. The author writes that economic and political crises lead to violence among "specific segments of the population," which may include youth; the author certainly doesn't rule out that possibility. Further, because boredom and lack of vision lead to habitual youth violence, that doesn't mean that *only* boredom and lack of vision lead to youth violence. The two explanations aren't mutually exclusive.

(D) also goes too far out on a limb. The author mentions two effects of the propaganda—it downplays the extent of the crisis and restores faith in the government. However, we don't know that an alteration in people's "fundamental beliefs" is inherent in either one of these cases; we simply know that the propaganda has an effect on their immediate actions at the time of the crisis.

(E) does the trick: Since the author does not directly link habitual youth violence to economic or political crises, or to the decrease in faith which such crises create, propaganda probably doesn't decrease that violence by restoring faith in the country's leaders. The author says that habitual youth violence is not caused by a loss of such faith, so restoring the faith probably wouldn't help matters any. If propaganda helps to quell habitual youth violence, then it probably does so in some other way.

A 180 test taker is wary of extreme answer choices that make overeager claims. He knows that the right answer to an inference question doesn't intensify the argument.

Explanation: Computer Crash

8. C

The computer in this one does a crash and burn, as do many test takers faced with this question. Formal Logic is the name of the game here, if you hadn't guessed. This question is a good example of a Formal Logic question that requires you to combine many statements, which makes it among the most difficult and time-consuming questions on the exam.

A 180 test taker begins a tough Formal Logic question by scoping out the most concrete information and using it to set off a chain of deductions.

What's the most concrete info here? It's the fact that the hard drive was not damaged. What other formal logic statements tell us something about the hard drive? Well, if there's no error message, then the hard drive *is* damaged. The correct implication of this statement is that if the hard drive is NOT damaged, then there cannot be "no error message," which means that there *is* an error message. So since we know the hard drive was not damaged, we know there must have been an error message. This would make for a fine choice, were it not for the further information at the end regarding the particulars of error messages. We're told that usually, the processor doesn't work quickly enough to produce an error message, and that such a message could instead result from an electrical surge. But what if there was no surge? Since we've deduced already that an error message must have appeared, we can further deduce that in the absence of an electrical surge, the processor must have worked unusually fast during the crash, choice (C). This is a particularly tough question because the formal logic statements combine to lead to a nice deduction, but that deduction isn't the answer; it only *leads* to the answer.

(A) There's no stated connection between the speed of the processor and the hard drive, so we can eliminate (A).

(B), (D) Even if the passage blew you away, you should still be able to eliminate these two fairly quickly. The intention behind the 401's construction is never addressed; it's way outside the scope.

A 180 test taker uses every method at her disposal in order to increase her odds of getting the point.

(E) is impossible. A crash is characterized by a "freeze," so after a crash no additional functions can be performed.

Explanation: Home Births

9. A

Here's a very typical example of how surveys appear in LSAT Logical Reasoning. A social worker surveys 100 women who chose to give birth in a hospital, and 100 who chose to have their babies at home. The social worker concludes that the home is the safer environment in which to give birth, based entirely on the fact that in the sample studied, there were more cases of complications in the hospital. She assumes that the environment was responsible for the number of complications, and overlooks any other possible reason for the survey results. (A) weakens the argument by providing such an alternative reason for the statistical disparity: Women who were at high risk for complications all decided to give birth in a hospital. In other words, the study was skewed; the women in the two groups (the 100 who gave birth in the home and the 100 who gave birth in the hospital) were not equally likely to have complications to begin with.

> A 180 test taker scrutinizes the sample groups used in surveys presented in Logical Reasoning questions, looking for disparities in the data or characteristics of the groups involved that may invalidate the survey.

(B) and (E) both make inappropriate appeals to authority—the fact that many doctors prefer hospital births alters neither the results of the study nor the conclusion drawn from these results.

> A 180 test taker is not fooled by appeals to authority. She knows that conclusions must be backed up by solid evidence, not by the opinions or actions of experts.

(C) provides the opposite of what we're looking for—it strengthens the argument by providing a possible reason why home births are safer.

(D) The point at issue is where it's safer to give birth, not the respective labor times. Since there's no evidence that *shorter* labors are *safer* labors, (D) doesn't weaken the argument. Later on we'll refer to such slight deviations as "scope shifts."

Explanation: Mitchell and Basketball

10. A

Poor Mitchell. Seems as if he's all ready to play, but Allyson and Lisa are standing in his way. Obviously this is our Parallel Reasoning question of the bunch, and as you'll see, there are generally two varieties: ones that ask you to mirror the logic of an argument, and ones that ask you to mirror the *flawed* logic of an argument. If the stem doesn't designate the reasoning in the original as flawed, then we can safely assume that the logic is valid and that the logic of the right answer will be valid in the same way. And there's nothing wrong with the conclusion here: Since Lisa has *not* borrowed a car, Allyson will *not* take the day off, and therefore Mitchell *cannot* play basketball.

Notice the Formal Logic element present here; in fact, it's extremely common to find Formal Logic constructions in Parallel Reasoning questions. When the statements are linked as closely as these, it's possible, and often helpful, to represent them algebraically.

A 180 test taker looks to simplify the content of Parallel Reasoning questions as much as possible, recognizing that the underlying logic is what's important, not the specific subject matter presented.

This pattern of reasoning breaks down to:

If A (Mitchell plays) → then B (Allyson takes off)

If B (Allyson takes off) → then C (Lisa borrows car)

Since NOT C (Lisa does NOT borrow car) → then NOT A (Mitchell does NOT play)

It's fairly linear and perfectly logical, as we noted above. Let's attack the choices, in search of the same pattern.

(A) If A (Kurt will travel upstate) then B (Jeannie goes out to dinner). If B (Jeannie goes out to dinner) then C (Sheila goes out to dinner). Since NOT C (Sheila cannot go out) therefore NOT A (Kurt will not travel upstate). No problem. We have a winner.

A 180 test taker understands that the statements in the correct answer to a Parallel Reasoning question need not be in the same order as those in the original.

(B) Comparing conclusions is enough to eliminate (B). The original predicts that something will not happen, but (B) indicates that something will happen. Also, there is no "or" scenario present in the original, so this can't be parallel.

(C) Close, but no cigar: If A (Matthew goes to amusement park) then B (Jack goes). If B (Jack goes) then C (fee is inexpensive). Since NOT C (fee is NOT inexpensive), NOT B (Jack will NOT go). The conclusion doubles back on Jack, instead of coming full circle to Matthew, as it should.

(D) cites *two* conditions which together would be sufficient for Sean to go bowling. There's nothing parallel to this in the original.

(E), like (B), predicts that something *will* happen.

What's Next?

Need more practice with these types of Logical Reasoning questions? We've got just the thing for you—in the very next chapter.

CHAPTER EIGHT

A Closer Look

Now it's time to really dig in and drill on the common types of tough Logical Reasoning questions we touched upon in chapter 7. We'll begin with five straight Formal Logic challenges, then move on to Parallel Reasoning, Numbers and Statistics, Surveys and Studies, and Just Plain Tough questions. Enjoy!

PRACTICE SET 1: FORMAL LOGIC

1. In ancient Mondavia, only members of the ruling council had access to classified information, and only people born into the elite class were members of the ruling council. Although some historians believe that a Mondavian peasant uprising was solely responsible for overthrowing the ancient Mondavian regime, the perpetrators of the successful coup must have known the location of the state's armament supplies as well as the inner layout of Mondavia's fortresses and strategic strongholds. This information was classified.

   The argument is structured to lead to the conclusion that

   (A) Mondavian peasants in the ancient Mondavian regime knew as much about the state's classified security information as did members of the Mondavian elite
   (B) all members of the Mondavian elite class had access to the state's classified security information before the overthrow of the ancient Mondavian regime
   (C) the accidental discovery of state secrets allowed the Mondavian peasants to overcome great odds in overthrowing the ancient Mondavian regime
   (D) at least one member of the Mondavian elite class helped in the overthrow of the ancient Mondavian regime
   (E) the ancient Mondavian regime could not be overthrown by people lacking knowledge of armament locations and the design of strategic strongholds

2. If ad pages in *Fission* magazine have increased in December, then either ad rates have decreased or circulation has increased for the month, but not both. If circulation has increased in December, then the editors will receive year-end bonuses. If ad pages have not increased in December, then the editors will not receive year-end bonuses.

   If all of the above statements are true, which one of the following can be concluded from the fact that the editors of *Fission* will not receive year-end bonuses?

   (A) Ad rates have not increased in December.
   (B) Ad pages have increased in December.
   (C) Ad pages have not increased in December.
   (D) Circulation has increased in December.
   (E) Circulation has not increased in December.

3. Participants in Smallville's Annual Easter Egg Hunt search for special plastic Easter Eggs containing valuable prizes. The top prize in the contest is an egg containing a three-carat diamond ring. The only way to locate the hidden eggs is by using clues provided to participants by the contest organizers. If every participant receives a complete list of clues for locating the eggs, then no participant will have any more information than any other participant regarding the whereabouts of the eggs. If no participant has any more information than any other participant, then no participant has a better chance of finding the diamond ring. However, the contest organizers did not provide a complete list of clues for locating the eggs to every participant. Therefore, some participant has a better chance of finding the diamond than all of the other participants.

   Which one of the following statements is consistent with the facts of the above argument in such a manner that it points to a flaw in the argument's reasoning?

   (A) Even if one participant received a more extensive clue list than all of the other participants, that participant might not necessarily find the diamond ring.
   (B) None of the participants received a complete list of clues.
   (C) Some participant may share a particular clue with other participants who did not receive that clue.
   (D) All of the participants received identical clue lists.
   (E) Some participants who did not receive a complete list of clues will nonetheless be able to locate the egg containing the diamond ring.

Questions 4–5

Unless public transportation becomes much more popular, traffic will become more congested and pollution from cars will get worse. Yet public transportation will only become much more popular when the railway system is modernized and expanded. Such modernization and expansion, however, will take place only when the state becomes convinced of the importance of improved public transportation, or when rail technology improves to the point that high-speed railroads become profitable for private investors.

4. Which one of the following can be properly inferred from the passage?

 (A) If the state becomes convinced of the importance of improved public transportation, then high-speed railroads will become profitable for private investors.
 (B) If rail technology does not improve enough for high-speed railroads to become profitable for private investors, then traffic will become more congested.
 (C) If public transportation has gotten much more popular, then the railway system has been expanded.
 (D) If the railway system is modernized and expanded, public transportation will become much more popular.
 (E) If public transportation does not become more popular, then the railway system either has not been modernized or has not been expanded.

5. If all the statements in the passage are true, and if it is also true that rail technology will not improve to the point that high-speed railroads will become profitable for private investors, then which one of the following CANNOT be true?

 (A) Either the state will become convinced of the importance of improved public transportation, or traffic will become more congested and pollution from cars will get worse.
 (B) The railway system is modernized and as a result traffic congestion is reduced.
 (C) The railway system will be modernized and expanded, but traffic congestion will continue to get worse.
 (D) The state is not convinced of the importance of improved transportation, but traffic congestion and pollution from cars will be reduced.
 (E) Although traffic congestion continues to get worse, public transportation does not become more popular, and the state is not convinced of the importance of improved public transportation.

PRACTICE SET 1: ANSWERS AND EXPLANATIONS

Explanation: Mondavian Uprising

1. D

In chapter 7's "Computer Crash," we advised that in tough Formal Logic problems it often pays to begin with the most concrete piece of information. Here, that honor goes to the last sentence of the stimulus, specifically the notion that Mondavian supply locations and fortress layouts were classified. We can combine this with the sentence immediately before to reasonably infer than the perpetrators of the coup must have known classified information, which then relates back to the first sentence: Only the members of the ruling council had access to classified info, which means that the rebels must have had help from the ruling council. Perhaps at this point you feel like the restless kid in the back seat—*are we there yet?*" Not quite; one final step. Since only members of the elite class are on the ruling council, the rebels must have had help from at least one member of the elite class. It's a bit windy, but the deductions here eventually bring us to (D).

A 180 test taker perseveres until the answer is found.

(A) is contradicted by the passage, since only those born into the ruling class had access to classified information.

(B) Being in the ruling class is necessary, but not *sufficient*, for access to classified info.

(C) The "accidental discovery" in (C) is neither stated nor implied.

(E) is quite close, but fails on one particular count. The perpetrators *of this particular peasant coup* needed such strategic info, but that doesn't imply that it's impossible in another situation (such as attack from a much stronger empire) for the regime to be toppled without knowledge of armament locations and strongholds.

A 180 test taker develops a knack for finding the flaw in even the most tempting wrong answers, knowing that there is no "second best" choice.

Explanation: Ads and Bonuses

2. E

This one has a real Logic Games feel to it, but happily provides a pretty user-friendly question stem as well, since it tells us which part of the argument the inference will address. And with so many formal logic statements to choose from, it's a good thing we know where to start.

A 180 test taker uses the information in the question stem to provide a starting point whenever possible.

The question stem gives us the first half of an if-then statement; the correct answer will likely be the second half. So, if the editors don't receive year-end bonuses, then what do we know? Scoping out the part of the stimulus that deals with bonuses, we come to sentences 2 and 3. Let's see if sentence 2 helps: If circulation has increased, then editors get their bonuses. The proper implication of this is that if editors DO NOT get bonuses, then circulation has NOT increased. We're given the first part, the "if" clause in the stem; the second part, the "then" clause that must follow is found in correct choice (E).

(A) deals with ad rates, about which we can make no inferences based on what we're told about bonuses.

(B) and (C) offer the two options regarding ad pages, but neither is right because, according to what we know, ad pages might have increased or not. There's no accurate inference that we can draw on this subject based on the information we're given.

(D) As we saw above, under these circumstances circulation must not have increased.

Explanation: Easter Egg Hunt

3. D

The author describes an Easter Egg hunt and the top prize, and informs us that one can locate the prize *only* through the contest organizers' clues. It therefore follows that if everyone has equal information about the clues, then everyone has an equal chance to find the diamond. So far, so good. The author then moves away from the hypothetical situation to describe what really happened. The contest organizers didn't give everyone all of the information, but that doesn't necessarily mean that one person has more information than others. Just because the organizers didn't give a complete list to everybody, it doesn't follow that they gave more complete lists to some people than others.

Once again our formal logic skills come into play: We were originally told that if people are fully informed, then nobody has an advantage. It doesn't follow that if people are *not* fully informed, then somebody *does* have an advantage. That's a common formal logic error, and since the author commits it, the right answer choice will likely identify this as the flaw in the argument. (D) accomplishes this by stating what still could be true given the argument; everyone could have received the same incomplete list. In concluding categorically that some lucky participant has a leg up on the others, the author doesn't allow for the possibility stated in (D), and so (D) legitimately points to a flaw in the argument.

(A), (E) Probably the easiest way to eliminate (A) is to recognize that the author discusses who has the best *chance* of finding the diamond ring. The author never suggests that having a better chance of finding the ring means actually finding the ring. If the author had made such a suggestion, it would be a flaw, but since the author never did, it isn't. (E) takes this issue from another angle by suggesting that people with incomplete lists might still find the ring. The author never suggests otherwise, since again the author solely discusses who has the best chance of finding the ring, not who will therefore actually find it. So while (A) and (E) are indeed consistent with the stimulus, they don't point to a logical flaw in the argument.

A 180 test taker notices small shifts in scope between the information in the passage and the focus of the choices.

(B) is close, but not fully there. Even if nobody receives a complete list (which is possible), there still exists the possibility that some people receive more complete lists than others, a situation that wouldn't by itself expose a flaw in the argument.

(C) just states one possible consequence of handing out different lists. The scenario in (C) is consistent with the facts in the stimulus, so it's okay on that count; but like (B), (C) still allows for the possibility that some person has a better chance than others, as the author maintains. In other words, it doesn't point to a flaw in the argument. Only the plausible possibility stated in (D) and overlooked by the author would show the author's conclusion to be unwarranted.

Explanation: Railway System

4. C

Translating (and abridging) the "unless" statement in the first sentence, we get: "If public transport isn't more popular, then we'll have more traffic and pollution." We can make this translation because the formal logic statement "X unless Y" is really just another way of saying "if not Y, then X." The next two sentences present two complicated "only if" statements: Public transport will become more popular only when (that means "only if") the railways are both modernized and expanded. The modernization and expansion, then, are prerequisites for increased popularity.

> A 180 test taker knows that the easiest way to handle an "only-if" statement is to turn it into a straightforward "if-then" statement.

In this case, turning the statement into "if-then" language yields: "If public transport is much more popular, then the railways were modernized and expanded." The last statement links right up. The only way the railways will get modernized and expanded is if . . . actually, there are two possible ways these results could occur—either the state becomes convinced of the importance of improved public transportation, or technology improves so that high speed railroads become profitable. Turning that into a regular "if-then," we get: "If the railways are modernized and expanded, then either the state has been convinced of the importance of improved public transport, or high speed railways have become profitable investments." Let's go to the choices, looking for the one that's inferable based on this mess of information.

(A) We're told only that the two ways in which the railways can become modernized and expanded are the state's being convinced and high-speed railways becoming profitable. There isn't, however, any causal connection between the two, as (A) would have it.

(B)'s pessimism is likewise unfounded. Even if high-speed railways don't become profitable investments, the state could become convinced of the importance of improving public transport. That would, ultimately, allow traffic to not become more congested.

(C) is inferable; in fact, it's nothing more than the basic if-then rewrite we formed from the second sentence. That's very LSAT-like. One of the test makers' favorite tricks in questions like this one is to hound us with a lot of statements and implications, and then present a correct choice that's a mere rewrite of one of them.

(D), (E) (D) confuses "if-then" and "only-if" statements. We're told that public transport can grow more popular only if the railways are modernized and expanded. This doesn't mean that it *will* grow more popular simply because the railways have been modernized and expanded—there may be other factors involved. (E) is just another way of stating the sentiment in (D): Since it means exactly the same thing, it's wrong in exactly the same way.

> A 180 test taker recognizes what are essentially identical choices, and if she has any doubt as to their validity, simply eliminates both on the grounds that there can be only one right answer.

5. D

No sense allowing such a plethora of information to go to waste—may as well squeeze another question out of this maze of formal logic statements. The stem effectively kills one of the only two possible ways that modernization and expansion can occur; namely, technology improving so that high-speed railroads become profitable. With that possibility nixed, we can deduce that modernization and expansion depend solely on the other factor: the state's becoming convinced of the importance of improved public transportation. If, as (D) has it, the state *doesn't* come around on this issue, then we can work backward from there. Coupled with the info in the stem, we can now conclusively infer that modernization and expansion won't happen, which, in turn means that public transportation will *not* become more popular. Relating this new fact back to the first sentence, we can deduce that traffic and pollution will both increase. Remember, as we noted in the previous question, the "unless" statement in the first sentence translates as "If public transport isn't more popular, then we'll have more traffic and pollution." So under these circumstances set forth in the stimulus, the question stem, and choice (D), the upshot for sure is an increase in traffic and pollution. Since the second part of (D) comes to the opposite conclusion, (D) is the statement that can't be true.

> A 180 test taker meticulously analyzes formal logic statements and has the ability to deduce what must, can, and cannot be true on the basis of them.

(A) could be true. If the state is not convinced of the importance of improved transportation, then the results will follow as stated above and pollution will get worse.

(B) Modernization is a prerequisite for popularity, so if we throw in expansion as well, it's possible that public transportation will get more popular, which in turn makes a reduction in traffic congestion possible as well. So (B) could be true.

(C) Modernization and expansion are necessary for increased popularity, but don't guarantee it. (We'll deal with this issue of necessary and sufficient conditions more extensively a little later in the book.) So (C) is possible as well.

(E) All of these things can happen without violating any conditions. In fact, working backward, if the state is not convinced, then that will cause the other things in the choice to occur (in conjunction, of course, with the condition in the question stem).

PRACTICE SET 2: PARALLEL REASONING

6. Most of the time, Doug has no stomach problems whatsoever when he eats dairy products. So it is unreasonable to claim that he has an allergy to dairy foods solely based on the fact that he has had stomachaches after eating dairy products on several occasions.

The argument above is most similar in reasoning to which one of the arguments below?

(A) A significant number of artists who take this Fine Arts program are later selected for fellowships to pursue their art. It is therefore unreasonable to believe that there is no connection between taking the program and receiving an art fellowship, even though many artists who attend the program never receive such fellowships.

(B) In some cases, dogs will display anxiety in the moments before an earthquake strikes. But it is unreasonable to conclude on this basis that dogs have the ability to sense earthquakes before they strike. In the vast majority of cases in which dogs display anxiety, no earthquake follows.

(C) Many people who try this diet show no long-term weight loss. So it is unreasonable to believe that this diet is effective for weight loss, even though many people have lost weight on the diet.

(D) Most theories must apply to a large number of cases before they are considered valid theories. It is therefore unreasonable to believe that a theory is valid when it has been applied to only a few cases, even if it has been applied successfully to those cases.

(E) Even though many businesses with decentralized operational structures earn a profit, it is unreasonable to believe the success of these businesses is solely attributable to their choice of operational structure. Only businesses with extensive capital resources can adopt a decentralized operational structure.

7. Most of the office complexes designed by Valentine Brown have a central open area around which the buildings are grouped. But it is also true that most of the office complexes designed by Mr. Brown have underground walkways between the buildings. So most of the office complexes designed by Valentine Brown combine a central space around which the buildings are grouped with a system of underground walkways between the buildings.

Which one of the following arguments contains flawed reasoning most similar to the flawed reasoning in the argument above?

(A) Most of the children in class say that dessert is their favorite meal, and that pecan pie is their favorite dessert. So the favorite food of most children in class is pecan pie.

(B) Excessive reading can weaken a person's eyesight. Excessive reading can also make a person round-shouldered. Excessive reading, therefore, can make a person round-shouldered and near-sighted.

(C) The majority of customers at Torrance Autos wish to buy a four-door sedan. But the majority of customers at Torrance Autos also wish to purchase a red car. So the majority of customers at Torrance Autos wish to purchase a red, four-door sedan.

(D) People who spend the most time watching television say they most prefer to watch sports programs and situation comedies. Thus, sports and situation comedies are probably the most frequently watched varieties of programming on television.

(E) Constance will live only in an apartment that has a playground attached. Philip will live only in an apartment that allows pets. Therefore, if Constance and Philip live together, they will live only in an apartment that has a playground attached and allows pets.

8. One morning, George Petersen of Petersen's Garage watches as a 1995 Da Volo station wagon is towed onto his lot. Because he knows that nearly 90% of the 1995 Da Volo station wagons brought to his garage for work in the past were brought in because of malfunctioning power windows, he reasons that there is an almost 9 to 1 chance that the car he saw this morning has also been brought in to correct its faulty power windows.

Which one of the following employs flawed reasoning most similar to that employed by George Petersen?

(A) Mayor Lieberman was re-elected by a majority of almost 75%. Since Janine Davis voted in that mayoral election, the chances are almost 3 to 1 that she voted for Mayor Lieberman.

(B) Each week nine out of 10 best-selling paperback books at The Reader's Nook are works of fiction. Since Nash's history of World War II was among the ten best-selling paperback books at The Reader's Nook this week, the chances are 9 to 1 that it is a work of fiction.

(C) 90% of those who attempt to get into Myrmidon Military Academy are turned down. Since the previous 10 candidates to the academy were not accepted, Vladimir's application will almost certainly be approved.

(D) Only one out of 50 applications to bypass zoning regulations and establish a new business in the Gedford residential district is accepted. Since only 12 such applications were made last month, there is virtually no chance that any of them will be accepted.

(E) Nearly 95% of last year's Borough High School graduating class went on to some type of further schooling. Since only a little more than 5% of that graduating class took longer than the usual four years to graduate, it is probable that everyone who did graduate within four years went on to further schooling.

9. Although striped bandicoots and bilbies are very similar in appearance, their diets come from entirely different sources. Since the bilby does not eat plants, the striped bandicoot's diet must include plants.

Which one of the following is an argument that contains flawed reasoning most similar to the flawed reasoning in the argument above?

(A) Only currently enrolled students may use the athletic facilities at the Appleton school. Since Patricia does not use the athletic facilities at the Appleton school, she cannot be a currently enrolled student.

(B) Diaz and Freund never play tennis at the community center on the same day. Since Diaz played tennis at the community center on Sunday, Freund could not have played tennis at the community center on Sunday.

(C) Although they are both respected scientists in the field of physical chemistry, Chatterjee and Myers have never served on the same peer review panel. This is hardly surprising, however, given that Myers only serves on peer review panels during the month of August, when Chatterjee is on vacation.

(D) Rob and Janet always go to the movies each week, but never to the same movie as each other. It is certain that Janet sometimes sees comedies, since Rob never sees comedies.

(E) All of the marbles in this bag have the same weight. Therefore, if a single marble were removed and weighed, it would be possible to determine the total weight of all the marbles in the bag.

10. Public service announcements attempt to persuade teenagers to follow useful advice, but cause them to resent being preached to. Teenagers will follow advice only if they do not resent being preached to. Therefore, public service announcements are ineffective, and should be discontinued.

Which one of the following exhibits reasoning most similar to the reasoning displayed in the argument above?

(A) Mandatory seat belt laws are directed at those who do not like to feel constricted when they drive. Freedom from unnecessary restrictions is one of the fundamental principles of this country. Thus, mandatory seat belt laws damage one of the fundamental principles of this country, and should be repealed.

(B) Zoning restrictions prevent the development of neighborhoods that include both industrial and residential buildings. Including both industrial and residential buildings in the same neighborhood is dangerous and very harmful to residential property values. Therefore, including both of these types of buildings in the same neighborhood should be prevented.

(C) The estate tax applies to those who possess large estates when they die, but encourages them to reduce their savings. Savings are needed to stimulate growth in the economy. Thus, the estate tax causes more economic harm than good, and should be repealed.

(D) Conservation laws are intended to protect endangered species and induce their expansion into land presently occupied by people. People will not support conservation laws when their land is occupied by the animals under protection. Thus, the conservation laws are self-undermining, and should be abandoned.

(E) The use of 12-hour shifts at a company is intended to maximize production by employees, but encourages them to work inefficiently. Employees must work efficiently in order for a company to maximize production. Therefore, the use of 12-hour shifts fails to further the company's objective, and should be abolished.

PRACTICE SET 2: ANSWERS AND EXPLANATIONS

Explanation: Doug's Stomachaches

6. B

The author argues that Doug usually doesn't have bad reactions to dairy products. Thus, he doesn't have a dairy allergy even though he has had several stomachaches following his consumption of dairy products. Considering, then, the structure of the argument, the author states that something (the consumption of dairy products) doesn't usually create a certain result (stomachaches), and then concludes that something which might explain a causal relationship between the two (allergies) doesn't exist. In other words, if a causal relationship isn't usually present, then it isn't present.

A 180 test taker is adept at abstracting arguments; that is, rephrasing them in general terms, a skill that's particularly rewarded in Parallel Reasoning questions.

Looking for another choice that demonstrates the same structure, we can hold on to (B): There the author states that dog anxiety does not usually indicate coming earthquakes, and therefore argues against a necessary relationship between the two. It matches the original in all the major elements.

(A) is wrong because its conclusion argues *for* a correlation while the stimulus argues *against* a correlation between two occurrences (the consumption of dairy products and stomachaches).

(C) begins by saying that something sometimes doesn't create a certain result. Already it isn't parallel, since the evidence in the stimulus states that something doesn't *usually* create a certain result. "Many people" in (C) doesn't parallel the "most of the time" in the stimulus. Moreover, (C) argues about the efficacy of a program, whereas the original and correct choice (B) are concerned with the relation between two events.

(D) presents an entirely different argument, arguing that a claim isn't valid because there isn't enough evidence to support it. The original argument says that a claim isn't valid because two factors usually aren't related. The notion of "validity," like "efficacy" in (C), is one step removed from the gist of the terms in the original argument.

(E) argues against a causal relationship, but it doesn't parallel the original evidence because it mentions what "many" businesses do, not what "most" do. More centrally, the conclusion veers away from the evidence: the evidence suggests that decentralized operations often yield a profit, while the conclusion suggests that the two aren't directly related. In the original, both the evidence and conclusion argue against a causal relationship.

Explanation: Office Complexes

7. C

Remember "*Light* Tanks" in chapter 7? In that one, we said that the author misunderstood the sets involved. The author of this stimulus simply doesn't understand sets either. Just because most of Brown's office complexes have underground walkways, and most of Brown's office complexes have a central space, doesn't mean that most of Brown's office complexes have *both* of these features.

Perhaps most of those office blocks that have underground walkways do not have central spaces. For instance, say Brown put up 10 office complexes. Six of them have central spaces; six of them have underground walkways. It's then fair to say that most (six out of 10) have walkways and most (six out of 10) have central space. But it's still entirely possible that only two complexes have both features; there might be four complexes with walkways only and four with central spaces only. (C) makes the same mistake of not seeing that the overlap of two large sets might be a much smaller set. It's possible that few of those Torrance Auto customers who want four-door sedans want them red, and that most of the customers who want red cars are among those who don't want four-door autos.

A 180 test taker has a solid grasp on the nature of sets and understands how certain sets with characteristics in common can, or need not, overlap.

(A) doesn't work the same way. What we get here is a narrowing of sets; the set of desserts exists *within* the set of meals. There is no overlap of two different sets as there is in the stimulus.

(B), (E) Nothing wrong with the logic in these two: (B) simply describes two possible effects of excessive reading, and then says that it's possible for both of these effects to follow from excessive reading at the same time. There's no claim that this happens in the majority of cases. There's nothing intrinsically flawed about this reasoning, which disqualifies this choice immediately. (E) deals with absolute conditions, and also draws a valid conclusion. *Every* place Constance will live must have a playground; *every* place Philip will live must allow pets. So any place they both live must fulfill both conditions.

A 180 test taker knows that the first requirement in a "Parallel Flaw" question is that the logic of the correct choice must actually be flawed. He knows that if it ain't flawed, it ain't right.

(D) is a simple, and *tentative* conclusion, that doesn't require figuring out the overlap of two sets as does the original argument in the stimulus. (D) simply says: TV addicts like these types of programs, so these programs are probably watched the most—not parallel.

Explanation: Petersen's Garage

8. B

Given this kind of reasoning, Petersen's garage must be an interesting place to work. Think about it this way: If 90% of a particular doctor's patients go to the doctor for treatment of strep throat, and Joe arrives with blood gushing out of his head, would the doctor figure that the odds are overwhelming that Joe is suffering from strep throat? We hope not; after all, one has to take some form of statistics course en route to becoming a doctor.

Evidently, George Petersen missed that course. In fact, Petersen gives us a little lesson on how *not* to use statistics. He knows that 9 out of 10 Da Volos are brought to his shop because of malfunctioning windows, so he reasons that this particular Da Volo, which is being *towed in*, has probably also been brought in for malfunctioning windows. Surely the fact that the car is being towed indicates that there must be some more serious problem. Petersen has mindlessly applied a numerical formula while ignoring additional information. Where else, besides the doctor example above, do we see such reasoning? Why, in choice (B), of course. (B) uses previous figures to conclude that there's a 9 to 1 chance that Nash's history of World War II is a work of fiction. (B) ignores the compelling contrary evidence (namely, that this book is a *history*) and mindlessly applies a numerical formula where it clearly shouldn't be applied. The author of (B) would no doubt feel right at home at Petersen's Garage.

You'll notice that we don't include this one in the Numbers and Stats section. While you might have been led to think that numbers are the key, the fact is that the actual numbers don't matter in this particular case; the flaw is one of ignoring pertinent information when formulating a statistical conclusion. The key to this question is therefore non-numerical.

A 180 test taker gets to the heart of the matter, recognizing which logical elements are most likely to be relevant to the right answer.

(A)'s use of statistics is reasonable. We don't know anything special about Janine Davis; she's just a voter. Therefore, since almost 3 out of 4 voters chose Lieberman, there's an almost 3 out of 4 (or 3 to 1) chance that Janine voted for Lieberman.

(C) reasons that Vladimir's chances of being admitted into the academy have been improved by the rejection of the previous candidates. That's not a persuasive line of argumentation, but it's nothing like the stimulus.

(D) is a straight numerical argument. The conclusion seems overstated (even 1 out of 50 isn't "virtually no chance"), but it's not at all like the stimulus; we're not shown a particular case with special information that goes against the numbers.

(E)'s mistake is to assume that all those who took more than four years to graduate did not go on to further schooling; this allows (E) to conclude that the 95% who graduated in four years did go on. It's statistically flawed, certainly, but no special case is discussed, and therefore there's no similarity to the stimulus.

Explanation: Bandicoots and Bilbies

9. D

Bandicoots? Bilbies? No matter: Exotic names aside, in the world of Parallel Reasoning they could just as easily be widgets or geraniums, for all we care. The key in this question type is to paraphrase the situation in general terms. Here, the problem with both the stimulus and choice (D) is the assumption that because two things differ in some fundamental way, they must differ in some other fundamental way. Just because the two creatures in the stimulus have different diets, and one of them never eats plants, doesn't mean that the other one *does* eat plants. It's equally possible that both creatures eschew plants in their two, very different, diets. By the same token, just because Rob and Janet go to different movies, and one of them never attends comedies, doesn't mean that the other person *does* attend comedies. For all we know, neither Rob nor Janet ever attends comedies in their different moviegoing experiences.

(A)'s conclusion is a statement of that which cannot be true—not so in the stimulus—and includes a necessary condition ("only") that the stimulus lacks.

(B), like (A), is a statement of that which cannot have been true, so it's not parallel to the stimulus. Also, (B)'s conclusion can be properly drawn from its evidence, so (B) doesn't qualify as "flawed reasoning."

A 180 test taker notices immediately whether a Parallel Reasoning question is asking for a parallel flaw or not. If so, then the first requirement of the right answer is that it be flawed, and only after determining that it is should one investigate whether it's flawed in the same way as the original. Top test takers recognize logic that's sound, and dismiss such choices immediately in Parallel Flaw questions.

(C) is an explanation of a phenomenon ("This is hardly surprising . . . given . . ."). The stimulus argument is not.

(E)'s conclusion is conditional (If so and so occurred, then such and such would be possible . . .), but the conclusion in the stimulus is not.

Explanation: Teen Angst, Part II

10. E

Remember the disaffected youths of poor countries back in chapter 7? Well, we see that their counterparts here, bombarded with preachy public service ads telling them what to do, aren't much happier. The "only-if" in the second sentence denotes Formal Logic, which we've seen is a common component of Parallel Reasoning questions. The stimulus starts off by telling us that public service announcements try to advise teens but really just annoy them. Then comes the "only-if" statement, which, when properly translated, means that IF teenagers follow advice, THEN they do not resent the delivery of that advice. The author then concludes that the announcements should be discontinued. As with all Parallel Reasoning questions, we should get a better sense of the general structure of the passage. The author shows that a certain program has a goal and an unintended negative side effect. The author then explains that the goal can't be met if the side effect exists (which we know it does), and concludes therefore that the program doesn't work and should be scrapped. It's a pretty solid argument, and we can proceed to look for the same elements in the answer choices.

(A) identifies the goal of a certain program (here, seat belt laws), but never identifies an unintended negative side effect. We can stop right there, without having to delve too deeply into the touching patriotism in the remainder of the choice.

A 180 test taker spends only as much time as is necessary to eliminate a choice, knowing that one slip-up could trash it.

(B) never discusses the goal of zoning restrictions, and so never survives past consideration of the very first element of the stimulus.

(C) never explains the goal of the estate tax—eliminate it. Don't be fooled by the fact that it does include what could be called a side effect and a negative consequence of it. If every element is not present, then you have to move on.

(D) identifies the goal of a certain program (here, conservation laws) and explains a negative side effect. But in the second sentence the issue shifts away from the success of the conservation laws to their ability to get support. The original argument stays focused only on the program's potential for success.

(E) is correct because it outlines the goal of a program (the use of 12-hour shifts), discusses an unintended negative side effect, shows that the program can't succeed in the presence of that side effect, and concludes that the program should be eliminated. All the necessary elements are present.

PRACTICE SET 3: NUMBERS AND STATISTICS

11. In the years 1971 to 1980, the population of the state prison system was, on average, about 82 percent of maximum occupancy. During those years, the average number of prisoners entering the system each year was equivalent to 9.1 percent of maximum occupancy. From the years 1981 to 1984, the average number of prisoners entering the system each year fell to 7.3 percent of maximum occupancy, yet the population of the state prison system rose to almost 89 percent of maximum occupancy.

Which one of the following, if true, helps to resolve the apparent discrepancy?

(A) The average sentence of a prisoner in the state system increased from 1981 to 1984.

(B) Beginning in 1981, many of those entering the state prison system had been transferred from prisons in other states.

(C) Between 1981 and 1984, the percentage of prisoners incarcerated for violent crimes increased by 26 percent.

(D) In 1981, a legislative fact-finding committee proposed a revision of the state's parole and work release programs.

(E) Between 1971 and 1984, the proportion of active criminals actually caught and incarcerated in the state prison system has steadily increased.

12. A local department store hires college students for one month every spring to audit its unsold inventory. It costs the department store 20 percent less to pay wages to students than it would cost to hire outside auditors from a temporary service. Even after factoring in the costs of training and insuring the students against work-related injury, the department store spends less money by hiring the student auditors than it would by hiring auditors from the temporary service.

The statements above, if true, best support which of the following assertions?

(A) The amount spent on insurance for college-student auditors is more than 20 percent of the cost of paying the college students' basic wages.

(B) It takes 20 percent less time for the college students to audit the unsold inventory than it does for the outside auditors.

(C) The department store pays its college-student auditors 20 percent less than the temporary service pays its auditors.

(D) By hiring college students, the department store will cause 20 percent of the auditors at the temporary service to lose their jobs.

(E) The cost of training its own college-student auditors is less than 20 percent of the cost of hiring auditors from the temporary service.

13. In order to promote off-season business, Mt. Dunmore Lodge made the following "Welcome Back" offer to their winter guests: guests who rent a room for at least a week during ski season can come back during the summer and get 25% off the standard summer price of any room they rent. After the summer passed, the owners of the lodge determined that the majority of their guests had taken advantage of the "Welcome Back" offer and paid the reduced rates. However, they were surprised to find they still managed to rent more rooms at full price than they did at the discount rate.

Which one of the following, if true, most helps to explain the apparent discrepancy in the passage?

(A) Most of the guests who stayed at Mt. Dunmore Lodge during the winter did not stay for a full week.

(B) Those guests taking advantage of the "Welcome Back" discount were more likely to bring their families with them than were those guests who were paying full price.

(C) Some of the guests who received the "Welcome Back" discount also received a 10% rate reduction through their auto club.

(D) In order to pay for the construction of a new gymnasium and a new pool, the owners of the lodge raised their summer prices considerably.

(E) On average, guests who took advantage of the "Welcome Back" discount spent more money at the hotel on additional goods and services than guests who paid full price for their rooms.

Questions 14–15

The incidence of suicide in the country of Travonia has increased dramatically in recent years, as evidenced by the fact that since the introduction of several nonprescription brands of sleeping pills, the number of deaths from overdoses alone has nearly doubled. However, certain types of suicides have not increased in number during this period. It is true that elderly suicides have seen a greater than 70 percent increase, but teen suicides now account for only 30 percent of all suicides in the country. This is a significant decrease over 1985, when teen cases represented 65 percent of all country-wide suicides.

14. The argument above is most vulnerable to criticism on the grounds that it does which one of the following?

(A) It discounts the possibility of suicides occurring in groups other than the elderly and teenagers.

(B) It takes for granted that the introduction of nonprescription sleeping pills has had the same effect on two different demographic groups.

(C) It assumes that a decrease in the percentage of teen suicides necessarily signifies a decrease in the number of teen suicides.

(D) It overlooks the possibility that the total number of deaths in Travonia has increased since 1985.

(E) It relies on evidence that contradicts its conclusion.

15. The assertion that suicides are increasing in Travonia is most justified if which one of the following is assumed?

(A) The elderly suffered the greatest number of overdoses from the nonprescription sleeping pills.

(B) Overdosing on sleeping pills was not the most pervasive method of suicide in Travonia ten years ago.

(C) The number of deaths from natural causes in Travonia has decreased in recent years.

(D) The majority of deaths resulting from overdosing on nonprescription sleeping pills were not accidental.

(E) Travonia's suicide rate is higher than the worldwide average suicide rate.

PRACTICE SET 3: ANSWERS AND EXPLANATIONS

Explanation: Prison Paradox

11. A

Here we have a case in which an apparent paradox stems from a misunderstanding of statistics. Clear up the misunderstanding, and the paradox vanishes—that is, the rise described at the end no longer seems surprising.

> A 180 test taker knows that Numbers and Statistics is a fertile ground for all sorts of questions. Maybe she'll be asked to find a choice that points out a flaw or weakens an argument, or maybe one that explains away an apparent discrepancy. Either way, she recognizes that understanding the ways in which numbers and percentages are used or misused is the key to answering these types of questions.

Here are the facts: In the early years, the prisons were 82% full, and just over 9% of the total possible occupancy arrived each year in the form of new prisoners. Now that the latter figure is down to 7.3%, the author is surprised that the prisons are more full: 89% full. She evidently expects that as one figure drops, so should the other. The key is seeing that she is focusing on the trend in incoming prisoners only, when the totals take into account all prisoners. Consider the long-termers. If the average length of sentences of all prisoners is increasing, then it's small wonder that the prisons are more crowded now, even if a smaller percentage of the inmates are newcomers. That's what (A) is all about.

(B) Where the prisoners came from has no impact on how many are, or should be, here in this state.

(C) Nothing in the evidence concerns the nature of crime, so no information about the nature of the crimes that land these people in jail in the first place can resolve the paradox.

(D) A "proposed revision" is way too weak. Was it instituted? And even if it was, what effect would it have? There's no way to know, so (D) is irrelevant and does nothing to clear up what the author considers to be a surprising result.

(E), even if true, begs the question of why the percentage of the prison total entering the system is lower than years ago, but the prisons are fuller. All (E) says is that fewer criminals are getting off scot-free.

Explanation: Student Auditors

12. E

The question stem directs us to find the assertion best supported by the evidence in the stimulus. All we have given here is evidence: The department store pays college students 20 percent less than it would pay employees from a temporary service. Add the costs of training and insurance, and the store *still* pays less for college students. The correct answer must arise from the facts: college students cost the store up to 20 percent less than do employees from a temporary service—even after training and insurance. Prephrasing an answer would be tough, so we should move right to testing the choices.

> A 180 test taker has an intuitive sense of when to try to prephrase answers and when to simply use a solid understanding of the given information to test the choices. In either case, he attacks the choices aggressively.

(A) attempts to relate the amount spent on insurance for student auditors to the total amount of their wages, but we have no basis for which to make this comparison. The amount spent on insurance for college-student auditors can be more, less, or equal to 20 percent of their basic wages without violating the numerical facts presented.

(B) and (D) should have been fairly easy kills. (B) involves time, a subject not included in the stimulus, while (D) mentions the loss of jobs at the temporary service, even though we know nothing about the overall demand for their auditors.

(C) is a little more subtle, but it involves how much the temporary service *pays* its auditors, not how much it charges the store for them. A classic "scope shift," something we'll be talking more about later.

> A 180 test taker always pays attention to the scope of the argument, which helps him to axe easy and difficult choices alike.

(E) fits, and one way we can verify that it's correct is to see what happens if it's *not* true. If the cost of training college students is *more* than 20 percent of the cost of hiring auditors from the temporary service, the overall cost of college students must be higher than the cost of temporary-service auditors. That would contradict the stimulus, so (E) must be true.

> A 180 test taker has many tricks up her sleeve. She knows that one way to verify an answer in an assumption or inference question is to see what happens when she denies or negates the choice. If doing so makes the argument fall apart, then she knows she's found the winner.

Explanation: Mt. Dunmore Lodge

13. B

One of the toughest things about this question is fully understanding the puzzling phenomenon described. Here's the discrepancy we're asked to resolve: How can it be that most winter guests availed themselves of discounted pricing, yet the lodge nevertheless rented more rooms at full price? Clearly it's a numerical mystery, which will require a numerical solution. (B) provides such an answer: If the discounted folks were comprised mainly of families, packing in more guests per room, while the full-price guests tended to come solo with fewer guests per room, then it's easier to explain how there could be lots of discounted guests wandering around the hotel but more rooms rented at full price.

Notice that the solution to the paradox hinges on the recognition that elements in the evidence and conclusion that appear to be similar are in fact totally different things (number of guests vs. number of rooms). This question furnishes another example of what we'll introduce later on as a "scope shift."

A 180 test taker suspects that in Paradox questions, some sort of shift between the argument's evidence and conclusion may be at the heart of the seeming contradiction.

(A) These guests aren't even eligible for the summer discount, so they play no part in the argument or the confusing result.

(C) That some people got an added discount doesn't serve to explain the paradox. The relevant comparison is between discounted guests and non-discounted guests, so the fact that some discounted guests are enjoying even larger discounts doesn't change a thing.

(D) The argument centers on a full vs. discounted rate. What that rate is is irrelevant; it does nothing to explain why more rooms were rented at full rate in light of the evidence.

(E) goes beyond the scope of the passage. Other charges above and beyond room rates are never discussed and are therefore not an issue.

A 180 test taker doesn't hesitate to work out actual examples to clarify her understanding of a numerical concept.

Here, imagine, for instance, that the hotel has 10 rooms, and rents three at a discount and seven at full price. Now suppose that the discounted rooms contain five people per room, while the full-price rooms each contain one person. Voilà! More full-priced rooms than discounted, but more discounted guests than full-priced ones.

Explanation: Suicide in Travonia

14. C

Where do the test makers find these depressing places? Earlier we read about the peasant uprising and coup in Mondavia. Now we have people in Travonia killing themselves in record numbers. No matter; let's see what's going on. The author states that Travonia's suicide rate has increased, citing an increase in the number of overdoses following the recent release of certain brands of sleeping pills. Getting to the heart of the argument, the author then asserts that certain types of suicides have not increased in number, conceding that the percentage of elderly suicides has increased but noting that the percentage of teen suicides has decreased. The latter fact sounds like good news on the face of it, but is tempered by the fact that the author blurs the distinction between numbers and percents. Just because the percentage represented by teen suicides has decreased, that doesn't mean that fewer teens are committing suicide. A decreased percentage needn't signify a decreased number of suicides, and the author's flaw comes in failing to recognize this, as (C) expresses. A common logical flaw, indeed.

(A) The argument doesn't explicitly discuss other groups (we don't really know where they fall), but it certainly doesn't discount the possibility that other groups might exist.

(B) Not really, since the author doesn't link the sleeping pill takers to either demographic group, as mentioned in the explanation for (A).

(D) The total number of deaths in general is outside the scope of the argument, which deals exclusively with deaths from suicides and overdoses. The author need not consider the overall death figures in Travonia in order to make this argument.

(E) is vague, and wrong. The evidence about percentages doesn't contradict the author's conclusion, it just doesn't necessarily support it in the way the author suggests.

A 180 test taker is crystal clear on the distinction between numbers and percentages.

---

15. D

Now for part 2 of "Suicide in Travonia." Re-evaluating the argument, we can see that the author presents one piece of evidence in support of her assertion: Deaths resulting from sleeping pill overdoses have almost doubled since new nonprescription sleeping pills have been released. In order to use these overdoses to support the assertion that suicides have increased dramatically, the author must assume that the overdoses were indeed deliberate and hence qualify as suicides. (D) clearly expresses this assumption.

(A) brings up the same problem that we saw in the previous question's answer choices: the author makes no links between the people overdosing on the sleeping pills and the teens and elderly folk discussed later in the stimulus. The author needn't assume such a connection in order to assert that suicides have increased dramatically.

A 180 test taker understands the relationship between groups represented in the stimulus, and what connections are necessary, and not necessary, between them.

(B) Knowing what was the most pervasive suicide method 10 years ago doesn't have any real bearing on the claim in the first sentence of the passage. Maybe the method of choice was overdosing on sleeping pills, maybe not. Either way, this doesn't help justify the assertion that recent suicides are up.

(C) is far outside the scope. Deaths from natural causes have no necessary relation to this argument about suicide.

(E)'s relative comparison of Travonia's suicide rate to the world's is not relevant to the assertion in question. The author only asserts that suicides in Travonia have increased; there is no mention of their relative increase or of the suicide rate in other countries.

PRACTICE SET 4: SURVEYS AND STUDIES

Questions 16–17

A consumer survey of independent feature films revealed that the percentage of action films that received the survey's highest rating was greater than the percentage of romance films that received the highest rating. Yet, the survey organizers were probably erroneous in their conclusion that subject matter determines a feature film's popular appeal, since the action films were all directed by filmmakers with at least one hit film to their credit, while the romance films were directed by newer filmmakers, many of whom had not produced a previous film.

16. The statements above, if true, support which one of the following inferences?

   (A) Fewer romance films than action films received the survey's highest rating.
   (B) There is no relationship between the popular appeal of the feature films evaluated in the survey and any previous successes of the directors of those films.
   (C) If consumers were surveyed regarding their impressions of big-budget mainstream films, the percentage of romance films that would receive the survey's highest rating would be lower than the percentage of action films that would receive the highest rating.
   (D) Experienced filmmakers are more likely to produce hit films than are new filmmakers.
   (E) Among directors with the same number of hit films to their credit, differences in the subject matter of their feature films may not affect the way the films are popularly rated.

17. Each of the following, if true, supports the author's contention that the organizers misinterpreted the survey data EXCEPT:

   (A) The fact that one has directed a previous hit film is a positive indicator of that director's filmmaking talent.
   (B) Consumer ratings of a new film are influenced by the previous history of success of the film's director.
   (C) Action films generally require larger budgets than romance films and are thus prohibitive for many first-time film directors.
   (D) It is rare for the films of first-time directors to attain the popular appeal of films directed by filmmakers with at least one hit film to their credit.
   (E) Directors who have produced a previous hit film generally obtain the largest budgets and attract the most talented and well-known actors for their subsequent films.

18. Candidate: I am worried about the effects that the recent media coverage of my personal life will have on my chances of gaining office. Even though the reports are untrue, some voters interviewed on television, in response to these reports, have already expressed doubts regarding my ability to lead.

   Campaign manager: Your concern is unfounded. Of 1,000 people in this city randomly surveyed by email, only 25 have responded that their perception of your ability to lead has been negatively impacted by the recent media coverage.

   The campaign manager's argument is most vulnerable to criticism on the ground that it fails to acknowledge the possibility that

   (A) future media reports that follow up on the story of the candidate's personal life will further damage the public's perception of the candidate's ability to lead
   (B) the candidate's main opponent will use the opportunity created by the recent media coverage to conduct her own survey to assess the damage done to her opponent's credibility
   (C) the voting public would understand that its reaction to the recent media coverage of the candidate's personal life was the intended primary focus of the survey
   (D) opinions expressed in television interviews are not always the most reliable indicator of how interviewees are likely to act in given situations
   (E) many of those surveyed who are skeptical of the candidate's ability to lead due to the recent reports did not respond to the survey

19. A certain laboratory is studying the incidence of fatal liver damage in rats. Sixty-five percent of all rats whose environments exposed them to low levels of the toxin sulfur dioxide died of liver disorder. Ninety percent of all rats who died of liver disorder, however, were not exposed to any environmental toxins.

    Which one of the following would provide a feasible explanation for the statistics above?

    (A) Environmental and nonenvironmental causes of liver disease in rats are mutually exclusive.
    (B) There is only one cause of fatal liver disease in rats.
    (C) Environmental toxins are not particularly dangerous to the livers of rats.
    (D) Only a small portion of the entire group of rats studied was exposed to environmental sulfur dioxide.
    (E) Most rats will not suffer from exposure to low levels of sulfur dioxide.

20. Researchers, perplexed by the development of measles immunity in children who were not given the measles vaccination, believe that they now understand this phenomenon. The children in question were all raised from birth on a baby formula produced by the manufacturer Dihydro. The Dihydro formula contains a synthetic chemical known as dihydron-X, which has been shown in lab tests to rapidly destroy cells infected with measles. Researchers have concluded that those children who ingest the Dihydro formula maintain dihydron-X in their bloodstreams indefinitely. When measles-infected cells proliferate in the child's body, the dihydron-X responds to the invasion by quickly killing off all infected cells, thus arresting the progress of the disease so rapidly that the child is perceived to have a measles immunity.

    Which one of the following most accurately characterizes the role played in the passage by the unstated assumption that some children who receive measles vaccinations develop an immunity to measles?

    (A) It is a point that, taken together with the fact that some children who do not receive the measles vaccine develop an immunity to measles, generates the problem that motivated the research described in the passage.
    (B) It is a generalization assumed by the researchers to prove that the explanation of their puzzling case must involve a reference to the chemical composition of measles-resistant cells.
    (C) It is a generalization that, if true, makes impossible the notion that some children who do not receive a measles vaccine develop an immunity to measles.
    (D) It is a hypothesis that the researchers take to be proven conclusively by the findings put forth in the passage.
    (E) It is a conclusion that is overturned by the researchers' discovery that some children who do not receive vaccines nonetheless develop a measles immunity.

PRACTICE SET 4: ANSWERS AND EXPLANATIONS

Explanation: Indie Films

16. E

In this one we get two opposing views presented in a single argument. A survey showed that as a group, action films were rated higher than romance films. Viewpoint number one comes from the survey organizers, who concluded from this that subject matter of popular movies must determine their appeal. Seems reasonable, but the author, making use of the Contrast Keyword "yet," states that this conclusion is probably wrong and offers an alternative explanation. She notes that the producers of the action films were more experienced in successful film production. Notice that the author doesn't disagree that action films receive better ratings, but rather supports a different explanation for that superiority; the effect is the same in both viewpoints, but the causes differ. We're looking for an inference based on this argument, so once you have a firm grasp of the content, it's time to move to the answer choices.

(A) This answer choice confuses percents and numbers. The survey is based on the percentage of films in each category to receive the highest rating, not on the actual number of films to receive the top rating. For instance, according to the argument it could be possible that 50% of 10 action films receive the high rating, and 20% of 100 romance films receive the high rating, in which case fewer actions films receive the highest rating, despite the action films group receiving the higher percentage of top ratings. As we've just seen quite clearly in "Suicide in Travonia," question 14, a lower percentage does not necessarily mean a lower number.

(B) On the contrary: The author *does* suggest a relationship between previous directorial successes and the popular appeal of the survey films, so this answer choice contradicts the author's argument.

(C) The argument is about independent feature films. Based on that argument, we cannot infer anything about what a survey of big-budget mainstream films would show.

(D) distorts the information in the stimulus. Sure, of the filmmakers whose work is represented in this particular survey, some have a hit film to their credit, while some have never even made a movie before. Does that allow us to conclude who's "more likely" to produce a hit? For all we know, the folks with previous hits were new filmmakers themselves when they produced those hits. The absolute statement in (D) is not inferable.

(E) is all that's left. The author suggests that having a previous hit film to the director's credit is more important than subject matter in determining ratings, so it logically follows that subject matter may not be a significant factor in the popular ratings of films made by directors with an equal number of previous hits. By positing another factor besides subject matter that accounts for the survey results, the author's argument certainly does allow for the possibility that subject matter *may* have no effect on the ratings.

The wrong choices here contain some fairly common wrong answer types: confusing numbers and percentages (A); a choice that suggests the opposite of what's in the passage (B); a choice that strays outside the scope (C); and a classic distortion (D).

A 180 test taker is intimately familiar with the kinds of wrong choices that appear again and again on the LSAT.

---

17. C

The second question based on this stimulus asks us to locate the one answer choice that *doesn't* strengthen the author's argument. (We'll have more to say about this wrinkle later on.) We therefore want to eliminate the four choices that strengthen the connection between the popular appeal of a director's film and that director's having a past hit film; or that strengthen the connection between lack of a hit film and lesser popular appeal. The right answer will be the choice that *doesn't* support the author's causal link between previous directorial success and the popular appeal of that director's other films.

A 180 test taker expects that some question stems will not be written in the clearest possible manner. Before proceeding to the answer choices in such questions, she pauses for a moment to consider what she's being asked and what kind of answer choice she's looking for, even when it's impossible to specifically prephrase an answer.

(A) If previous hits indicate talent, then the author's theory of the link between previous hit films and popular appeal of the survey films seems more plausible, and we're more likely to believe that the organizers' *are* wrong, as the author maintains, about the effects of subject matter.

(B), (D), and (E) all strengthen the argument by tying past experience of success to present cinematic successes. (B) links previous experience to ratings directly. (D) takes it from another angle and explains that the films of first-timers do not often achieve the same popular appeal as that attained by previous hit-makers. It still strengthens the argument by offering a direct relationship between past success and appeal. (E) links prior experience of success to the ability to obtain the best actors, offering another benefit that accrues to experienced directors and makes them more likely to produce hit films. Like (A), all of these choices make it seem more reasonable to argue that the organizers have misunderstood the role of subject matter in the survey ratings. That is, they all support the author's alternative explanation.

(C) *Why* many first-time directors don't make action films has no impact on this argument. The fact remains that of the films in this particular survey, the action films were made by more experienced directors while the romances were made by novices, and the author uses this fact to counter a previous conclusion. (C) gives us one possible explanation for this fact, but has no effect on how this fact is *used* by the author, which, after all, constitutes the crux of her argument. This is the one choice that does not strengthen (or, for that matter, even affect) the author's argument, so it is the right answer here.

Explanation: Candidate and Media

18. E

With most elections being largely conducted via the media these days, it's no surprise that this candidate is worried that apparently negative media coverage will weaken his chances of getting elected. His manager tries to reassure him that he's wrong to worry by providing information from a survey. She recaps the results of an email survey of 1,000 people, only 25 of whom responded negatively to the candidate as a result of the media coverage. The question stem directs us to find a weakness in the manager's argument, and it lies in the survey. What if others who are skeptical about the candidate *simply didn't respond* to the survey? The fact that only 25 responded negatively does not necessarily mean that the other 975 are okay with the reports and have confidence in the candidate's ability to lead, although this is the interpretation the manager implies.

> A 180 test taker, when presented with a survey, asks whether the supposed results accurately represent the views of the whole group surveyed.

(E) picks up on this problem in the manager's argument: If the skeptics were disinclined to respond to the survey, then the conclusion that the candidate need not worry may be unfounded, and the candidate's concern may be legit. The fact that we're looking for a vulnerability in the manager's argument and that her argument is based on a survey is no coincidence. To a 180 test taker, (E) jumps out as a most common logical flaw associated with surveys: the failure to accurately interpret the response.

(A) is beyond the argument's temporal scope. The candidate and his manager discuss only the impact of the recent media coverage; the possible effects of future coverage don't play a relevant role in that discussion.

(B) identifies a possible use to which the candidate's opponent might put the media coverage, but that too is outside the scope. Maybe the opponent's survey won't show any residual concerns based on the survey, or maybe it will. By itself, (B) doesn't point out a weakness in the argument.

(C) There's no indication that the survey was intended to hide its main focus; presumably, those surveyed knew that the survey was intended to measure the fallout from the media coverage. So (C) need not be something that the campaign manager's argument fails to acknowledge.

(D) deals with television interviews, which show up in the candidate's argument but not in his campaign manager's. Therefore, (D) doesn't identify a problem with the manager's argument.

Explanation: Rats and Liver Damage

19. D

Here's another study to ponder, and the stem alerts us to the fact that we need to find a plausible explanation for the statistics cited. That alone suggests that the stats are puzzling, or at least a bit unusual, which is reinforced by the word "however" in the final sentence.

> A 180 test taker takes careful notice of "Keywords"—structural signals that authors employ in order to help convey their ideas. Contrast Keywords like "however" are especially powerful, as their job is to signal that something new is about to follow.

So what's going on in this one? We have a significant number of rats dying of liver disorder after being exposed to sulfur dioxide, but most of the rats who died of liver disorder were not exposed to any environmental toxins. This is not unlike what we've seen previously: a situation in which what seems like the same groups are actually not. Specifically, you should have realized immediately that the 65% and the 90% figures refer to two different groups, and thus that there is no discrepancy in the statistics. The 65% figure represents all rats exposed to sulfur dioxide; 90% represents the percentage of all rats that died of liver disorder. (D) points this out. If only a small number of rats were exposed to sulfur dioxide, then it's not surprising that 90% of the rats that died of liver damage died of something other than sulfur dioxide exposure. After all, only a small number of them were exposed to sulfur dioxide in the first place.

(A), the exclusivity of causes of liver damage, is irrelevant to this study. Any of the rats could have had both causes, but only one seriously enough to cause death.

(B) explains nothing. If there is only *one* cause of liver disease in rats, then what killed the rats that were *not* exposed?

(C) As for this one, why did 65% of the exposed rats die, if environmental toxins are not very dangerous? This seems counterintuitive, and so it can't possibly help to explain the statistics.

(E) says basically the same thing as (C), with different wording. It's wrong for the same reason, namely, that it contradicts the evidence. If 65% of the rats exposed to low levels of sulfur dioxide died, then most rats probably *will* suffer from such exposure.

Explanation: Measles Immunity

20. A

Were you feeling unchallenged? Probably not, but here's a little twist just in case you were. We're directed in this one to determine the role played not by just any piece of information, but rather by a certain assumption in the argument which is given to us in the stem. Strange!

> A 180 test taker rolls with the punches. When he sees something a bit unusual, he relates it to something more familiar and proceeds from there. With definite strategies for both Role of a Statement and Assumption questions at his command, there's no need to panic over a minor deviation.

The first task is to see where the given assumption exists in the argument. The author begins by explaining a paradox: Kids who weren't vaccinated seemed to be immune to measles. This is the only place in the stimulus where the author discusses vaccination, so it must be where the stem's assumption comes in. Indeed, in this first sentence the author does assume that vaccinations give kids immunity, or else the researchers wouldn't have been so surprised by this nonvaccination-based immunity. Now for the question at hand: How does this function in the argument? Well, it helps to set up the unusual situation that the rest of the stimulus will strive to explain or, in other words, the problem that requires a solution provided in the argument. (A) captures this by noting that the first sentence (statement plus assumption) creates the confusion which the researchers then worked to explain.

(B) would tie the assumption into the evidence regarding dihydron-X, but this assumption doesn't come from that part of the passage.

(C) contradicts the passage, which explains how the kids were able to achieve such an immunity. Therefore, such immunity is not impossible.

(D) This assumption is not what the researchers seek to prove; they seek to prove how the kids who *don't* receive the vaccination could get such immunity.

(E) Just because the kids became immune through their formulas, that doesn't overturn the assumption that vaccinations also create immunity. The researchers' conclusion does not contradict or undermine this particular assumption.

PRACTICE SET 5: JUST PLAIN TOUGH

21. Candidates for public office who begin their campaigns early and maintain a continuous barrage of campaign rhetoric have an almost insurmountable advantage over their opponents. Money is the single resource that allows these candidates to mount this sort of sustained effort. Politicians with a personal fortune or wealthy backers have instant access to a wide variety of media. They can even buy access to the most important and influential political tool of all—television. Well-heeled candidates can thus ensure that they are consistently before the public eye whether or not they have done anything newsworthy. Less monied candidates can usually afford a certain amount of media exposure, but they must start their campaigns late. It is an unfortunate fact that money, not merit, is the deciding factor in most elections.

    Which one of the following statements, if true, would most seriously weaken the author's conclusion that money is the deciding factor in most elections?

    (A) Even the most impoverished candidates can afford a minimal amount of television air time.

    (B) Most candidates who cannot afford television exposure can at least afford substantial amounts of radio air time.

    (C) Sometimes less wealthy candidates can acquire great sums of money by election day by collecting a very large number of small contributions.

    (D) Candidates who start their campaigns late are nonetheless as familiar to the voters by election day as those who begin early.

    (E) People often consider such factors as a candidate's stance on the issues and his or her personality before deciding whom to vote for.

22. John's Father: John has complained frequently that his psychoanalysis sessions are not helpful. But John has no knowledge of psychology, and he cannot accurately judge his analyst's techniques. His dissatisfaction in no way indicates that his analyst's methods are unsound, and is therefore no reason for him to discontinue his counseling sessions.

    John's Mother: But the purpose of his therapy is to help him adjust to our divorce. While it is true that John is not qualified to assess the analyst's methods, the only way to know if John is being helped by the therapy is through his evaluations of his own progress. If he believes that the sessions are a waste of time, he should stop seeing the analyst.

    Which one of the following is an assumption upon which John's mother's argument depends?

    (A) John's father is correct in concluding that John is unhappy with his counseling sessions.

    (B) Involvement in the therapeutic process does not hamper John's ability to perceive the value of his counseling sessions.

    (C) Psychoanalysts do not need to have extensive qualifications in order to be helpful to their clients.

    (D) If a psychoanalyst employs a sound method, then his or her clients will perceive the counseling sessions as helpful.

    (E) John is entitled to act on any belief concerning his own well-being, regardless of the origin or merits of that belief.

23. Boz: Scots Gaelic, an ancient and unique language, is now spoken only in a few places in the Western Highlands and in the remoter Scottish islands. It does not have a population base of native speakers sufficient to survive on its own. Unless drastic action is taken to preserve Scots Gaelic, we will probably witness the tragic loss of this distinct and irreplaceable language within the next century.

   Gertrude: You are wrong in considering Scotland only. Scots Gaelic and Irish Gaelic are essentially different dialects of the same language. As long as Irish Gaelic is still spoken in Ireland, it would be inaccurate to say that a language has been lost even if Scots Gaelic ceases to be spoken in Scotland altogether.

   Boz and Gertrude are committed to disagreeing with each other on which one of the following statements?

   (A) The population base currently speaking Scots Gaelic in the Western Highlands and remoter Scottish islands is enough to sustain the language into the future.
   (B) Scots Gaelic is properly considered a separate and distinct language.
   (C) Scots Gaelic is only spoken in a few places in the Western Highlands and in the remoter Scottish islands.
   (D) Without drastic action, the Gaelic language will probably be lost in the next century, because of the shortage of native speakers.
   (E) The population base of Irish Gaelic speakers is enough to sustain that branch of the Gaelic language into the next century without drastic action.

Questions 24–25

The proliferation of colloquialisms is degrading the English language. A phrase such as "she was like, 'no way!' you know?'", a meaningless collection of English words just a few decades ago, is commonly understood by most today to mean "she was doubtful." No language can admit imprecise word usage on a large scale without a corresponding decrease in quality.

24. The argument relies on which one of the following assumptions?

   (A) Colloquialisms always evolve out of a meaningless collection of words.
   (B) The colloquialisms appearing in the English language introduce imprecision into the language on what would be considered a large scale.
   (C) The Russian, French, and German languages cannot admit imprecise word usage on a large scale without an inevitable decrease in the quality of those languages.
   (D) The English language would not be degraded if there did not exist an alternative informal way to express the sentiment "she was doubtful."
   (E) The widespread use of colloquialisms represents the most serious form of language degradation.

25. Which one of the following, if true, most weakens the argument above?

   (A) Linguists have shown that the use of imprecise language on a small scale does not generally impair understanding.
   (B) Many colloquialisms that appeared in earlier forms of the English language disappeared over time as the people who used those particular phrasings were assimilated into larger groups with different language patterns.
   (C) Dissemination of a new word or phrase by the mass media is an important factor in whether or not the new word or phrase will become a colloquialism.
   (D) Colloquialisms are more likely to be coined by the youth in a culture than by any other segment of the population.
   (E) Languages of the highest quality often evolve over time out of a collection of colloquial usages woven into the formal dialect of a given people.

PRACTICE SET 5: ANSWERS AND EXPLANATIONS

Explanation: Media and Candidates

21. D

We saw, back in "Candidate and Media," question 18, a candidate worrying about how negative media coverage might hurt his election chances, and now we get the other side of the story. In this little tale of media and politics (two popular LSAT topics), the media play an indispensable role in a candidate's bid for office; and access to the mother of all media, television, takes moolah, and lots of it. According to the author, money allows a candidate to mount a sustained media barrage, and gain access to "the most important and influential political tool of all—television." We're asked to find the statement that weakens the claim that money is the deciding factor in elections, which means we need to break down the connection between the two that the author attempts to establish. In simple terms, we're looking for something that, if true, would suggest that money is *not* as important in deciding elections as the author would have us believe. That's about as good a prephrase as we're likely to form.

A 180 test taker attempts to determine what a right answer will look like or do when it's impossible to predict exactly what the right answer will say.

(A) What good is a minimal amount of air time? The wealthy, who could purchase lots of air time, would still have an "insurmountable advantage" over the poor.

(B) ignores the passage's claim that television is "the most important and influential political tool;" the fact that poor candidates can afford some radio coverage doesn't offset the TV advantage of the rich.

(C) The key to the mistake in this one is the phrase "by election day." The whole argument is based around the notion of using money to begin campaigning *early* and to maintain a "constant barrage of campaign rhetoric." Getting the dough by election day is too late.

(D) is what we want: It strongly suggests that the supposed financial advantage isn't so important after all. If candidates who start their campaigns late are just as familiar to voters by election day as candidates who wage sustained media campaigns, the conclusion that money is the deciding factor (because it buys recognition) is seriously damaged.

(E) is tricky, and perhaps sucked you in because it discusses the importance of nonmonetary concerns such as candidates' views and personalities. But in actuality this plays right into the author's argument: Before the public can judge a candidate's stance or personality, that candidate must be known, and what better way to get known than the author's "money and media barrage" approach?

A 180 test taker sees all angles, and recognizes subtle nuances that others miss.

Explanation: John's Therapy

22. B

Here's another question that doesn't fall into any major category, but is difficult nonetheless. John's mother argues that John should stop seeing his analyst if he believes that the sessions aren't helping him to adjust to his parents' divorce. She explains that there is only one way to know if the therapy is actually helping him, which is by looking at John's own feelings. If he believes that the sessions aren't helping, then the sessions should stop. Notice that she never says that John is actually right in his perceptions. She identifies one goal for the therapy: to help John adjust to his parents' divorce. Just because John doesn't *think* it's working, that doesn't necessarily mean that it *isn't* working. In order for the mother to conclude from her evidence that the sessions should end, she needs to assume that John is capable of accurately analyzing the sessions' usefulness. If he's not, then his feelings on the matter may not be an accurate indicator of the value of the sessions, and it may not be a good idea to base any decisions on them. Basically, John's mother assumes that John's is right in believing that the sessions aren't helping him, which is where answer choice (B) comes in. If she's assuming that John is right, then she must also assume that his judgment hasn't been impaired.

(A) is wrong because John's mother just discusses what should be done *if* John is unhappy with the sessions. Her conclusion does not depend on him being happy or unhappy.

(C) is far outside of the scope of the mother's argument. She never addresses the issue of the psychoanalyst's qualifications; she just discusses John's feelings and their indication of the sessions' value.

(D) Again, whether or not the analyst's methods are sound is not the issue for John's mother. For her, the central issue is John, and how his feelings determine the helpfulness of the sessions. Therefore, the validity of her conclusion doesn't rest on whether John's perceptions accurately indicate the soundness of the analyst's methods, but whether they indicate the value of the sessions in helping him to adjust to his parents' divorce. She cares about only two things: John's feelings and their role in determining whether he's adjusting. The analyst's methods needn't play a part in this equation.

(E), by stating that John should "act on *any* belief," exceeds the argument's scope. The argument does not deal with anything so broad as whether John should always act on his beliefs. Rather, it addresses whether his beliefs should be acted upon in this particular situation.

A 180 test taker quickly eliminates Assumption choices that are simply too broad in their scope to be necessary to the argument in question.

Explanation: The Death of Scots Gaelic

23. B

No, it's not a person, although "Scots Gaelic" would make a mighty fine name. We're talking about the possible death of a language here, or at least Boz and Gertrude are talking about that. Boz predicts the death of Scots Gaelic if "drastic action" isn't taken to preserve it, and he says that the death of Scots Gaelic would constitute the tragic loss of a *distinct* language. Gertrude disagrees with this diagnosis; she takes issue with Boz's focus on Scots Gaelic as a unique language. She says that Scots Gaelic is but one *dialect* of a larger language (i.e., Gaelic); therefore, as long as some type of Gaelic is spoken somewhere (specifically, Irish Gaelic in Ireland), the death of Scots Gaelic would not be the death of a distinct language, but merely that of a dialect. Since Boz insisted that Scots Gaelic is a "unique" and "distinct" language, the two speakers are committed to disagreeing on the proposition set forth in (B).

A 180 test taker pays attention to the adjectives used by the test makers, knowing that they often set the terms of the debate.

In this question, Boz describes Scots Gaelic twice, once as "ancient and unique" and again as "distinct and irreplaceable." It's that idea of Scots Gaelic's uniqueness that's the key to the disagreement.

(A) Gertrude never said that the population base currently speaking Scots Gaelic was enough to sustain it, only that the loss of Scots Gaelic wouldn't be the loss of a distinct language.

(C) While Gertrude said that Boz was wrong to limit his focus to Scotland, her point was that *other* types of Gaelic are spoken elsewhere, not that *Scots* Gaelic is spoken elsewhere.

(D) Boz only spoke of Scots Gaelic, so we have no idea what he would make of (D). Similarly, Gertrude never took a firm position as to whether Gaelic as a whole could survive into the next century without drastic action; her point was only that Scots Gaelic is a part of a larger Gaelic world.

(E) Boz never even mentioned the existence of Irish Gaelic, so he's not committed to believing anything about (E). Gertrude also never takes a position on (E), limiting herself to saying that *if* Irish Gaelic survives there will be no loss of language.

A 180 test taker knows that for a choice to be correct on a "point-at-issue" question, it must be a statement on which both speakers have taken clear, and contradictory, positions.

Boz never says *anything* about either Irish Gaelic or Gaelic as a whole, so he hasn't taken a position on (D) or (E), which means that these choices simply cannot be correct.

Explanation: "Like, No Way! You Know?"

24. B

How's that for eloquence? The strange part is that most of us really have no problem understanding the meaning of this phrase. Which is, in fact, the author's beef in the stimulus. He gets right to the point: the conclusion that the increase in colloquialisms degrades the English language. For evidence, the author (1) gives us an example of a colloquialism, the illustrious phrase in the title above, and (2) states that imprecise word usage present on a large scale basically decreases the quality of the language—hence, the tie in with the conclusion in the first sentence. The assumption resides in the gaps between these pieces of information; we were never told that these colloquialisms were rampant or imprecise. Indeed, the author states that *imprecise* words admitted on a *large scale* decrease a language's quality, without showing that colloquialisms really fall into either category. For the author's conclusion to be valid based on this evidence, he must assume that the evidence is relevant to the conclusion, and that colloquialisms are both imprecise and prevalent in English. The right answer choice, (B), picks up on both: colloquialisms are both imprecise and appear on a large scale. Without this, the evidence simply doesn't lead all the way to the conclusion.

(A) focuses on the source of colloquialisms, which the author addresses but which plays a central role in neither the evidence nor the conclusion. This could or could not be true without impacting the conclusion.

(C) basically restates the evidence. If "no language" can permit such laxity, then these three languages would logically follow along, but since the stimulus already tells us this much, (C) is not a necessary assumption here.

A 180 test taker recognizes the difference between a stated piece of evidence and an unstated yet required part of an argument (i.e., its assumption).

(D), if anything, presents us with a flawed inference, which would be accurate only if the author assumed that the stated colloquialism were the *only* colloquialism in English, and that *only* colloquialisms degrade the English language. He assumes neither, so if this were an inference question, (D) would be wrong on these counts. As far as being assumed—that is, being something that's *required* by the argument—(D) is even further off base.

(E) is too extreme. The author identifies one cause (proliferating colloquialisms) which leads to one effect (*like, um, degraded English*). To make this argument, he does not need to assume that this cause is more or less serious than any other. Even if colloquialisms were a minor part of this problem, the author's conclusion could still be valid.

25. E

Okay, it's, like, um, time for the second question on this passage about degraded English, you know? We're asked to weaken the same argument. To recap: The author concludes that the proliferation of colloquialisms degrades English. He then gives an example of a colloquialism and asserts as evidence that lots of imprecise word usage decreases the quality of a language. The right answer probably won't involve denying the argument's assumption, since the first question for this stimulus already focused on that element. Therefore, we can go through the choices one by one looking for a choice that will decrease the viability of the conclusion.

(A) discusses imprecise language "on a small scale" while the stimulus focuses on such language "on a large scale." Therefore, (A) is outside of the argument's scope.

(B) Since the author's argument relates colloquialisms to the quality of a language, information about their historical longevity does not impact the argument one way or the other. The real issue is the damage they do to the language while they're around.

(C) explains the media's role in determining the fate of a potential colloquialism. Since the argument itself does not concern itself with the media or with the mechanisms by which a colloquialism becomes a colloquialism, (C) has no effect on this argument.

(D) Like (C), (D) brings up the issue of the source of colloquialisms. The argument focuses on the *effect* of colloquialisms; their source plays no role in that focus.

(E) breaks apart the author's causal argument. The author asserts that colloquialisms lower the quality of a language, while (E) explains that they actually often contribute to the "highest quality" languages in the long run. (E) thus addresses a possibility which the author doesn't consider and which would weaken the author's argument.

A 180 test taker knows that the two most common ways to weaken an argument are by breaking down the argument's central assumption, and by asserting alternative possibilities relevant to the argument.

What's Next?

This concludes our in-depth look at the five major categories of tough LR questions. In the next chapter we'll look at other structural and logical formulations that present difficulties for LSAT test takers on the Logical Reasoning sections. The concept of "alternative explanations"—nicely highlighted here in "Like, No Way! You Know?"—is among them.

CHAPTER NINE

Other Logical Reasoning Challenges

Aside from the major categories of tough LR questions discussed thus far, there are also a number of other logical elements that appear somewhat regularly on the LSAT that are notorious for giving test takers trouble. These logical features and question types often appear in conjunction with the major categories discussed in chapters 7 and 8—indeed, we've noted en route those questions that contain some of these logical nuances. But let's now have a better look at them as challenges to reckon with in their own right. Sink your teeth into the following questions, one at a time, focusing on the specific logical elements and/or distinguishing features of each.

PHILOSOPHERS' CORNER

The difficulty of some LR questions resides in the sheer language of the stimulus. The question below is a long-winded discussion of the nature of good and evil, qualifying it as an example of what we at Kaplan call "Philosophers' Corner"—dense prose concerning esoteric topics and laden with abstraction.

1. There are those, Mr. Hobbes foremost among them, who maintain that before any positive laws were instituted, there could be no distinction between the good and the evil, the just and the unjust. In the state of nature, each had the "right" to lop off the head of any other. This frightening situation prompted those in a state of nature to form a social body and enact positive laws that forbid murder. It was only with the formation of these laws that good and evil were born; and it was only as a result of these laws that murder could be termed evil. This description is inaccurate. If murder was deemed so unfit and unreasonable an act that men entered into contracts to preserve themselves, then murder must have been understood as unfit and unreasonable before such contracts were formed. This being the case, these thinkers' supposition that there is neither "good" nor "evil" antecedent to the institution of law is self-defeating: If the distinction between good and evil is once admitted to exist, then it has always existed.

    The author intends to discredit the view of Mr. Hobbes and similar thinkers by attempting to

    (A) present historical evidence in support of his view
    (B) show that their argument contains circular reasoning
    (C) show that their account of the origin of morality presupposes a contradiction
    (D) point out the unacceptable consequences of their views on morality
    (E) impugn the motives of these thinkers themselves, rather than dealing with their argument

You'll see this category resurface later on in the Reading Comprehension section of this book, and the little morality piece we have here in this question certainly seems much like a mini Reading Comp passage in its own right. Let's see how you did with Hobbes and company.

Explanation: Beyond Good and Evil

Perhaps the philosophically minded among you recognize the title of this question as the title of the famous book by German philosopher Friedrich Nietzsche. Nor is this the last we'll hear from Mr. Nietzsche in this chapter—but more from him later.

The author argues that morality—or the distinction between good and evil—has always existed. This contradicts the claims of Hobbes and others that morality is an effect of law, and that where there is no law, there is neither good nor evil. Hobbes and the others presume that in the state of nature—man's condition before laws—there was no distinction between good and evil. They then claim that men entered into a social contract, and with the formation of the contract, good and evil were born—evil being that which breaks the contract (such as murder), and good being that which upholds the contract. The author's point is that, in order to explain the later prohibition against murder, one must assume that in the state of nature men found murder to be unreasonable, and therefore, evil. Thus, the author believes, thinkers such as Hobbes assume *first*, that the state of nature *is* free of moral judgment, and *second*, that this state is *not* free of moral judgment. Pretty dense stuff, but if we boil it down correctly we see that the author attempts to show that his opponents' view is self-contradictory. A contradiction is presupposed in this line of thinking, according to the author, so (C) is correct.

(A) is incorrect because the author presents no historical evidence. The argument concerns history, as it is an argument about origins, yet no actual history is given as evidence.

(B) is wrong because self-contradiction is not the same as circular reasoning. (We'll discuss what circular reasoning is in just a little bit.) Both are serious flaws, but they are not the same flaw.

(D) While the author likely feels that his opponents' views on morality can have unfavorable consequences, this is not what his argument rests on. He is concerned with refuting their argument on logical grounds, not on moral grounds.

(E) is incorrect because there is no *ad hominem* attack here; that is, a situation in which the author attacks his opponents personally rather than the *views* of his opponents. That's not the method employed here.

A 180 test taker is familiar with all forms of argumentation, valid and not, that are known to appear on the LSAT.

CIRCULAR REASONING

Advertisement: "If you plan to go to law school, you should take the Kaplan LSAT course because, all things considered, it is very much in the interest of all aspiring lawyers to enroll in and complete Kaplan's preparation program for the LSAT."

How do you like this reasoning? Now, while there are dozens of good reasons to take the Kaplan LSAT course (excellent teachers, world-class materials, access to every released LSAT question with explanations, killer software, etc.), not one is actually mentioned in the ad.

(**Disclaimer:** Not an actual ad. The Kaplan Marketing department is far more on the ball than this.)

In fact, the hypothetical ad above says nothing; or, more precisely, *its conclusion says nothing different from its evidence*. And that's the essence of what's known as "circular reasoning," a type of flawed logic that shows up occasionally on the LSAT. The argument in the ad above essentially boils down to "future law students should take Kaplan's LSAT course because future law students should take Kaplan's LSAT course." Of course, the language is dressed up a bit, and on the LSAT these can actually be quite tricky. Choice (B) in question 1 above wrongly suggests that the author is accusing Hobbes of employing circular reasoning, but Hobbes and the others do not use evidence that mirrors their conclusion, nor do they assume the truth of their conclusion in proving it. But the argument in question 2 below is another story. Practice recognizing Circular Reasoning with this example.

2. Censorship is poor policy and should be abandoned. Those who promote censorship, and there are more than one might believe, simply refuse to see that it is a far worse state of affairs when people are not free to express themselves than it is when they are free to express themselves.

   Which one of the following best describes the author's method of argument?

   (A) It attempts to establish the validity of an argument by denying the truth of the opposite of that argument.
   (B) It appeals to a false authority.
   (C) It makes a general conclusion based on one segment of the population.
   (D) It employs circular reasoning.
   (E) It draws a conclusion about a whole group from evidence about some members of the group.

Did you catch the circularity of the reasoning in this question?

Explanation: Censorship

Not much to say after the discussion above, other than to spell out exactly how the argument is circular, making (D) our correct answer. The argument concludes that censorship is bad because it's much worse when there *is* censorship than when there isn't. Sounds pretty unpersuasive, doesn't it? The reasoning literally goes in a circle, using its own conclusion as evidence: X is a poor policy because it's much better when there's no X than when there is X. But that's the very definition of something that's bad, so the argument essentially says nothing and only winds back on itself. Which is to say, it's circular.

(A) The opposite argument isn't presented—we simply don't know why some people would promote censorship—so the truth of it isn't denied and (A) isn't correct.

(B) The author doesn't use an authority, false or not, to establish credibility, so (B) is out.

(C) and (E) are both incorrect for the same reason. There isn't any generalizing here. Censorship is bad for all people, the author argues, because it's bad for all people. That's a circle, not a generalization.

It's worth noting that circular reasoning shows up more often on the LSAT as a wrong choice than as a right answer, but either way it's important to understand what this faulty kind of reasoning is all about. (Hey, if nothing else, it may help you to point out holes in your friends' arguments. And people just love that kind of thing . . . .)

PRINCIPLE APPLICATION

Principle questions are among the more difficult questions on the LR sections, and of the few different types of Principle questions, the kind that asks you to find the choice among the five that conforms to a given Principle in the stem is probably the most difficult of these. Applying a principle to specific situations is, of course, a very lawyer-like thing to do, so it's not surprising that the test makers want to see if you're able to home in on the relevant aspects of the principle and recognize situations that accord with a principle and those that do not. Most Principle questions come with difficult choices, and "Free Press" below is no exception.

3. A free press always informs the public of all aspects of a country's current military operations except for cases in which the safety of troops or the success of a mission would be jeopardized by the public's right to know.

    Which one of the following adheres most closely to the principle set forth above?

    (A) A free press would publish editorials supporting a current military campaign, but could repress dissenting opinions regarding the campaign.

    (B) An unfree press would release information on the country's prisoners of war taken during a current military campaign, unless such information would hamper efforts to secure the prisoners' release.

    (C) A free press would accurately report the number of casualties suffered on both sides of a battle, but could withhold information regarding the possible targets for a future military strike.

    (D) An unfree press would print inflammatory accounts of an international event in order to garner public support for an unpopular war.

    (E) A free press would reveal any new information regarding the country's past involvement in secret military operations as soon as that information became available.

Did you breeze through the choices to the correct answer, or did you have difficulty relating them back to the principle in question?

Explanation: Free Press

The opposite of censorship is freedom of the press, so in this one we have a complete about-face from the previous question. When asked for a situation that conforms to a principle, your best bet is to understand the principle thoroughly, and then test the choices against this understanding. The author offers an absolute truth with two restrictions. First the rule: A free press always reports all information about a country's military operations. There are two cases, and only two cases, in which this might not be true. First, if such information would jeopardize the safety of the troops. Second, if such information would jeopardize the success of a mission. With such clear rules, we'll be looking for the answer choice that follows them faithfully.

(A) To make this answer choice work, you'd have to assume that such dissenting opinions would jeopardize the troops and/or the success of the mission. This choice supports no such assumption, so based on the information that it alone provides, it is not consistent with the stimulus' principle.

(B) and (D) discuss unfree presses, and therefore fall outside the scope of the argument. The rules pertain only to a free press, and we can't infer how an unfree press would behave in regard to these issues.

(C) This answer choice succeeds where (A) fails because, while it doesn't directly state that the publication of future military targets would jeopardize the success of a mission, the link between the two is far clearer and more logical. According to the principle, a free press *could* withhold information that endangers the troops or mission, and it's reasonable to say that the info discussed in (C) could fall into that category. In this question, (A) could be correct with some amendments, but (C) is correct without that extra step.

A 180 test taker understands that the right answer will never require any extra work; that is, it must be correct on its own merit, without requiring us to introduce extra information.

(E) The principle deals with *current* military operations, and therefore doesn't shed any light on what's appropriate behavior in regard to previous engagements. Clandestine past military operations are outside the scope.

SCOPE SHIFTS

Have you ever been in an argument in which you just know that your opponent is pulling a fast one, but you can't quite put your finger on the flaw in his argument? Perhaps, somewhere along the way, he subtly changed the direction of the argument. This is a classic argumentative technique; in fact, one that the LSAT test makers are quite fond of. In a number of LR questions, the author introduces a subtle distinction that slightly alters or shifts the scope or focus of the argument, as in the following example:

> Educators have been complaining that salaries are not high enough to draw enough top applicants to teaching jobs at the high school level. This is clearly absurd; there is fierce competition for teaching jobs at all levels, with many candidates vying for each new job that opens up.

Do you see the scope shift? The claim that the author attempts to refute deals with *top* applicants, whereas the evidence that the author provides for her rebuttal involves applicants *in general*. It may seem like a minor difference, applicants vs. *top* applicants, but it opens up a logical chasm. This is exactly the type of subtle distinction the test makers like to exploit. Such distinctions provide great material, especially for Assumption, Weaken the Argument, and Logical Flaw questions. They show up both in passages and choices. We've seen examples above in "Home Births" in chapter 7 and "Mt. Dunmore Lodge" in chapter 8. Now give this question a try:

4. It is mistaken to attribute Zanco's failure to the publicity about the supposedly inhuman working conditions in the foreign factories that furnish Zanco with many of its parts. Zanco's failure has more to do with defects in its products than with any boycott on moral grounds. After all, plenty of other companies are supplied by factories with working conditions just as bad as those in Zanco's suppliers, and the public does not hesitate to buy their products.

    The argument in the passage is based on which one of the following assumptions?

    (A) People are unlikely to let moral considerations affect what products they decide to purchase.
    (B) People who patronize companies supplied by factories where working conditions are as bad as those of Zanco's suppliers are aware of those conditions.
    (C) The working conditions in the factories that supply Zanco with parts are not as bad as has been claimed.
    (D) Zanco's sales did not dip sharply after the poor working conditions in its suppliers' factories became known.
    (E) The poor quality of Zanco's products is not a result of the working conditions in the foreign factories where its parts are manufactured.

Did you catch the scope shift here in "Zanco's Failure"?

Explanation: Zanco's Failure

The assertion that Zanco's failure is not due to publicity about poor working conditions in its suppliers' factories only makes sense if those who buy the products of those other companies are *aware* of those conditions in their suppliers' factories. After all, if people bought products from the other companies without knowing that they too were supplied by sweatshop-style factories, the comparison would be moot and the logic of the argument would go down the drain. The scope shift centers around the word "publicity." The conclusion that Zanco's failure was not due to publicity about bad working conditions is backed up by evidence concerning companies with bad working conditions *that says nothing about publicity*. Publicity is a key feature of the conclusion, but drops off the map in the evidence, and therein lies the scope shift and the necessity of (B).

(A) Even if people are likely to base purchasing decisions on moral considerations, it doesn't weaken the conclusion that people didn't do this in the case of Zanco.

(C) The point isn't that the working conditions of Zanco's suppliers have been unfairly exaggerated, but that these conditions are not a factor in the company's failure. It wouldn't affect the argument if, contrary to (C), working conditions are just as bad as the negative publicity claims.

(D) Even if Zanco's sales did dip sharply after people found out about the poor working conditions, we couldn't conclude that the dip resulted from the public's refusal to buy Zanco's products on moral grounds; the sales dip could have easily resulted from something else and merely coincided with the public's learning of the factory conditions.

(E) It doesn't matter whether or not there's a connection between the poor quality of the products and the lousy working conditions—the existence or lack of such a connection doesn't affect the logic of the argument.

ALTERNATIVE EXPLANATIONS

Perhaps, when arguing in real life, you've used the "Oh yeah? But what about . . ." defense. We look for alternative explanations for situations all the time, to prove our own points or argue against others. This is another common feature of Logical Reasoning questions; for example, take a look at question 25 in chapter 8, "Like, No Way! You Know?" In that one, choice (E) addressed a possibility that the author overlooked, thus weakening the argument. Some arguments are flawed, or can be weakened, because their authors fail to see that a piece of evidence can lead to more than one possible conclusion, or that a situation or result can have more than one possible explanation. See if you can spot the relevant alternative that would weaken the argument below.

5. Some sports historians claim that professional tennis players develop unique playing styles that result from a combination of the peculiarities of each player's physical attributes and the influence of coaches during their early adaptation to the game. But when the increase in strength and endurance of modern players is discounted, it becomes readily apparent that the playing styles of the current crop of professional tennis players are no different from the styles of players from previous generations. Clearly, there is a universally efficient tennis style to which all professional tennis players conform.

    The argument above is most weakened by which one of the following statements?

    (A) The differences in physical attributes among tennis players are even more pronounced than the sports historians believe.
    (B) Few current professional tennis players are familiar with the professional tennis players of fifty years ago.
    (C) The increased strength of current tennis players contributes more to the development of individual playing styles than does increased endurance.
    (D) All of the early coaches of today's professional tennis players were professional tennis players themselves earlier in their lives.
    (E) Weight training and greater attention to diet are the primary factors in the increased strength and stamina of the current generation of professional tennis players.

Explanation: Tennis Styles

The author begins by describing the view of some sports historians, who subscribe to a basic formula: physical attributes + a coach's influence = a player's "unique" tennis style. After dismissing the relevance of modern players' greater strength and endurance, however, the author argues that current styles are really no different from previous styles, implying that the historians' claim of the existence of "unique" tennis styles is bogus. And this implication is stated outright in the last sentence, where the author posits the existence of a universally successful tennis style shared by all professionals. In other words, the author uses the fact that tennis styles haven't changed over the years to argue that there's simply one best way to play tennis; in contrast to the historians' theory of "unique," the author proposes the theory of "universality." But the author ignores a plausible alternative explanation; namely, the role of the tennis coach. If, as (D) has it, the early coaches of today's players were the professionals of yesteryear, then it's reasonable to believe that the style that the author considers "universal" may simply be the style (one possible one among many) that was handed down from one generation to the next. Perhaps if the current crop of tennis stars doesn't go on to teach the next generation, whole new styles will develop. If the current style is *learned*, then it may not be universally inherent to the game. If (D) is true, the author's claim of "universality" is weakened.

(A) emphasizes the truth of the first part of the sports historians' view regarding the individuality of physical attributes. Since the author doesn't explicitly disagree that players vary in terms of some attributes, this choice doesn't weaken the argument.

(B), if anything, strengthens the argument. If most current players don't know of the players of previous generations, yet their styles are for the most part similar to that of those players, then we'd be more likely to believe that the author is on to something with the claim that a universally efficient style exists in the world of professional tennis.

(C) makes an irrelevant distinction between strength and endurance. Saying that one has a greater impact than the other has no effect on the argument, which never even begins to rank those two factors.

(E) The factors that contribute to the greater strength and weight of today's players are beyond the scope of this argument. The argument focuses on the similarity of styles that is evident once these factors are discounted. *Why* the current players are stronger and heartier than the previous bunch is not the issue.

THE "ODD MAN OUT"

Next up in our potpourri of tough questions are questions that ask you to locate the one choice that *doesn't* satisfy a particular requirement; in other words, to find the "odd man out." These are difficult because the right answer may do the opposite of what's required, or may simply be irrelevant to the situation at hand. At the same time, the wrong choices are *all* relevant, and sometimes look and sound the same, lulling us into a state of mind in which every choice, including the bogus right answer, sounds reasonable. Finally, some test takers simply blow past the word "EXCEPT" or "NOT" in the question stem, and blow the question on that account.

These come in a number of varieties. Back in chapter 8's "Indie Films," question 17, we saw a "Strengthen EXCEPT" question. Later on we'll see a few other types. The following question is of the "which is *not* assumed" variety.

6. A political candidate committed to the principal tenets of a political party may not always explain the implications of his or her party commitment to the voters in full detail. Adele Richardson, for example, is a minor-party candidate in contention for a seat on the school board. She is not likely to inform conservative voters in her district that the national leadership of her party has recently recommended that school curricula be more closely monitored by agencies of the federal government.

Which one of the following is not assumed or implied by the passage above?

(A) A political candidate is likely to be more interested in winning an election than in proselytizing the electorate.

(B) The candidate of any party is likely to support the policy decisions made by the national leadership.

(C) All candidates for such community positions as membership on the school board must have commitments to national parties.

(D) Conservatives in Adele Richardson's district do not support federal intervention in decisions made by community school officials.

(E) Voters in Adele Richardson's district are not fully aware of the policy statements made by the national leadership of her party.

How did you make out?

Explanation: School Board Candidate

Four assumptions means we must be dealing with a pretty shaky, or at least, incomplete, argument. The author states a general point in the first sentence: A candidate who has faith in the beliefs of a party may not find it in her interest to explain those beliefs to voters. Enter Ms. Richardson, school board hopeful. Her party would like to see tight government regulation of school curricula, but in accordance with the claim in the first sentence, the author thinks that she's not likely to explain this to conservative voters. Since there are four assumptions here, our best bet is to go right to the choices, looking for the "odd man out."

(A) If (A) is *not* true, then the argument is weakened, which shows that (A) must be assumed. If a candidate is interested in proselytizing the electorate rather than winning an election, then, contrary to the author's assertion, the candidate would have no reason to conceal her opinions from voters likely to disagree with her.

(B) must be assumed because if a candidate is *not* likely to support the national leadership's policy decisions, then the author's assertion about Richardson makes no sense.

(C) is the only nonassumption here—the argument doesn't depend on candidates for community positions having commitments to national parties. The author addresses only those candidates who *are* committed to a political party's central tenets; he says nothing about what's required to run for community positions. Adele Richardson happens to be committed to a national party, but this needn't be true of all candidates for such positions.

(D) is a fairly obvious assumption: Why would Richardson conceal her party's recommendation from conservatives if conservatives supported it? Instead, she'd be more likely to parade the party recommendation in order to garner conservative votes.

(E) is also assumed: The only way Richardson can conceal her party's recommendation from voters is if they're not fully aware of it already.

TOUGH CHOICES

We've covered all kinds of tough Logical Reasoning questions, but we would be remiss to overlook questions that are difficult simply due to the fact that they contain tough choices. Tough choices are especially prevalent in Method of Argument and Principle question types—both of which often include choices with general, somewhat abstract descriptions of what's going on in the passage—but there's really nothing stopping tough choices from showing up in any question type. Some of the questions you've seen already contain tough choices, and there's more to come later on. As for the question below, there's nothing inherently difficult about the story told in the stimulus, but the choices are a different matter altogether.

7. Playing in a rock band during college has caused Matthew's grades to suffer, which in turn has decreased his chances of being accepted to a prestigious graduate program. But being active in extracurricular activities such as music can in some cases compensate for bad grades and help a candidate's chances for admission to graduate school by demonstrating that one is a well-rounded individual with varied interests. However, the dean of Wentworth Business School refuses to allow Matthew's participation in the band to positively impact on his acceptance chances.

    Which one of the following principles best justifies the dean's position?

    (A) The consequences of an action can only be evaluated with respect to the possible consequences of an opposing alternative action.
    (B) Nothing that causes a condition can be used to compensate for the consequences of that condition.
    (C) The overall value of an activity must not be overridden by a negative result of a single aspect of that activity.
    (D) A decision that affects the future of an individual must not discount any factor relevant to that decision.
    (E) A factor that eliminates a candidate from consideration in one instance should not be used to eliminate that candidate from consideration in a dissimilar situation.

Explanation: Matthew's Rock Band

The question stem tells us to focus on the dean's position, but the author gives us a good deal of background information before we hear about the dean. Apparently, Matthew's membership in a rock band has lowered his grades, which has hurt his chances of getting into a good business school. Matthew might be able to rock on, however, because extracurricular activities like his could compensate for the lower grades. Finally we get to the dean, who will not allow Matthew's musical escapades to better his chances of getting into Wentworth Business School. Focusing on this last piece of information, let's hack our way through these tough choices to find one that generalizes the dean's position.

(A) sounds extremely official and yet says relatively nothing that relates to this situation. What "action" does (A) refer to? If it's Matthew's rock playing, then "consequences" probably would have to refer to his lower grades. If the action is the dean's refusal, the consequences for Matthew may be that he won't get in. Either way, there's no way to relate any of this to an evaluation of the action in light of "possible" consequences of an "opposing alternative action."

(B) is consistent with the dean's position and would support the validity of it. Participating in the band has hurt Matthew's chances for admission, so if something (like playing in a band) can't simultaneously hurt and help an applicant, then it makes sense that the dean sees no way for the rock band to increase Matthew's chances of getting in. (B) would therefore justify the dean's view that the band can have no positive effect. All the terms match up: The "cause" is playing in the band; the "condition" is lower grades; the "consequence of that condition" is a lowered chance of admission.

> A 180 test taker is adept at matching up the general terms in tough choices with the specifics of the passage.

(C) is inconsistent with the dean's position, since she is not stressing the positive value of Matthew's activities over their negative results. Rather, she sees no positive value in Matthew's musical activities. (Nor, perhaps, did his audience, considering that most rock stars don't take time out for business school.)

(D) We have no idea how many factors go into admitting someone to business school, and whether this particular dean has considered them all or missed a few. Either way, it's not relevant to her position here regarding the value of Matthew's musical activities.

(E) No: Matthew is never eliminated from consideration. The dean won't give him credit for playing in the band, but that doesn't mean that she's tossed his application.

NECESSARY AND SUFFICIENT CONDITIONS

If I throw a baseball at the window, the window will break.

Considering the statement above, if I *don't* throw a baseball at the window, can we conclude that the window has *not* broken? No. While the baseball is enough to break the window—that is, is *sufficient* to break the window—nothing in the statement above indicates that the baseball is *necessary* to break the window. The window may break some other way, such as from a sonic boom, or from an egg thrown at it on Halloween.

Questions that test an understanding of the difference between necessary and sufficient conditions are perennial LSAT favorites. The Formal Logic example in chapter 8, "Mondavian Uprising," contains a necessary/sufficient element, and choice (B) in particular was wrong for mistaking one for the other. Questions 4 and 5 in chapter 8, "Railway System," are other Formal Logic questions you've seen earlier that involve necessary and sufficient conditions. In question 4, we say the following for (D) and (E): "We're told that public transport can grow more popular only if the railways are modernized and expanded. This doesn't mean that it *will* grow more popular simply because the railways have been modernized and expanded." What that means in this context is that modernization and expansion are *necessary* for increased popularity, but not *sufficient*. Other factors may need to come into play.

The question below is a complex Formal Logic question that's centered squarely around this notion of necessity vs. sufficiency.

8. In order to justify the merger of two banks, two things must be accomplished: First, the cost of the merger must not exceed one billion dollars; second, the bank created by the merger must retain the two former banks' customers. The newly formed bank cannot keep those customers, however, unless it avoids claims of discrimination by earmarking at least ten billion dollars for loans to low-income customers. If the bank cannot keep its customers, it cannot keep the cost of the merger from exceeding one billion dollars. So, it follows that if the new bank earmarks ten billion dollars in loans, it will keep the cost of the merger from exceeding one billion dollars.

    The reasoning in the argument is not valid because it fails to establish that

    (A)   many successfully merged banks have earmarked loan money
    (B)   some unsuccessful mergers cost less than one billion dollars
    (C)   earmarking loan money is sufficient to guarantee customer loyalty
    (D)   earmarking loan money is necessary for guaranteeing customer loyalty
    (E)   many merged banks that experienced costly mergers have not earmarked loan money

Explanation: Bank Merger

We hope you noticed the landslide of necessity going on here: Earmarking loan money to low-income customers is *necessary* to retain customer loyalty (earmarking is *necessary* to prevent claims of discrimination, avoiding discrimination claims is *necessary* to customer loyalty), which in turn is *necessary* to keep merger costs from going over the one billion mark.

A 180 test taker can translate complex formal logic constructions such as "cannot . . . unless" into familiar, easy-to-work-with statements.

From the introduction above, you can probably see where this is going. Despite these necessary conditions, note the definite nature of the conclusion: If the new bank earmarks ten billion dollars in loans, then it *will* keep the cost of the merger under one billion dollars. What the author fails to consider is that, just because earmarking loan money is *necessary*, that doesn't mean it's *sufficient* to guarantee loyalty. That's choice (C). Nor, for that matter, is it established that maintaining customer loyalty will guarantee that the deal won't cost more than one billion dollars; again, loyalty is *necessary* for this outcome, but we can't conclude that the cost will be kept down simply because loyalty is maintained; other factors may involved.

(A), (B), and (E) all offer useless background information; it's not necessary to the logic of the argument for the author to provide examples of past mergers. Therefore, these choices are all beyond the scope of the argument.

(D), actually, is valid. As noted above, the argument does succeed in establishing this point.

CAUSATION

The great German philosopher, Friedrich Nietzsche, put it perfectly in his 1888 book *Twilight of the Idols*:

"There is no more dangerous error than that *of mistaking the consequence for the cause*: I call it reason's intrinsic form of corruption." (italics Nietzsche's)

The LSAT test makers have apparently taken the philosopher's words to heart; LSAT test takers mistake cause and effect at their own risk. Some Logical Reasoning questions even contain precisely the same kind of reasoning as the example Nietzsche furnishes on the same page as the quote.

"Everyone knows the book of the celebrated Cornaro in which he recommends his meager diet as a recipe for a long and happy life—a virtuous one, too . . . I do not doubt that hardly any book . . . has done so much harm, has shortened so many lives, as this curiosity, which was so well meant. The reason: mistaking the consequence for the cause. The worthy Italian saw in his diet the *cause* of his long life: while the prerequisite of long life, an extraordinarily slow metabolism, a small consumption, was the cause of his meager diet." (italics Nietzsche's)

What Nietzsche is saying is that a meager diet didn't cause Cornaro to live long; a necessary condition of long life caused him to eat little. A perfectly LSAT-like example, right down to the name—we certainly wouldn't be surprised to find "Cornaro" in a Logic Game or as a contestant in a Logical Reasoning dialogue debate.

The LSAT test makers are fond of all kinds of causation problems. In some, one causal element is mistaken for another. In others, correlation is mistaken for causation, or occasionally, vice versa. You've already seen a few questions that contain causal elements. See for example "Doug's Stomachaches," "Indie Films," and "Like, No Way!, You Know?" Later on you'll also see examples in which cause and effect are reversed—that's a popular one.

The following question illustrates another very common and basic way that causation is tested on the LSAT. See what you can make of the reading predicament in Gotham.

9. Reading skills among high school students in Gotham have been steadily declining, which can only be the result of overcrowding in the schools.

    Which one of the following, if true, most seriously weakens the argument expressed above?

    (A)   The high school system in Gotham succeeds in giving students a good education at considerably less cost than do most systems.

    (B)   Several cities have found that overcrowding in the schools is not always associated with lower reading scores.

    (C)   Gotham schools have a greater teacher-to-student ratio than most other school systems.

    (D)   Students' reading skills have not declined in other cities where the high schools are just as crowded as those of Gotham.

    (E)   Schools are not overcrowded in many cities where high school reading scores have declined more than they have in Gotham.

Explanation: Gotham Reading Skills

The important word in the author's conclusion is the word "only." She states that the problem of declining reading skills can only have one cause—overcrowding. Anything that renders doubtful the causal connection between Gotham's overcrowding and Gotham's declining reading scores will seriously weaken the argument. (E) does this by pointing out a case in which skills have declined, yet there is no overcrowding. So something *other* than overcrowding *can* account for a decline in reading skills. (Notice how this ties in with the notion of Alternative Explanations discussed earlier.)

(A) just tries to make an excuse for Gotham schools by pointing out that they spend less money. While this may furnish a reason for the overcrowding, it does nothing to hurt the argument that the overcrowding causes declining scores.

(B) and (D) point to overcrowding without declining scores. Yet the author didn't say that overcrowding always leads to declines in skills, but rather that declines in skills are always a result of overcrowding. Be careful to keep the causal mechanism straight!

(C), if anything, strengthens the argument by pointing out that the decline in reading scores cannot be attributed to a low teacher-to-student ratio. It must, therefore, be attributed to some other cause (e.g., overcrowding).

What's Next?

You've now heard about five major categories and nine subcategories of the most difficult LSAT Logical Reasoning material. What do you need to reinforce this learning and to match your wits against the conquests presented? More questions, of course. Onward to chapter 10.

CHAPTER TEN

Putting It All Together

By now, you should have a very definite idea of the many kinds of challenges presented in LSAT Logical Reasoning. While we've broken down these challenges into major and minor categories, roughly based on the prevalence of certain kinds of questions on the test, the truth is that difficult questions are often combinations of the various logical elements you've just encountered. In other words, the logical elements and question types presented in chapters 7, 8, and 9 may, and often do, overlap in a single question. And just like in Logic Games "Hybrid/Mixture" games, the existence of multiple logical elements within questions complicates matters significantly.

In this chapter, you'll get practice with plenty of complex Logical Reasoning questions. Not every question contains more than one logical element, but many do, and we've taken the liberty to cite in the explanations the distinguishing logical or structural characteristics of each. We've arranged the questions in small groups so that you can learn as you go along and get practice recognizing the logical patterns that recur throughout the Logical Reasoning sections of the test.

Enjoy!

PRACTICE SET 1

1. Studies of trauma victims suggest that shock brought on by violent or life-threatening situations causes damage to the hippocampi, structures in the brain that play a crucial role in learning and memory. Researchers found that in combat veterans suffering from post-traumatic stress symptoms, which include nightmares and vivid flashbacks, the hippocampi were eight percent smaller in volume than in combat veterans who suffered no such symptoms. The researchers concluded that the hippocampi had lost cell mass as a result of trauma.

   Which one of the following, if true, would most seriously weaken the researchers' conclusion drawn above?

   (A) In another study, subjects who had experienced the death of a close relative were found to have no reduction in the volume of their hippocampi when compared to those whose close relatives were all still living.

   (B) In the study, the traumatized veterans were compared with other veterans of similar background, body size, and other characteristics that might have a bearing on brain size.

   (C) Some individuals are born with hippocampi whose volume is smaller than average, and this reduced volume makes them more susceptible to post-traumatic stress symptoms.

   (D) Combat veterans who experience post-traumatic stress symptoms perform significantly worse on tests of verbal memory compared with veterans who suffer no such symptoms.

   (E) Further study revealed that veterans who had seen more intense combat and had more severe post-traumatic symptoms exhibited even greater reduction in the volume of their hippocampi.

2. Over the past seven years, private college tuition rates have increased, resulting in a large decrease in private college attendance across the country. Private college revenues, however, have progressively increased in each of the seven years during this period, and researchers predict further increases in the years to come.

   Which one of the following, if true, offers the best explanation for the situation described above?

   (A) Most private colleges increase tuition rates approximately once every two years.

   (B) Attendance at vocational schools generally exceeds attendance at private colleges in most cities.

   (C) The increase in tuition rates at private colleges has influenced many prospective students to seek a state scholarship to attend a public university.

   (D) The decrease in students attending private colleges over the last seven years has been more than offset by the increases in tuition.

   (E) Private colleges gain a larger percentage of their revenue from alumni contributions than do public universities.

3. When attempting to understand the world of art, it is necessary to distinguish between an artist's conception of his or her own particular work and the conception of the public who will experience that work of art. It is true that anyone can ascribe his or her own personal meaning to a work of art. Some art scholars, however, argue that only the artist's own conception of a work of art constitutes the "true" meaning of that work. Furthermore, they believe that only when an individual's conception of a work of art matches the "true" meaning of that work is it possible for an individual to experience art's power of transcendence.

If the views of the art scholars discussed in the passage above are correct, then which one of the following can be properly concluded from the passage?

(A) If an artist has a particular conception of a work of art, then no individual is justified in ascribing a personal meaning to that work.

(B) The stronger the personal meaning an individual ascribes to a work of art, the more likely that individual will experience art's power of transcendence.

(C) Some art scholars believe that an artist's conception of a work of art can never match the conception of individuals experiencing that work of art.

(D) There are some works of art that could never invoke art's power of transcendence.

(E) If art's power of transcendence is realized, then some artist's conception of his or her work matches the conception of some individuals experiencing that work of art.

4. A person should not take an action that involves a serious physical risk to another person unless the person thereby placed at risk is aware of the risk incurred and consents to it, or unless the risk that person faces as a result of the action is likely to be less serious than the risk that person would face if the action were not taken.

Which one of the following actions would most clearly violate the principle expressed above?

(A) In order to avoid a water landing, the pilot of a stricken plane crash lands in a thinly populated community, endangering its inhabitants without their knowledge.

(B) An officer summons an all-volunteer bomb-disposal unit to the front lines to neutralize a minefield.

(C) Following the outbreak of a deadly disease especially threatening to kids, the board of education inoculates school children without their parents' knowledge, despite the danger of painful side effects to some of those inoculated.

(D) A person in charge of a trust fund invests some of the money in risky stocks, without the knowledge or consent of the trustees.

(E) The government raises the tax on cigarette sales in order to curtail tobacco smoking, despite abundant evidence that smokers understand and accept the risks entailed in smoking.

PRACTICE SET 1: ANSWERS AND EXPLANATIONS

Explanation: Trauma Victims

Distinguishing Features: Study, Causation

1. C

Here we have a cause-and-effect argument presented in the context of a study. The trauma of the vets must have caused the loss of hippocampi cell mass, the doctors conclude, because those with stress symptoms had smaller hippocampi than those without the symptoms. We're looking for something that would weaken the argument, and a classic way of attacking cause-and-effect is illustrated by (C), which points out that the cause and effect could actually be working in reverse—it could be that the symptoms are the result of the small hippocampi, rather than vice versa. This should remind you of Nietzsche's Cornaro example presented in chapter 9.

A 180 test taker knows all the potential weaknesses of a causal argument. When confronted with the proposition that X caused Y, he considers the possibility that Y may have in fact caused X; that some third factor, Z, caused both X and Y; or that the two things are merely correlated and thus not causally related at all.

(A) The argument concerns the effects of "violent or life-threatening" events. The death of a close relative is traumatic, to be sure, but it isn't "violent or life-threatening," as those terms are used here. So (A) is irrelevant.

(B) and (E) do the opposite of what we're looking for here. The very fact that (B) asserts the similarity among all the veterans studied tends to support, rather than weaken, the study's findings. And (E), if anything, strengthens the argument by cementing the connection between trauma and tiny hippocampi.

A 180 test taker keeps her eye on the ball at all times, and does not carelessly choose a strengthener when asked for a weakener, or vice versa.

(D) omits the main issue—the connection between trauma and hippocampi damage—and hence cannot have any effect on the reasoning.

Explanation: Tuition Rates

Distinguishing Feature: Numbers and Statistics

2. D

Here we have a specific, and common kind of number question: an increase/decrease problem. The author discusses two simultaneous trends that might seem to contradict one another. Tuition has increased at private universities, leading to a decrease in enrollment—so far that's logical. However, revenue at these universities has continued to increase despite the decreased enrollment.

The correct answer must offer some source of revenue that more than compensates for the decrease in revenues created by the lower enrollment. That's where (D) fits in: If the tuition hikes have brought in more revenue than the loss of enrollment has taken away, then it's easy to see how both trends discussed in the stimulus can simultaneously co-exist.

(A) The frequency with which private schools increase tuition doesn't begin to explain the revenue situation in the stimulus. The relevant fact is that tuitions are increasing, which triggers the rest of argument. In what specific manner they're increasing is irrelevant.

(B) offers an irrelevant distinction between vocational schools and private colleges that doesn't contribute any new information to the stimulus. Vocational schools are outside the scope, which focuses only on the situation related to the decrease in enrollment at private colleges.

(C) tells us what happens to some students who can no longer afford private universities. Their fate, sorry to say, doesn't matter, and again it doesn't add any new information to the scenario. We already know that enrollment decreased; this choice just gives us a human-interest story when we really want to know how it's possible under these circumstances for revenues to actually increase.

(E) is similar to (B) in that it provides another irrelevant distinction. It compares the role of alumni contributions at public and private colleges, while the stimulus does not express any interest in public universities or in alumni contributions. Even if private colleges do get a larger percentage of money from alumni, decreasing enrollment shrinks the number of alumni and would, if anything, seem to decrease revenue even further, deepening the mystery but not explaining it.

A 180 test taker knows that in Explain questions, the information provided in the stimulus remains true, and that his task is to reconcile, not to change, the presented facts.

Explanation: The Meaning of Art

Distinguishing Features: Philosophers' Corner, Formal Logic, Necessary Conditions

3. E

This one is long and complicated, but the key to the right answer comes from two statements of *necessity*: Understanding the "true" meaning of art requires one to have the artist's conception; and experiencing art's power of transcendence requires an understanding of the "true" meaning. Putting these together, we know that if the scholars are right, if transcendence is realized, then someone must understand the true meaning, and therefore someone must have the same conception as the artist. This powerful prephrase is paraphrased in choice (E).

A 180 test taker uses her Formal Logic skills to provide shortcuts in tough inference questions.

(A) "Justified"? A viewer of art can come up with any meaning he wants. The question is what's necessary for him too experience the transcendental powers of art.

(B) "Personal meaning" is devalued because anyone can ascribe any old meaning to a work. What's important is "true" meaning. No matter how strong "personal meaning" is, transcendence is impossible if one's interpretation doesn't match the artist's conception.

(C) "Never"? There is no evidence here that suggests that there is at least one art scholar who is so pessimistic.

(D) is possible but not inferable. For all we know, the right viewer is out there for every work of art, in which case no work of art would fail to invoke art's power of transcendence.

Explanation: Risk to Others

Distinguishing Feature: Principle Application

4. A

The difficult part about this one is working through the principle and getting it organized in your mind. Once you do, (A) is a pretty clear violation. The pilot crash-landing in the community is placing the people there at risk; moreover, since the landing is taking place "without their knowledge," it can't be true that they are aware of the risk and consent to it. The only question that remains is: Are the people in the community being placed at greater risk by the crash-landing than they otherwise would face? Clearly, yes: it's riskier to have a plane land on your house than it is *not* to have a plane land on your house. The pilot is violating the principle in every way, and we have our answer.

A 180 test taker boils down the principle as much as possible before attempting to find the choice that conforms.

In question 4, that means recognizing a basic rule ("don't place another person at risk") that allows for two specific acceptable exceptions.

(B) Since the bomb-disposal unit is "all volunteer," we can presume that all of its members understand and accept the risks involved in disposing of bombs or mines.

(C) The people placed at risk by the inoculations are the children. Although we're told that the parents are unaware of the procedure, for all we know the children themselves are aware of the risks and consent to them. More importantly, if the students did *not* get the inoculation and risk "painful side-effects," it seems likely that they would be facing a greater risk from the "deadly disease." So (C) is in accordance with the principle; the situation presented represents one of the special cases where placing another person at risk is justified.

(D) contains a scope shift: The principle only concerns placing a person at serious *physical* risk; there's no hint that the unauthorized investments involve a physical risk to the trustees (though there may be some physical risk to the investor when the trustees find out what's going on).

(E) The government's action does not place smokers at physical risk; more likely, the action is motivated by the desire to place them at *less* risk, even without their consent.

PRACTICE SET 2

5. The recent proliferation of newspaper articles in major publications that have been exposed as fabrications serves to bolster the contention that publishers are more interested in selling copy than in printing the truth. Even minor publications have staffs to check such obvious fraud.

The above argument assumes that

(A) newspaper stories of dubious authenticity are a new phenomenon
(B) minor publications do a better job of fact-checking than do major publications
(C) everything a newspaper prints must be factually verifiable
(D) only recently have newspapers admitted to publishing erroneous stories
(E) publishers are ultimately responsible for what is printed in their newspapers

6. For exactly 10 years, it has not been legal to bungee-jump in state A. All of the members of the Rubberband Club must live in state A and have bungee-jumped at least once in the last two years. The Rubberband Club is currently taking applications for new members.

Which one of the following necessarily follows from the information provided above?

(A) Every current member of the Rubberband Club has bungee-jumped outside of state A.
(B) No current applicant to the Rubberband Club has legally bungee-jumped in state A.
(C) The current members of the Rubberband Club have bungee-jumped illegally at least once.
(D) Current members of the Rubberband Club who have never bungee-jumped outside of state A have broken the law in state A.
(E) The Rubberband Club does not include members who have bungee-jumped legally in state A.

7. If 400 or more students are enrolled for the next school year, Shady Creek Junior High School in Washburn county will be able to offer electives in psychology and economics only if additional teachers are hired before the start of the next school year. Proposition 307, if passed, would mandate that all schools in Washburn county hire three to seven additional teachers before the start of the next school year.

Which one of the following can be properly concluded from the statements above?

(A) If Proposition 307 passes, Shady Creek may be exempted from the requirement to hire additional teachers before the start of the next school year.
(B) If Proposition 307 does not pass, hiring additional teachers at Shady Creek before the start of the next school year will not allow Shady Creek to offer electives in psychology and economics during the next school year.
(C) If current students at Shady Creek show no interest in psychology or economics, Shady Creek should not look to hire additional teachers for the next school year.
(D) If fewer than 400 students are enrolled at Shady Creek for the next school year, representatives of Shady Creek should vote against Proposition 307.
(E) The passing of Proposition 307 could ensure that a condition necessary for Shady Creek to offer electives in psychology and economics during the next school year would be met.

8. A team of pediatricians recently announced that dogs are more likely to bite children under age 13 than any other age group. Their finding was based on a study showing that the majority of all dog bites requiring medical attention involved children under 13. The study also found that the dogs most likely to bite are German shepherds, males, and non-neutered dogs.

    Which one of the following, if true, would most weaken the pediatricians' conclusion that dogs are more likely to bite children under age 13 than any other age group?

    (A) More than half of dog bites not requiring medical attention, which exceed the number requiring such attention, involve people aged 13 and older.

    (B) The majority of dog bites resulting in the death of the bitten person involve people aged 65 and older.

    (C) Many serious dog bites affecting children under age 13 are inflicted by female dogs, neutered dogs, and dogs that are not German shepherds.

    (D) Most dog bites of children under age 13 that require medical attention are far less serious than they initially appear.

    (E) Most parents can learn to treat dog bites effectively if they avail themselves of a small amount of medical information.

PRACTICE SET 2: ANSWERS AND EXPLANATIONS

Explanation: Publishers and Fraud

Distinguishing Features: Just Plain Tough, Scope Shift

5. E

The distinguishing features listed above pretty much say it all. The question is just plain tough, although deceptively so—it doesn't really appear to be a difficult argument to follow. The trouble comes from the subtle shift in scope that's introduced as the argument proceeds. If you caught it, then this is a fairly doable question. If not, then you're likely to end up staring at the choices, wondering if there actually is one that's correct. The argument is based on a scope shift: The author concludes that publishers are more interested in selling copy than in printing the truth. The evidence is that many newspaper articles have recently been exposed as frauds. The assumption—that is, the necessary yet unstated premise here—is contained in (E): that publishers *know about*, or must take responsibility for, the truth of every article in their newspapers. If that's not the case, then the author cannot fairly blame publishers for the rash of bogus stories. So (E) must be assumed in order for this argument to stand.

Now, this assumption—and the scope shift that creates the need for it in the argument—may be a bit subtle; you may say, "well, of course publishers are responsible for what is printed in their newspapers."

> A 180 test taker understands that the "reasonableness" of a piece of information doesn't disqualify it from being an assumption. Any fact that's required by the argument but is not explicitly stated by the author qualifies as an assumption.

Even 180 test takers can't be expected to prephrase every right answer, and it's quite possible that even many top test takers would not have come up with this answer on their own. No matter; that's what the choices are on the page for.

> A 180 test taker recognizes the validity of an answer choice when she sees it, even if the concept contained in the choice didn't occur to her up front. Top test takers know how to let the choices help them to succeed.

Eliminating the wrong choices here may have been more than half the battle. Many people are at least able to get it down to (C) and (E).

(A) and (D) are pretty much out of left field. The conclusion doesn't have anything to do with the relative novelty of inauthentic articles (or admissions thereof), despite the tangential reference in the stimulus to "recent" proliferation.

(B) contains a distortion. Minor publications' fact-checking apparatus is mentioned in order to emphasize that the big publications ought to check too; it's not there as the basis of a quality comparison.

(C) is a popular wrong choice, but is too extreme. "Everything a newspaper prints must be factually verifiable" encompasses the movie clock, the weather forecast, today's horoscope, and *Dilbert*. The author's not peeved because *Beetle Bailey* was inaccurate, but because false stories are appearing without adequate checking. The issue isn't lies, but *willful* lies. If you proved to this author that every one of those bogus stories was thoroughly checked and published in good faith, her complaints would fade away.

Explanation: Bungee-Jumping

Distinguishing Feature: Formal Logic

6. D

This inference question is an exercise in keeping track of the many discrete Formal Logic statements given in the stimulus. Everyone in the Rubberband Club lives in state A. Everyone in the Rubberband Club has bungee-jumped at least once in the past two years. The club's still chugging along, despite the fact that it's been illegal to bungee-jump in state A for the past ten years. Even though it may seem like there's a possible contradiction in the stimulus, don't seek to resolve the seeming discrepancy; rather, remain faithful to the four primary pieces of information while searching for a proper inference.

A 180 test taker answers the question that's asked, and uses the question stem early on to set him on the right path.

(A) is too extreme. The stimulus doesn't tell us that they *can't* bungee-jump in state A, but that it's illegal to do so. While each current member must have jumped in the last two years, some of them may have broken the law and jumped away in state A for all that we know.

(B) and (E) take us too far also: It's quite possible that one or more of the current applicants (B) has taken the plunge legally in the state A ten or more years ago, before the ban was enacted. Bungee-jumping has only been illegal in state A for the past ten years, during which it's safe to infer that no member has jumped in the state legally, but current members (E) might have also done so before the prohibitive law went into effect.

(C) is yet another overly extreme option. As mentioned above, while each must have jumped at least once in the last two years, they needn't have jumped in state A; perhaps they're getting all of their kicks in another state where jumping is legal.

A 180 test taker recognizes statements that are too extreme to fit the scenario at hand. He avoids all choices that make overly generalized claims.

(D) is perfect. If they didn't jump outside of state A, then they must have jumped within state A sometime in the last two years to fulfill the club's requirements. And if they did that, then they must have bungee-jumped illegally. There are no unsupported steps in this chain of reasoning, so it's the logical inference we seek.

Explanation: Shady Creek Electives

Distinguishing Features: Formal Logic, Necessary Conditions

7. E

Here's another Formal Logic question; perhaps you were tipped off by the "if . . . only if" construction in the first sentence. "Only if" usually denotes a necessary condition, and that's what we get here. Like many inference questions, this question doesn't lend itself to prephrasing. Don't worry: You may not know exactly what the right answer will look like, but a strong grasp of the formal logic statements in this stimulus should be all that's needed to recognize the right answer when you see it. We know what the first sentence says; now, what does it *mean*? If the school has more than 400 students, then offering both electives will require hiring more teachers; that is, extra teachers will be necessary for offering the electives under these circumstances.

A 180 test taker paraphrases statements and doesn't simply parrot the stimulus. He knows that understanding the passage on his own terms is the key to most questions.

A rule like this—and we *can* simply look at it as a rule, just like the kind we find in Logic Games—is very specific; it tells us one thing in particular, and leaves open many possibilities that we simply don't know anything about. For example, can we deduce anything if *fewer* than 400 students are enrolled? No, which incidentally kills (D) right off the bat. We can do the same with the next sentence. If 307 passes, then Shady Creek will hire more teachers. What if it *doesn't* pass? Who knows . . . which means we can chop (B) as well.

A 180 test taker immediately recognizes what she can't infer from a statement.

At this point, we're better off using our understanding to put the remaining choices through their paces. We've already axed (B) and (D). As for the rest:

(A) 307's passage would lead to the fulfillment of a requirement, not an exemption from that requirement.

(C) "Should"? The stimulus is purely descriptive, and does not go into evaluation or prescription. The stimulus deals with what's required for offering electives, and what's mandated if a proposition passes. What Shady Creek should *look to do* is not inferable here. And that leaves only (E):

(E) If 307 passes, we know that extra teachers will be hired, which means that the necessary condition for offering electives would be satisfied. It may not be as strong a statement as the other choices, but it's a valid inference and therefore gets the point.

Explanation: Dog Bites

Distinguishing Features: Scope Shift, Study, Numbers and Statistics

8. A

There sure are a lot of things going on in this question, which touches on a number of the logical elements we've been discussing. We don't have to look far for the conclusion; it's restated right in the question stem: Dogs are more likely to bite children under age 13 than any other age group. The evidence is found in the second sentence dealing with the findings in the study. The last sentence expands on the study, but essentially adds nothing of value to the logic of the stimulus; it's basically "filler" material.

So what's the scope shift? The conclusion is about dogs biting children under 13, but the evidence is based on dog bites *requiring medical attention*. (A) weakens the argument by addressing this scope shift. It basically says that many dog bites that *don't* require medical attention (bites that are within the scope of the conclusion) happen to people *over* 13. Now, this doesn't *disprove* the argument; it merely weakens the link between the stated evidence and the stated conclusion. The pediatricians counted up all the people bitten by dogs who came in for medical attention, found most of them to be under age 13, and concluded *from this alone* that dogs are more likely to bite children under age 13. This general conclusion is based on evidence about a very specific group. If it's true, as (A) says, that many who don't seek treatment are over 13, then the argument is weakened.

A 180 test taker has a sure-fire method for spotting scope shifts. She asks herself: (1) What's the focus, subject, or scope of the conclusion? (2) What's the focus, subject, or scope of the evidence? (3) Are they the same?

(B) We're not concerned with the results of the dog bites, only the frequency of bites by age group. Even if everyone over 65 who's bitten dies, it could still be true that children under 13 are most likely to be bitten.

(C) is a takeoff on the filler sentence—once again, it's the sheer number of bites that's important, not the kinds of dogs inflicting them.

(D) Same thing—the number of bites, not the seriousness of them, is the issue.

(E) is irrelevant; what *can* happen plays no role in the study and the conclusion based on it.

PRACTICE SET 3

9. Tsumi bats are a rare breed of omnivorous bat found only in highly temperate climates. Most Tsumi bats living in captivity develop endocrine imbalances from their normal zoo diets, which consist mostly of fruits and berries. The healthiest way to feed the bats, therefore, is to provide them primarily with nuts, grubs, and vegetables and only minimal amounts of fruits and berries.

Which one of the statements below does NOT reflect an assumption upon which the argument depends?

(A) Those who care for Tsumi bats in captivity should avoid feeding them diets that produce endocrine imbalances.

(B) Tsumi bats living in captivity will not be malnourished on diets that contain minimal fruits and berries.

(C) Tsumi bats living in captivity will consume diets that consist of nuts, grubs, and vegetables but no fruits or berries.

(D) Tsumi bats living in captivity will be adequately nourished on a diet that consists primarily of nuts, grubs, and vegetables.

(E) For Tsumi bats living in captivity, no health problem stemming from diets consisting mostly of nuts, grubs, and vegetables would surpass in severity the health problems associated with endocrine imbalances.

10. Movie pirating, the illegal videotaping of a new theater release and subsequent selling of the tape on the black market, is a major concern to the film studios that produce today's mainstream movies. When pirating sales are high, individual studios whose movies are being taped and sold illegally lose a large amount of revenue from black market viewers who would otherwise pay the full theater price. A low level of pirating sales during a specific period, however, is a fairly reliable indicator of an economic downturn in the movie industry as a whole during that period.

Which one of the following, if true, most helps to reconcile the discrepancy noted above?

(A) The film studios that produce today's mainstream movies occasionally serve as distribution outlets for smaller budget independent films that are also susceptible to pirating.

(B) Movie piraters exclusively target blockbuster hits, the existence of which is inextricably tied to the financial success of the movie industry during any given period.

(C) Most movie piraters use small, handheld video cameras that are specially designed to record images in the darkened environment of a movie theater.

(D) The five largest film studios take in a disproportionate amount of movie revenue compared to hundreds of smaller and independent film studios, regardless of whether pirating activity during a specific period is high or low.

(E) A movie pirater who is highly active in selling movies on the black market can sometimes make a full living doing so, while a less active pirater will usually have to supplement the income generated from pirated movies.

Questions 11–12

No one who listened to the debates and thought that the Democrat argued more convincingly than the Republican is a registered Republican, but some of them intend to vote for the Republican candidate anyway.

11. If the statements above are true, which one of the statements below must also be true?

(A) No one who thought the Republican argued more convincingly than the Democrat intends to vote for the Republican candidate.

(B) No one who heard the debates is a registered Republican.

(C) Some of those who intend to vote for the Republican candidate thought the Republican argued more convincingly.

(D) Not everyone who intends to vote for the Republican candidate is a registered Republican.

(E) Everyone who thought the Democrat argued more convincingly than the Republican is a registered Democrat.

12. If it is also true that all those who thought the Democrat argued more convincingly than the Republican are registered Democrats, which one of the following must be false?

(A) No registered Republicans intend to vote for the Democrat.

(B) Some registered Republicans intend to vote for the Democrat.

(C) No registered Democrats intend to vote for the Republican.

(D) Some registered Democrats thought the Republican argued more convincingly than the Democrat.

(E) Some of those who thought the Democrat argued more convincingly than the Republican intend to vote for the Democrat.

PRACTICE SET 3: ANSWERS AND EXPLANATIONS

Explanation: Tsumi Bats

Distinguishing Feature: Odd Man Out

9. C

Four valid assumptions in the answer choices? The stem itself prepares us to expect a pretty weak argument. Our job is to locate the statement that's not assumed in the argument. The author concludes that, to achieve maximum health, Tsumi bats should be fed certain nuts and veggies and a minimum amount of fruits and berries. The evidence comes in the second sentence: These bats, who are now fed mostly fruits and berries, develop endocrine imbalances. It's not worth the effort to try to prephrase all the assumptions inherent in this argument, but if a few ideas jumped out at you, great. At the very least, you should proceed to the answer choices with a clear understanding of the evidence and conclusion.

(A) is a valid assumption. The author suggests that the bat's endocrine imbalance is a problem, and that a revised diet might fix that problem. Thus the argument does assume that bats should not be fed endocrine imbalance-producing foods.

(B) and (D) are valid assumptions too. If the proposed diet will make the bats "healthiest," then the argument assumes that it will adequately nourish them (D) and that it won't malnourish them (B). Negate these choices and the argument falls apart, confirming that these are necessary assumptions here.

> A 180 test taker confirms whether a statement is a necessary assumption in an argument by seeing what happens to the argument when that statement is denied or negated. If the argument crumbles, that's proof positive that the statement is necessary and thus must be assumed.

(C) The conclusion states that the bats will be fed a minimal amount of fruits and berries, while this choice says that they will eat none. Must that be a necessary part of this argument? No, it's too extreme: The author says straight away that some fruits and berries is okay, so it need not be assumed that the bats are denied these foods altogether. (C) is therefore our winner—our "odd man out."

> A 180 test taker reads the answer choices extremely carefully and notices even very subtle inaccuracies.

Here, (C) is correct because it discusses a diet with "no" fruits and berries instead of "minimal" fruits and berries.

(E) focuses again on the author's claim that the recommended diet will make the bats healthiest. If that is true, then the author must assume that it won't create any health problems that are more detrimental to the bats' health than the endocrine imbalances that inspired the proposed diet in the first place.

Explanation: Movie Pirating

Distinguishing Feature: Just Plain Tough

10. B

Nothing fancy here; just a difficult paradox to resolve. Our first task is to understand the discrepancy. The author tells us that a high volume of pirating sales causes studios to lose a great deal of money. However (a "contrast" keyword which signals the discrepancy in the stimulus), a low volume of pirating sales generally indicates a period of economic weakness in the movie industry.

> A 180 test taker keys in on structural signals that illuminate the author's purpose. Words like "but" and "however" indicate contrast and are especially important because they signify that a twist is upcoming.

Why does a low level of pirating sales, which would seem to benefit the industry, actually signal a period of economic weakness in the industry? This is the question that we need to answer, so let's proceed to the answer choices.

(A) doesn't address the issues involved in the discrepancy, focusing as it does on whether these studios distribute smaller films.

(B) is correct because it creates a direct connection between pirating and the financial success of the entire industry. If pirating is related exclusively to big hits, then a low level of pirating signals a lack of blockbuster hits, in which case it's more understandable how a low level of pirating would correspond to periods of economic downturns in the industry.

(C) is off base, focusing as it does on the methods of pirated tape production and not on the connection between pirating and the economic health of the movie industry.

(D) is similarly off base, since it offers a comparative analysis between the largest and not so large studios, which isn't a comparison relevant to the original discrepancy.

(E) gives us information about the profitability of selling pirated movies, which may be interesting but doesn't explain why low pirating sales would signal an economic low point in the entire movie industry.

> A 180 test taker identifies the primary issues involved in complex discrepancy questions, and then searches for a choice that addresses those issues while eliminating choices that violate that scope.

Explanation: Democrats and Republicans

Distinguishing Features: Formal Logic, Tough Choices

11. D

Occasionally Formal Logic is tested in particularly nasty ways. In this relatively short blurb we get two formal statements telling us about three groups of people, and it's certainly not easy keeping it all straight. The first group comprises those who found the Democrat more convincing. We're told that not one person in this group falls into the second group, the group of people who are registered Republicans. So far, then, we have those two mutually exclusive groups, with no person overlapping. The third group comprises those who intend to vote for the Republican. We know that some of the people in this group are also members of the first group. That is, there are people who found the Democrat more convincing, and who nonetheless intend to vote for the Republican. And since we know these people are not registered Republicans, we know that (D) is correct: Some who intend to vote for the Republican are not themselves registered Republicans. It's a bit circuitous, but it all adds up to the deduction in (D).

A 180 test taker uses his Logic Games skills wherever they may apply on the LSAT, and one good place is in Logical Reasoning Formal Logic questions.

We included this one in the "Tough Choices" category because all of the choices sound alike, which is a common feature in strict Formal Logic questions. Here's how those pan out:

(A) and (C) are out because they draw inferences about those who found the *Republican* more convincing. We are told nothing about such persons, and therefore cannot infer anything about them.

(B) infers that no registered Republicans heard the debates. That's not necessarily true. Many may have heard the debate, just so long as they found the Democrat *less* convincing than, or only *equally* convincing as, the Republican.

(E) is out because although those who were more convinced by the Democrat are not registered Republicans, it does not necessarily follow that they are registered Democrats. They may be independents, or they may not be registered at all.

12. C

As if this Democrat-Republican business isn't bad enough as it is, now the plot thickens.

The second question of the pair adds the new information that all those who found the Democrat more convincing are registered Democrats. This information is added because it is *not* inferable, and seeing it here may have tipped you off to the fact that choice (E) in the previous question was incorrect, had you not thought so earlier.

A 180 test taker, whenever possible, uses information provided in questions to help him deal with later questions.

Since most LR questions are independent entities, the opportunity to reuse information from previous questions rarely presents itself in this section, although we do see a case of it in this question. (This strategy applies much more often in the Logic Games and Reading Comprehension sections, since each game and passage is accompanied by a question set, which allows for much greater interplay between questions.)

With this new information included, we're asked to recognize the statement that must be false. Let's take them in order and see which one contradicts the total scenario.

(A) and (B) speak of registered Republicans. (A) concludes that none of them intend to vote for the Democrat, whereas (B) concludes that some intend to vote for the Democrat. Since we don't know whether anyone intends to vote for the Democrat, either could be true.

(C) says that no registered Democrats intend to vote for the Republican, and this is the statement that must be false. Since, according to the question stem, all of those who found the Democrat more convincing are registered Democrats, and some who found the Democrat more convincing intend to vote for the Republican, there must be at least one registered Democrat who intends to vote for the Republican.

(D) suggests some registered Democrats found the Republican more convincing. Perhaps; there's nothing to prevent this from being true.

(E) There's no reason under these circumstances why some who found the Democrat more convincing couldn't intend to vote for the Democrat. All we know for sure regarding voter intentions concerns votes for the Republican.

A 180 test taker, when faced with a "must be false" question, asks herself: "Could this be true?"

PRACTICE SET 4

13. Peacocks with spectacular plumage are almost always free of parasites. While the naive might conclude that a brilliant display of feathers somehow provides a defense against parasites, the evidence shows that the peacocks with parasitic infections are rarely capable of maintaining spectacular plumage.

The pattern of reasoning displayed in the argument above is most closely paralleled by that in which one of the following arguments?

(A) Corporations that reimburse employees for educational expenses are almost always profitable. The X Corporation reimburses its employees for educational expenses, but it also produces superior products.

(B) Almost every student in the honors program at Overton High School wears a tie to school each day. Therefore, it is certain that school uniforms enhance academic achievement.

(C) The best-selling cars are almost always reliable and moderately priced. However, since measures to guarantee reliability always increase production costs, the most reliable cars are probably not bestsellers.

(D) Candidates endorsed by the *Post-Dispatch* are almost always elected to office. However, endorsement by the *Post-Dispatch* does not influence the electorate one way or the other, as the *Post-Dispatch* only endorses candidates that are strongly favored to win.

(E) Household electricity use is at its highest in the summer, when there are more daylight hours. While longer days do contribute to increased demand for electricity, the increased use of air conditioners in the summer is known to be a more significant factor.

14. Our conception of our self-interest shapes and influences our behavior, from the sentences we utter to the actions we undertake. As a result, we can see that this self-interest is not the product of ethics, for ethics alone cannot influence our behavior. Our conception of our self-interest necessarily determines our behavior, at least in part, influencing us to act in some way and not in another. Ethics alone, on the other hand, has no such power.

Which one of the following points to an assumption the author makes in the argument above?

(A) If our conception of our self-interest is not the product of ethics, it will have a detrimental influence on our behavior.

(B) If our conception of our self-interest were the product of ethics, then ethics would have some influence on our behavior.

(C) If our conception of our self-interest is not the product of ethics, the standards of proper conduct will be more difficult to derive.

(D) If our conception of our self-interest influences our behavior, it is unreasonable to act on our self-interest.

(E) If ethics influences our behavior, immoral acts would decrease.

<u>Questions 15–16</u>

Center director: The number of volunteer applications for our elderly care center has doubled over the past five years. This clearly shows that community members are taking a greater interest in working with their aging parents.

Nurse: Unfortunately, my research indicates that just the opposite is true. If you look closely at our records, applications from patients' family members have decreased by 20% over the past five years. This would indicate that, contrary to your conclusion, community members' interest in working with their elderly parents has actually decreased.

15. If the statistics cited by both the center director and the nurse are correct, which one of the following must be true?

   (A) The center has had a decline in its patient population over the past five years.
   (B) The quality of care provided to patients at the facility has improved over the past five years.
   (C) The center has received volunteer applications from individuals who are not related to patients at the center.
   (D) The cost of maintaining adequate staff to care for the center's patients has risen enough to warrant the need for additional volunteers.
   (E) Only a small percentage of all the people who apply to volunteer at the center actually assume volunteer positions.

16. Which one of the following, if true, would most seriously weaken the nurse's argument?

   (A) Many community members living near the center have moved into newly constructed housing developments on the outskirts of town.
   (B) Over the past five years, center funding for family-oriented activities has decreased significantly.
   (C) Volunteering in elderly care facilities requires training for which most individuals do not have the time.
   (D) Due to a recent change in policy, many family members who volunteer at the elderly care center do not fill out formal applications.
   (E) The time commitment required by volunteers at elderly care centers is relatively modest compared to other volunteer opportunities in the region.

PRACTICE SET 4: ANSWERS AND EXPLANATIONS

Explanation: Peacock Plumage

Distinguishing Features: Parallel Reasoning, Causation

13. D

The stimulus presents a correlation found in some peacocks: beautiful plumage and being parasite-free. The "naive" believe that the former causes the latter, but the author indicates that only parasite-free peacocks can maintain beautiful plumage. Remind you of the reasoning of someone you know—Cornaro, for instance, in the Nietzsche example back in chapter 9? Same thing. Or how about the weakener to the argument in "Trauma Victims," the first question in this chapter? Yet another example of reversing cause and effect. Here, we can summarize the argument in the stimulus like so: Beautiful plumage doesn't lead to being parasite-free; rather, being parasite-free is a precondition for having beautiful plumage. Which choice mimics this? (D)'s the one: The newspaper's endorsements don't improve anyone's chance of winning. Instead, having a strong chance of winning is a precondition for receiving the endorsement. In all of these arguments, we're forced to confront the possibility that a stated causal relation may actually work the other way around.

(A) proceeds from a general correlation (reimbursement policy and profitability) to a specific case about the specific X Corp. The original did not do so.

(B) proceeds from a correlation (honors program and uniforms) to the claim that the latter cause the former. This is closer to the "naive conclusion" cited in the stimulus than the author's actual logic.

(C) begins with a correlation between three factors: sales, reliability, and price. On that ground alone you can reject it. Plus, (C) goes on to suggest a tradeoff between two factors (reliability and price) which has no parallel in the original.

(E) concedes that the number of daylight hours has a causal impact on electricity use, whereas the original explains why plumage does not cause peacocks to be parasite-free. Also, (E) brings in a supplementary "more significant factor" influencing electricity use, unlike the original, which sticks to parasites and plumage.

A 180 test taker meticulously analyzes every facet of Parallel Reasoning answer choices, and immediately tosses the ones that deviate in even the slightest way.

Explanation: Self-interest, Ethics, and Behavior

Distinguishing Features: Philosophers' Corner, Tough Choices

14. B

This one, laden with abstract conceptual issues such as "self-interest" and "ethics," falls squarely into the Philosophers' Corner category. In addition, we can designate the choices as tough since they all sound fairly alike and are all formulated as conditional statements, beginning with the hypothetical "if." Such things in the context of an Assumption question usually make for a difficult time. But Assumption questions are often about connecting the dots, and we can make our task easier by sorting out the evidence from the conclusion and looking for the missing link between them. The argument can be summed up as follows: Self-interest influences our behavior (evidence), and " . . . we can see that" (a strong conclusion signal) this self-interest is not the product of ethics (conclusion). Why not? "For (note the structural signal "for," meaning "since") ethics alone cannot influence our behavior" (evidence).

A 180 test taker uses structural signals to determine the function of an argument's components.

The author continues: Conception of self-interest determines some part of behavior, but ethics does not. This last part is merely intended to reinforce the conclusion that self-interest doesn't come from ethics. But just repeating the evidence for the conclusion doesn't establish it; the case is still not fully made. Just because ethics has no bearing on something (behavior) that self-interest does influence, doesn't mean we can rule out any possible connection between ethics and self-interest. The missing piece that would make the conclusion valid is found in choice (B). The author must assume that if self-interest came from ethics, then ethics would influence behavior, in order to disregard the connection between ethics and self-interest based solely on the fact that ethics does not influence behavior. It's a little roundabout, and made more complex by the factors cited above, but (B) contains the necessary piece of information that completes this puzzle of an argument.

(A) Exactly *how* self-interest influences behavior is beyond the scope of the argument, which is concerned simply with the fact that it does influence behavior. Nothing need be assumed regarding any detrimental, or for that matter, beneficial influence.

(C) How difficult it is to derive proper conduct—presumably, in this context, that means to set ethical standards—is also beyond the scope of the argument, so nothing about that need be assumed here.

(D) The circumstances in which it is proper to act on our self-interest are not discussed in the passage, so (D) need not be assumed in order for this argument to stand.

(E) We're told flat-out that ethics does not influence our behavior, so what the effect on morality would be if they did has nothing to do with the line of reasoning.

A 180 test taker knows that a choice dealing with superfluous issues cannot contain an assumption required by the argument.

Explanation: Elderly Care Center

Distinguishing Features: Numbers and Statistics, Alternative Explanation

15. C

Here's an interesting use of statistics. Usually, when stats are bandied around in a two-person dialogue, the question deals with how one or both disputants botch or misinterpret them. That's, in fact, a bit of what we get in next question, where we're asked to weaken the nurse's argument. But in this question, we're to assume that both the director's and the nurse's statistical assertions are correct, and we need to find the choice that must be true based on both facts presented. So let's have a look at the stats in question. Over the past five years, the elderly care center has seen an increase in its applications from volunteers—the director says they've almost doubled. The nurse points out, however, that applications from patients' family members have actually decreased by 20%. If overall applications have increased, but family members' applications have gone down, what can we infer? (C) provides a logical deduction—that the center is receiving applications from volunteers who are not patients' family members. Think of it this way: If the clinic received no applications from persons who were not related to patients, then the statistics cited would not make sense.

(A) does not necessarily follow from the statistics in the passage. The statistics concern volunteer applications, not the size of the patient population. The data that we're given about the volunteer applications tells us nothing about the patient population one way or another.

(B) might be tempting, but does not provide us with the inference we need. Based on the statistics given, we cannot know whether patient care has improved or not. We're told that the number of volunteer applications has increased, but we don't know whether the number of accepted volunteers has grown—and we certainly don't know whether the volunteers are providing *better* care to the patients.

(D) Again, we cannot be sure that this statement is true, simply based on the passage. It may be the case that the center needs more volunteers—but we don't know that definitively. We merely know that more people are interested in volunteering. This doesn't necessarily mean that the extra volunteers are *needed*, and it tells us nothing about *why* they might be needed if they are.

(E) is again beyond the limits of what we can infer here. We are told that the number of applications has increased and that the number of applications from family members has decreased. But that's all that we're given. This is not enough information to tell us anything about the selection process for volunteers—for all we know, every person who applies may actually become a volunteer.

A 180 test taker sticks to the facts, and realizes that just as important as understanding what we can tell from the facts is understanding what we cannot tell from them. In tough questions, that allows her to eliminate wrong choices.

---

16. D

Next we're asked to find a statement that weakens the nurse's argument. Before we can choose a weakener, we must first isolate the nurse's conclusion and evidence. The nurse concludes that the director's interpretation is wrong, and that community members are less interested in working with their parents than they were five years ago. She bases this conclusion on one piece of evidence: that applications from patients' family members have decreased over this time period. To weaken the argument, we might find another explanation for why volunteer applications from family members are down. (D) provides just such an alternative: If family members are no longer required to fill out formal applications, their applications will obviously not be on file, which could easily explain the 20% decrease. But they may continue to volunteer just the same. (D), if true, would weaken the nurse's argument considerably.

A 180 test taker thinks "alternatives and assumptions" when faced with weakening an argument. Chances are that the right answer will relate to at least one of these two mechanisms.

(A) doesn't affect the nurse's argument one way or the other, because it refers to "community members" in general. We do not know if these community members are volunteer applicants, or if they are related to the elderly at the center. This choice provides irrelevant information.

(B) touches on the issue of family activities, but it doesn't tell us anything about the center's volunteers. Like (A), it neither strengthens nor weakens the nurse's argument because it doesn't address the reason why family member applications are down.

(C) might be tempting, because it provides another reason—other than lack of interest—for why an individual might not volunteer. The problem with (C) is that it addresses individuals in general, and makes no distinction between family members and nonfamily members. Even if (C) is true, the fact remains that family member applications are down, and (C) does nothing to damage the conclusion that the nurse bases on that fact.

(E) If anything, this choice might serve to strengthen the nurse's argument. If the volunteer commitment is relatively not extensive, this might reinforce the notion that relatives don't volunteer because they lack interest. Whether we see it as a slight strengthener or not, (E) contains nothing that weakens the argument.

PRACTICE SET 5

17. Membership in the Theta Delta Psi fraternity is easily obtained by those who have previously had strong social connections with existing fraternity members before college. However, one must have attended high school with one or more of the members in order to forge such strong social connections. People who lack these social connections because they have not attended high school with one or more current fraternity members will therefore find it difficult to join the fraternity.

This argument displays flawed reasoning because it neglects to consider the possibility that

(A) many of those who went to high school with Theta Delta Psi fraternity members did not themselves become members of the fraternity

(B) it is more important in the long run to socialize with nonfraternity members than to develop strong connections with fraternity members

(C) it is more difficult to forge social connections with fraternity members than with non-fraternity members

(D) one may easily obtain membership in the fraternity through means other than having strong social connections with existing fraternity members

(E) some current members of the fraternity did not go to high school with other members

18. Many international correspondents believe that the formation of opposing political parties within country X demonstrates that the president of country X no longer retains absolute control over the government. However, if the president had lost his grip on power, he would no longer be able to censor the local media. Since the media in country X uniformly reflect the views of the president, the president must have retained his power to censor, and thus these international correspondents must be mistaken.

The argument in the passage proceeds by doing which one of the following?

(A) arguing that since censorship of the media is against a state's long-term interests, external action will be required to bring about a revolution in country X

(B) concluding that since an event occurred under one set of circumstances, that event can be expected to occur under all similar circumstances

(C) arguing that since two sets of circumstances are mutually exclusive and exhaust all possibilities, exactly one must have occurred

(D) concluding that since an expected result of an event did not take place, the event itself did not occur

(E) arguing that since the evidence supporting a claim is balanced by evidence weakening that claim, more information is required to make a proper judgment

19. A wave of incidents of unusual violence, from murder to acts of self-destruction, plagued the small medieval town for a period of five years, nearly wiping out the population. At the same time, there was an unusual shift in the area's weather pattern. Rainfall was so heavy and continuous that the wheat crop probably fell prey to the ergot fungus. When eaten, grain thus affected can cause ergotism, a disease associated with hallucinations and other disturbing psychological side effects. In the end we can conclude that the violence was the result of freakish weather conditions.

Which one of the following is the most effective rebuttal to the contention made above?

(A) It is based upon a series of plausible suppositions rather than upon contemporary evidence.
(B) No clear distinction is drawn between cause and effect.
(C) Explanations of historical events cannot be convincing when too great a role is assigned to chance or the irrational.
(D) The author makes no distinction between probable occurrence and actual occurrence.
(E) Such crucial terms as "unusual violence" are not adequately defined in regard to the specific historical event.

20. A study found that last year roughly 6,700 homeless people in the United States were admitted to hospitals due to malnutrition. In the same year, a little more than 7,200 nonhomeless people were admitted to hospitals for the same reason. These findings clearly show that the nonhomeless are more likely to suffer from malnutrition than are the homeless.

The answer to which of the following questions would be most likely to point out the illogical nature of the conclusion drawn above?

(A) What is the relative level of severity of the malnutrition suffered by each group cited in the study?
(B) To what extent, on average, are the nonhomeless better off financially than are the homeless?
(C) To what extent are the causes of malnutrition in the nonhomeless related to ignorance of proper dietary habits?
(D) What percentage of each group cited in the study suffered from malnutrition last year?
(E) What effect would a large increase in the number of homeless shelters have on the incidence of malnutrition among the homeless?

PRACTICE SET 5: ANSWERS AND EXPLANATIONS

Explanation: Fraternity Membership

Distinguishing Features: Formal Logic, Necessary and Sufficient Conditions

17. D

Did you have trouble isolating the logical feature at work here? The formal logic element present is extremely subtle, but is nonetheless the key to the question. The argument begins by offering one route through which a student can gain a coveted membership to the Theta Delta Psi fraternity. For those aspirants who attended high school with a current member of the house and developed a strong social connection with that member before college, entrance into the fraternity is easy. People who didn't attend high school with a current member can't easily attain membership through this route, but we were never told that this was the *only* way to easily get into the fraternity. The author concludes that the unconnected individuals will have difficulty joining the fraternity, but that's only valid if the route the author describes is the only possible easy route. But the author never says that. (D) thus gets at the major point the author fails to consider in issuing her hasty conclusion: the possibility that there might be other ways to easily get into the frat. In "necessary/sufficient" lingo, the social connections described are *sufficient* to easily get one into the frat, but nowhere does the author state or imply that such connections are actually *necessary*; maybe there are other means of easy entry.

(A) First of all, those who attended high school with fraternity members are not necessarily the same people who have forged strong social connections with them. So the "many" referred to here may not even be relevant to the argument. Secondly, even assuming these guys *are* good high school buddies of the members, the author argues about only what conditions make for easy entry into the frat, and need not consider the possibility that many high school classmates of the members would choose not to join.

(B) Associations with nonfraternity members are not relevant to the argument and fall outside of its scope. Additionally, this choice discusses the long-term benefits of such connections; we only care about entrance into the fraternity, not about lifelong happiness.

(C) The relative difficulty of building these connections has nothing to do with their necessity for membership. This choice also shares with (B) an interest in nonfraternity members, whom the author never mentions.

(E) is perfectly consistent with the author's argument, as it totally avoids the issue of the ease with which these "current members" got in. This choice falls outside of the author's scope, which is about the possibility of getting into the fraternity with ease, and we therefore can't fault the author for neglecting the possibility raised here.

A 180 test taker always pays close attention to author's topic and scope.

In this question, choice (D) is the only one to address the difficulties of obtaining membership; most of the others fall outside of that scope.

Explanation: Presidential Control

Distinguishing Features: Tough Choices, Formal Logic

18. D

While there is a touch of Formal Logic present in this one, it's in fact not crucial to picking up the point. Still, it's good practice to recognize and understand formal logic statements when you see them.

A 180 test taker sees the LSAT as an integrated whole, and brings all her skills to bear on every question. It doesn't matter if certain insights turn out to not be required in a particular instance; it doesn't hurt to know too much.

The statement "if the president lost control, then he would no longer be able to censor the media" is essentially a simple "if A, then B" statement. The correct implication of this is that if the president is able to censor the media, then he must not have lost control. The last sentence, which contains the author's conclusion, plays off of this logic. Since the media's views are in line with the president's, the author concludes that correspondents who assert that the president has lost power are wrong. The formal logic element is thus entirely self-contained, and we're not asked about *it*, per se. And here's another difficulty with this question: The argument is actually flawed, but we're not asked about that, either. (Did you catch the flaw? Just because the media reflect the president's views doesn't necessarily establish that he's maintained power of censorship; perhaps they all just think alike.) So there's formal logic in here, but we're not asked to crunch through that. And there's a subtle logical flaw, but recognizing that doesn't get us the point, either. Rather, we're asked about what the author is *doing* in the argument; that is, about the author's method of argument. And here's where the final difficulty lies—in the choices. They're mostly dense and abstract, consisting of phrases like "one set of circumstances . . . similar circumstances" and "mutually exclusive." But if we hang in there and compare the choices piece by piece to the argument, it's not too bad.

(A) Huh? The state's "long-term interests" are outside the scope.

(B) and (C) start off okay, or at least not obviously wrong, but the reference to "all similar circumstances" in (B) has no relation to the action of the stimulus. And (C) says that *exactly one of two events has occurred*, whereas this conclusion is more definite. That's enough to chop that one.

(D) is the winner. An "event" that may or may not have occurred (the president losing power) is connected to an expected result that would have taken place if the event in question *did* occur (loss of the power to censor the media). Since this expected result didn't happen, the author argues that the event itself didn't happen; that is, that the president did not lose power. (Note that even that is not stated explicitly, but is implied by the conclusion that the commentators are wrong.) It's a little tricky, but it does match the situation in the stimulus.

(E) What balancing evidence? That's just not there.

A 180 test taker cuts past abstract language and is not swayed by impressively worded phrases.

Explanation: The Case of the Poison Grain

Distinguishing Features: Causation, Scope Shift

19. D

This passage tells a story similar to the anonymous fable of the poison grain, in which all of a kingdom's grain crop is mysteriously poisoned, causing anyone who ate it to go insane. The author describes a wave of unusual violence that swept over a medieval town for a period of five years, characterized by acts ranging from self-destruction to murder. That's followed by a description of a chain of events, beginning with an unusual shift in weather patterns that coincided with the violent period. Due to unusually heavy rainfall, the wheat crop probably fell prey to the ergot fungus, which can cause ergotism, a disease characterized by hallucinations and other psychological abnormalities. The author then concludes that the violence was caused by ("was the result of") the freakish weather conditions. There's the element of causation alluded to above.

A 180 test taker recognizes causation in the all of the various ways in which it is suggested by the wording of arguments.

When presented with a causal argument—especially when looking for a rebuttal to that argument—the first thing to do is check to see that the causal mechanism described is appropriate. The author blames the unusual acts of violence in the town on ergot fungus. However, he doesn't know for a fact that the ergot fungus was present in the town's wheat. He knows conditions were ripe for the formation of the fungus (i.e., lots of rain), and he knows fungus-infected wheat *can* cause psychological disturbances—but the crucial point, the actual presence of the fungus, is mere supposition. (Note how the author says that the wheat crop "probably" fell prey to the fungus.) As (D) points out, the conclusion treats the probable occurrence of the fungus as if it were a certain, actual occurrence. And therein lies the scope shift as well; the author argues from probability in the evidence to a clear-cut, definite statement of actual causation in the conclusion. In arguing against this reasoning, it would be perfectly appropriate to point out that the author misses the distinction described in (D).

(A) Contrary to (A), the argument does use contemporary evidence: the shift in the area's weather patterns at the time of the incidents of violence.

(B) Actually, the author *does* set up a clear chain of cause and effect—rain causing fungus which causes psychological abnormality. The causes and effects are perfectly distinct; the question is whether the causal mechanism described is *valid*.

(C) distorts the argument, since no role at all is assigned to the chance or irrational in causing the psychological disturbances.

(E) The term "unusual violence" is reasonably well defined as involving acts of murder and self-destruction so pervasive as to endanger the town's very survival. We really can't ask for a more comprehensive definition than that.

Explanation: Homeless, Nonhomeless, and Malnutrition

Distinguishing Features: Numbers and Statistics, Study

20. D

The LSAT test makers have an incredible knack for writing short, unassuming arguments that nonetheless pack a major wallop. This one's an example of this type. It's one of the shortest arguments you'll see, and it doesn't even contain any difficult words, but it sure gives people fits—and that's because of the statistics involved. It goes to show that it really doesn't take much more than a few well-placed statistics to, shall we say, liven things up. The first thing you might have noticed is that the argument contains both numbers and statistics. The 6,700 and 7,200 figures represent actual numbers of people, while the conclusion states what's "more likely" to happen—a clear reference to an element of probability. Knowing from the stem that the argument is fatally flawed, this should have already raised a red flag. Here's the specific lowdown: Since only 6,700 homeless people suffering from malnutrition were admitted to U.S. hospitals last year, compared to 7,200 nonhomeless people, the nonhomeless must be more likely to suffer from malnutrition. Perhaps the argument immediately struck you as a little wacky, as it well should have given the clues in the question stem.

A 180 test taker is suspicious whenever she sees raw numbers side by side in an argument with rates, percentages, or probabilities—and even more so in a Logical Flaw question.

We're asked to find a question whose answer would most effectively illuminate the problem with the argument, and, as strongly suggested above, this boils down to a numbers versus percentages game: We cannot figure the odds of suffering from malnutrition solely from the number of malnourished people in each group. We must also know the overall total number of people in each group before we can create ratios and thus figure out the "likelihood" of suffering from this condition. The only way for this conclusion to be valid is if the total number of homeless people in the United States was close to or greater than the total number of nonhomeless people. Then, the 7,200 hospitalized nonhomeless, as opposed to the 6,700 hospitalized homeless, would suggest that the nonhomeless are more likely to suffer from malnutrition. But this is clearly a ludicrous assumption (at least at the present time)—there's no way the number of homeless comes close to the number of nonhomeless people in the United States. The answer to the question in the correct choice will somehow point this out, thus making the flaw in the reasoning (using raw numbers as the basis for a conclusion about likelihood) plain to see. Choice (D) provides the question whose answer would provide the information we need to correctly understand the odds. Since the United States has far fewer homeless people than it has people with homes, the 6,700 figure would form a far higher percentage of homeless people who suffer from malnutrition than the percentage of nonhomeless people based on the 7,200 cases of malnutrition among this group. The answer to this question would allow us to see how the raw numbers cited do not support the author's counterintuitive conclusion that the nonhomeless are more susceptible to malnutrition than are the homeless.

(A) goes beyond the scope of the argument. The argument involves the likelihood of suffering from malnutrition, not the relative levels of severity.

(B) also introduces a new issue—finances. No matter how much people with homes are better off financially than are the homeless, the fact remains that more nonhomeless than homeless were hospitalized for malnutrition, and the answer to this question would do nothing to reveal the illogical conclusion that's drawn from this data.

(C) introduces another new issue. The argument draws no conclusion about the causes of malnutrition within these groups, only about the likelihood of malnutrition. Nailing down the precise causes of malnutrition in one of the groups wouldn't change the numbers in the evidence nor point out the problem with the logic.

(E) is irrelevant to the argument as presented: The future possibility of remedying homelessness to some degree does not impact upon these numbers and this particular conclusion drawn from them. The reasoning still seems off, but the answer to the question will not show how the logic goes astray.

PRACTICE SET 6

21. The plastics commonly used in household garbage bags take, on average, 100 years to decompose in landfills. From an environmental standpoint, the plastic bag industry should be forced to switch to newly developed plastics, which begin to decompose after only 20 years.

Which one of the following pieces of information would be most helpful in evaluating the argument above?

(A) the rate of growth or decline in sales of plastic garbage bags

(B) the number of plastic garbage bags sold last year that eventually wound up in landfills

(C) the feasibility of enforcing legislation that regulates the plastics used in garbage bags

(D) the length of time it takes the newly developed plastic to fully decompose in landfills.

(E) a comparison of the production cost of one bag made with the old plastics and of one bag made with the new plastics

22. Superintendent: Teachers in our district must refrain from intervening in student conflicts in order to encourage students to hone their social interaction skills, except for cases in which physical violence is involved.

Which one of the following is an application of the Superintendent's principle of teacher intervention?

(A) A gym teacher watches while students break up a fistfight between the players of two teams that was ignited over a disputed call.

(B) An English teacher takes the side of one student in an argument concerning a school locker, and sends the other student to the principal's office.

(C) A parent instructs her child who is having difficulty getting along with certain schoolmates to work it out on his own.

(D) A philosophy teacher instigates a heated debate between students holding radically different opinions on a controversial topic.

(E) A math teacher allows a group of students to tease another student about her new haircut.

23. A useful philosophy, unless conceived simply as a means of indulging its creator's ego, is incomplete unless it interprets major recent historical events and offers specific prescriptions for the future. Ernesto's philosophy Neo-Futurism is full of advice on how to live in the world of the future, but makes no mention of the invention of atomic energy or the dawning and ramifications of the computer age, two of the most significant events of the twentieth century. Therefore, one can only conclude that Ernesto's philosophy is incomplete.

Which one of the following is an assumption on which the argument relies?

(A) The prediction of future events is the central tenet of Ernesto's philosophy.

(B) Ernesto's philosophy includes no other elements besides discussions of the past and prescriptions for the future.

(C) Ernesto's prescriptions for the future are unrealistic.

(D) Ernesto's philosophy was not conceived simply as a means of indulging his ego.

(E) Ernesto's philosophy includes no interpretations of current trends.

24. Some companies calculate the number of employee vacation days based strictly on the employee's length of service to the company, while other companies use the employee's position in the company hierarchy as the sole basis for determining vacation days. All other companies take both factors into consideration. Since Cathy and Joe have different positions in the hierarchy of CMA Inc., but receive the same number of vacation days per year, CMA Inc. must therefore base its vacation policy partly or fully on length of service.

The pattern of reasoning in which one of the following is most similar to that in the argument above?

(A) In figure skating competitions, a contestant's total score is based on independent scores in the categories of technical merit and artistic expression. For this reason, if two contestants receive different scores in technical merit, yet finish with the same total score, then they must have received different scores in artistic expression.

(B) A company with high revenue may be profitable, and a company with low expenses may be profitable, but the likelihood of profitability increases significantly if a company has both high revenue and low expenses. Therefore, a business seeking to maximize profitability should attempt to increase revenue whenever reducing expenses is impossible.

(C) On days when Sheila has early morning classes, she wakes up at 7 A.M. However, on days when she has only afternoon classes, or no classes at all, she always wakes up at 10 A.M. Since Sheila woke up at 7 A.M. this morning, she must have early morning classes today.

(D) Car rental charges are influenced by either the number of days a car is rented, the distance traveled during the time of rental, or a combination of both. Therefore, if a customer is charged the same amount for two different cars rented from the same car rental agency, yet kept each car for a different number of days, then part if not all of the charge associated with renting a car from that specific agency must be attributed to distance traveled.

(E) The Rapido Shipping Company bases its package delivery prices on at least one, and sometimes both, of two factors: package weight and speed of delivery. Therefore, if the company's shipping foreman quotes identical cost estimates for two packages that have identical weights, it must be because he believes that the amount of time that it will take to deliver the two packages will be the same.

PRACTICE SET 6: ANSWERS AND EXPLANATIONS

Explanation: Landfill Plastics

Distinguishing Feature: Scope Shift

21. D

Some questions test nothing more than whether you've recognized a scope shift, and this one falls into that category. The question stem complicates matters, however, and requires a bit of translation. A piece of information that would help us evaluate the argument is essentially a piece of information that would strengthen or weaken the argument. The right choice will need to have one of those effects in order for us to be able to say that this argument is good or bad. In other words, the operative question one has to ask to test each choice is: "Does this help me pass judgment on the argument?"

> A 180 test taker interprets question stems in light of what they tell him to do with or look for in the passage.

Now, if you picked up on the scope shift, then you would have known that the right choice will somehow address it. The shift is subtle, but definite, and perhaps if you didn't see it up front on your own, you would have recognized the shift when you came to correct choice (D). The author argues for the switch to the new plastics, but takes no account of the fact that there's a difference between 100 years *to decompose* and 20 years to *begin* to decompose. The newly developed plastic takes only 20 years to *begin* to decompose, but we need to know how long it takes for it to *fully* decompose in landfills before we can pass judgment on the argument. Only then would we be able to compare the new plastics to the current bags. (D) provides this information and is therefore correct.

(A) and (B) present irrelevant issues. We're trying to evaluate whether the change from one plastic to another is environmentally beneficial. Neither of these pieces of information helps us to differentiate between the environmental impact of the old vs. new bags.

(C) Whether or not the industry will be able to switch over to and legally maintain the new plastic bags is outside the scope. The question is whether or not it *should*.

> A 180 test taker understands that when an argument is based around the notion that something "should" be done, whether or not it "can" be done is logically irrelevant.

(E) offers up an irrelevant distinction. The argument is made from an environmental standpoint; the cost per bag has no logical bearing on this.

Explanation: Teacher Interventions

Distinguishing Feature: Principle Application

22. E

In order to apply a principle, the first step is to have a very strong grasp of the principle as the author originally presents it. The Superintendent argues that teachers should not intervene in student conflicts except when violence is involved. The Superintendent therefore provides a general rule and offers one definite exception to it. The argument also contains a justification of this hands-off policy: it hones student interaction skills. It's pretty much impossible to prephrase an answer to such a question, so once you have a solid grasp of the principle presented, proceed to the answer choices, looking for the one that best conforms. And remember—every element of the correct choice must match up with the tenets of the principle.

(A) presents a hands-off gym teacher, but the teacher's non-involvement contradicts the stimulus' principle by not intervening even though violence is involved. Since violence justifies intervention, the situation in (A) doesn't accord with the principle in the stimulus.

(B) presents a teacher intervening in a dispute that is not clearly defined as violent. We therefore can't tell whether it demonstrates the original principle or not.

(C) is outside of the author's scope, which specifically concerns *teachers'* intervention in student conflicts. Parents have no role in the principle as it is originally presented, so they can't be centrally present in a situation that applies that original principle.

(D) Generating debate in philosophy class seems like a fully justifiable teaching activity. This is not the type of student conflict toward which the principle is geared, especially when it is instigated *by* a teacher. The principle simply doesn't apply to the situation in (D).

(E) While we may pity the student with the new 'do, this is the right choice because it precisely follows the rules of the Superintendent's principle. The teacher does not intervene in a clearly nonviolent (teasing doesn't suggest violence) student conflict situation. Perfect.

> A 180 test taker recognizes that principle questions are often similar to inference questions—in both types, the right answers are strictly consistent with the information in the original argument.

Explanation: Ernesto's Neo-Futurism

Distinguishing Feature: Formal Logic

23. D

Don't be fooled by the use of the word "philosophy" in the first sentence—this is not a Philosophers' Corner type of problem, as the stimulus is really not that difficult to understand. Rather, we have a Formal Logic problem on our hands (signaled by the word "unless"), albeit a subtle one at that. A useful philosophy—*unless* conceived simply for ego's sake—is *required* to have two elements. Ernesto's philosophy has one requirement covered (he's got advice for the future), but comes up short on the second (he neglects important recent historical events). So is his philosophy incomplete? If his philosophy is intended to indulge his ego, then he's excused from the dual requirement, and therefore Neo-Futurism would be off the hook. The problem with the argument, as it stands, is that the conclusion is formulated as if the entire "unless" clause in the beginning didn't exist. So (D) the notion that this philosophy was *not* conceived merely to stroke Ernesto's ego—must be assumed in order for the conclusion "Ernesto's philosophy is incomplete" to stand.

A 180 test taker understands that single words (especially when they're powerful Formal Logic words like "unless") can radically alter the meaning of a text. These words are always important, but sometimes, the entire point hinges on them.

(A) First of all, "prescriptions for the future" in the stimulus is not the same thing as "predictions of future events" here in (A); the former speaks to what should happen, the latter to what *will* happen. But even if these were the same, there's no requirement that this be the central tenet of the philosophy.

(B) So what if Neo-Futurism is chock full of other meaningful (or not) platitudes? There's no reason to assume that these are the only elements of his philosophy.

(C) Unrealistic? Nothing in the argument touches on the *value* of Ernesto's work, so this needn't be assumed.

(E) is not necessary for this argument to work. Including interpretations of current trends wouldn't damage the argument, since "interpretations of current trends" is different from "interpretations of major recent historical events." In any case, discussing the latest fad wouldn't save Neo-Futurism.

Explanation: Vacation Days

Distinguishing Features: Parallel Reasoning, Scope Shift

24. D

The sheer length makes this one fairly intimidating, but recognizing how the scope shifts between the conclusion in the stimulus and the conclusion of some of the choices helps to eliminate a good number of choices right off the bat.

A 180 test taker does not allow the length of a question to overwhelm him, but rather looks for ways to cut the text down to size.

Let's rephrase the action of the stimulus and put it into general terms. We're told that either one factor (length of service), another factor (hierarchical position), *or a combination of both*, brings about a specific result (number of vacation days). Already, recognizing this "one or the other or both" scenario allows us to eliminate choices that don't contain this same element, and we'll see some choices drop like flies in just a bit. (D), however, conforms: Number of days rented, distance traveled, *or both* contribute to a car rental charge. The conclusions of the stimulus and (D) match perfectly as well. If two different situations have the same result (Cathy and Joe have the same number of vacation days/two rentals cost the same), but are different according to one of the considerations (different hierarchical positions/different number of days traveled), then the other consideration (length of service/distance traveled) must have been a factor in the result.

(A) lacks the element of "one or the other or both" present in the stimulus. Since all skating scores are influenced by both factors, it's not possible for a skating score to be entirely determined by one factor alone, as opposed to the stimulus, which does allow for this possibility.

(B) can be eliminated solely on the basis that its conclusion concerns what a business *ought* to do in the future, which has no parallel in the original. Also, the stimulus applies a general rule to a specific example, whereas (B) does not.

(C) lacks the element of two factors working in combination. In the case of Sheila, it's either one or the other; she can't possibly wake up at 7 and at 10 on the same day.

(E) has two factors working alone or in combination, but shifts the scope of the conclusion. The original states that one consideration (length of service) must have been a factor in the policy decision, whereas (E) makes a decision concerning what the foreman *believes*, which has no parallel in the original. Also, the conclusion in (E) concerns the particular packages, whereas the conclusion in the original concerns the general policy adopted by the company.

A 180 test taker faces down even the hardest of Parallel Reasoning questions by comparing conclusions and eliminating choices containing conclusions that don't match that of the original.

In this case, the scope shifts of the conclusions in (B), (C), and (E) are enough to disqualify these choices.

PRACTICE SET 7

25. If Larry studied harder, he would have more confidence in his abilities. He would feel better about himself, and he would be glad that he had made the decision to study harder. His whole outlook on school would improve. Clearly, then, Larry's increase in study time will lead to increased confidence.

Which one of the following arguments contains flawed reasoning that most closely parallels the flawed reasoning in the argument above?

(A) If voters were to research our candidate's background, they would understand why she is the best person for the job. She has made great strides in the area of human rights, she has lowered taxes, and she has improved our school system. Clearly, therefore, if voters make a well-informed choice, they will probably choose our candidate.

(B) If students with difficulties in specific subject areas seek tutoring, they will probably improve. Tutoring also allows superior students to review their own work while helping classmates to learn. Tutoring leads to overall scholastic improvement. Thus, all schools should implement tutoring programs.

(C) If television were made more educational, more parents would approve of it. Parents would recommend programs for their children, and let them choose their own viewing patterns. Their entire opinion of TV would be revised. Obviously, therefore, a rise in educational programming will lead to an increase in parental approval of television.

(D) If historians want to know how people lived, they should stage reenactments of historical events. They would learn more about customs, while coping with some of the same hardships that historical personages had to cope with. Therefore, reenactments are one of the most powerful tools that historians can use.

(E) Obviously we should pay more attention to the effects of workplace pollutants on our employees. Not only will the number of insurance claims rise if we continue to ignore health hazards, but we will also be faced with an increasing number of lawsuits. Clearly, therefore, we should form a committee to investigate the sources of workplace pollutants.

26. Kopke: In the past 10 years, most of the new clothes that I have purchased have fallen apart within a few short years. However, all of the clothes that I have purchased at vintage clothing shops are still in excellent condition, despite the fact that they were all over 30 years old at the time that I bought them. Clearly, clothes are not manufactured as well today as they were when those vintage clothes were made.

Which of the following is a weakness in the argument above?

(A) It fails to demonstrate that the clothes manufactured 30 years ago were of higher quality than clothes of all other eras.

(B) It neglects the possibility that the clothes of 30 years ago, when prices are adjusted for inflation, cost more than clothes manufactured today.

(C) It confuses the number of clothing items sold with the proportion of those items that are no longer useful.

(D) It does not explain why clothing manufacturing standards have fallen over time.

(E) It fails to take into account clothes made over 30 years ago that are no longer fit for sale.

27. A man cannot lie unwittingly. He is not properly a liar who, while thinking he speaks truly, utters a falsehood. He may be said to be in error, and this perhaps because his will to know has overstepped the boundary of his reason; yet such a man does not lie, for knowledge of the falsity of one's assertions is essential to the act of lying. Thus, when the ancients propounded ridiculous notions concerning the nature of the heavenly bodies, they did not lie, as a proper understanding of celestial phenomena was not within their grasp.

Which one of the following best describes the argument in the passage above?

(A) The argument attempts to draw a false conclusion from an inaccurate definition by using an analogy.

(B) The argument draws a conclusion about the past from evidence about the present.

(C) The argument denies a proposed effect by first denying its proposed cause.

(D) The argument uses a specific definition as evidence, and draws a conclusion from the definition.

(E) The argument concludes the truth of a general principle from evidence about one instance of the principle.

28. The overall rate of emphysema has declined 15 percent over the last 15 years in region A. During that period, the total cost of care for emphysema sufferers in region A, after accounting for inflation, declined by 2 percent per year until eight years ago, at which time it began increasing by approximately 2 percent per year, so that now the total health care cost for treating emphysema is approximately equal to what it was 15 years ago.

Which one of the following best resolves the apparent discrepancy between the incidence of emphysema in region A and the cost of caring for emphysema sufferers?

(A) The overall cost of health care in region A has increased by 7 percent in the last 15 years, after accounting for inflation.

(B) Improvements in technology have significantly increased both the cost per patient and the success rate of emphysema care in the past 15 years.

(C) About seven years ago, the widespread switch to health maintenance organizations halted overall increases in health care costs in region A, after accounting for inflation.

(D) The money made available for research into the causes and cures of emphysema had been declining for many years until approximately eight years ago, since which time it has shown a modest increase.

(E) Beginning about nine years ago, the most expensive-to-treat advanced cases of emphysema have been decreasing in region A at a rate of about 5 percent per year.

PRACTICE SET 7: ANSWERS AND EXPLANATIONS

Explanation: Larry's Studying

Distinguishing Features: Parallel Reasoning, Circular Reasoning

25. C

This is not just a search for a similar argument, but also a search for an argument similarly flawed. Since the author is trying to assert that if Larry studied harder, he would have more confidence, the evidence should back this up by showing how studying leads to confidence. Instead, the evidence (Larry is feeling better about himself, is glad he decided to study more, and has a better outlook) are effects caused by the increased confidence—which, lo and behold, is the conclusion the author is trying to establish. In other words, the conclusion is being used to set the evidence in motion; the evidence and conclusion are for all intents and purposes, identical. This is precisely how we described circular reasoning earlier. So we can make our lives easier in this lengthy intimidating Parallel Reasoning question by simply searching for the choice that also contains circular reasoning. (C)'s the winner: If TV were made more educational, more parents would approve, but the first piece of evidence (parents recommending programs for their kids) depends on parents approving of TV.

(A) Although this sales pitch may not work on everyone, the reasoning is certainly not circular. Also, the word "probably" in the last sentence makes the argument more qualified, whereas the conclusion in the original is stated in more absolute terms.

(B) is similar to the original in content, dealing as it does with students and tutoring, a form of studying. But the reasoning couldn't be more different; in fact, it's not flawed at all. The merits of tutoring seem plausible, and the conclusion seems justified based on the evidence. No flaw, no parallel.

A 180 test taker is not fooled by Parallel Reasoning choices written about the same subject matter as the original. This is an old trick of the test makers, intended to catch those who are not aware that they are to mimic the structure, not the content, of the stimulus.

(D) Perhaps there is a slight flaw here, in that the evidence doesn't fully support the conclusion, which is worded very strongly in the last sentence. But not any goofy choice will do. The correct answer has to be goofy in the same way as the original, which in this case means it must be circular. Here, the evidence may be insufficient, but it's not identical to the conclusion.

(E) is not circular either. It begins by concluding that something needs to be done, and ends with a specific recommendation for how to go about it.

Explanation: Kopke's Vintage Clothing

Distinguishing Features: Alternative Explanation, Scope Shift

26. E

The stem alerts us to the fact that there's a flaw afoot, so we should expect something in Kopke's speech to get all fouled up. In more official LSAT lingo, that simply means that the evidence won't adequately support the conclusion. And what is that conclusion? Kopke maintains that clothes manufactured 30 years ago were constructed better than clothes manufactured today. His evidence is that clothes he's purchased within the last 10 years have fallen apart, while the clothes he bought in vintage shops are all in excellent shape despite their age. This might sound persuasive so far, but we know from the stem that this is a flawed argument. Think about where Kopke's logic goes astray. For one thing, he compares all the clothes he's bought within the last 10 years to only the clothes that have *survived* 30 years before he purchased them. That's a subtle shift, but a shift nonetheless. The correct answer should point out the dubious nature of this comparison, and indeed, choice (E) points out the inappropriateness of this kind of comparison. The only "vintage" clothes he takes into account are those that have proven to be extremely durable. So it isn't much of a surprise that they're still functional. Kopke doesn't consider the clothes made long ago that have fallen apart, so he can't evaluate the overall standards of that era. Comparing only the extremely durable vintage clothes to all modern clothes is like comparing apples and oranges, so choice (E) gets to the heart of the flaw here. It suggests an alternative explanation for the "favorable" comparison that Kopke relies on in forming his conclusion.

(A) The argument doesn't address all eras, so Kopke doesn't have to compare the clothes made 30 years ago with those of every other era.

> A 180 test taker doesn't fault an author for failing to do something he's not logically obligated to do.

(B) Kopke's argument does not address cost at all—just quality. Considering cost would not affect the validity of the argument.

(C) Kopke doesn't take into account vintage clothes that are no longer fit for sale (see choice (E) above), but he never equates the proportion of tattered clothes with the total number of clothing items sold. So choice (C) doesn't describe a weakness in the argument.

(D) The argument doesn't hinge on explaining why standards have fallen, just that they have.

> A 180 test taker notes the scope of the argument from the get-go, and immediately discounts choices that violate it.

Explanation: Liar, Liar

Distinguishing Features: Philosophers' Corner, Tough Choices

27. D

The answer choices in Method of Argument questions are often laden with abstraction, and the subject matter here—a discussion of what constitutes lying—is no picnic, either. The argument begins with a wordy expression of the idea that one cannot lie without being aware that one is lying. In other words, "lying" is defined in such a way that only people who *know* that they are not telling the truth can be considered liars. On the other hand, those who make incorrect statements without knowing that what they say is false are merely in error. In order to lie, then, you must be aware that you aren't telling the truth. This definition of lying is then used as evidence to draw the conclusion that the "ancients," who said erroneous things about the moon and planets, weren't lying. Why not? Because they couldn't know that what they said was false. Thus the argument uses a specific definition of lying as evidence to draw a conclusion about the ancients. (D) therefore offers the best description of this argument.

(A) is incorrect because irony is never used in the argument. Nor is it acceptable to consider the author's definition "incorrect" or her conclusion "false." (A) is little more than a judgment, and not a very objective one at that.

(B) goes astray in that the author's evidence is a general, presumably timeless, principle. It is not evidence about "the present."

(C) would describe this argument as one dealing with cause and effect. Yet there is no cause and effect at work here. The argument concerns whether or not it is legitimate to consider ancient stargazers "liars." And it proceeds from the *definition* of "lying."

A 180 test taker understands a logical mechanism such as causation to the point of knowing perfectly well when that mechanism is not employed. She uses her understanding of such logical elements to both pick out correct choices and eliminate wrong ones.

(E) has it backwards. The argument uses a general principle (in this case a definition) as *evidence*, not as a conclusion. And the one instance of this principle (the ancient stargazers) is the argument's *conclusion*, not its evidence.

Explanation: Emphysema Rates and Costs

Distinguishing Features: Numbers and Statistics, Alternative Explanation

28. B

On the LSAT, "apparent discrepancy" is just another way of saying "paradox," and here it is: Despite the fact that the rate of emphysema has declined 15 percent within the past 15 years in region A, the cost of caring for emphysema sufferers in the region is now roughly equal to what it was 15 years ago. In other words, the decline in the percentage of emphysema sufferers has not been accompanied by a corresponding decrease in the cost of treating such sufferers. Without trying to predict what might resolve this discrepancy, let's look to the answer choices for some sort of explanation.

A 180 test taker attempts to prephrase answers whenever possible, but knows when it's best to let the choices do some of the work for her.

(A) deals with the overall cost of health care in the region, which goes beyond our concern with one particular category of costs: the money spent on emphysema sufferers. Thus, knowing that the region's overall health care costs have increased doesn't help to explain what's going on with the cost of emphysema care in particular.

(B) addresses both parts of the paradox and does help to explain it. If improved technology has increased the cost of caring for emphysema sufferers, then a decline in sufferers wouldn't necessarily yield a decrease in costs, since the cost per patient would increase. Also, if the technology worked, then there would be fewer sufferers. This technology would thus decrease the overall incidence of emphysema without necessarily decreasing the costs attending such care. A perfect explanation for the passage's surprising result.

(C) tells us that the region's overall health care costs haven't really increased in the past seven years, which, if anything, would only heighten the paradox. After all, the stimulus informs us that the costs of emphysema care *have* increased in the past eight years. After reading this choice, we still don't know what might account for that.

(D) doesn't connect the dots enough to really help. It only contributes to explaining the paradox if we assume that the research funds which have recently increased have actually been used, and then assume that the "modest increase" in such funds would counteract the savings offered by the decline in the rate of emphysema sufferers. (D) doesn't tell us this much.

(E), like (C), would if anything only exacerbate the problem: If the most expensive cases are becoming more rare, why hasn't the cost of caring for emphysema sufferers declined?

A 180 test taker expects some choices in Paradox questions to deepen the mystery at hand.

PRACTICE SET 8

29. All of the business seminars offered by Speakers-R-Us cost more than $1,000, while all of the personal achievement seminars offered by this company cost less than $1,000. Most of the seminars offered by Speakers-R-Us are over two hours in length. All of the seminars offered by a rival seminar company, Consultant Connection, are under two hours in length and cost less than $1,000. The Brookdale Community Center presents the seminars of these two companies only, and presents only seminars that cost less than $1,000. Last Sunday, The Brookdale Community Center presented the business seminar "Taking Corrective Action."

If the statements above are true, which one of the following must be true on the basis of them?

(A) The Brookdale Community Center does not present seminars on any other topic besides business and personal achievement.

(B) "Taking Corrective Action" is under two hours in length.

(C) "Taking Corrective Action" is a seminar offered by Speakers-R-Us.

(D) The Brookdale Community Center does not offer personal achievement seminars.

(E) All of the seminars offered by Speakers-R-Us are longer than any seminar offered by Consultant Connection.

30. Sarrin monks practice the Pran meditation technique only when extremely damaging weather conditions confront the farming villages surrounding Sarrin monasteries. Pran meditation is a more highly disciplined form of the ritual meditation that the monks practice daily, and involves unique practices such as isolation and fasting.

Which one of the statements below does NOT follow logically from the passage above?

(A) Some meditation practices are less disciplined than Pran meditation.

(B) Pran meditation among Sarrin monks does not take place according to a precisely regulated schedule.

(C) The ritual meditation that a typical Sarrin monk practices daily does not take place in an atmosphere of isolation.

(D) Monks practice some types of meditation in response to threats faced by the local population.

(E) The ritual meditation that Sarrin monks practice daily is largely undisciplined.

31. History has shown that severe and sudden political instability strikes country Y roughly once every 50 years. The most recent example was the attempt on the president's life in 1992. The reaction of average investors in country Y to crisis situations in the country cannot be predicted in advance. The government's fiscal affairs department has introduced an electronic protection mechanism into the stock market of country Y in the hopes of avoiding a prolonged large-scale selloff. The mechanism is triggered in specific instances based on estimations of how average investors will react to changes in corporate data and economic indicators.

If the statements above are true, which one of the following conclusions can be drawn regarding the electronic protection mechanism?

(A) Sometime within the next 50 years an attempt on the president's life will trigger the protection mechanism.

(B) Whether the protection mechanism will function appropriately in response to a sudden political event depends on whether the event is seen by investors as positive or negative.

(C) It is unclear how well the protection mechanism would work in the event of a sudden political coup if such an event is partially or wholly unrelated to changes in corporate data and economic indicators.

(D) There would be no way for the protection mechanism to differentiate between market fluctuations resulting from economic factors and those that are caused by political instability.

(E) The protection mechanism would be purposely destroyed by political insurgents if they were able to infiltrate the government's fiscal affairs department.

32. Poor health is best understood as merely a symptom of deeper spiritual problems. Therefore, the only way to improve a patient's physical health is to address that patient's spiritual well-being. While this conclusion has been met with unrelenting criticism from the medical establishment, consider this: Since the only way to remedy poor health is to address spiritual well-being, then other methods relied upon by the medical establishment are useless in promoting good health.

    The reasoning in the argument is flawed because it

    (A) presupposes what it sets out to prove
    (B) overlooks the possibility that some members of the medical establishment might also be practitioners of "alternative medicine"
    (C) is based on premises that are inconsistent with each other
    (D) bases its conclusion on an attack on the character of members of the medical establishment
    (E) relies on experts outside of their area of expertise

PRACTICE SET 8: ANSWERS AND EXPLANATIONS

Explanation: Speakers-R-Us
Distinguishing Feature: Formal Logic

29. B

We're given loads of information on the nature of the seminars offered by two different companies, and then have to figure out the deal with the seminar actually offered at a community center. "All," "most," and "only" give away the formal logic element in this one; there's no doubt that interpreting and combining statements will be the way to go. In fact, this one's almost like a mini Logic Game, with each of the statements in the stimulus representing rules. Our job, accordingly, is to make deductions.

So how did you do? As we've said before, the best place to start a complicated Formal Logic question is with the most concrete piece of information given, which in this case is the fact that the Brookdale Community Center presented a business seminar. ("Taking Corrective Action"? Sounds kind of ominous, no?) What other formal logic statements mention either the BCC or business seminars? Well, we're told that the BCC presents only seminars from the two companies, and only seminars costing under $1,000. All the business seminars from Speakers-R-Us cost more than $1,000. We can combine these conditions to deduce that "Taking Corrective Action" must have been offered by Consultant Connection. Is that one of the choices? Ha! Maybe in any easier question, but certainly not in the questions contained in this book of challenge material. However, in general, it does pay to look.

A 180 test taker uses any skills gained in her LSAT preparation wherever they may apply on the rest of the test. In Logic Games, top test takers scan the choices as soon as they discover a new deduction, and they do the same in Logical Reasoning questions that structurally resemble Logic Games challenges.

No, we're not there yet, but this deduction certainly leads us to the point. All Consultant Connection seminars are under 2 hours, which brings us squarely to choice (B). It takes a few steps, but you're used to that from Logic Games, right?

(A) is too broad. The BCC is restricted to the two companies mentioned, not to the two topics mentioned.

(C) On the contrary. As we deduced, "Taking Corrective Action" must have been offered by Consultant Connection.

(D) is possible only. Either company could offer personal achievement seminars at the BCC.

(E) would be true if *all* of the Speakers-R-Us seminars are more than 2 hours, but we only know that most are over 2 hours, which leaves open the possibility that some S-R-U seminars are shorter than those of Consultant Connection.

Explanation: Pran Meditation

Distinguishing Features: Odd Man Out, Formal Logic

30. E

Since we need to find the one choice which *isn't* an inference, we should keep careful track of the boundaries around the argument. That way we'll be better prepared to spot what *isn't* there. The author begins by noting that the Sarrin monks use Pran meditation only in cases of severe weather. The author then explains the differences between Pran meditation and ritual meditation. Understanding the differences will likely be key to getting this question right. Pran meditation is different from ritual meditation because it's more highly disciplined and uniquely involves isolation and fasting. Thus there are three specific ways in which Pran meditation is different from ritual meditation. Let's go to the choices.

(A) The author states that Pran meditation is more disciplined than ritual meditation, so (A) must be true. Since we have one example of a less disciplined form of meditation, we can rightfully infer that *some* practices are less disciplined. The formal logic element in this one comes into play thanks to the word "some" here and in choice (D), as well as the "only" in the stimulus.

> A 180 test taker understands that on the LSAT, the word "some" strictly means "one or more."

(B) The monks practice Pran meditation only when there's severe weather and, since weather isn't precisely scheduled, then Pran meditation must not be precisely scheduled either. Sure, that's an inference.

(C) If Pran meditation involves the *unique* practice of isolation, then no other meditation, including ritual meditation, involves isolation. This is therefore also inferable from the passage.

(D) Again, "some" means "one or more," so since the monks practice Pran meditation in response to local weather threats, then some types of meditation do in fact exist as a response to local threats.

(E) is correct because, even though the author implies that ritual meditation is *less* disciplined than Pran meditation, that doesn't mean that it's UNdisciplined. (E) takes us beyond what the passage supports, so it's not a valid inference and is therefore the correct answer here.

> A 180 test taker has a keen eye and ear for distortions of the passage text.

Explanation: Market Protection Mechanism

Distinguishing Features: Just Plain Tough

31. C

The president of country Y is sure having a harder time of it than the president of country X in question 18. The president of X has solidified control with the media under his wing, while this one's being shot at. No matter. The real issue here is this electronic market regulation gizmo that's supposed to help the country avoid a major economic disaster. Our job is to draw a conclusion about it.

Once again, there's a lot going on here, so let's recap: Roughly every 50 years, country Y experiences political instability. The reaction of average investors to such crises cannot be predicted. Country Y has created an electronic protection mechanism for its financial market that relies on estimates of how average investors will react to changes in corporate data and economic indicators. The purpose of the mechanism is to avoid a major market selloff. The correct answer will draw an inference that logically connects the different ideas stated in the evidence. It's difficult to prephrase the correct answer here, so your best bet is to test the choices rigorously, looking for the one that absolutely must be true.

(A) goes too far in its inference that an attempt on the president's life will happen within 50 years. The 1992 attempt was only an example of the political instability that occurs roughly every 50 years, and the 50-year period was an average, not an absolute limit. Furthermore, even if there is an attempt on the president's life, it is unclear how investors will react because their behavior in such situations cannot be predicted in advance. For all we know, the market will go up and the mechanism will not be needed.

(B) goes beyond the scope of the argument. Whether investors perceive sudden political events positively or negatively isn't mentioned in the stimulus, so we can't infer that that perception makes any difference to the accuracy of the mechanism.

(C) draws a reasonable conclusion based on the evidence. If political instability involves changes in corporate data and economic indicators, then the mechanism should work the way it is designed to work. But if the incident does not involve those elements, then the way the mechanism will work becomes unclear, because the behavior of investors will be unpredictable.

(D) The statement in (D) goes too far to be inferable here. The mechanism might be able to differentiate between various types of market fluctuations, even though it might not be able to trigger appropriate responses to some of them.

(E) takes the argument far beyond its original scope. Nothing in the stimulus leads to a prediction of what might happen to the protection mechanism in the event of political instability.

Explanation: Poor Health and Spirituality

Distinguishing Feature: Circular Reasoning

32. A

It's funny, isn't it, how an argument can sound persuasive, yet not really say anything at all? To understand why this is an example of circular logic, consider what follows "Consider this": Other methods are ineffective because improving spirituality is the only effective method. In other words, other methods are ineffective because other methods are ineffective. Hello? We are given no independent evidence to the effect that the spiritual approach works and others don't; thus, the author is assuming (instead of providing evidence) that that method works (addressing spiritual well-being is "the only way to remedy poor health") in order to prove that it works. This is what (A) is saying. "Presupposes what it sets out to prove" is just a fancy way of accusing the author of employing circular logic.

(B) "Unrelenting criticism" of alternative treatment still leaves open the possibility that some doctors practice or approve of it, so the author doesn't overlook the possibility in (B). But even if the author *had* overlooked that possibility, (B) wouldn't describe a flaw in the argument. If anything, a crossover between members of the medical establishment and practitioners of alternative medicine would tend to rebut the "unrelenting criticism" from that medical establishment.

(C) Nothing in the argument is self-contradictory. How could it be? The evidence and conclusion are functionally identical.

(D) No doctors are maligned in the course of this argument.

(E) The argument doesn't rely on any outside expertise at all—just on the author's unsupported claims.

A 180 test taker understands that wrong choices in Flaw questions often wrongly accuse the author of doing something he hasn't done, or wrongly fault the author for failing to do something he isn't logically obligated to do.

PRACTICE SET 9

33. Julia: No one knows exactly how the Russian wheat aphid made its way to the United States, but it has caused tremendous damage to certain crops around the country. If the aphid continues to infest these crops, then this damage will be irreparable.

Hector: So we can save those crops just by stopping the aphid infestation.

Which one of the following statements is consistent with Julia's claim but not with Hector's claim?

(A) The aphid infestation is stopped and the crops suffer irreparable damage.

(B) The aphid infestation continues and the crops suffer irreparable damage.

(C) The aphid infestation is stopped and the crops do not suffer irreparable damage.

(D) The aphid infestation is kept under control but not stopped and the crops do not suffer irreparable damage.

(E) The aphid infestation is kept under control but not stopped and the crops suffer irreparable damage.

34. General: The commander of the Air Force has recommended that we deploy the G28 aircraft in the reconnaissance mission, because the G28 can fly lower to the ground without being detected and could therefore retrieve the necessary information more efficiently than the currently stationed D12. But the D12 is already in the area and poised for takeoff, and would have just enough time to accomplish the mission if deployed immediately, while the G28 would require four days just to arrive in the area and get outfitted for the mission. Since the mission's deadline is immovable, I am forced to overrule the commander's recommendation and order the deployment of the D12.

Which one of the following is assumed in the general's argument?

(A) The quality of information retrieved from the mission would be higher if the D12 were deployed than if the G28 were deployed.

(B) By the time the G28 arrived in the area and was outfitted for the mission, the D12 would have already completed the mission if deployed immediately.

(C) The ability of an aircraft to fly low to the ground is not a significant consideration when choosing aircraft for a reconnaissance mission.

(D) It would take longer for any aircraft not currently in the area besides the G28 to arrive in the area and get outfitted for the mission.

(E) Any time saved during the mission due to the operation of the more efficient G28 would not offset the additional time required to deploy the G28.

35. If foods that require refrigeration are not kept at the proper temperature, they can become fertile environments for the growth of bacteria that invariably cause food poisoning in those who ingest it. Since the number of customers stricken with food poisoning at the Panhandler Restaurant rose significantly last month, the Panhandler must have served food that was not stored at the proper temperature.

    Which one of the arguments below contains flawed reasoning similar to that in the argument above?

    (A) Men over 65 with high blood pressure are at high risk for heart disease. Men over 65 from the Tonare tribe do not have high blood pressure, so they must not be at high risk for heart disease.

    (B) Magelli is the only cabinetmaker who could have crafted a cabinet similar to this one. But the records show that Magelli died 15 years ago. This cabinet must therefore be a copy.

    (C) PaintAll paint is sold at Decorator Outlet stores. PaintAll paint is very popular among housepainters because of its brilliant pigment and its stain-resistant finish. Therefore, Decorator Outlets must sell more cans of PaintAll than any other kind of paint.

    (D) Relief-O! is a new pain reliever that has been known to cause blurred vision in some people who take it. When Molly took a pain reliever last week to relieve a migraine headache, she experienced a bout of blurred vision. So the pain reliever Molly took last week must have been Relief-O!

    (E) If tigermint is allowed to grow out of control in a garden, it can overrun other plants and kill them. Sally recently noticed that a number of plants in her garden looked better than ever. Clearly, her tigermint problem must be under control.

36. Psychologists who wish to have one of their book reviews nominated for the prestigious *Boatwright Psychology Review* award should not submit book review articles that review more than three books at a time. This is because editors for the *Boatwright Psychology Review* will not publish a book review article if it is too lengthy and cumbersome to read. In their submission guidelines, the editors explicitly state that review articles that cover more than three books at a time are considered too lengthy and cumbersome to read.

    Which one of the following statements represents an assumption upon which the argument above depends?

    (A) The books review article that covers the most books must be the lengthiest and most cumbersome article to read.

    (B) If a book review article is published in the *Boatwright Psychology Review*, that article will receive the prestigious *Boatwright Psychology Review* award.

    (C) All articles published in the *Boatwright Psychology Review* must be limited to a certain length specified by the editors.

    (D) The *Boatwright Psychology Review* editors generally prefer book review articles that cover one book rather than two books.

    (E) To be nominated for *Boatwright Psychology Review* award, a psychologist's book review article must be published in *Boatwright Psychology Review*.

PRACTICE SET 9: ANSWERS AND EXPLANATIONS

Explanation: The Russian Wheat Aphid

Distinguishing Features: Formal Logic, Necessary and Sufficient Conditions, Tough Choices

33. A

Here's a dialogue question, and both speakers, whether they know it or not, are employing a form of formal logic. And the choices are difficult because they all present various combinations of the same terms—quite easy to confuse if you're not paying careful attention. According to Julia, the mysterious Russian wheat aphid is devastating crops around the country, and here comes the formal logic element: If this infestation continues, soon the damage will be permanent. That's a statement of sufficiency. It means that continuation of the aphid infestation will guarantee that the damage will be irreparable. It's not, however, a statement of necessity—we can't infer that the continuation is necessary to bring about irreparable damage to the crops; perhaps other factors are at work that could completely damage the crops as well. Now, evidently Hector doesn't understand this distinction. He states that the crops can be saved just by eliminating the aphid infestation, but that's not a proper interpretation of Julia's statement. Eliminating the aphid infestation will get rid of a factor that would certainly bring about total ruin of the crop, but we don't know that the crop would be guaranteed survival simply by removing this one factor. Now, what makes the question more difficult is the fact that we're not asked for the flaw in Hector's response, but rather for a statement that's consistent with Julia's claim but not with Hector's. So, with a reasonable understanding of the respective claims, we can proceed confidently to the choices, looking for the one that meets this requirement.

(A) does the trick. As we saw, according to Julia's statement, stopping the infestation is necessary, but not sufficient for halting the damage. While the damage will surely be irreparable if the infestation is not stopped, the fact that it *is* stopped doesn't ensure that the crops won't suffer irreparable damage. So (A) satisfies the first part of the stem—it's consistent with Julia's claim. Seeing that is the tough part; it's a bit easier to see how (A) is inconsistent with Hector's reasoning. He says flat out that stopping the infestation is the only thing needed to save the crops. In (A), however, the infestation is stopped, but the crops bite the dust anyway. So (A)'s the choice we seek.

(B) is perfectly consistent with Julia's argument, but does not contradict Hector's. He speaks only to the issue of what will happen if the infestation is stopped.

(C) The easiest way to eliminate (C) is to recognize that it mirrors Hector's argument precisely. He says that stopping the infestation will save the crops, so this choice is consistent with his claim, and therefore incorrect.

(D) Forget about this "kept under control" business—the key point in (D) is that the infestation is *not stopped*, which, according to Julia, means that the crops are goners. So this one is inconsistent with Julia's claim.

(E) Also discounting the "kept under control" phrase, which essentially adds nothing, (E) is the same as (B), and is therefore wrong for the same reason.

A 180 test taker is familiar with the terms "consistent" and "inconsistent,"
and understands the ways in which these concepts are tested on the LSAT.

Explanation: D12 Versus G28

Distinguishing Features: Numbers and Statistics, Scope Shift, Alternative Explanation

34. E

Next up we have "Logical Reasoning meets *Top Gun*." The last general we encountered was trying to defend a city from attack, way back in "Regiments and Areas" in the Logic Games section. This one's trying to determine which of two types of aircraft would better fit the needs of the Air Force for an upcoming mission, and as you can tell from the list of distinguishing features above, there are many logical elements present here. While the commander of the Air Force prefers the G28 because it could perform the necessary task more efficiently, the general orders that the D12 be used instead. He provides one piece of evidence to support this decision: Only the D12 can perform the task in time to meet the mission's deadline. When an author argues for one option over another, the author must assume that the benefit provided by the preferred option can only be found in that option. In other words, the author must assume that the G28 would not fulfill the mission in the allotted period of time. But perhaps there's an alternative? The general says that it would take four days for the G28 to be ready for the mission, but he never explicitly says that the G28 *couldn't* meet the deadline. Perhaps the plane's greater efficiency would enable it to still complete the mission in the allotted period of time, despite the later start. That's a plausible alternative that the general has overlooked. In order for the general's conclusion to be valid, he must assume that the G28 could not perform the mission by the immovable deadline. Thus he assumes that the G28's efficiency would not recoup the extra time that it would take for the G28 to begin the mission.

The number issue is a common one: The test makers like to create situations in which a decrease in one area is made up, in fact, even surpassed, by an increase in something else. And one could see this scenario in terms of a scope shift, as well: The general speaks of the efficiency of the G28 early on, but then makes his recommendation based solely on the time factor. Recognizing that shift is key to understanding the assumption here.

A 180 test taker has the ability to see situations in Logical Reasoning questions from a number of angles, and to think through problems on a number of different levels. The more tools in your test-day arsenal, the better.

(A) The stimulus never states that one aircraft retrieves higher quality information than the other; one is simply *more efficient*. So (A) is not relevant to the general's decision.

(B) goes too far. The author never states how long the mission would take, so there's no basis for assuming that the D12 would be done before the G28 arrived.

(C) The ability to fly low to the ground is a significant consideration to the commander, and the general never contests the importance of this consideration. He just overrides it by making the deadline a *more* significant consideration, so he need not assume (C) in order to formulate his recommendation.

(D) focuses on aircraft other than the G28. Aren't two enough to deal with? The author seems to think so, because she discusses only the D12 and the G28. How long it would take *other* kinds of planes to get to the scene is irrelevant to the general's argument, which specifically deals with a choice between these two.

Explanation: Food Poisoning

Distinguishing Features: Parallel Reasoning, Causation

35. D

Here's a cheery topic: food poisoning. This Parallel Reasoning question lends itself well to algebraic characterization. The question stem itself gives us some critical information. We're told that the argument in the stimulus is flawed and that we're looking for an answer choice that is flawed in a similar manner. Since this example contains formal logic statements, we can reduce the action of the stimulus to letters to help us determine the flaw. If foods aren't stored properly, they can give people food poisoning (if X, then possibly Y). Since people at the Panhandler got food poisoning, the restaurant must have served food that wasn't properly stored (Y, therefore X). This argument makes the mistake of concluding that a "reverse cause and effect" relationship is operating: because the consequence occurred, the cause must have been in effect also. We know from formal logic that we simply can't get from "if X then Y" to "if Y then X." So all we need to do is find the choice that commits the same error. There's of course no way to prephrase the specifics of the right choice, only its structure, so the best bet is to simply work through the choices:

(A) tells us that if a man over 65 has high blood pressure, he is at risk for heart disease (if X, then Y). That has the first part of the argument right. But the second sentence tells us that Tonare males over 65 do not have blood pressure, so they are not at risk for heart disease—which translates into not X, therefore not Y. This conclusion simply negates the terms without switching them as in the original.

(B) and (C) can both be eliminated because neither of them presents a "reverse cause and effect" argument; in fact, neither one contains anything that can be translated into a formal logic if-then statement. (B) contains a temporal flaw; for all we know, Magelli might have crafted the cabinet before he died. We would need information that the cabinet is less than 15 years old before the conclusion would be valid. And (C)'s conclusion is certainly premature as well, but again does not contain the same formal logic structure as the original; there's nothing in there that can be translated into "if X, then Y."

(D) contains the kind of flaw we seek. This choice states that Relief-O! has been known to cause blurred vision in people who take it. We can translate that sentence as: "if people take Relief-O!, they may experience blurred vision" (if X, then possibly Y). So far so good. The following sentences then tell us that Molly took a pain reliever and experienced blurred vision (Y), so she must have taken Relief-O! (therefore X). Perfect.

(E) This argument deals with cause and effect, but not in the same manner as in the stimulus. (E) lays out an initial cause: if tigermint grows out of control, it can kill other plants (if X, then Y). But its second sentence introduces a negative condition: Sally's plants did *not* get killed—in fact, they look better than ever. Therefore, the tigermint must not be out of control. This reduces to not Y, therefore not X—not parallel.

Explanation: Boatwright Award

Distinguishing Feature: Scope Shift

36. E

The author concludes that psychologists who want their work to be nominated for the *Boatwright Psychology Review* award should only submit articles containing reviews on three or fewer books. The evidence follows: the *Boatwright Psychology Review* basically will not publish any book review article that reviews more than three books. Look back over the conclusion and evidence, and you'll realize that they aren't really talking about the same thing. The conclusion is about what one should do in order to get his work *nominated* for the award, and the evidence is about what one should do in order to get his work *published*. That's a classic scope shift. The only way to make these two different subjects relate to one another is to assume that one must have a review article published in the *Review* in order to be eligible for the award. Otherwise the evidence about publication requirements would have no relevance to the conclusion about nomination requirements. (E) expresses this central assumption faithfully, tying the evidence concerning publishing to the conclusion concerning nominations.

A 180 test taker knows that the logical gap that results from a scope shift can often be bridged by an assumption.

(A) While the stimulus suggests that articles covering more books are longer, it nowhere suggests that this proportional relationship carries out to the extremes. What makes for the longest articles isn't central to the evidence and conclusion, and hence need not be assumed in order for this argument to work.

(B) overstates the link between the two subjects. The argument in the stimulus assumes that publication is necessary for a book to be *nominated*, while (B) says that publication guarantees that a book will *win* the award. The argument doesn't concern itself with which book might win the award, so (B) isn't directly relevant to it.

(C) is too broad to be necessary here. The argument concerns book review articles, which do come with certain length restrictions. But (C) deals with *all* articles, and we don't know nor do we really care anything about articles besides book reviews that *Boatwright* may contain (editorials, feature articles, etc.). These may or may not have length restrictions, but this particular argument doesn't depend on this issue.

(D) makes an irrelevant distinction that doesn't directly pertain to the central issue: what must be done with an article before it can be nominated for the prestigious award. One book and two books are both on the acceptable side of the length restriction—no distinction between them need be assumed here.

PRACTICE SET 10

37. Lillian has expressed concern about maintaining cohesion in her drug addiction recovery group that she leads at her youth center. She has worked to develop cohesion by encouraging group members to share their experiences openly with the group. But some of the group members take advantage of this opportunity for openness by sharing long, violent stories primarily intended to shock the others. Aversion to these stories has caused some members to quit the group. These violent lengthy stories also take time away from other members, preventing them from sharing their experiences. To ensure cohesion in the group, then, Lillian should delineate a specific time slot for each member to speak during each session.

Which one of the following best describes the logical flaw in the argument above?

(A) Two actions that merely occur simultaneously are presented as actions that are causally related.

(B) A hypothesis is presented that runs counter to a proposal related to that hypothesis.

(C) A course of action is proposed to resolve a problem that would in actuality address only one cause of the problem.

(D) A conclusion is based on evidence that is unrelated to the issue at hand.

(E) A conclusion is supported by evidence that contradicts the conclusion.

38. An international study recently examined the effects of secondhand smoke on health. Surprisingly, although the dosages of harmful chemicals from secondhand smoke are so small that their effect should be negligible, the study found that nonsmoking spouses of smokers displayed an incidence of heart disease that was significantly greater than that of nonsmokers who were not as regularly exposed to secondhand smoke.

Each of the following, if true, could contribute to an explanation of the unexpectedly high incidence of heart disease in smokers' spouses EXCEPT:

(A) A disproportionately high number of people married to smokers are among the older segment of the married population, a group that inherently has a higher-than-average risk of heart disease.

(B) On average, more alcohol and coffee, both of which have been linked to heart disease, are consumed in the homes of smokers than in the homes of nonsmokers.

(C) A disproportionately high number of smokers are married to other smokers, and the risk of heart disease increases in proportion to the number of smokers living in a household.

(D) Smokers generally tend to live in higher-stress environments than do nonsmokers, and stress is a factor associated with above average incidence of heart disease.

(E) A disproportionately high number of smokers live in areas with a high level of industrial pollutants, which have been shown to be a factor in increased risk of heart disease.

PRACTICE SET 10: ANSWERS AND EXPLANATIONS

Explanation: Lillian's Recovery Group

Distinguishing Features: Tough Choices, Causation

37. C

Lillian's goal is simple: to create cohesion in her drug addiction recovery group. In order to achieve this goal, she has encouraged members of the group to share their personal experiences openly, but this approach isn't working. The problem is that some members have begun telling long and violent stories to shock the others, causing some members to quit and leaving inadequate time for others to share. This is all a long setup for the conclusion, which is that Lillian should limit the time available for each member to speak. The stem alerts us that there's a flaw in this argument, and that flaw becomes apparent in the conclusion. The problem that the conclusion seeks to resolve stems from two causes: members telling long *and* violent stories. The conclusion as it stands might prevent the stories from being long, but it doesn't prevent them from being violent. Therefore, the argument is flawed because its conclusion would only remedy one of two factors which create the problem it seeks to resolve. All the choices are wordy and cumbersome, but (C) states the flaw precisely.

> A 180 test taker fights his way through tough choices to locate the idea that he prephrased, or, if no prephrase came to mind, the one that holds up best under close scrutiny.

(A) Apparently, "two actions" refers to the telling of long scandalous stories and members dropping out. (A) is most immediately wrong because the author does not suggest that these incidents occur simultaneously. On the contrary, the author presents them sequentially: According to the argument, the stories "cause" other members to quit. So while there is an element of causation present here, the author does not commit the causality flaw described in (A).

(B) is perplexing because there is no hypothesis in this argument. Also, there is no contradiction within the elements of this argument. The conclusion is flawed because it's incomplete, not because it runs counter to anything.

> A 180 test taker puts all choices through their paces, especially tough choices in Logical Flaw and Method of Argument questions that accuse the author of doing all sorts of things. She focuses on each key element of the choice ("hypothesis," "runs counter to") and asks herself "Is that in there?"

(D) The evidence is all perfectly relevant to the conclusion. They are, after all, both focused on the same issues, so there's no scope shift here.

(E), like (B), suggests that the elements of the argument contradict one another, but that is not true in this case. Lil's evidence is consistent with the conclusion—the problem is that the recommendation in the conclusion simply doesn't go far enough.

Explanation: Secondhand Smoke

Distinguishing Features: Study, Causation, Odd Man Out, Alternative Explanation, Scope Shift

38. C

Perusing the list of distinguishing features, you're likely to ask "what's *not* in this one?"—and the answer is "not much." This one nearly has it all, and we can take the features in order to describe what's going on. First of all, we're dealing with another study, and you should be fairly familiar by now with the kinds of mishaps, misconceptions, and downright mistakes that can arise when researchers get their hands on things. The study involves the nonsmoking spouses of smokers; that is, people who are presumably in contact with a decent amount of secondhand smoke. While the author contends that secondhand smoke shouldn't really have any effect, the study found that the incidence of heart disease in nonsmokers married to smokers is actually much higher than that of nonsmokers not exposed to secondhand smoke. So while there shouldn't be any causal mechanism at work here, the author implies that the study's finding suggests that there is. Now, we're asked to evaluate possible explanations of the unexpectedly high incidence of heart disease in smokers' nonsmoking spouses, and to choose the one that *wouldn't* contribute to an explanation. So there are the odd man out and alternative explanation features—four of the choices will provide plausible alternative explanations for the surprising results, while the right answer will not. And let's jump right to our Odd Man Out, since it relates to the final feature mentioned above—Scope Shift. As difficult as this question may be for a number of reasons, the right answer is actually quite simple if you noticed the shift that takes place between the scope of the study and the scope of choice (C): The study focuses entirely on nonsmokers married to smokers. Cases in which *smokers* are married to other smokers fall outside of this scope, so (C) has no power to clear up the mystery at hand.

As for the wrong choices—that is, the valid explanations—they all hinge on the causation issue; or, more specifically, breaking down the notion of causality in order to show that the study's finding is not so surprising after all. Remember, the author is surprised at the finding because supposedly, secondhand smoke shouldn't cause a higher incidence of heart disease. Each wrong choice lessens the surprise by suggesting that secondhand smoke is in fact *not* to blame here; that is, by suggesting that some other factor *correlated* with smoking is responsible for the higher incidence of spousal heart disease.

A 180 test taker recognizes the difference between causation and correlation, and is intimately familiar with the ways in which the LSAT tests this distinction.

(A) If the spouses of smokers tend to be on the old side, and older people are more prone to heart disease, this helps explain the findings in a way that would satisfy the author—in other words, in a way that's consistent with her belief that secondhand smoke, by itself, shouldn't cause the increased incidence of heart disease noted in the study.

(B) Same thing: If smoking homes are generally homes with increased alcohol and coffee intake, and these things are associated with heart disease, then we'd be less surprised by the findings in light of the fact that the effects of secondhand smoke should be negligible.

(D) and (E) Same thing: If smoking is correlated with higher stress and higher pollution levels, both of which are related to heart disease, the mystery would be lessened.

KAPLAN

section three

READING COMPREHENSION

CHAPTER ELEVEN

The Reading Comprehension Challenge

See Spot run.

According to the passage, Spot engaged in which one of the following activities?

(A) growling
(B) sleeping
(C) digging
(D) running
(E) eating

Ever since you learned to read, you've been tested on your comprehension of written material, so it's no surprise that Reading Comprehension is the most familiar section in all of standardized testing. Medicine, business, archaeology, psychology, dentistry, teaching, law—the exams that stand at the entrance to study in these and most other fields all have one thing in common: a Reading Comprehension section. No matter what academic area you pursue, you have to make sense of dense, even unfamiliar prose. And the passages don't get much more dense, difficult, or unfamiliar than those contained on the LSAT.

As with all LSAT material, Reading Comp passages and question sets run the gamut from cake to killer, and naturally for the purposes of this book we've compiled for your test-taking pleasure a group of the densest, nastiest passages we could find. Keep in mind that the passages that follow represent the toughest material you're likely to encounter on your LSAT. If you can ace these, it's safe to say you have absolutely nothing to fear from the Reading Comp section come test day.

The following offers some guidelines on how to get the most out of the passages in this book.

USING THE READING COMPREHENSION PASSAGES IN THIS BOOK

The Reading Comp passages in this book are broken up into three categories:

Just Plain Tough

Blinded by Science

Philosophers' Corner

You may wish to build up to the ones in the final category, as these are particularly complex. Here are a few general pointers that should help guide your attack.

Read for the author's purpose and main idea. It's easy to get bogged down in details, especially in difficult passages like the ones in this book. But if you keep the author's purpose—that is, the reason he or she wrote the passage—and main idea in mind, you'll be able to answer many general types of questions immediately, and will know where to find the answers to the others.

Pay attention to passage structure. Many questions ask about how the author strings ideas together to present his or her overall point, or how certain elements function in relation to the passage as a whole. Paying attention to passage structure as you read will give you a leg up on these questions.

Paraphrase the text. You'll be able to process and apply the information in any passage, including these toughies, if you simplify the passage's ideas and translate them into your own words.

A 180 test taker cuts past impressive-sounding text and boils it down to the basic idea the author is trying to express.

Observe timing guidelines. Four passages in 35 minutes allows for roughly eight and a half minutes per passage, but considering the difficulty level of the readings in this book, it's reasonable to allow a little extra time. Try, however, not to exceed nine to ten minutes per passage. If you can knock out tough ones like the ones in this book in that amount of time, you should have no problem finishing easier passages in less than the average time allowed per passage, and your timing will all work out in the end.

Read the explanations. Review the key points of each passage, comparing your own synopsis of the passage to ours. Notice whether you are consistently weeding out the main idea and focusing on the relevant parts of the passages. As in the Logic Games and Logical Reasoning sections, the thought processes and habits of 180 test takers are highlighted throughout the explanations. Study these as you go along, and try to make these habits your own.

Have fun. No doubt this advice is easier to take for Logic Games than Reading Comp. However, it still behooves you to approach the Reading Comp section with enthusiasm and a good-natured appreciation for the challenges presented. Who knows, you may even come across some material that's *interesting* to you. Once again, approaching the section with the right attitude is half the battle.

Oh yeah: Regarding that ubiquitous canine of children's literature, Spot, choice (D) is correct—just in case you were wondering.

CHAPTER TWELVE

Just Plain Tough

Technical science and abstract philosophical passages often give test takers trouble, and you'll cut your teeth on examples of these soon enough. But it's important to remember that the difficulties of the Reading Comp section are not confined to these types alone. Any passage from any other category commonly represented in LSAT Reading Comp—humanities, social science, law—can pose serious problems for the unsuspecting test taker. The following four examples epitomize difficult passages that are neither scientific nor particularly philosophical in nature, but nonetheless present their own unique challenges. They are, as the title of this chapter states, just plain tough—and it's up to you to be tougher. See how you do.

PASSAGE 1

Sensing that government defined by the Articles of Confederation did not meet the needs of the newly born United States, the Congress of the Articles of Confederation authorized
(5) commissioners to "devise such further provisions as shall appear to them necessary to render the Constitution of the federal government adequate to the exigencies of the Union." These provisions were to be reported to Congress and confirmed by
(10) every state, and were to consist of alterations of the Articles of Confederation. Having given these instructions, Congress was quite surprised by the terms of the Constitution as submitted, and even claimed that the commissioners did not have the
(15) legal authority to submit such a revolutionary Constitution.

In the Federalist Papers, James Madison defended the commissioners by returning to the terms of their mandate. Given the goals expressed
(20) by Congress, and the principle that conflicts ought to be resolved in favor of more important goals, Madison argued that the degree to which the Constitution departs from the Articles cannot make the Constitution illegal. Where the goal of
(25) amending the Articles conflicts with the goal of creating good government, the Articles must yield, since the goal of "good government" is an overriding consideration. This same argument, however, does not apply to the commissioners'
(30) decision to allow the Constitution to be ratified by only three-quarters of the states. Unanimous approval was a fundamental aspect of national government under the Articles. Requiring nonratifying states to be bound by the new
(35) Constitution was thus a powerful diminishment of their sovereignty, as the Constitution changed the national government from a weak union of independent states to a strong union in which the interests of the many states could outweigh the
(40) protests of the few. Although history has validated the wisdom of the change, the question of whether the change was legal is another matter.

In authorizing the commissioners, the independent states requested a proposal for the
(45) alteration of the national government, but never intended to waive their veto power. So even if Madison is correct, and the commissioners could have proposed anything they deemed likely to fulfill the goal of good government, it does not
(50) follow that their proclamations should impinge upon the legal rights of the states. This does not, however, imply that the Constitution ratified by the states has no moral authority. No government ought to have the power to entrench itself against
(55) amendment, and so the fact that the government

under the Articles of Confederation did not consent to the alteration of the ratification process does not establish the moral illegitimacy of the Constitution. The case for rebelling against the
(60) government under the Articles is further strengthened by the fact that the government itself admitted its unfitness for the exigencies of the Union.

1. It can be inferred that Congress's surprise over the radical nature of the Constitution submitted by the commissioners could be attributed in part to the fact that its members did not foresee

(A) the inevitability that the Constitution it requested would be adopted without the unanimous ratification of the states
(B) the possibility that the Constitution it requested would contain provisions that jeopardized the government's moral authority
(C) a conflict between the modification of the Articles of Confederation and the creation of a Constitution adequate to the needs of the nation
(D) the possibility that the Constitution it requested would differ from the Articles of Confederation
(E) the likelihood that one such as Madison would invoke a principle as part of an argument attempting to justify the legality of the Constitution submitted

2. Which one of the following views can be attributed to Madison?

(A) In the case of conflicting interests, priority should be given to the course of action that best promotes peace in the nation.
(B) Applications of conflict resolution principles can be used to determine the legality of an action.
(C) Unanimous approval is the most important objective in drafting a new Constitution.
(D) The Constitution drafted by the commissioners corresponded precisely to the expectations of the Congress of the Articles of Confederation.
(E) In drafting the new Constitution, the commissioners had a moral obligation to forge a strong nation out of the weak union of independent states.

3. If a government decrees that it is illegal to make any changes to the structure or practices of the state, the author would most likely view a group within the state that attempts to violate the decree

   (A) with skepticism regarding its motivations
   (B) with admiration since any law passed by such a government has no moral authority
   (C) with concern regarding the government's reaction to the group's act of dissent
   (D) with disdain for its violation of the orders of the state
   (E) with approval regarding its moral right to disobey the decree

4. Which one of the following, if true, would most seriously weaken the argument put forth in defense of the legality of the Constitution submitted by the commissioners?

   (A) Non-unanimous ratification of such a new Constitution is incompatible with the goal of creating a good government.
   (B) Extensive debate among statesmen is necessary in order to create a fair and legal Constitution.
   (C) It is nearly impossible to create an effective Constitution out of the pieces of a previous Constitution.
   (D) No legal Constitution can include provisions to safeguard the power of the ruling elite that commissioned the document.
   (E) In regard to heated political issues, arguments presented orally are generally more persuasive than arguments presented in written form.

5. According to the passage, which one of the following provided justification for the revolutionary nature of the new Constitution?

   (A) The current government's admission of its inadequacy in national affairs
   (B) The right of any given state to refuse to ratify the new Constitution
   (C) The moral right of a new government to entrench itself against amendment
   (D) The recommendation that the new Constitution be created from alterations of the current Articles of Confederation
   (E) The analysis presented by Madison that showed that the new Constitution did not differ from the Articles of Confederation to the extent asserted by Congress

6. Which one of the following relationships between legal and moral authority is implied by the author?

   (A) The morality of a Constitution is the primary determinant of its legality.
   (B) A principle lacking moral authority can still be legally binding.
   (C) The morality of an action can never be determined irrespective of the legality of that action.
   (D) A document lacking legal authority can still carry moral weight.
   (E) The moral justification for an action can be used by a court to override the illegality of that action.

7. The primary purpose of the passage is to

   (A) reconcile two opposing viewpoints
   (B) illustrate the argumentative power of a principle
   (C) argue for the reconsideration of an established doctrine
   (D) support the establishment of one form of government over another
   (E) assess the authority of a political event on two grounds

Passage 1: Illegal Constitution

What Makes It Difficult

This passage offers a long and complicated political story intertwined with legal and moral issues—perhaps a potboiler to legal scholars, but a snoozer to many of the rest of us. Twists and turns abound, and the distinction between moral and legal legitimacy adds to the complexity of the subject matter. Madison's arguments are complex and based around abstract principles, and the author's assessment of Madison's argument likewise relies on principle for its power: "No government ought to have the power to entrench itself against amendment . . . ." It all adds up to some fairly difficult reading followed by challenging questions. Let's look at the key points.

Key Points of the Passage

Purpose and Main Idea: The author's purpose is to evaluate whether the Constitution is legal and morally legitimate. The main idea is that while the Constitution may not be legal (because its adoption by three-quarters ratification violated the sovereignty of nonratifying states), it nonetheless carries moral weight.

Paragraph Structure: The first paragraph tells us that although Congress authorized a group of "commissioners" to create the U.S. Constitution by revising the Articles of Confederation, Congress was surprised by the revolutionary nature of the Constitution that the commissioners submitted.

Paragraph 2 starts by explaining James Madison's argument that the commissioners were justified in submitting a revolutionary Constitution because the document served the goal of creating good government, a goal that was more important than adhering strictly to the Articles. Despite Madison's argument, the author questions the legality of the Constitution because it was ratified by only three-quarters of the states.

In the final paragraph, the author expands her argument from paragraph 2 by showing that the "three-quarters ratification" provision violated the rights of nonratifying states. At the same time, however, she claims that the Constitution's questionable legality does not cast doubt on its moral legitimacy, and gives two reasons why this is so.

Note the strategically placed "however"s in the middle of paragraphs 2 and 3: Both are fundamentally related to the author's main idea. The first prefaces the notion that despite Madison's justifications, the new Constitution may not be legal, while the second sets up the idea that despite its possible illegality, it nonetheless may carry moral weight.

A 180 test taker uses Keywords to follow an author's twists and turns. One of the most popular and powerful Contrast Keywords is "however," a word that is used by authors to signal a change in direction.

Answers and Explanations

1. C   2. B   3. E   4. A   5. A   6. D   7. E

1. C

This inference question asks us for a reason why Congress may have been surprised by how much the Constitution differed from the Articles of Confederation. What possibility might the Congress have overlooked? This topic is discussed in the very beginning of the passage where we see that Congress authorized the commissioners to revise the Articles to create an "adequate" federal government. They asked for some alterations, and got back something they deemed to be an illegal revolutionary document. To carry out Congress' wish, the commissioners felt they had to radically depart from the Articles, not just modify them. We can infer from its reaction that Congress did not foresee that mere modification of the Articles would not suffice to carry out its charge, choice (C).

(A) distorts information from the text. While the Constitution was adopted without unanimous ratification, this fact is not described by the author as an "inevitability," or as something that was bound to occur. Any lack of foresight on this issue cannot be blamed for Congress' surprise.

(B) Moral authority appears later in the passage, and has no recognizable connection to Congress's surprise over the revolutionary Constitution. Congress certainly felt that the document submitted lacked legal authority, but the issue of moral authority is not raised at this point.

(D) On the contrary: Congress was presumably aware that the Constitution would differ from the Articles, because it specifically commissioned a revision of the Articles. What the Congress did not anticipate was the *extent* of this difference.

(E) The reaction of an individual such as Madison is irrelevant to Congress' surprise. The question concerns why Congress was surprised about the content of the Constitution, not how or why someone would later justify this content.

A 180 test taker is not tempted by a choice simply because it contains familiar words or characters found in the passage.

---

2. B

Next up is a question that asks us to draw an inference based upon Madison's views. In other words, given the discussion of Madison's perspective, which statement could he be expected to uphold? Since Madison's views are primarily discussed in paragraph 2, we can look to that paragraph to determine an answer. Madison based his argument about the legality of the Constitution on the principle that conflicts ought to be resolved in favor of more important goals, so choice (B) represents a statement he would be likely to agree with. Presumably, Madison would believe that conflict resolution principles can be relevant to a determination of legality, since this is the very type of principle he resorts to.

(A) Madison used the principle that conflicts should be resolved in favor of more important goals, but the author never stated or implied that Madison viewed "peace in the nation" to be an overriding national goal that should be used to resolve conflicts of interest.

(C) misrepresents the author's meaning in the passage. The author never specifies that unanimous approval is the most important objective in drafting a new Constitution, nor does he imply that Madison believed this. The issue of unanimous approval comes up later in a different context.

(D) No, just the opposite. The reason why Madison raised his voice to justify the new Constitution in the first place was because it did *not* meet Congress's expectations.

(E), like (C), appeals to an issue that comes up later in the passage: moral obligation. The author states that the result of the Constitution was to forge a strong union of the states, but he does not indicate that Madison believed that the commissioners were *morally obligated* to create a Constitution that did so.

A 180 test taker quickly dismisses choices that focus on irrelevant elements of the passage.

---

3. E

Next we get our third inference question in a row—we're asked for a deduction based on the author's views. Where are we given the author's views about the legality of making changes to government? In paragraph 3, the author states flat out that "no government ought to have the power to entrench itself against amendment." So the author would be likely to support a group that rebelled against a state's decision to protect itself from changes. (E) summarizes this view nicely.

(A) and (D) violate the spirit of the author's view on this matter. These choices can be eliminated at first glance, because we're looking for a positive or supportive attitude. The author would be likely to support such a group, not view it skeptically or with disdain.

A 180 test taker understands that many of the wrong choices in Reading Comp are written to go against the grain of the passage, and eliminates such choices quickly.

(B) starts off better than (A) and (D)—at least "admiration" is in the ballpark, as opposed to (A)'s "skepticism" and (D)'s "disdain." However, it goes a bit too far. First of all, it can be argued that "admiration" is too strongly positive; the author's views are more moderate than that, and "approval" matches her tone a little better. In any case, the rest is too extreme as well: Certainly the author would believe that opposition to the law in question would carry moral weight, but would she believe that "*any law* passed by such a government has no moral authority"? We can't tell— that's a different issue. We can speculate, but this is too extreme to be fully inferable here.

(C) The most we can infer here is how the author would react to the legitimacy of such an act of dissent. That's as far as the scope of the passage takes us. How she would feel about the reaction *to* the reaction against such a law is one step beyond the scope. While we can infer that she would support such dissent on moral grounds, there's no way to tell if she would be concerned about government reprisals or not.

A 180 test taker conducts a quick scan of the main verbs in each answer choice in questions asking about the author's attitudes, quickly eliminating those that are blatantly inappropriate.

---

4. A

In order to choose the best weakener, we must first understand which argument the question is referring to. We are asked to determine which statement would best weaken the argument put forth in defense of the legality of the Constitution. Where is this argument made, and by whom? Madison argued in defense of the Constitution's legality, and this argument is presented at the beginning of paragraph 2. Here Madison claims that the Constitution is justified despite its radical nature because it upholds the overarching goal of creating a good government. Choice (A) serves as a good weakener: If one of the Constitution's provisions (nonunanimous ratification) prevented it from creating a good government, then Madison's argument would be far less convincing.

(B), (D), (E) These choices are irrelevant to Madison's argument. The issue of "extensive debate" is not addressed in his justification. Neither are the issues of safeguarding the power of the ruling elite or the relative merits of oral versus written arguments. Since an argument can only be weakened on its own terms, these answer choices do not accomplish the task at hand.

(C) If anything, (C) supports the necessity for the radical nature of the Constitution handed in by the commissioners. However, it does not relate to Madison's specific reason for why he believed the Constitution to be legal. He viewed it as justified because it upheld the overriding goal of good government. If anything, (C) might strengthen Madison's *cause* (defending the Constitution), but since it does not address Madison's reasoning, we can say that it has no real effect on his particular argument.

5. A

"According to the passage" lets us know that we're being asked for something that is found directly in the text. We need to find something that provided justification for the revolutionary nature of the new Constitution. Justification is given in two places: Madison justifies the Constitution's legality, and the author justifies the Constitution's moral authority. Choice (A) relates to the final sentence of the passage in which the author justifies rebelling against the government under the Articles on the grounds that that government itself admitted it wasn't up to the task of dealing with the "exigencies"—that is, pressing needs—of the nation. (A) is a good paraphrase of this.

(B) The author uses this reason to argue against Madison's justification of the Constitution's legality.

(C) On the contrary: In paragraph 3, the author states that no government has the right to entrench itself against amendment.

(D) also presents the opposite of what we're looking for: If the commission followed Congress's recommendation, it would not have submitted such a radical document. Far from justifying the revolutionary Constitution, (D) describes a factor that would presumably guard against the creation of such a document.

(E) Madison does no such thing: His analysis attempted to justify the differences between the Articles and the Constitution. Nowhere does the author state that Madison questioned the extent of these differences.

6. D

Nowhere does the author *directly* relate legality to morality, but since we know about the author's attitude toward each independently, we must be able to infer a connection—otherwise, this question wouldn't exist. Briefly review what we learned about each: The author believes that the legality of the Constitution is questionable, but that its moral authority is not. It's a simple matter of putting these facts together: Inferably, the author believes that moral authority can exist without legality, choice (D).

The remaining choices are difficult insofar as they include all of the same terms as the correct choice, but each choice somehow fouls up the relationship between morality and legality:

(A) goes against the spirit of the passage. In stating that a document with questionable legal validity can nonetheless carry moral weight, the author evidently sees moral authority and legality as two separate issues.

(B) First of all, the author is concerned with the morality and legality of a written document, not a principle. But even if we overlook that fact, (B) reverses the situation in the passage, where there's something that could be illegal yet moral. Would the author think that something lacking morality can be legal? It's doubtful, since morality seems to carry lots of weight with this author. But still, there's no real way to tell.

(C), like (B), switches the scope from documents to "action." Still, had you overlooked that, you should still have recognized that (C) runs counter to the author's beliefs: *Despite* its possible illegality, in the author's mind the new Constitution can still have moral authority.

(E) goes beyond the scope of the passage. The author's argument does not address court decisions, but rather the country's governing documents.

A 180 test taker quickly recognizes choices that shift the scope from the focus of the passage.

---

7. E

Your initial reading should have revealed the author's purpose in writing the passage: to evaluate the legality and moral legitimacy of the Constitution. Answer choice (E) expresses this purpose in a more general manner, to "assess the authority of a political event [i.e., the Constitution] on two grounds [i.e., legal and moral]."

(A) What two viewpoints are *reconciled*? The author argues against Madison's view, but that's about as close as we come in this passage to opposing viewpoints.

(B) The author does make an argument, but she isn't interested in illustrating the "argumentative power" of anything (except perhaps the evidence she provides).

(C) This choice misrepresents the author's purpose. She doesn't argue for a "*reconsideration*" of the Constitution (after all, she states that "history has validated the wisdom of the change"), but apparently for an *initial* consideration of it. And besides, the Constitution can be considered a governing document, not a "doctrine" *per se*.

(D) The author's argument does not support the establishment of the Constitution over the Articles as much as it reviews some legal and moral considerations of the Constitution itself.

What's Next?

Let's move on to our next tough passage. In this one we make the leap from political philosophy to economics, and from the early United States to the former Soviet Union (although, as you'll see, the United States does make a cameo appearance in this one as well). See what you can make of our friends "Gerschenkron and Hough."

PASSAGE 2

Both Alexander Gerschenkron and Jerry Hough view the former Soviet Union as an "anomalous" nation in certain fundamental respects. Gerschenkron focuses on the degree to which the
(5)   Soviet Union deviated from the expected European pattern of industrialization, while Hough emphasizes how the Soviet Union differed from the standard type of bureaucratic organization. Despite this difference in
(10)   orientation, both authors share a similar theoretical approach.

First, both authors react in their works to specific explanations already existing in their fields. Gerschenkron responds to the prevailing
(15)   belief that all countries pass through similar stages of industrialization that can be modeled after England's industrial growth. He also reacts to the accepted notion that states must possess certain specific prerequisites before they can
(20)   industrialize. Hough as well develops his argument in reaction to an existing view, the notion that the only type of bureaucracy that can operate efficiently is one that embodies the conventional American image of the ideal
(25)   organization. This American image, known as monism, sees efficiency as maximized when bureaucrats perform only those duties passed down to them from a central authority.

Second, both Gerschenkron and Hough also
(30)   clearly attempt to use their work to supplement the existing explanations prevailing in their fields. Gerschenkron expands W. W. Rostow's industrialization model by defining a causal factor that he calls the "degree of economic
(35)   backwardness." Specifically, he argues that backwardness impacts the speed, organizational structure, institutional instruments, and ideology of a country's industrialization. In a similar vein, Hough broadens the conventional explanation in
(40)   his field, concluding from his findings that the centralized, monistic model of organization must be expanded if it is to enable efficient administration. He uses the Soviet experience to show that overlapping bureaucratic duties can
(45)   actually promote organizational efficiency in certain cases.

While Gerschenkron and Hough differ sharply regarding the focus of their research in their works, both authors portray the Soviet Union as
(50)   anomalous with respect to the phenomena of industrialization and bureaucratic organization that they study. Both authors also attempt to use the anomalies that they discover to enhance the explanatory value of the theories already existing
(55)   in their fields. Ultimately, Gerschenkron and

Hough succeed at their similar tasks, because they develop explanations for their anomalous cases that enable the existing theories to more accurately explain the issues under investigation.
(60)   Not only do both authors provide enough evidence to document the anomalous nature of the cases they investigate, but they use their anomalous cases to increase the explanatory range of the existing theories without altering those
(65)   theories beyond recognition.

1. The author's main point in the passage is reflected most accurately in which one of the following statements?

    (A)   Gerschenkron and Hough share a similar theoretical enterprise in their works, and both manage this enterprise successfully.
    (B)   In their research, both Gerschenkron and Hough react to prevailing theories within their fields.
    (C)   Gerschenkron and Hough both use evidence from the Soviet case to highlight the anomalous features of the former Soviet experience.
    (D)   The works of Gerschenkron and Hough are expansive because both authors attempt to refute existing theories within their fields and to replace these theories with better explanations.
    (E)   The works of Gerschenkron and Hough are similar with respect to the specific central tenets of their research.

2. According to the author, the works of Gerschenkron and Hough are similar in that they both

    (A)   provide evidence to show how the experiences of the former Soviet Union invalidate prevailing theories in their fields
    (B)   adhere to the standard interpretations of prevailing theories in their fields
    (C)   develop the explanatory power of existing theories through the investigation of anomalous cases
    (D)   address anomalies in the stages of industrialization experienced by the former Soviet Union
    (E)   portray the development of the former Soviet Union in a generally critical light

3. The passage states which one of the following about Hough's portrayal of the former Soviet bureaucratic system?

   (A) The former Soviet bureaucratic system mirrors the monistic model of bureaucratic organization exemplified in the American bureaucratic system.

   (B) The experiences of the former Soviet bureaucratic system support the notion that bureaucracies must be organized according to the monistic model if they are to run efficiently.

   (C) Throughout its development, the former Soviet bureaucratic system underwent growth stages similar to that experienced by England during its industrial growth.

   (D) The development of the former Soviet bureaucratic system was impeded by the system's degree of economic backwardness.

   (E) The experiences of the former Soviet bureaucratic system demonstrate that bureaucratic efficiency can be enhanced through the overlapping of organizational functions.

4. Which one of the following best describes the function of the third paragraph in the context of the passage as a whole?

   (A) It demonstrates that despite similarities in their approaches, the two authors cited study fundamentally different subjects.

   (B) It suggests that the most effective method for comparing the works of Gerschenkron and Hough is to focus on their research concerning the former Soviet Union.

   (C) It illustrates the role of W. W. Rostow's industrialization model in influencing Gerschenkron's analysis of the former Soviet Union.

   (D) It provides additional support for the notion that Gerschenkron and Hough share similar theoretical goals in developing their works.

   (E) It serves to refute the contention that the works of Gerschenkron and Hough exhibit any fundamental similarity.

5. The passage suggests that both Gerschenkron and Hough would be most likely to agree with which one of the following statements?

   (A) Scientific studies of the former Soviet Union should be limited to an emphasis on industrialization patterns or methods of bureaucratic organization.

   (B) W. W. Rostow's industrialization model can be expanded by incorporating the variable of economic backwardness.

   (C) All countries pass through stages of industrialization similar to those experienced by England during its early growth.

   (D) Empirical research into anomalous cases can broaden the explanatory range of current theories.

   (E) Empirical research should focus on attempting to falsify theories through emphasis on disconfirming cases.

6. The author refers to the concept of monism in the second paragraph in order to

   (A) support the claim that the former Soviet Union deviated in its development from the normal European pattern of industrialization

   (B) refute the notion that Hough provides an alternative conception of bureaucratic efficiency

   (C) demonstrate that Hough's work takes issue with the conventional view that efficient bureaucratic organization must conform to the American idealized image

   (D) support the claim that Hough portrays the former Soviet Union as similar to most industrialized nations in its bureaucratic structure

   (E) provide evidence for the conclusion that the former Soviet case displayed many elements of the idealized American model of bureaucratic organization

Passage 2: Gerschenkron and Hough

What Makes It Difficult

The names alone are a pain, but maybe keeping track of them as simply G and H, as we would in Logic Games, is the way to go. As for serious considerations, the subject matter is fairly dry and it's fairly difficult to visualize what these guys are talking about. The concept of the Soviet Union as an "anomalous" nation is a tough one to assimilate, and the various repetitions of "anomalous" throughout the final paragraph magnify this complexity. The "compare and contrast" passage structure, while common to LSAT Reading Comp, is blurred a bit by the presentation of similarities between the work of Gerschenkron and Hough. Keeping the two theorists views straight in your mind is no easy task, and the questions continually test your ability to distinguish one from the other. The choices are long and complex. Overall, a very tough passage. Let's break it down to its key points.

Key Points of the Passage

Purpose and Main Idea: The author's purpose is to compare how Gerschenkron and Hough approach the case of the former Soviet Union in their scholarly works. The main idea is that both authors share a similar theoretical approach in their works, and both are successful in their theoretical endeavors.

Paragraph Structure: Paragraph 1 introduces the passage by noting that both Gerschenkron and Hough view the former Soviet Union as an anomalous nation. Although they focus on different aspects of the former Soviet anomaly, they nonetheless share a similar approach in their research.

Paragraph 2 explains one aspect of similarity between the authors' approaches: Both develop ideas in reaction to existing theories in their fields. We are told first what Gerschenkron reacts to and then what Hough reacts to in his work.

Paragraph 3 provides a second aspect of similarity between the authors' approaches: Both attempt to supplement existing theories in their fields. Again, we are given a description of Gerschenkron's attempt, and then a description of Hough's.

The final paragraph summarizes the points made in paragraph 2 and paragraph 3. It also draws a final conclusion: Not only are the authors' tasks similar, but they both succeed in these tasks.

> A 180 test taker knows that a good "Roadmap" doesn't include every detail of a passage, and that such a Roadmap should recap the points of each paragraph and remind her where the evidence is to support these points.

Answers and Explanations

1. A   2. C   3. E   4. D   5. D   6. C

1. A

This question asks for the author's main point, or the main idea of the passage. This question would be a good one to prephrase, since a careful focus on purpose and structure should make the main idea clear. In this case, the main idea has two parts and is summed up in paragraph 4: The theorists share similar tasks, and they succeed at these tasks as well. This is well-stated in choice (A).

(B), (C) These choices describe only parts of the author's claim; they are not broad enough to reflect the main idea. Choice (B) summarizes the point of paragraph 2, while choice (C) discusses a point raised in paragraph 1 about the anomalies of the former Soviet case.

(D) contradicts the author's argument as laid out in paragraph 4. The author specifically states that the theorists use their anomalous cases to "enable the existing theories to more accurately explain the issues under investigation." In other words, their works supplement the existing theories. This is a far cry from replacing the theories, as choice (D) suggests.

(E) Again, the opposite is suggested: The author tells us in paragraph 1 that Gerschenkron and Hough focus on different aspects of the Soviet experience—Gerschenkron on industrialization and Hough on bureaucratic organization. Their specific central tenets differ, but their overall theoretical *approach* is the same.

2. C

How are the works of the two theorists similar? Maybe you were able to prephrase an answer here—after all, the first sentence tells us that both theorists view the Soviet Union as an anomalous case, and perhaps that stuck in your head. Or the fact that despite differences in their specific concerns, they share a similar overall theoretical approach. Either of these ideas would work. Unfortunately, however, the test makers decided to cull the answer to this one from paragraph 4, where it's stated that "Both authors also attempt to use the anomalies that they discover to enhance the explanatory value of the theories already existing in their fields." Choice (C) is a very close paraphrase of this. (Technically, the notion of expanding theories in their fields appears earlier in paragraph 3, but the idea of using anomalous cases toward this end is stated more explicitly in paragraph 4.)

(A) This answer choice contradicts the author's point. The author specifically tells us in paragraph 4 that the works of Gerschenkron and Hough enhance the explanatory power of existing theories—they do not invalidate these theories.

(B) Again, this goes against the grain: In paragraph 2 we're told that Gerschenkron and Hough react to existing theories in their fields, and later that they expand upon them. Thus it cannot be said that they adhere to these interpretations.

(D) Gerschenkron addresses industrialization, but Hough investigates bureaucratic organization. This is not a similarity in their works.

(E) misrepresents the author's meaning in the passage. She says that Gerschenkron and Hough use the former Soviet experience to draw attention to factors that expand existing theories. Nowhere are we told that their portrayals of the Soviet case are critical.

A 180 test taker is extremely sensitive to distortions of the text.

---

3. E

Here we're presented with another detail question, this time regarding Hough's work. Hough's work is discussed in detail in two places—paragraph 2 and paragraph 3—so now is a good time to return to the passage and examine those paragraphs to answer the question.

A 180 test taker does not hesitate to return to the passage to reread text in greater detail when it's necessary to pick up a point.

The author states at the end of paragraph 3 that Hough believes that the Soviet experience shows that overlapping bureaucratic duties can promote organizational efficiency—a point reflected in choice (E).

(A), (B) On the contrary: The author states in paragraph 3 that the former Soviet Union has an overlapping model of bureaucratic function that differs from the American monistic model. As we saw with correct choice (E), he also states here that the Soviet overlapping model may promote efficiency in certain cases.

(C) and (D) confuse Hough's work with that of Gerschenkron. England's industrial growth is part of Gerschenkron's work, and nowhere is this compared to the growth of Soviet bureaucracy (C). Similarly, the degree of economic backwardness is another element of the Gerschenkron discussion of paragraph 3, and nothing is stated about its effect on Soviet bureaucracy. Gerschenkron deals with industrialization, while Hough deals with bureaucratic organization. Choices (C) and (D) try to combine them, and thus must be tossed.

A 180 test taker can keep multiple theories straight in his mind, and doesn't fall for choices that attempt to mix them together.

---

4. D

This question asks us to determine the role played by one part of the passage in upholding the author's main idea. The paragraph focuses mainly on the way both theorists attempt to supplement existing theories in their fields. That's the specific gist of paragraph 3, but we're asked what this has to do with the passage as a whole. The best clue is the first word of the paragraph: "Secondly." This structural signal tells us that what's about to follow harks back to the earlier claim, back in paragraph 1, that their overall theoretical approaches were similar. Paragraph 2 presented the first similarity, and now in paragraph 3 we get the second. So this paragraph simply serves as additional support for the author's claim in the last sentence of paragraph 1, and (D) captures the gist of this nicely.

(A) It is true that Gerschenkron and Hough study different aspects of Soviet development. This point is raised in paragraph 1 and may even be reinforced in paragraph 3, where again we see how

Gerschenkron is concerned with industrialization while Hough is into bureaucratic structures. However, this is not related to the *function* of paragraph 3. These illustrations merely support the larger point that their overall goals are similar despite the fact that their specific subject matter differs.

(B) This answer choice distorts the author's argument. Nowhere does she state that Gerschenkron and Hough's works can *most effectively* be compared by reviewing their research on the former Soviet Union.

(C) This choice captures part of what *occurs* in paragraph 3, but it does not describe the function of paragraph 3 in the entire argument. It merely describes one idea that is developed in that paragraph.

A 180 test taker understands the difference between the content and function of a specific part of the passage.

(E) is yet another choice that flies in the face of the passage: The third paragraph supports the notion that Gerschenkron and Hough have similar approaches by showing that both theorists attempt to supplement existing theories in their fields. That's the overall point of the paragraph, differences in their specific topics notwithstanding.

5. D

Next we're asked to choose a statement about which both Gerschenkron and Hough would likely agree. Rather than attempt to prephrase the answer (the possibilities could be very broad), we should scan the choices to determine the correct one. (D) provides the best summary of a statement that would align with both theorists' views, since paragraph 4 tells us that both men use research into anomalous cases to broaden the explanatory value of existing theories. Presumably, since both theorists use such cases to broaden such explanations, they would agree that using such research in this way is possible.

(A) The author doesn't suggest that studies of the former Soviet Union should be limited to any subjects, and neither does she imply that Gerschenkron and Hough believe this. All we know is that industrialization and bureaucracy are their respective areas of concern. We can't infer that they think that Soviet studies should be limited to their subjects.

(B) Gerschenkron would agree with this, but the passage does not indicate Hough's views on Rostow's model.

(C) Not even Gerschenkron would buy this one—the author states in paragraph 2 that Gerschenkron reacts against this notion. And of course, we don't know what Hough's views would be on the subject.

(E) Again, on the contrary: As we saw with choice (D) in question 1 and choice (A) in question 2, Gerschenkron and Hough do not attempt to falsify the existing theories they deal with—they attempt to supplement them. They would therefore, if anything, probably *disagree* with the notion that empirical research should focus on falsification.

> A 180 test taker knows that similar ideas are tested throughout the question set, and that the thought process employed in an earlier question can sometimes be applied later on.

6. C

This question asks us to determine what function is served by the introduction of the concept of monism in paragraph 2. Paragraph 2 demonstrates that both authors react in their works to existing theories. Without looking at the answer choices, we can prephrase that "monism is introduced to show that Hough's work reacted to an existing theory." Do we find such an answer with a scan of the choices? In fact, (C) conveys just this idea—albeit a bit more specifically than our prephrase.

> A 180 test taker attempts to prephrase answers to Reading Comprehension questions, and when successful is adept at spotting the choice in each question that conveys the gist of that prephrase.

(A) This choice refers to the subject discussed by Gerschenkron, not Hough.

(B) and (D) present yet two more notions that go against the grain of the passage. Hough reacts against the American system known as monism, and according to paragraph 3, Hough's examination of the former Soviet case results in an alternative conception of bureaucratic efficiency. In addition, the author tells us in paragraph 1 that Hough portrayed the former Soviet Union as anomalous, or different, in its bureaucratic structure. The mention of monism in paragraph 2 is in no way included to show otherwise.

(E) Again, the author states that Hough portrayed the former Soviet Union as *different* from the American monistic model.

> A 180 test taker understands that choices that reflect the opposite of what the passage, author, or characters in the passage believe or suggest are quite common in passages that include a number of theorists and theories. He realizes that in such cases, the test makers are simply testing whether or not he's able to keep the various elements of the passage straight.

What's Next?

Had enough of tackling the global issues of nations and their various political and economic problems? Next up is a topic a little closer to home; in fact, as close as your front-yard mailbox. But don't get caught napping—just because the concept is a bit easier to grasp doesn't mean that the questions are easy. Prepare yourself for a deluge of "Junk Mail."

THE NEXT READING COMPREHENSION
PASSAGE BEGINS ON THE FOLLOWING PAGE

PASSAGE 3

Every day the mailboxes of America are filled with millions upon millions of solicitations provided by the direct marketing industry. Most often they are straightforward advertisements for
(5) goods and services, but they also include such things as fund-raising solicitations, sweepstakes entries, and free trial offers. America's response to this deluge has been strangely mixed. On the negative side, poorly executed direct marketing
(10) produces unwanted, annoying and wasteful solicitations, also known as "junk mail." The deluge of these solicitations constitutes an imposition on each household, putting a condition on that household's use of the mail system. Even
(15) worse, aggressive direct marketing techniques represent a serious threat to informational privacy. Rapid increases in technology have allowed direct marketers to have access to the personal characteristics of virtually everyone. Further,
(20) sophisticated computer matching programs can produce intrusive personal profiles from information which, standing alone, does not threaten individual privacy. Direct mailers disseminate this personal information originally
(25) revealed with an expectation of privacy. This information is disclosed without the subject's consent, and the target is typically never notified of the transfer.

The 1991 Harris-Equifax Consumer Privacy
(30) Survey addressed popular attitudes toward direct mailing practices and their impact on informational privacy. When asked how they viewed direct mail offers in general, 46 percent said they were a "nuisance," 9 percent considered
(35) them to be "invasions of privacy," and only 6 percent said they were "useful." But if Americans have such a negative opinion of the direct marketing industry, they have a strange way of showing it. Direct marketing is an effective
(40) technique that has grown in influence. Direct mail advertising expenditures rose from $7.6 billion in 1980 to $23.4 billion in 1990. The laws of the market dictate that companies would not have made these efforts without prospects of success.
(45) Moreover, in the Equifax survey mentioned above, almost half of the citizens who considered direct mail offers to be "invasions of privacy" had themselves bought something in response to a direct mail ad in the past year. Why, then, did not
(50) more of them express more positive opinions of direct marketing offers?

Analysis of this seeming contradiction reveals the central problem of regulation in this industry: Everyone hates receiving "junk mail," and
(55) everyone ought to be concerned about informational privacy.

Still, direct marketing offers real advantages over other means of shopping, and the industry as a whole probably offers something for everyone.
(60) Even those who believe that the direct mailing industry has a generally negative societal impact probably would prefer to remain on some mailing lists. We like shopping by mail, and we don't want to throw out the good with the bad.

1. Which one of the following best expresses the main idea of the passage?

   (A) Increases in technology have been the main catalyst for the direct marketing explosion during the 1980s.

   (B) Concerns over privacy issues as expressed in popular opinion polls have influenced the way direct marketers have targeted their audience.

   (C) The discrepancy between the public's stated views of unsolicited "junk mail" and individuals' actual reaction to direct marketing materials has fueled the recent boom in the direct marketing industry.

   (D) The mixed response of Americans toward direct marketing stems from aggressive marketing techniques that threaten individual privacy.

   (E) The success of the direct marketing industry in the face of apparent public opposition to its practices can be explained in the light of consumer tendencies.

2. Which one of the following, if true, would best strengthen the author's explanation of the "seeming contradiction" expressed in line 52?

   (A) Awareness of commercial infringements on the rights of citizens has never been higher.

   (B) The number of people on more than one mailing list has increased in direct proportion to the increase in direct marketing expenditures.

   (C) Consumers do not perceive a connection between their individual purchasing behavior and infringements on their personal rights.

   (D) Some people believe that the benefits associated with the recent success of the direct marketing industry will filter down to consumers over time.

   (E) Some opinion polls on other topics indicate a similar discrepancy between what people say about an issue and how they act in relation to that issue.

3. Which one of the following critiques most approximates the logic underlying the author's concern regarding the effects of the computer matching programs mentioned in lines 20–23?

   (A) An ecologist who states that since each of three species individually would not damage an ecosystem, it is safe to introduce all three into the ecosystem overlooks the possibility that the dominance of one species may lead to the extinction of one or both of the other two species.

   (B) An ecologist who states that since each of three species individually would not damage an ecosystem, it is safe to introduce all three into the ecosystem overlooks the possibility that the three species taken together may very well pose a serious threat to the ecosystem.

   (C) An ecologist who states that since each of three species individually would not damage an ecosystem, it is safe to introduce all three into the ecosystem overlooks the possibility that the addition of the three species to the ecosystem may preclude the addition of any further species.

   (D) An ecologist who states that since each of three species individually would not damage an ecosystem, it is safe to introduce all three into the ecosystem overlooks the possibility that the ecosystem may not be the optimal environment for the species in question.

   (E) An ecologist who states that since each of three species individually would not damage an ecosystem, it is safe to introduce all three into the ecosystem overlooks the possibility that any one of three species may have posed a risk to the previous ecosystem in which it lived.

4. Which one of the following can be inferred from the passage about direct mail advertising expenditures in the years between 1980 and 1990?

   (A) The rise in expenditures during this period is suggestive of the expectations of companies engaged in direct marketing at the time.

   (B) The profit derived from sales linked to these expenditures in 1990 was more than double the profit derived from such sales in 1980.

   (C) The lowest yearly expenditure on direct mail advertising during this period occurred in 1980.

   (D) Direct marketing companies expect the pattern of expenditures during this period to continue in the decades to come.

   (E) The rise in expenditures during this period closely parallel the laws of the market.

5. According to the passage, the author believes that the American public's reaction to the direct mail phenomenon

   (A) is in accordance with the true dangers posed by the enterprise

   (B) demonstrates an unusual willingness of people to consistently act against their deeply held convictions

   (C) stems primarily from its fear of the loss of privacy that results from direct mail practices

   (D) is unusual at first glance but more understandable once the motivations of the public are considered

   (E) signals that the direct mail industry will need to alter its practices to respect informational privacy

6. The opinions expressed in the Harris-Equifax Consumer Privacy Survey in lines 32–36 serve as

   (A) a justification for the increase in direct mail advertising expenditures in the 1980s

   (B) the basis for the solution to a seemingly paradoxical situation

   (C) the primary evidence for the author's conclusion about computer matching programs

   (D) a contrast to additional evidence derived from another part of the survey

   (E) an indication that the boom in direct marketing is not likely to continue

7. The author would most likely agree with which one of the following statements?

   (A) Despite its drawbacks, direct marketing has had an overall positive effect on American society.

   (B) The attitudes revealed in opinion polls can provide insight into actual behavior.

   (C) Regarding the effects of commercial enterprises, presenting a nuisance is a more serious offense to society than is invasion of privacy.

   (D) Everyone who would prefer to remain on at least one mailing list thinks that direct marketing negatively affects society in some way.

   (E) The growth in direct marketing would be even more significant in the future if the percentage of people who find direct mail offers to be a nuisance were to decrease.

Passage 3: Junk Mail

What Makes It Difficult

We've all been the victims of junk mail at some point or another, so the concept behind this one is not intimidating in the same manner as, say, the "overdemandingness problem in moral philosophy"—a cheery topic you'll encounter later on.

> A 180 test taker attempts to relate the content of Reading Comp passages to her own experience, but only as an aid, and never a substitute, for understanding.

And the writing itself isn't too difficult to understand, either. The real problem lies in the questions. Question 2 is a "Strengthen the Argument" question, common on the Logical Reasoning sections but more rare and cumbersome in Reading Comp. Question 3 is a real monster: incredibly long, it's a mixture of a Reading Comp application type of question and a Parallel Reasoning question found on every Logical Reasoning section. We're asked to go outside the passage in search of a situation that mirrors the underlying logic of a critique. Not fun. Some of the other questions present formidable challenges as well. Here's the lowdown on the passage.

Key Points of the Passage

Purpose and Main Idea: The author's purpose is to explain why direct mail marketing has been so successful despite Americans' seemingly negative attitudes toward direct mail techniques. The main idea is that even though Americans dislike receiving "junk mail," they value the advantages of shopping by mail and continue to respond positively to direct mail marketing, increasing the industry's success.

> A 180 test taker persistently searches for the overriding main idea, and hangs in there even when the author's full point isn't revealed until late in the passage.

Paragraph Structure: Paragraph 1 introduces us to the notion that Americans' response to direct mail marketing has been "strangely mixed." We get the "negative side" of the American response in the first paragraph, as the author explains why Americans view direct mail marketing as annoying and invasive.

Paragraph 2 then helps us to see why the American response can be considered "mixed." It starts out by providing evidence from an opinion survey that supports the author's claim that Americans view direct mail negatively. It then shows that despite their attitudes, Americans' behaviors in response to direct mail have been positive: direct mail has become a highly successful marketing industry. Evidence from the same opinion survey cited earlier is given to show that Americans buy items through direct mail even though they dislike its techniques.

This "seeming contradiction" is explained in paragraph 3, where the author tells us that Americans shop by direct mail even though they dislike it because it is convenient and offers distinct advantages over other types of shopping. In essence, Americans like shopping by mail—so they put up with the drawbacks of direct mail techniques.

Answers and Explanations

1. E   2. C   3. B   4. A   5. D   6. D   7. B

1. E

First off is a standard question looking for the main idea of the passage. If you've properly developed a "Roadmap" of the passage and put some thought into the author's purpose and main idea up front, this question shouldn't pose much of a problem. The author argues that direct mail has been successful, despite negative attitudes about it, because people like the advantages of shopping by mail. This point is nicely summarized in choice (E).

(A) distorts the technology issue presented in the passage. Increases in technology are seen as responsible for the fact that direct mail marketers now have access to individuals' private information, but technology is not cited as a reason for the success of direct marketing. Not even an inferable statement, (A) is far from being the passage's main idea.

(B) We are never told that concerns over privacy issues have affected the targeting of direct mail audiences. In fact, the opposite may be true—direct marketers seem to ignore individuals' concerns over privacy.

(C) misrepresents the author's argument. The boom in direct mail marketing appears to be the result of individuals' actual reaction to the technique, not a result of the discrepancy *between* attitude and reaction.

(D) discusses only part of the author's argument and is therefore too narrow to reflect the main idea. Part of America's "mixed response" does stem from the perceived threat to privacy caused by aggressive marketing techniques—but what about the other reasons for this mixed response, especially the positive reasons?

> A 180 test taker avoids choices that are too narrow or too broad when searching for the answer to a "main idea" question.

2. C

This "strengthen the argument" question requires that we first understand how the author explains the "seeming contradiction" in paragraph 3. He argues that Americans respond to direct marketing because of its conveniences, even though Americans don't like the annoyance or the invasion of privacy. This evidence assumes that Americans are willing to maintain certain shopping habits despite the drawbacks associated with them. Choice (C) bolsters this assumption and therefore strengthens the argument. If consumers don't perceive a connection between their shopping behaviors and infringements on their rights, they are more likely to react as the author says they do: to continue shopping by mail despite its disadvantages.

(A), (B) These choices focus on one portion of the author's argument but do not help strengthen it as a whole. The fact that awareness of infringement is high (A) would strengthen only one part of the author's claim—that people don't like direct mail. It doesn't bolster the full argument that direct mail marketing is successful *despite* these infringements due to the fact that Americans like to shop by mail. Similarly, with (B), the increased number of people on multiple mailing lists does not necessarily strengthen the argument that people use direct mail despite its drawbacks because they like its conveniences. These individuals may be on multiple lists simply because their names were sold to direct mail companies.

(D) This choice can be seen as contradicting the author's explanation of why direct mail marketing is successful. (D) states that direct marketing may eventually benefit consumers—its success will filter down to consumers over time. But the author tells us that people respond to direct mail marketing because they like its advantages—in other words, they benefit from it now, as they are using it. That's why they put up with its annoyance and invasion of privacy. If (D) is true, perhaps there's more to the story than the author perceives.

(E) The only thing that (E) may strengthen (and it's tenuous at best) is the notion that the "seeming contradiction" that the author describes *exists*. Even that's a stretch. Either way, the implications of the opinion polls in (E) have no bearing whatsoever on our author's *explanation* for the discrepancy at hand.

A 180 test taker understands that just like in Logical Reasoning, strengtheners and weakeners in Reading Comp often work by bolstering or damaging the assumptions in an author's argument.

---

3. B

Ouch. Here's one of the nightmares referred to above, but it's really not as hard as it looks. We're asked to identify the criticism that most closely approximates the logic of the author's concern over the use of computer matching programs. Well, why is the author concerned about these? The line reference brings us right to the crux of the matter: "Further, sophisticated computer matching programs can produce intrusive personal profiles from information which, standing alone, does not threaten individual privacy." Extracting the general logical structure of this, we have a situation in which harmless individual elements, when combined, become harmful in some way. That's the situation we need to find among the choices, and (B) best approximates this situation: the species alone aren't dangerous to the ecosystem, but put them together and look out! The mechanism at work in (B) mirrors the mechanism the author describes in paragraph 1—namely, the way the computer matching systems can combine non-intrusive independent bits of information into a profile that threatens individual privacy.

It's helpful to restate exactly what we're looking for in order to eliminate the wrong choices: The logic of the original example in the passage states that things (bits of information) that individually don't have a certain effect (i.e., threaten privacy) DO have that effect when put together.

(A) Here, we have species that individually don't harm the ecosystem (so far so good), but when put together may harm *each other*. Not the same thing.

(C), like all of the wrong choices, starts out okay with individual species that by themselves don't harm the ecosystem, so we have to look to the end of the choice to see where it goes awry. In this case, the ecologist is chastised for asserting the safety of throwing the three species together into the ecosystem on the grounds that they may not allow other species to join later. Boo hoo. This result would not necessarily cause damage to the ecosystem, which is the result that we're looking for in order for this critique to match the logic of the computer matching example in the passage.

(D) This time the ecologists' assertion is bashed on the grounds that the species in question may be happier somewhere else. Again, the "overlooked possibility" is not one that necessarily causes harm: The ecosystem might not be an optimal environment for the species, but that doesn't necessarily mean that the ecosystem itself will be damaged.

(E) Their *previous* ecosystems? What does that have to do with putting them together here in the ecosystem in question? This is far from the logic underlying the example in the passage.

A 180 test taker is able to apply what she learns in the passage to other issues in different contexts.

---

4. A

The mention of expenditures from 1980–1990 brings us squarely to paragraph 2, where the author informs us that expenditures rose significantly during that stretch, and that "companies would not have made these efforts without prospects of success." Inference questions are not great candidates for prephrasing, so you probably moved on to the choices at this point. Hopefully you saw that (A) is a reasonable inference based on this information. It stands to reason that companies spent more money on advertising because they expected to benefit from it (in accordance with the "laws of the market"). Therefore, the rise in direct marketing expenditures can be reasonably said to reflect their expectations regarding success.

(B), (C), (D) The passage implies that companies benefited from direct marketing—meaning, they made greater profits—but we have no idea how much they benefited. Thus, a specific claim like (B)'s assertion that they made "more than double" the profit at the end than at the beginning of the period is not warranted. Similarly, we are told that expenditures rose from 1980 to 1990, but we don't know how much they rose in any given year. In fact, we can't be sure that expenditures rose every single year—we're only told that the 1990 figure was greater than the 1980 figure. For all we know, expenditures could have decreased in 1981, thus making this the lowest expenditure year. So we don't have enough information to infer choice (C). The same is true of choice (D). We're only told that expenditures rose from 1980–90. We cannot infer anything about what companies might expect expenditures to be in the future.

(E) distorts information in the passage. The author tells us that "the laws of the market dictate" that companies would not have invested in direct marketing unless they expected it to be successful. But to say that the rise in expenditures "parallels" the laws of the market is a distortion of this concept. The rise in expenditures may be explained with reference to the laws of the economic market, but that's about it. (E)'s manner of combining these two elements of the passage is unwarranted.

5. D

The answer to a detail question like this will most likely not restate the passage's information directly, but will often be recognizable, nonetheless, as a close paraphrase. Since a number of parts of this passage deal with Americans' reaction to direct mail, perhaps the best method is to move right to the choices, seeing if any jump out. (D) is, in fact, a very close paraphrase of the author's main idea that emerges along the way and is summarized rather explicitly in the final paragraph. The author thinks the public's reaction to direct mail is "strangely mixed" but explainable, a view that is captured nicely by choice (D).

(A) goes beyond the scope of the passage. The author does not discuss the "true dangers" of the enterprise (whatever these may be).

(B) This choice exaggerates material from the passage. The author states in paragraph 3 that Americans are willing to put up with the drawbacks of direct mail because they like its conveniences. We might interpret this as meaning that people are willing to overlook some problems in order to receive certain benefits. To say that people "consistently act against their deeply held convictions," however, is going too far. Besides, the dislike of direct mail probably doesn't qualify as a deeply held conviction in most people's books.

A 180 test taker recognizes and quickly eliminates extreme-sounding answer choices.

(C) This choice only gives us part of the author's view, and is a distortion to boot. The author distinctly tells us that the public's reaction is mixed—it's not just negative, as this answer choice portrays it. In addition, the negative attitude of the American public revolves around both the privacy issue and the "annoyance" factor. It's a distortion to say that privacy is the primary issue.

(E) The author states no such thing. In fact, the author tells us that the industry has been very *successful* despite the public's negative attitudes. There is no indication that the industry will need to alter its practices.

6. D

Next we're asked to determine what function is served by the opinions expressed in the survey mentioned in the beginning of paragraph 2. These opinions are provided as evidence for the public's negative view of direct mail. But, later in paragraph 2, these opinions seem to contradict further findings of the same survey, which show that people who don't like direct mail buy from direct mail ads anyway! This function is captured in choice (D)—these opinions are brought up to form a contrast to the behavior of consumers described later in the paragraph, which in turn forms the basis of the author's main concern.

A 180 test taker looks to weed out the function of each paragraph, which puts him in an excellent position to determine how any given part of the passage serves the whole.

(A) goes beyond the scope of the passage. The negative attitudes revealed in this part of the survey would make it rather unlikely that the opinions were used by the author to justify increased direct mail spending.

(B) The author does not provide a "solution" to a paradoxical situation but rather an explanation for a seemingly contradictory phenomenon. If anything, the opinions cited contribute to a contradictory phenomenon, not to its explanation.

(C) The information about computer matching programs is presented in paragraph 1 and is unrelated to the author's discussion of the survey. The author develops his conclusion about the problem of the matching program without resorting to any opinion data.

(E) The opinions expressed in the survey *could* reasonably be used to argue that the direct marketing industry will fall on hard times; after all, the opinions expressed are quite negative. But that would be a different passage altogether—here, the author goes on to say that the industry seems to be booming *in spite of* these opinions.

7. B

This inference question requires us to determine which statement could most likely be attributed to the author, based on the information presented in the passage. Again, our grasp of the author's purpose in writing the passage comes into play. This passage looks at the difference between Americans' attitudes about direct mail and their behaviors in response to it. Evidence for the public's attitudes is provided through opinion surveys, which suggests that the author believes that the attitudes revealed in surveys can help us understand public behavior, choice (B). Think of it this way: If the author *didn't* agree with (B), then there would be no contradiction to resolve, because the data from the opinion polls would be meaningless. The passage as is can exist only if the author believes that polls can provide insight as stated in choice (B).

(A) exaggerates the author's conclusion. We are told that Americans respond to direct mail because they perceive its benefits, but it would be going too far to conclude from this that the author believes that direct mail has "an overall positive effect on American society."

(C) presents an unwarranted comparison that in no way can be attributed to the author. Nuisance and privacy invasion are two categories of responses from the poll of paragraph 2, with the former outranking the latter in the public's mind, but we can't infer from this that the author believes that presenting a nuisance is a greater offense than invading privacy when it comes to direct marketing, no less in the context of "commercial enterprises" as a whole.

A 180 test taker zeros in on comparisons presented in choices to determine whether they are warranted or unwarranted.

(D) switches the terms of the second-to-last sentence of the passage, which reads "Even those who believe that the direct mailing industry has a generally negative societal impact probably would prefer to remain on some mailing lists." Not only does (D) get this backwards, but it also fails to take into account the qualified nature of the author's assertion indicated by the word "probably."

(E) Again, we are not given enough information to draw this inference. The author does not discuss the future growth of direct marketing, so it's too much of a stretch to infer how the author thinks the industry might increase or decrease. In addition, the passage states that the direct marketing industry has grown *despite* people's negative attitudes about it. Growth in the industry does not therefore seem directly proportional to negative attitudes, which is another reason why it is unwarranted to ascribe the belief in (E) to the author.

What's Next?

How's it going so far? Next up we present one more legal-minded author to contend with before moving on to the more specialized and esoteric material. We call this one "Evolutionary Models of Law." Do what you can with it and then check out the explanation.

PASSAGE 4

To understand the special appeal that evolutionary models and metaphors hold for legal scholars, one must first appreciate that scholars mean something quite different by "the law" than

(5) do most lawyers or citizens. To someone who may be affected by a legal decision, the important issue to predict is how a particular case will be decided. This rarely interests legal scholars. They typically focus on patterns in legal decisions which emerge

(10) over many decades.

Evolutionary models and metaphors are a particularly useful device for talking about changes of this sort in the law. One of the distinctive features of evolutionary theories is that

(15) they may be used to describe the nature and direction of changes in a complex phenomenon even though little is known about its constituent parts and the mechanisms connecting them. Darwin knew almost nothing about the

(20) mechanisms of heredity; yet he was able to formulate simple, powerful statements at higher levels of abstraction about the patterns of change that result from these forces. Similarly, writers in the evolutionary legal tradition—from Savigny

(25) and Maine to Hirshleifer and Rodgers—aspire to describe global patterns of change in the law without specifying the details of why particular officials decide particular cases as they do. They are not abusing evolutionary metaphors. Rather,

(30) they are attempting to use a unique aspect of the power of evolutionary models to make relatively refined statements at an abstract level.

To say that evolutionary models have particular advantages for describing gradual patterns of

(35) change in the law is not, however, to assert that the function of jurisprudence is primarily descriptive. Theories of law are rarely written to describe; their aim is more often to advocate and to legitimate. Here too, on a normative level,

(40) evolutionary models have a particular appeal. In one guise or another, the question, "by what right do courts and bureaucrats make law?" has occupied a large percentage of the energy of American legal scholars. If law is to be more than

(45) the record of commands backed by superior force, a jurisprudential theory is needed which gives meaning to arguments that law is right or wrong (rather than simply *is*). It is here that the normative power of evolutionary theories comes

(50) into play. Lawyers have fastened on evolution as an alternative to intuition or economics as a source of natural law principles by which human law may be judged.

As a context for thinking about law,

(55) evolutionary metaphors offer both perils and

strengths. The peril is insidious, if well known. Evolutionary theories can be, and have been, invoked to maintain that existing legal arrangements are the natural, even inevitable,

(60) products of evolution. But it does not follow that an evolutionary jurisprudence leads inevitably to legal scholarship which rationalizes the status quo. On the contrary, the evolutionary tradition encourages debate of diverse opinions and

(65) interpretations in that it does not dictate a single definite theory of law; at most, an evolutionary approach to law creates a context, a distinctive kind of conversational setting, within which dialogue about law may occur. It provides the

(70) intellectual atmosphere in which legal scholarship may be at once constructive and creative, critical and vigorous. At its best, evolutionary jurisprudence leads scholars to take legal doctrine seriously but not glorify it.

1. The primary purpose of the passage is to

(A) compare two models of law and advocate one of them
(B) describe the uses and advantages of one model of law
(C) distinguish between two aspects of a legal model and determine which is more appropriate
(D) explain how American legal scholars have answered questions about the legitimacy of law
(E) discuss the work of one group of American legal scholars

2. The author indicates that an evolutionary model of law serves primarily as

(A) A predictor of specific legal decisions
(B) An intuitive approach to jurisprudential theory
(C) A description of legal reforms
(D) A conceptualization of broad legal trends
(E) A rationalization of the status quo

3. The author refers to Darwin in order to

   (A) support the view that evolutionary models of law do not depend on detailed factual knowledge
   (B) warn against the abuse of evolutionary models by nonscientists
   (C) show that the abstract approach of legal theorists is superior to that of lawyers and citizens
   (D) contend that evolutionary theories have been slipshod in their uses of evidence
   (E) draw a comparison suggesting that evolutionary legal theory is in its infancy

4. The author would probably express sympathy with which one of the following statements?

   (A) Law requires moral legitimation.
   (B) Power is its own justification.
   (C) The present is inevitably better than the past.
   (D) Evolutionary jurisprudence should reinforce the status quo.
   (E) Legal scholars should focus more on the details of evolutionary change than on global patterns.

5. The author makes all of the following points about evolutionary models EXCEPT that they

   (A) describe change at high levels of abstraction
   (B) provide answers to questions about the legitimacy of law
   (C) can be utilized to rationalize the legal status quo
   (D) focus on long-term patterns of change
   (E) strive for detailed precision in their description of legal phenomena

6. It can be inferred that which one of the following is most likely to be the subject of a work by Savigny?

   (A) a discussion of how the law has been changed by the impact of specific cases
   (B) an essay concerning the sources of judges' authority to define the law
   (C) an inquiry into the derivation of human law from principles of natural law
   (D) a historical study of how Roman law developed into medieval law
   (E) a treatise on personal property law

7. The author would most likely describe the view that legal codes merely reflect the power of dominant social groups as

   (A) laudable
   (B) debatable
   (C) objectionable
   (D) astonishing
   (E) far-sighted

Passage 4: Evolutionary Models of Law

What Makes It Difficult

What does evolution have to do with law? There's no common sense connection between the two, so for most people the subject matter of this one begins in foreign territory, which always makes it more difficult to handle. And since the main thrust of the passage revolves around this link, those who don't eventually get the connection down are in for a long haul. The author never even bothers to formally define "evolutionary models and metaphors," and leaves us to infer the context from such things as references to Charles Darwin and descriptions of the features of evolutionary theories. Furthermore, the difference between a "model" and a "metaphor" isn't described, but turns out to be unimportant, as these two terms are used interchangeably with "theory." All of this adds to the passage's complexity. As usual, we can paraphrase the key ideas and break the passage down into manageable chunks. Here are the key points:

Key Points of the Passage

Purpose and Main Idea: The author's purpose is to discuss the evolutionary approach to law and the attraction and uses that it has for legal scholars. The main idea is that viewing law in an evolutionary context, while posing some possible problems, has many advantages while giving lawyers a context through which to judge legal morality.

Paragraph Structure: Paragraph 1 establishes the connection between models of evolution and legal issues, so a good first step is a common sense reading of the term "evolutionary model." "Evolution" most likely conjures up an image of Charles Darwin and his description of long-term changes in the development of species. Might this term, used in this legal context, refer to gradual change over a period of time, as Darwin's type of "evolution" does? This reading is confirmed by the last sentence of the paragraph: "They typically focus on patterns in legal decisions which emerge over many decades."

Paragraph 2 cements this interpretation with the use of phrases such as "aspire to describe global patterns of change in the law" and "make relatively refined statements at an abstract level." The latter relates to Darwin's method discussed earlier in the paragraph, so on the whole this second paragraph merely reinforces the notion that law can be viewed in the context of evolutionary theories.

The second half of the passage touches on the subject of morality in law. Paragraph 3 assures us that viewing law in an evolutionary context need not imply that legal scholars do so simply to describe what's going on; the function of legal theories is to "advocate and legitimate." Law needs to be more than simply commands backed by force, and evolutionary metaphors give legal scholars an alternative to other rationales backing legal structures such as intuition or economics.

The problem in this arrangement is touched on in the beginning of paragraph 4: The evolutionary paradigm may encourage some "to maintain that existing legal arrangements are the natural, even inevitable, products of evolution." This is akin to the "but that's the way it's *always* been" argument used to justify certain laws—slavery, for example. While this can happen, the author contends that an evolutionary model of law will not inevitably lead in this direction, since such a model encourages debate, dialogue, and interpretation. The final few sentences speak to the promise that the evolutionary approach of law presents.

Answers and Explanations

1. B   2. D   3. A   4. A   5. E   6. D   7. C

1. B

We're looking for the primary purpose, so let's quickly review the passage structure: paragraphs 1 and 2 are primarily descriptive, telling us what evolutionary models and metaphors do ("focus on patterns," "describe the nature and direction of changes") and don't do ("predict how a particular case will be decided"). Paragraphs 3 and 4 lean more toward what these "models and metaphors" can and should do: "advocate and legitimate," lead scholars "to take legal doctrine seriously but not to glorify it." This is summed up by correct choice (B). Key words in each paragraph— "appeal," "useful device," "advantages," "strengths" (paragraphs 1, 2, 3, and 4, respectively)—justify (B)'s speaking of "advantages" as well as "uses."

(A) *Two* models? No, there's just one. "Models and metaphors" do not count as two things; these terms are used interchangeably.

(C) may serve as a summary of the primary purpose of paragraph 4, but not of the entire passage; it neglects those early descriptive paragraphs.

(D) also focuses narrowly on the last two paragraphs. Yes, the author does talk there about "the legitimacy of law," but this is not the purpose of the *entire* passage.

(E) is intended to recall that reference in paragraph 3 to "American legal scholars." But the author always discusses these people as if all legal scholars should be lumped together; they are never mentioned in smaller, separate, or distinguished groups.

2. D

Another way of phrasing this question stem is to ask, "What is the primary purpose of an evolutionary model?" Scanning the first few words of each choice is a good approach here, since several give themselves away just in a word or two:

(A) says such evolutionary models serve as a "predictor," which directly contradicts paragraph 1, where we're told that "to predict . . . how a particular case will be decided . . . rarely interests legal scholars."

(B) calls it "an intuitive approach," directly contradicting paragraph 3, which informs us that "Lawyers have fastened on evolution as an alternative to intuition."

(E) The reference in (E) to "rationalization" should make you suspicious, since the only place that subject comes up is in paragraph 4, where the author discusses the "perils and strengths" of this model of law. Moreover, the author is critical of rationalizing the status quo, but generally approving toward evolutionary models.

A 180 test taker reads only as much as is necessary to eliminate a choice. If one word of a choice is off-base, she chops that choice on that account alone.

(C) is faulty because of the word "reforms." What evolutionary models and metaphors describe, according to paragraph 1, is "patterns which emerge over many decades." Such patterns could include both reform and no change at all. (This is backed up by paragraph 4, where the author discusses maintaining the status quo through evolutionary theories.)

(D) is correct not only by default but by virtue of what it says. Notice how the neutral language ("broad legal trends") matches the neutral description in the passage ("patterns . . . which emerge over many decades").

3. A

This one's not too tough, mainly because Darwin and his theories are so well-known that his presence in the passage not only makes sense in the context but helps us make sense *of* the context. On the most basic level, the author refers to Darwin because he, like the legal scholars of the passage, was interested in a long-term pattern, an evolution. Does the Darwin example support the legal scholars, contradict the legal scholars, give a concrete example of the abstract work a legal scholar does? Near the middle of paragraph 2 we're told that Darwin "knew almost nothing about the mechanisms of heredity; yet he was able to formulate simple, powerful statements at higher levels of abstraction about the patterns that result from these changes." In other words, he didn't know *how* or *why* heredity works; he knew nothing about genes and chromosomes; yet he was able to see the patterns it caused and describe them. The very next sentence begins with "similarly"—right there you should know what's coming, that legal scholars do the same—and the rest of the sentence confirms it. This is all neatly paraphrased by correct choice (A).

(B) One sentence later we're told: "They are not abusing evolutionary metaphors." So much for choice (B).

(C) is a classic wrong answer type in that it takes a point made in the passage (there is a difference between legal scholars on the one hand and lawyers and citizens on the other) and gives it a twist the author never suggested (legal theorists are *better*).

(D) is a misinterpretation of the author's statement that neither Darwin nor legal scholars specify the detailed mechanics of the evolution they study. This is not a result of carelessness, as (D) suggests, but of focus; the details are not necessary to the work done by these people.

(E) misinterprets the same part of the passage by suggesting that like Darwin, evolutionary legal theorists are perhaps pioneers in their field, whose work is necessarily primitive because it's only a beginning. This is nonsense—in fact, at one point the author refers to the "evolutionary legal tradition," which is certainly indicative of something well-established.

A 180 test taker can recognize distortions of passage ideas a mile away.

---

4. A

This is a very general inference question asking for a view with which the author might agree. The best thing to do is keep focused on what's already known about the author's opinion while testing out the choices.

A 180 test taker works out what the author does think as it is explained in the passage before speculating about what the author might think.

KAPLAN

Basically, our author supports evolutionary models and metaphors as a "useful device for talking about [long-term] changes . . . in the law" (paragraph 2). They may help scholars prove that "law is right or wrong (rather than simply is)" (paragraph 3). Turning to the choices now, (A) immediately looks good. It echoes paragraph 3, where the author says that evolutionary legal theories should "advocate and . . . legitimate," and strongly implies that the law itself should be "more than the record of commands backed by superior force." In other words, "might" should not "make right"; laws themselves should be morally legitimate.

(B) contradicts this sentiment; it translates as "might *does* make right."

(C) is too sweeping. While evolutionary legal theorists clearly believe that the law changes over decades, the author never goes so far as to suggest that the present is *always* better than the past.

(D) goes against the first half of paragraph 4, where the author discusses the "perils" of evolutionary law. Far from saying that evolutionary jurisprudence *should* reinforce the status quo, the author warns against this as one of the "perils" of using evolutionary metaphors. In fact, the author specifically defends the evolutionary model by arguing that "it does not follow that an evolutionary jurisprudence leads inevitably to legal scholarship which rationalizes the status quo."

(E) contradicts paragraph 2, where the author says that "writers in the evolutionary legal tradition . . . aspire to describe global patterns of change in the law without specifying the details of why particular officials decide particular cases as they do." So evolutionary legal scholars focus on the global patterns, *not* on the details, and the author supports this methodology.

5. E

We've no option but to try out the choices, crossing off those in accordance with the tenets of evolutionary law as presented by the author.

(A) is quite true; the author refers throughout paragraph 2 to "higher levels of abstraction" and "refined statements at an abstract level." And in fact, we may as well mention here that this is the very reason why (E) is correct: "Detailed precision" is the opposite of high-level abstraction. Precision certainly sounds like a good thing, but as we've seen before, this is not what Darwin or the proponents of the evolutionary approach to law are seeking.

(B) raises an issue just addressed in the last question, the "legitimacy of law"; we noted then that answering questions on this issue is a possible role for evolutionary models and metaphors.

A 180 test taker expects the same ideas from the passage to appear repeatedly, perhaps in different forms, throughout the question set.

(C) should be quite familiar by now; it describes one of the perils of such models.

(D) recalls the very first statement the passage makes about evolutionary models and metaphors; their very nature causes them to focus on the long-term patterns of law.

A 180 test taker gets stronger as she proceeds through the question set due to better and better assimilation of the author's ideas.

---

6. D

No matter whether a question asks about someone as well-known as Darwin or as obscure (to most of us, anyway) as Savigny, it's good strategy to relocate the name in the passage and check up on just who we're dealing with. In the middle of paragraph 2 we get the following facts: Savigny is a writer in the evolutionary legal tradition, and "aspires to describe global patterns of change in the law without specifying the details of why particular officials decide particular cases as they do." Credited choice (D) is right for two important reasons: first, it mentions an evolution (the development of Roman law into medieval law) and second, it deals with the big picture, as evolutionary legal writers do.

(A) is the opposite of what Savigny would care about, which becomes clear once we read the part about how Savigny and his cohorts look to describe global legal trends "without specifying the details."

(B) The author says that the question "by what right do courts and bureaucrats make law?" is relevant and important to legal scholars, but does not specifically connect Savigny's name with this issue.

A 180 test taker recognizes choices that try to connect elements from the passage that have no right to be connected.

(C) is playing around with that reference at the end of paragraph 3 to "natural law principles by which human law may be judged." But again, Savigny is not connected with this issue.

(E) "Personal property law" is too vague; to choose (E) we'd need to know what Savigny was saying about it, whether the treatise dealt with long-term changes or with details.

7. C

Try decoding the question stem first: "legal codes" is a fancy way of saying "laws," while "the power of dominant social groups" could be rephrased as "the people with the most power." In essence, the idea is that the only real function of a law is to enforce what powerful people want it to enforce. This should ring a bell: in the middle of paragraph 3 the author says "If law is to be more than the record of command backed by superior force, a jurisprudential theory is needed which gives meaning to arguments that law is right or wrong (rather than simply *is*)." The author, then, comes down on the side of judging laws, evaluating their morality, and would not agree with the statement made in the question stem. (A) and (E) are out at that point, since they have the author responding positively.

On the other hand, the author would not find the idea surprising, as (D) suggests; he or she treats it as a familiar and troubling issue, which legal theorists have dealt with before. Between (B) and (C), (B) is wrong because there is no debate in the author's mind: he or she is clearly in favor of distinguishing between good and bad laws. "Objectionable" (C) is a reasonable description of the author's probable reaction to a statement that completely contradicts what he or she believes.

A 180 test taker approaches "tone" questions (those that ask about the author's attitude regarding some subject or demeanor in general) methodically, first narrowing down the author's tone to positive, negative, or neutral. That alone helps eliminate at least a few choices, allowing him to put the bulk of his time into choosing among the remaining viable candidates.

What's Next?

Still there? Good. In the next chapter we'll explore the wonderful world of science. You don't have to be Einstein to handle these—but it probably wouldn't hurt.

CHAPTER THIRTEEN

Blinded by Science

This Reading Comprehension category could also be called "It's Not Brain Surgery—It's Rocket Science." Actually, neither brain surgery nor rocket science would be an unusual topic for the LSAT Reading Comp section. Nor, for that matter, would esoteric, mind-numbingly technical topics such as lake stratification, mitochondria, symbiotic stars, or plate tectonics—the very subjects of the passages that follow.

We at Kaplan designate these as "hard" science passages, not in the sense of being difficult (although they certainly are that), but rather to distinguish these technical science passages from "soft" science passages, which view scientific topics from other angles such as the history or social repercussions of scientific findings. There's not always a "hard" science passage on the test, but when they appear, they often give test takers fits—especially those coming to law from a nontechnical background such as humanities or social science. The key to successfully tackling science passages is to not allow yourself to be overwhelmed by the technical terms and processes described.

> A 180 test taker notes the location and purpose of intricate details, but doesn't attempt to memorize or even fully understand those details unless a question specifically asks about them.

Focus on the author's purpose and main idea, using the mass of details to fill in the big picture rather than to learn everything about the topics presented. You should dig deeper only when a point is at stake. Follow these keys, and when someone asks you how hard the science passages are on the LSAT Reading Comp section, you'll be able to proudly state, "hey, it's not *brain surgery*"—even when it is.

PASSAGE 5

One of the many remarkable properties of water is the unwillingness of bodies of water of substantially different temperatures to mix together. This property is responsible for the
(5) formation in freshwater lakes of a phenomenon known as the thermocline, a phenomenon that can play an important role in a lake's summertime ecology. Consider the annual temperature fluctuations in a typical deep-water impoundment
(10) in the southern United States. In late winter, usually sometime in February or March, whatever ice may have previously formed at the surface of the lake melts, and the water temperature measures a uniform 38–42 degrees. Wave action
(15) stirs oxygen into the water at the lake's surface, and the temperature uniformity allows distribution of this dissolved oxygen to all depths. With oxygen plentiful, many of the reservoir's fish species, both predator and forager, are found
(20) throughout the water column.

The windy, sunny days of early spring quickly warm the lake's surface. As the surface temperature increases, that water expands. Because 50-degree water is lighter than 40-degree
(25) water, a layer of warmer water builds at the surface of the lake, resting like a pillow on the mass of colder water below. The pillow of warm surface water slowly increases in thickness, as heat is transferred into the depths by the limited
(30) stirring of wave action.

By early summer, a remarkable stratification has occurred. A sharp boundary separates two independent bodies of water within the lake. The boundary is a temperature gradient called the
(35) thermocline, and it acts as a barricade to prevent any further mixing of oxygen into the chilly depths. The depth of the thermocline fluctuates with air temperatures and the prevailing winds. On July 1, the water temperature at the surface
(40) might be 86 degrees, 84 degrees at 10 feet, and 82 degrees at 20 feet—but at 24 feet, the temperature has plunged to 65 degrees. When winter ended, the depths were well-oxygenated and populated with fish. But as the thermocline set up in late
(45) spring, the supply of oxygen to the depths was abruptly shut off. In summer, the temperature barrier prevents oxygen from circulating downward from the surface to replace the oxygen consumed by fish and dying zooplankton. In order
(50) to survive, fish are forced upward into the relatively narrow zone between the thermocline and the surface.

The cold nights of autumn reverse the trend, as the surface cools to the point that it is heavier than
(55) the water below the thermocline. This initiates a process known as the turnover: A current of richly oxygenated water plunges to the bottom of the reservoir, forcing stagnant water back to the surface. The lake reaches equilibrium by early
(60) winter and remains there until the process repeats itself the following spring.

1. The passage suggests that which one of the following can be inferred about dissolved oxygen in a lake?

   (A) The colder the water, the less dissolved oxygen it can hold.
   (B) There is always more dissolved oxygen within six feet of the surface than at 60 feet beneath the surface.
   (C) The formation of ice can completely block the supply of dissolved oxygen.
   (D) Dissolved oxygen is not necessary for organisms other than fish and zooplankton.
   (E) Wave action at the surface is a significant source of dissolved oxygen.

2. Which one of the following most accurately describes the organization of the passage?

   (A) A problem is described, its potential effects are summarized, and a possible solution is critiqued.
   (B) A property is introduced, a process resulting from the property is described, and an effect is explored.
   (C) A process is outlined and then described in greater detail, and its benefits are explained.
   (D) A problem is defined, and its implications are considered and generalized.
   (E) A chronology is described, various events are fit into the chronology, and predictions are made.

3. The author states in the second paragraph that 50-degree water is lighter than 40-degree water primarily in order to

(A) refute a commonly held theory regarding the effects of temperature increases in the water near lake surfaces

(B) explain why warmer water tends to sink below layers of colder water in lakes of the southern United States

(C) prove that the number of fish occupying different water levels in freshwater lakes is directly related to the formation of the thermocline

(D) show how the decreased oxygen level in the depths of freshwater lakes during certain seasons could lead to the death of zooplankton

(E) supply background information relevant to an explanation of a step in the lake stratification process

4. The passage suggests that the effects of temperature stratification

(A) would be relevant to the interests of fisheries managers

(B) on an individual lake cannot be predicted

(C) represent the most important factor influencing a lake's ecology

(D) become more pronounced as a lake gets older

(E) are most severe in the lakes of the southern United States

5. Which one of the following is not mentioned in the passage as a step in the yearly lake stratification process?

(A) Fish congregate in the water layer above the thermocline in the summer.

(B) Water temperatures achieve a general uniformity by late winter.

(C) The thermocline reaches its maximum depth by early summer.

(D) Oxygen levels decline in the layer beneath the thermocline.

(E) The fall turnover replaces stagnant water in the depths with oxygen-rich water.

6. The author is primarily interested in discussing

(A) the effect of fish and other aquatic organisms on a phenomenon known as the thermocline

(B) the relationship between a lake's ecology and water purity

(C) the contribution of the thermocline to overfishing in Southern lakes

(D) an effect of the seasonal warming and cooling of water in freshwater lakes

(E) the changes in a lake's water temperature caused by fluctuating oxygen levels

Passage 5: Lake Stratification

What Makes It Difficult

A common thread to most science passages is the employment of jargon—technical terms and phrases peppered throughout the passage that serve to scare off, or at least befuddle, the unsophisticated test taker.

A 180 test taker cuts past jargon, returning to cumbersome technical details only when a question demands it.

This passage is no exception, introducing us to things such as the "thermocline" and a process called "the turnover"—heck, they even throw in "deep-water impoundment" as a synonym for the simple term "lake." We have to ask: Is that really necessary? But the jargon here isn't even as thick as in some of the others that follow. The problem in this passage is keeping track of the various processes at work. Lots of details, lots of mechanisms, lots of numbers to keep on top of—that's the challenge here. But if you break each part of the process down into simple ideas, it's not so hard to handle. The passage is, after all, mostly descriptive, so we simply need to follow the cycle described from winter through the rest of the seasons and back to winter again, bearing in mind that the author is interested, as stated early on, in the role this process plays in a lake's summertime ecology.

Key Points of the Passage

Purpose and Main Idea: The author's purpose is to explore the cyclical process of lake stratification and its effects on lake ecology. The main idea is that seasonal temperature differences within lake water cause the cyclical formation of water layers of various temperatures separated by the thermocline, which prevents oxygen from reaching the colder, deeper lake waters and periodically causes redistribution of fish within the lake.

Paragraph Structure: Paragraph 1 introduces the thermocline phenomenon and describes its development using the example of freshwater lakes in the southern United States. The description of the cycle that the author will present throughout the passage begins at the end of the paragraph with info about late winter, when lake water temperatures are uniform and fish species thrive at all depths of the lake.

Paragraph 2 describes the changes that occur in early spring: The water on the surface of the lake becomes warmer and lighter than the water below it. This warm water expands and forms a layer over the water below.

Paragraph 3 describes the development and results of the thermocline. In summer, the warm water on top of the lake becomes distinctly separated from the colder water below it by the thermocline, a temperature gradient that acts as a boundary between the two parts of the lake. The thermocline boundary prevents oxygen from reaching the lower depths of the lake, and this causes fish to swim up to the warmer surface of the lake to survive.

The final paragraph describes the reversal of the cycle. In fall, the water at the surface above the thermocline cools and becomes heavier than the water below the thermocline. This allows oxygen to plunge to the depths of the lake, and the lake reaches equilibrium again by early winter.

Answers and Explanations

1. E   2. B   3. E   4. A   5. C   6. D

1. E

This inference question asks about the subject of dissolved oxygen, which is raised many times in the passage. It's not easy here to pinpoint exactly which part of the passage we should review to answer this question, so the best tactic is to evaluate the answer choices, returning to the passage for verification when necessary.

> A 180 test taker knows when and how to allow the answer choices to guide her to the relevant portions of the text when a question is fairly open-ended.

We're told in paragraph 1 that wave action stirs oxygen into the water, making (E) the best inference in this set.

(A) We aren't given information relating water temperature to oxygen capacity. True, during certain months the thermocline prevents oxygen from reaching the cooler depths, but for all we know, cold water can hold just as much dissolved oxygen as warm water given the chance.

(B) On the contrary: The passage tells us in paragraph 1 that during late winter, oxygen is found plentifully throughout all of a lake's water levels.

(C) The only thing we're told about ice formation is that ice melts in February and March, which is not nearly enough information to allow us to infer the statement in (C).

(D) This choice misrepresents the author's claim in paragraph 3. We're told that fish and zooplankton consume oxygen below the surface, but not that they're the *only* organisms that do so.

If you're not sure where to look back for information in the passage, move to the answer choices and allow them to guide you back to the relevant sections. If you can kill a choice on sight, fine, but it's usually worth quickly verifying that a choice is bogus, especially in such a detail-heavy passage as this one.

2. B

Next up is a general question concerned with the organization of the passage. Hopefully you took the time to focus on the passage's structure; if so, a prephrase was certainly in order. Even though the details may be a bit cumbersome, the overall structure isn't that complex, and (B) provides a good summary of this structure: A "remarkable property" (the unwillingness of different temperature water to mix) leads to a process (the formation of the thermocline) which has some effects (determining the supply of oxygen and forcing the species of lakes to behave in certain ways).

> A 180 test taker is able to form and recognize general paraphrases of the specific action taking place in the passage.

(A) and (D) can be ruled out quickly because the author describes a property and a related phenomenon, not a particular problem or solutions.

(C) sounds plausible at first, but fails in the end. The "benefits" of the thermocline aren't related here.

(E) Events from winter, spring, summer, and fall are related in that order, so presumably it's okay to say that a "chronology is described," if only in the loose sense of the word. As in (C), the main problem comes at the end—no "predictions" are made. Describing results or effects of a process is not the same as making predictions.

A 180 test taker doesn't fall for half-right, half-wrong choices that start off pretty well, but go awry toward the end. He reads and pays careful attention to the entire answer choice.

---

3. E

This question ends with the words "in order to," which tells us we need to determine the purpose of some piece of information; in other words, how does a certain statement function in the context of the section in which it appears? In this case, why does the author mention that 50-degree water is lighter than 40-degree water? In general, he's attempting to explain the process of lake stratification—you might have prephrased this answer and scanned the choices for it. In fact, choice (E) comes pretty close: The author mentions the difference to help the reader better understand his explanation of a particular step in the lake stratification process—the step in which a layer of warmer water forms over a layer of cooler water.

If you weren't able to prephrase this answer, you needed to evaluate the answer choices to eliminate the ones that *don't* represent the purpose of this detail:

(A) can be ruled out quickly, because the author isn't attempting to refute any theories.

(B) On the contrary: The author explains in paragraph 2 why warmer water forms layers *on top of* colder water.

(C) is tricky because the author certainly does suggest that the number of fish dispersed through different layers of lakes is related to the thermocline, but showing this is not the reason the author included the bit about the 50-degree and 40-degree water. The comparison between these water temperatures doesn't prove anything, and besides, the information about the thermocline's effect on fish placement comes later.

(D) Zooplankton appear even later than the issue raised in (C), and is even further removed from the purpose of the author's comparison between 50-degree and 40-degree water.

4. A

Here we have another inference question, denoted by the word "suggests." What does the author suggest about the effects of temperature stratification? The most significant effect he discusses is how temperature stratification causes fish to move to the top layer of lakes during the summer. This might certainly be pertinent for fisheries, as choice (A) indicates.

(B) No, the passage shows that the effects of temperature stratification can be predicted to some degree, at least in terms of the general effect on lake ecology. It also shows that the general timing of these effects can be predicted as well. (Note that this doesn't conflict with the explanations above to question 2, choice (E), in which we say that the author doesn't make predictions. Suggesting that due to a stable process, results can be predicted is not the same as saying, from a passage structure point of view, that the author *himself* makes predictions.)

(C) and (E) exaggerate the author's claims in the passage. Paragraph 1 states that the thermocline plays an "important role" in lake ecology, but we don't know if it is the *most* important factor (C). It is also clear that temperature stratification affects southern U. S. lakes, but these effects aren't compared to those of other lakes, so we can't determine the relative severity of the effects (E).

A 180 test taker recognizes extreme wording that damages the plausibility of certain answer choices, and instinctively stays away from those that include exaggerated or extreme ideas.

(D) is outside the scope of the argument. The age of lakes is never brought up in the author's discussion, nor is anything implied regarding the way lake age may affect the stratification process described.

5. C

Here's a detail question asking us to look for something that was NOT mentioned in the passage— a bit harder than the traditional detail question. Fortunately, the wrong answers are all stated in the passage fairly clearly. (C) is the only choice that's not mentioned; in fact, it even tends to contradict the passage: Paragraph 3 tells us that the depth of the thermocline fluctuates with temperature and winds, so we can't be sure when the depth is at its maximum.

All of the other answer choices repeat information from the passage. Paragraph 3 tells us that fish move above the thermocline in the summer, so this eliminates (A). We're told in paragraph 1 that water temperatures are uniform in late winter, eliminating (B). Paragraph 3 helps us eliminate (D), because it states that the thermocline shuts off the supply of oxygen to the lower depths. Finally, choice (E) can be eliminated by paragraph 4, which describes how the turnover brings oxygen to deeper, stagnant water.

6. D

The stem itself gives away the fact that the author's purpose is "to discuss" something, so there's no need to choose among various verbs (discuss, argue, refute, etc.) —but what is he interested in discussing? The author's main concern should be firmly planted in your mind by now; he's simply interested in discussing the process and effects of lake stratification. Choice (D) comes very close to this prephrase, merely substituting "seasonal warming and cooling of water . . ." for the process described.

Both (A) and (E) reverse the direction of causality in the author's discussion. The author is interested in how the thermocline affects lake ecology, not vice versa (A). Similarly, he shows how changing water temperatures, by means of the thermocline, affect oxygen levels—not the other way around, as (E) would have it.

A 180 test taker is ultrasensitive to cause-and-effect relationships, and is not likely to mistake one for the other.

(B) and (C) go beyond the argument's scope. The author mentions "stagnant" water in paragraph 4, but does not focus on water purity throughout the passage. And the phenomenon of overfishing, if it exists, is not discussed.

What's Next?

Not so bad, huh? Well, of course, we're just getting started, and not surprisingly, things do get a bit worse. "Mitochondria," the next passage in our little group of nightmares, raises the bar, both in the density of the material and in technical jargon. We'll get back to you in the explanation.

THE NEXT READING COMPREHENSION
PASSAGE BEGINS ON THE FOLLOWING PAGE

PASSAGE 6

Some one and a half or two billion years ago, when the Earth was still poor in oxygen, a primitive bacterium that made a precarious living from the anaerobic fermentation of organic
(5) molecules engulfed a smaller cell that had somehow evolved the ability to respire. The event was a turning point in organic evolution. Respiration liberates far more energy than fermentation, and the growing abundance of
(10) oxygen in the atmosphere must have been the driving force behind a symbiotic relation that developed between the two cells, with the aerobic cell generating energy in return for shelter and nutrients from its larger host.
(15)   In time the engulfed cell and others like it were to become subcellular organelles, passed on by host cells to their progeny. Eventually the host cells themselves changed, developing other subcellular structures and internal membranes and
(20) segregating their genetic material in chromosomes within a nucleus. These cells were the ancestors of all modern eukaryotic (nucleated) cells: protozoans and algae and the individual cells of fungi, plants, and animals. The present-day
(25) descendants of those ancient symbiotic respiring bacteria are the mitochondria, the power plants of the eukaryotic cell.
Mitochondria are oval or worm-shaped organelles, about half a micrometer in diameter
(30) and from two to five micrometers long; this is roughly the size of many modern bacteria. The mitochondrion has an outer membrane and an extensively folded inner membrane that encloses a fluid matrix. The organelle is the site of oxidative
(35) phosphorylation, the primary source of cellular energy. In the fluid matrix, organic molecules derived from the breakdown of foodstuffs are oxidized in a series of chemical reactions known as the citric acid cycle. Electrons removed in the
(40) course of oxidation are passed along a chain of respiratory-enzyme complexes arrayed in the inner membrane, driving the phosphorylation of adenosine diphosphate to form adenosine triphosphate (ATP), the universal energy carrier of
(45) cells. The cytoplasm of eukaryotic cells (the region outside the nucleus) contains a few mitochondria to many hundreds; the greater the energy demands placed on the cell, the more mitochondria it has.
(50)   Perhaps because they are descendants of a free-living bacteria, mitochondria have their own genetic material and the machinery to express it. The possibility that the organelles might have their own genes, distinct from the genome in the
(55) cell nucleus, was raised as early as 1949, when

Boris Ephrussi found that the ability of baker's yeast to carry out oxidative phosphorylation seemed to be controlled by some factor in the cytoplasm rather than in the nucleus. It was only
(60) in 1966, however, that the first vertebrate mitochondrial DNA (that of the chick) was isolated and characterized. Since then the mitochondrial DNAs of many organisms have been under intensive study.

1. Which one of the following titles best reflects the content of the passage?

(A) The Structural Complexity of Eukaryotic Cells
(B) The Evolution and Significance of Mitochondria
(C) Reverse Evolution: From Cell to Subcellular Organelle
(D) Fermentation vs. Respiration: Which is More Efficient?
(E) The Origin and Role of Mitochondrial DNA

2. The author of the passage would most likely agree with which one of the following statements about the "symbiotic relation" in line 11?

(A) The new cell that developed out of the symbiotic relation between anaerobic and aerobic cells has not changed over the last one-and-a-half billion years.
(B) Neither anaerobic nor aerobic cells had a specific function to perform in the new cell.
(C) Anaerobic and aerobic cells combined to create a new cell because neither type of cell was capable of surviving for long on its own.
(D) Anaerobic and aerobic cells could not have joined to form a new cell in the absence of the proper atmospheric conditions.
(E) The chromosomes of eukaryotic cells were originally located in aerobic cells before aerobic cells combined with anaerobic cells to form a new cell.

3. The passage suggests which one of the following about "anaerobic fermentation" (line 4)?

(A) It occurs in the mitochondria located in cells' cytoplasm.

(B) It causes the breakdown of organic molecules during the citric acid cycle.

(C) It is the basis of energy production in modern eukaryotic cells.

(D) It can only be carried on by primitive bacterium in an oxygen-poor environment.

(E) It is not the most efficient way for cells to produce energy.

4. According to the passage, the energy released by a eukaryotic cell is

(A) generated by the mitochondria contained in its cytoplasm

(B) dependent on the transformation of adenosine triphosphate into adenosine diphosphate

(C) caused by chemical reactions that take place outside of the mitochondrion's inner membrane

(D) related to the number of chromosomes in the cell nucleus

(E) incorporated into the mitochondrion's genetic material

5. According to the passage, which one of the following occurs during the citric acid cycle?

(A) Organic molecules that are derived from food penetrate the mitochondrion's outer membrane.

(B) Electrons help to transform adenosine diphosphate into adenosine triphosphate.

(C) Mitochondria from a eukaryotic cell's cytoplasm are transported to the cell's nucleus.

(D) Eukaryotic cells develop subcellular structures, internal membranes and nuclei.

(E) The fluid matrix enclosed by the mitochondrion's inner membrane is transformed into organic molecules that are later broken down in a series of chemical reactions.

6. The author of the passage mentions Boris Ephrussi in the fourth paragraph most probably in order to

(A) demonstrate that eukaryotic cells have genetic material in both the nuclei and mitochondria

(B) suggest that genetic research has only just begun to understand how cells reproduce

(C) point out the historical roots of more recent research on the genetic composition of mitochondrial DNA

(D) prove that subcellular structures like mitochondria contain genetic material

(E) illustrate the difficulties involved in isolating vertebrate mitochondrial DNA

Passage 6: Mitochondria

What Makes It Difficult

Well, we were just talking about jargon in the previous passage, and this one is chock full of it. It's quite a chore to simply chop through the heavy biology in the beginning to get a sense of where this author is going. In fact, it takes a good long while before the main character, mitochondria, even hits the stage. By the time that we recognize that the details in the beginning are presented to shed light on the evolution of mitochondria, the focus shifts to a complex discussion of the characteristics and function of mitochondria, laden of course with complicated terms and descriptions of heavy-duty processes. As if digesting all this were not bad enough, the focus shifts *again* in paragraph 4 to mitochondrial DNA, with the introduction of a new character (Boris Ephrussi) and further findings.

Now, sometimes dense complicated passages are followed by easy questions, and these really aren't as bad as they could be. However, every question except for the first plays off in some way of the technical terms and complex mechanisms described in the passage. Recognizing the following key passage points will help, but you'll also have to go back to the passage at points to pick up a few of the details.

Key Points of the Passage

Purpose and Main Idea: The author's purpose is to describe the evolution of mitochondria and its function in present-day organisms. The passage is purely descriptive, and so there is no main idea, per se. It's simply about mitochondria.

Paragraph Structure: Paragraph 1 describes a turning point in organic evolution, the coming together of a host cell with a smaller respiring cell. The author speculates on how this may have occurred (increase in atmospheric oxygen), and describes the benefit to each of the participating cells. The passage is still pretty wide open at this point; there's no telling where it might go.

A 180 test taker constantly interrogates the passage and the author, asking "where are you going with all this?" until he's satisfied that he's nailed down the author's main area of concern and purpose in writing the passage.

Paragraph 2 continues the saga of "the little cells that could": The engulfed cell evolved into specialized subcellular organelles, and the host evolved other structures within a nucleus. The hosts are the forebears of modern eukaryotic cells, and the present-day version of the respiring symbiotic duo are the mitochondria.

Is the author going to settle down to one concept here, or what? Thankfully, yes. Paragraph 3 describes mitochondria in great detail—its size, its structure, its function. The latter is the key, although you don't have to (and shouldn't!) try to take in the mess of technical details just yet; we'll return to those when necessary (and unfortunately, it does become necessary). The main thing is to see is that mitochondria supply cells with energy. *How* exactly they do that is not worth getting into just yet.

Paragraph 4, as alluded to above, shifts the scope yet again, discussing mitochondrial DNA; specifically, the notion that mitochondria might contain genes distinct from the nucleus. Boris

Ephrussi raised this possibility in the middle of the 20th century after observing the behavior of baker's yeast, but it wasn't until 17 years later that real evidence began to support the theory. You may as well notice what's here, but don't let it distract you from the main gist of the passage. If a Boris/DNA question arises (and of course, one does), you'll know where to look.

Answers and Explanations

1. B   2. D   3. E   4. A   5. B   6. C

1. B

A "best title" question is just another way for the test makers to ask about the author's purpose in writing the passage. The point of a title (at least so far as academic prose is concerned) is to summarize in a few words what the author intends to convey in the text.

> A 180 test taker knows and is conversant with all of the variations of questions that the test makers might throw at her.

It takes a while to come to the forefront, but mitochondria is the star of this show, so any choice without at least that word in the title would be incomplete. That kills (A) and (C), which focus on details from paragraph 2. (D) is worse yet: Not only doesn't it include the word *mitochondria*, but its topic is raised and dropped in paragraph 1. (E) may be tempting, because "origin and role" seems very much to capture the scope of the passage. However, the other half of (E) is wrong— mitochondrial DNA is mentioned only in paragraph 4. Heck, mitochondrial DNA (in vertebrates, anyway) was isolated only in 1966; the events of the passage go back billions of years before that. Only (B) is broad enough to fully cover the passage's topic, scope, and purpose.

2. D

We're asked to infer something about the symbiotic relationship mentioned in paragraph 1, and there's a bunch of material relating to that early on, so we have no idea specifically what the test makers are after here. In other words, as is common in inference questions, prephrasing an answer is not a good option, so we should go right to the choices, looking to confirm or negate each based on the information in the passage.

(A) and (B) are both flatly contradicted by the passage: The new cell *did* evolve quite a bit, and each partner cell in the original symbiotic relation *did* have a specific function.

(C) Presumably, the cells managed pretty well on their own before the atmosphere became oxygen-rich, so there's no way we can infer that the combination occurred because the cells were in danger of dying out.

(D) is the winner: The reasonable implication of oxygen being the "driving force" is that, absent all of that oxygen, the symbiotic relation that led to the formation of the new cell would have been difficult if not impossible.

(E) not only distorts information in the passage—information in paragraph 2—but the information it plays on is located far from the cited lines.

> A 180 test taker knows that the correct answer to questions containing a line reference usually won't be located very far from that line reference.

3. E

The line reference brings us right to the concept in question, so it's best to quickly review what's said about anaerobic fermentation. And it's what comes a bit later that's really the key to the question; we're told that "respiration liberates far more energy than fermentation," which is just another way of saying that anaerobic fermentation isn't the most efficient way for cells to produce energy. (E) is therefore inferable here.

(A), (B), and (C) are all far removed from the detail in question. They misrepresent matters, anyway.

(D) might be tempting—after all, we're told that primitive bacterium in an oxygen-poor environment did employ anaerobic fermentation. But it's not valid to deduce from this that *only* primitive bacterium in an oxygen-poor environment can carry on anaerobic fermentation. Perhaps you put (D) on hold until you reached (E)—but we really have to work much harder to justify (D) than to justify (E).

> A 180 test taker doesn't bend over backwards to justify an answer choice, knowing that if a choice takes that much work to rationalize, it's almost certainly wrong.

4. A

"According to the passage" signifies a detail question, and we had to expect at least a few of those to make our lives somewhat miserable. But it's not that bad, really, as long as we find the subject in question and focus on what's said about it. The striking term that appears in this question is "eukaryotic cell," which appears only in lines 21–24 and then again in line 45. These references tell us a few major things: Mitochondria are located in the cytoplasm of eukaryotic cells, and they power these cells. And that's really all we need to know to answer the question—(A) paraphrases that very closely.

> A 180 test taker does not overestimate the amount of "comprehension" that Reading Comprehension requires; she seeks to understand only as much as she needs to pick up points.

(B) and (C) both contradict the passage: ADP is transformed into ATP, and the chemical reactions, according to information in paragraph 3, take place in the fluid matrix, which is *enclosed* by the mitochondrion's inner membrane.

(D) and (E) distort details taken from the wrong paragraphs—(D) a detail in paragraph 2 and (E) a detail in paragraph 4. Of the two, (D) is likely to be more tempting, since paragraph 4 makes no mention of eukaryotic cells. But neither is directly related to the energy released by a eukaryotic cell.

5. B

The detail "citric acid cycle" is even easier to skim for than the detail from the previous question—it shows up only in the middle of paragraph 3. There we see that the citrus acid cycle is a set of chemical reactions that oxidize molecules derived from food. If we keep reading, we sees that the oxidation moves the electrons along to turn ADP into ATP, just as (B) says. (B)'s wording is no mystery and no real challenge. The challenge lies in figuring out where the answer is going to come from, and translating the relevant text once found into simpler words.

> A 180 test taker often asks himself "where is the answer likely to come from?"

(A), like a few choices in the previous question, gets it backwards. The citric acid cycle takes place in the fluid matrix, which is part of the mitochondrion's *inner* membrane.

(C) and (E) distort information in the passage. The citric acid cycle is a process that takes place within the mitochondrion; it has nothing to do with the movement of a mitochondrion from one part of the cell to another (C). Nor does the citric acid cycle result in the transformation of the fluid matrix (E); rather, a transformation (of organic molecules) occurs *within* the fluid matrix during the citric acid cycle.

(D) plays on an irrelevant detail from paragraph 2. There's no reason why we should look at paragraph 2 in a question about the citric acid cycle.

6. C

As promised above, here's our cameo by Boris Ephrussi, and it certainly isn't hard to track him down. The purpose of paragraph 4 is to discuss the history of scientific research on mitochondrial DNA, and Boris Ephrussi is identified as the father of such research. (C)'s notion of "historical roots" is therefore on target.

(A) and (D) both focus on the substance of the detail rather than why the author has included it. Mentioning Boris doesn't demonstrate or prove anything regarding the possibility Boris himself investigated; that is, whether or not mitochondria actually contains genes. The reference is simply there to tell us when and how this idea was first formulated.

> A 180 test taker understands the difference between the "what" and the "why" of passage material. When asked why someone or something was included in the passage, he doesn't get distracted by the specifics of what was actually said, but rather focuses on the function of the detail.

(B) is way too broad to be the reason Ephrussi was mentioned. In the fourth paragraph, the author limits himself to a discussion of mitochondria, while (B) deals with the scope of genetic research in general and whether the field is in its infancy. Nothing about the Boris reference relates to that.

(E) distorts the situation: We can't infer that isolating the DNA didn't happen until '66 because it was so difficult. For all we know, 17 years is an incredibly short time to advance from Ephrussi's original insights to the accomplishment of 1966. Nothing about the Boris reference speaks to this issue of "difficulties."

What's Next?

We now move from one type of symbiosis to another. Having finished with microscopic biological symbiotic partners—the cells in the first paragraph that came together to eventually produce mitochondria—we journey to the other side of the spectrum and out into the universe to find "Symbiotic Stars."

All this helping out, both cells and stars working together so well; it's really very touching, isn't it?

THE NEXT READING COMPREHENSION
PASSAGE BEGINS ON THE FOLLOWING PAGE

PASSAGE 7

Among the several hundred million binary
systems estimated to lie within 3,000 light-years
of the solar system, and thus to be theoretically
detectable on sky-survey photographs, a tiny
(5) fraction, no more than a few hundred, belong to a
curious subclass whose radiation has a wavelength
distribution so peculiar that it long defied
explanation. Such systems radiate strongly in the
visible region of the spectrum, but some of them
(10) do so even more strongly at both shorter and
longer wavelengths: in the ultraviolet region and
in the infrared and radio regions.

This odd distribution of radiation is best
explained by the pairing of a cool red-giant star
(15) and an intensely hot small star that is virtually in
contact with its larger companion as the two travel
around a common center. Such objects have
become known as symbiotic stars. On
photographic plates only the giant star can be
(20) discerned, but evidence for the existence of the
hot companion has now been supplied by satellite-
borne instruments capable of detecting ultraviolet
radiation at wavelengths that are absorbed by the
earth's atmosphere (and therefore cannot be
(25) detected by instruments on the ground). Recently
two symbiotic-star systems, the first to be
detected outside our galaxy, have been observed
in the Large Cloud of Magellan, one of the
satellite galaxies associated with ours.

(30) The spectra of symbiotic stars indicate that the
cool red giant is surrounded by a very hot ionized
gas. The existence of the ionized gas marked such
objects as being peculiar several decades before
satellite observations finally identified the
(35) ionizing source as the radiation from an invisible
hot companion. Symbiotic stars also flared up in
outbursts indicating the ejection of material in the
form of a shell or a ring, reminiscent of the
recurrent outbursts of a nova. Symbiotic stars may
(40) therefore represent a transitory phase in the
evolution of certain types of binary systems in
which there is a substantial transfer of matter
from the larger partner to the smaller.

The exact evolutionary course that turns a
(45) binary system into a symbiotic one is a matter of
conjecture. The comparatively small number of
known symbiotics in our galaxy suggests that if
all binaries of modest mass normally pass through
a symbiotic phase in their evolution, the phase
(50) must be extremely brief, perhaps as short as a
million years. It is suspected that the evolutionary
course of a binary system is predetermined by the
initial mass and angular momentum of the gas
cloud within which binary stars are born. Since
(55) red giants and Mira variables are thought to be

stars with a mass of one or two suns, it seems
plausible that the original cloud from which a
symbiotic system is formed can consist of no
more than a few solar masses of gas.

1. The passage implies that symbiotic star systems
    differ from other binary systems in which one of the
    following ways?

    (A) Symbiotically paired stars emit a radiation
         pattern different from that of most binary
         stars.
    (B) In symbiotic star systems, one star is the
         center of the other's orbit.
    (C) Symbiotically paired stars are the only binary
         stars which are capable of exchanging
         matter.
    (D) Symbiotic star systems are more common
         than other binary systems.
    (E) Symbiotic star systems are the only binary
         systems that can be detected by satellite-
         borne instruments.

2. According to the passage, which one of the
    following is true about symbiotic star systems?

    (A) The majority of binary systems are symbiotic.
    (B) Most symbiotic systems lie outside our
         galaxy.
    (C) Evidence for the existence of each distinct
         partner in such systems is gathered via
         independent mechanisms.
    (D) Only symbiotic star systems are formed from
         clouds of gas.
    (E) The Large Cloud of Magellan obscures the
         view of most symbiotic stars.

3. The primary purpose of the passage is to

    (A) argue that a great percentage of binary star
         systems are symbiotic
    (B) criticize the theory of symbiotic stars as
         overly speculative
    (C) describe symbiotic stars as a distinct type of
         binary system
    (D) present evidence that binary star systems have
         evolved from gas clouds
    (E) compare symbiotic stars to red giants and
         Mira variables

4. According to the passage, the radiation emitted by symbiotic stars is distinctive in that it

   (A) is visible on photographic plates
   (B) consists partly of visible waves
   (C) cannot be detected by satellite-borne instruments
   (D) is strongest at the extreme ends of the spectrum
   (E) emanates primarily from the larger star

5. The author suggests that

   (A) the detection of radiation from an invisible hot companion star prompted scientists to investigate the peculiar ionized gas surrounding cool red giants
   (B) small hot stars attach to cool red giants because red giants have a mass of one or two suns
   (C) a million years is a brief period of time for the occurrence of many solar events
   (D) the only symbiotic star systems to be detected outside of our galaxy are in the Large Cloud of Magellan
   (E) if binary stars of modest mass passed through symbiotic phases lasting much more than a million years, it is likely that more of them would have been detected

6. The existence of which one of the following would weaken a hypothesis stated in the passage concerning a mechanism by which symbiotic stars evolve?

   (A) a cool red giant, involved in a symbiotic relation, that loses mass over time
   (B) a small hot star, involved in a symbiotic relation, that loses mass over time
   (C) millions of star systems that passed through symbiotic phases lasting one million years
   (D) stars that absorb matter emitted by a surrounding gas cloud
   (E) solar phenomena other than symbiotic stars that emit odd radiation distributions

7. The passage as a whole can be considered an answer to which one of the following questions?

   (A) How do binary star systems evolve into symbiotic systems?
   (B) Why are symbiotic stars surrounded by ionized gas?
   (C) What percentage of the binary star systems detected to date are symbiotic pairs?
   (D) Why are red giants usually accompanied by intensely hot, small stars?
   (E) Why do certain binary stars emit unusual radiation patterns?

Passage 7: Symbiotic Stars

What Makes It Difficult

This one has a structure common to many LSAT science passages: it introduces a mystery that has puzzled scientists for some time, and then proceeds to document various findings supporting a theory meant to explain the mystery. This passage holds together a little better than does "Mitochondria"; the structure is a bit more coherent. The author states the mystery up front, and then methodically presents the theory of symbiotic stars as a possible solution. But the theory contains a ton of details, which, of course, the test makers exploit in the questions. In passages in which the details are so technical and abstract, so difficult to connect to everyday experience, you have to pay extra careful attention to the reason why the author includes the details she provides. As always, it behooves you to break down the passage into its key elements.

Key Points of the Passage

Purpose and Main Idea: The author's purpose is to describe the phenomenon of symbiotic star systems; namely, their characteristics and possible origin. The passage is mainly descriptive, but if we had to settle on a main idea, it would sound something like this: The nature of symbiotic stars helps explain certain strange radiation distribution patterns that have long puzzled scientists.

Paragraph Structure: Paragraph 1 introduces a mystery that had "long defied explanation": certain binary star systems exhibiting quirky radiation patterns stronger on the extreme sides of the spectrum.

Paragraph 2 gets right to the explanation. Evidently, this pattern can be explained by the pairing of a cool big star and a hot little star. These two types of stars are attached to one another through a common center; hence, the notion of symbiosis. The paragraph goes on to explain how the big and small stars are detected, and where a few of these things have been found.

A 180 test taker paraphrases the author's ideas into the simplest terms possible.

Paragraph 3 throws in some more details about this partnership, and suggests that symbiotic stars represent a phase in the evolution of certain binary systems. There's no need to assimilate every detail just yet. You should simply mark this paragraph as the place where some of the mechanisms of these star systems are laid out.

In the last paragraph, the author continues this speculation as to the evolution of symbiotic stars, employing a good deal of scientific terminology in the process. Again, not to panic—get the gist and you'll know where to return to reread if a question demands it.

A 180 test taker knows that everything she needs to answer the questions is right there in the passage, and strives to keep the paragraph topics in mind if she has to hunt for answers later.

Answers and Explanations

1. A   2. C   3. C   4. D   5. E   6. B   7. E

1. A

Paragraph 1 states that symbiotic stars are distinctive from other binary star systems in the pattern of radiation that they emit. In fact, this is the basis of the whole mystery, right? So (A) must be true. It goes to show that sometimes the first few questions on even a difficult passage are very straightforward.

(B) The second paragraph specifically mentions that both stars in a symbiotic system travel around a common center, so (B) is wrong.

(C) and (E) are way too broad; neither one is implied by anything in the passage, which doesn't speculate on the case out there in the universe in general.

(D) contradicts the first paragraph, where we're told that symbiotic stars make up a tiny fraction of binary systems.

2. C

In the middle of the second paragraph, the author states that only the cool red giant stars show up in photographs, and that it took satellite technology to eventually produce evidence about the small hot invisible partners. (C) may be a bit wordy, but it's right on the money: Independent mechanisms are employed to supply to supply evidence of these distinct partners.

(A) As we saw in choice (D) above, paragraph 1 explicitly states that symbiotic systems represent a very small percentage of all binary systems.

A 180 test taker uses the thought process employed in one question to help with similar choices in later questions.

(B) Paragraph 2 mentions that two symbiotic star systems have recently been detected outside our galaxy, but the passage supplies no information that allows us to conclude where *most* such systems exist.

(D) Paragraph 4 states that all binary stars originate in gas clouds, so (D) contradicts the passage.

(E) distorts a detail found in the second paragraph: nothing suggests that the Large Cloud of Magellan obscures the view of symbiotic stars.

A 180 test taker is not fooled by choices containing familiar wording, knowing that it's quite simple for the test makers to take a concept directly from the passage and misrepresent it in a choice.

---

3. C

Since the gist of the passage is that symbiotic stars represent a special type of binary star system—one with a bizarre radiation pattern—choice (C) is correct. And the neutral verb "describe" fits the author's method to a T. The same, however, can't be said of choices (A) and (B), which we can dismiss on the basis of their verbs alone. The author doesn't "argue" or "criticize" anything in this passage: he or she simply describes a phenomenon.

A 180 test taker pays very careful attention the verbs in answer choices, especially in "Primary Purpose" or "Method of Argument" questions.

(D) The theory that binary stars are born in gas clouds is a detail from the last paragraph. It's certainly not the passage's main point, so (D) cannot describe the primary purpose of this passage. Notice how it doesn't even mention the main concept of the passage, symbiotic stars. It's very hard to describe the author's purpose without a reference to the passage's central character.

(E)'s out because the author doesn't even tell us what Mira variables are, let alone compare them to symbiotic stars.

4. D

Next up is a detail question that relates to the main idea. The last sentence of the first paragraph states that the type of binary system later defined as symbiotic radiates "even more strongly at both shorter and longer wavelengths" than in the middle of the spectrum. Choice (D) is a near perfect paraphrase of this.

(A) We know that only one star of the symbiotic pair shows up in photographs, and we aren't told whether radiation emitted by nonsymbiotic stars is visible on photographic plates, so there's no basis to choose (A).

(B) Although some of the radiation from symbiotic systems is visible, that's not what makes these systems' radiation patterns "distinctive," so (B) cannot be correct.

(C) contradicts information presented in the second paragraph about evidence provided by satellite-borne instruments. At least one partner in the symbiotic pair can be detected by satellites.

(E) The passage never suggests that the radiation primarily emanates from the larger star, and even if we somehow made this leap, it would still be incorrect to say that this is what makes their radiation distinctive. None of this is hinted at in the passage.

5. E

Next up is an open-ended inference question with no clues as to what the test makers are after, so we have no choice but to wade into the choices, looking for the one that's supported by the hard facts of the passage.

(A) bollixes up the order of things; in fact, pretty much gets it backwards. In paragraph 3 we learn that the ionized gas surrounding the cool red giant looked weird to scientists for decades before radiation from the invisible hot companion was discovered, so it can't be the detection of radiation that prompted scientists to look into the matter.

(B) tries to fashion a causal relationship out of two facts of the passage. True, the small hot stars attach to the big cool ones, and yes, we're told in paragraph 4 that red giants have a mass of one or two suns. But what has one thing to do with the other? Nothing, as far as the passage suggests, so (B) is out.

A 180 test taker is suspicious of choices that attempt to tie together two or more elements from different parts of the passage.

(C) A million years may not seem so "brief" to us, but according to the passage, that's a relatively short period of time for a symbiotic phase. Regardless, other solar events are outside the scope of the passage, so there's no way we can judge from the material at hand the time it takes for these to occur. For all we know, a million years is a long time for most solar events; all we know about is symbiotic stars.

(D) erroneously plays off the Magellan detail in paragraph 2. Just because a few symbiotics *were* found over there doesn't in any way suggest that the *only* symbiotic stars outside our galaxy are in the Large Cloud of Magellan.

(E) That leaves (E), which must be correct. In paragraph 4, the author says that the small number of symbiotics detected in our galaxy suggests that the symbiotic phase is brief—"perhaps as short as a million years." Evidently, the author sees a link between the length of the phase and our ability to detect symbiotic stars. Therefore, it's reasonable to infer that if these phases were much longer, we'd probably detect more of them.

6. B

There seem to be a number of hypotheses in the passage regarding the mechanisms of symbiotic stars, so it's not likely we'll be able to paraphrase this weakenener off the top of our heads. Let's therefore move right to the choices, looking for the one that contradicts some mechanism described in the passage.

(A) Does a cool red giant losing mass over time contradict, support, or have no effect on some hypothesis in the passage? In fact, it directly supports the notion, discussed at the end of paragraph 3, that symbiotic stars represent an evolution of star system in which matter goes from the big star to the small one. That means that the larger star, the red giant, loses mass while the small, hot companion gets bigger. The existence of a cool red giant that's in such a relationship and getting smaller over time would certainly supports this. The star in the next choice, however, would not.

(B) According to the same hypothesis just cited in (A), a small hot star involved in a symbiotic relationship would get bigger in time, as matter was transferred to it from the red giant. The existence of the shrinking small star in (B) would not bode well for the theory at the end of paragraph 3, so (B) is the weakener we seek.

(C) Nothing in the passage is blatantly overturned by the fact that millions of systems go through "brief" symbiotic phases. A million years, remember, is not always long enough to allow us to detect these, so there's nothing here in (C) that would weaken any claim in the passage.

(D) We're told that binary stars originate in gas clouds, so nothing in (D) seems to damage any theory in the passage.

(E) There's nothing in the passage that precludes the existence of other solar phenomena besides symbiotic stars emitting odd radiation patterns. Perhaps these other distributions are odd but have always been explainable. Perhaps they aren't odd in the same way as the patterns emitted from what turned out to be symbiotics. The facts in the first paragraph don't conclusively establish symbiotic stars as the only solar phenomenon ever to emit strange radiation.

A 180 test taker avoids unwarranted conclusions.

---

7. E

We need to keep the passage's main idea in mind in answering this question, which itself deals with the passage as an answer *to* a question. Interesting . . . Well, we merely have to return to the question that was set out in the beginning, namely: How can the odd distribution of radiation put out by some star systems be explained? According to the passage, symbiotic star systems provide the best explanation of the previously puzzling observation that some binary systems emit extremely unusual patterns of radiation. The author spends most of the passage presenting theories regarding the mechanisms of these systems, and yet never loses sight of the original question. Therefore, (E), dealing with the unusual phenomenon introduced in the beginning, is the question that can best be answered by information in the passage.

(A) Since the first sentence of paragraph 4 says that the way in which a binary star system evolves into a symbiotic system is conjecture, (A) can hardly be answered by the passage.

(B) First of all, the red giant is specifically surrounded by ionized gas, but even if we allow "symbiotic star" to substitute for red giant here, the passage as a whole isn't structured to answer this question, since this is merely one detail in the story of symbiotic stars.

A 180 test taker does not confuse a detail for an overriding point of the passage.

(C) We know only that few binary star systems are symbiotic—the passage doesn't address the precise percentage here.

(D) While paragraph 2 states that symbiotic stars involve a pairing of red giants and small hot stars, the passage never suggests *why* these two stars pair up, so (D) is wrong.

What's Next?

Three science passages down, and one to go. We come full circle and return to the Earth theme set out earlier in "Lake Stratification," which dealt with the ecology of lakes. This next passage, "Plate Tectonics," takes as its scope entire continents. More excitement for the geologically minded among you. Have fun.

THE NEXT READING COMPREHENSION
PASSAGE BEGINS ON THE FOLLOWING PAGE

PASSAGE 8

The basic theory of plate tectonics recognizes two ways continental margins can grow seaward. Where two plates such as the African plate and the South American plate are moving away from a

(5) mid-ocean rift that separates them, the continental margins on those plates are said to be passive, or rifted. Such continental margins grow slowly from the accumulation of riverborne sediments and of the carbonate skeletons of marine organisms,

(10) which are deposited as limestone. Suites— unbroken sequences—of such accretions, consisting of nearly flat strata, are called miogeoclinal deposits. Since most miogeoclinal deposits are undeformed and exhibit an unbroken

(15) history, it is evident that passive margins are generally not associated with mountain building.

Along active, or convergent, margins, such as those that ring most of the Pacific basin, continents tend to grow much faster. At an active

(20) margin an oceanic plate plunges under a continental plate, with the continental plate scraping off deep-ocean sediments and fragments of basaltic crust that then adhere to the continental margin. Simultaneously the plate plunging under

(25) the continental margin heats up and partially melts, triggering extensive volcanism and mountain-building. A classic example is the Andes of the west coast of South America.

In the original plate-tectonic model western

(30) North America was described as being a passive margin through the late Paleozoic and early Mesozoic eras (roughly 350 to 210 million years ago) after which it became an active margin. It was assumed that the continent grew to a limited

(35) extent along this margin as sedimentary and igneous rocks of oceanic origin were accreted in a few places, as in the Coast Ranges of California. The model was successful in explaining such disparate features as the Franciscan rocks of the

(40) California Coast Ranges, formed by local subduction processes, and the granite rocks of the Sierra Nevada, farther to the east, which clearly originated as the roots of volcanoes similar to those of the Andes.

(45) The basic plate-tectonic reconstruction of the geologic history of western North America remains unchanged in the light of microplate tectonics (the process by which the edge of a continent is modified by the transport, accretion

(50) and rotation of large crystal blocks called terranes), but the details are radically changed. It is now clear that much more crust was added to North America in the Mesozoic era (248 to 65 million years ago) than can be accounted for by

(55) volcanism along island arcs and by the simple

accretion of sediments from the ocean floor. It has also become evident that some terranes lying side by side today are not genetically related, as would be expected from simple plate tectonics, but

(60) almost certainly have traveled great distances from entirely different parts of the world.

1. Which one of the following best expresses the main idea of the passage?

    (A) The margin of the west coast of North America developed through a combination of active and passive mechanisms.

    (B) The growth of continental margins is only partially explained by the basic theory of plate tectonics.

    (C) Continental margins can grow seaward in two ways, through sedimentation or volcanism.

    (D) The introduction of microplate tectonics poses a fundamental challenge to the existing theory of how continental margins are formed.

    (E) Continental margins grow more rapidly along active margins than along passive margins.

2. The passage supplies information for answering all of the following questions regarding continental margins EXCEPT:

    (A) How have marine organisms contributed to the formation of passive continental margins?

    (B) What were some of the processes by which the continental margin of the west coast of North America was formed?

    (C) Are miogeoclinal deposits associated with mountain building along continental margins?

    (D) Were the continental margins of the east and west coasts of South America formed by similar processes?

    (E) How much crust added to North America in the Mesozoic era can be accounted for by the accretion of sediments from the ocean floor?

3. According to the passage, which one of the following is true about the formation of the Sierra Nevada Mountains?

    (A) They developed through the deposition of terranes.
    (B) They were formed during the Paleozoic era.
    (C) Their geologic origin is analogous to that of the Andes.
    (D) Their history can be traced back to the accretion of miogeoclinal deposits.
    (E) They are similar in structure to the California Coast Ranges.

4. The author mentions the Franciscan rocks of the California Coast Ranges in order to make which one of the following points?

    (A) The basic theory of plate tectonics accounts for a wide variety of geologic features.
    (B) The original plate tectonic model falls short of explaining such features.
    (C) Subduction processes are responsible for the majority of the geologic features found along the west coast of North America.
    (D) Passive margins can take on many geologic forms.
    (E) The concept of microplate tectonics was first introduced to account for such phenomena.

5. Which one of the following does the author mention as evidence for the inadequacy of the original plate tectonic model to describe the formation of continental margins?

    (A) Nearly flat, undeformed crystal blocks have been found along some continental margins where there are mountains further inland.
    (B) Sediments and fragments from the depths of the ocean accumulate along continental margins.
    (C) Large pieces of the Earth's crust that appear to be completely unrelated are found in the same area today.
    (D) Undeformed miogeoclinal deposits are usually not linked to mountain building.
    (E) Oceanic plates drop beneath continental plates along active margins.

6. According to the passage, a passive margin is more likely than an active margin to be characterized by which one of the following?

    (A) rapid growth
    (B) mountain-building
    (C) the aggregation of oceanic rocks
    (D) carbonate deposits
    (E) the accretion of terranes

7. The author seems to regard the basic theory of plate tectonics as

    (A) outdated
    (B) unassailable
    (C) insufficient
    (D) revolutionary
    (E) unlikely

Passage 8: Plate Tectonics

What Makes It Difficult

There's not much to say about the difficulty of this final science passage that hasn't already been said about the others preceding it. We're faced with the same challenges: An esoteric, difficult topic containing its own unique lingo. A mass of technical details, and questions to test your understanding of them. As always, you're best served by getting the basic gist of the passage, noting where specific details occur so you can return to them as needed. Here are the key points:

Key Points of the Passage

Purpose and Main Idea: The author's purpose is to describe the basic theory of plate tectonics. The main idea is that the theory ultimately falls short of explaining all the phenomena of growing continental margins.

Paragraph Structure: Paragraph 1 introduces the basic theory of plate tectonics, which posits that there are two ways in which continental margins can grow seaward. The paragraph goes on to describe one of those ways, a mechanism known as passive margins. Details regarding passive margins abound, but it's best to let those pass for now and see where the author's going with all this. As always, we'll return to this material if a question demands it.

Paragraph 2 describes the other way continental margins can grow, and that's along active margins. A simple distinction is presented which is worth noting; continents grow faster along active margins.

A 180 test taker pays careful attention to distinctions in passages that compare two or more people, theories, or phenomena.

Again, details are plentiful, as we'd expect in a science passage. We're told what actually happens at active margins, the results of such activity (volcanoes and mountains), and an example of these results (the Andes). Take in what you can, but again, there's no need to obsess over the particulars. All you really need to note is that this paragraph contains a process, some results, and an example.

A 180 test taker first and foremost picks up on what generally occurs in a paragraph.

Paragraph 3 applies the model to a concrete example (western North America), illustrating how the concepts of passive and active margins, taken together, can accurately describe the growth of a continental margin and successfully explain various specific continental features.

Things are humming along quite well until we get to paragraph 4, which introduces something new—the concept of microplate tectonics. Here, with the aid of specific examples, the author shows how this new theory helps to explain certain phenomena that "simple" or "basic" plate tectonics cannot account for. While remaining in general accordance with the story told by basic plate tectonics, microplate tectonics "radically" changes some of the details. Much of the paragraph is given over to examples of how this is so.

Answers and Explanations

1. B   2. E   3. C   4 A   5. C   6. D   7. C

1. B

First up is a main idea question, and we looked into that issue above while getting the passage squared away. While the basic theory of plate tectonics explains much about the growth of continental margins, the fourth paragraph suggests that it cannot fully explain certain geologic details. (B) captures this, and is the correct answer.

> A 180 test taker understands that the author's full main idea may not emerge until the end of the passage, and stays alert throughout.

(A) and (E) both represent true statements, but they're details from the passage, not the passage's main idea.

> A 180 test taker can distinguish between the main idea of a passage and facts that are merely reflected in the passage.

(C) distorts the notion of the two ways that continental margins can grow. Though the first paragraph mentions sedimentation as an example of passive margins, and paragraph 2 states that volcanism often results from active margin growth, the author never goes so far as to say that sedimentation and volcanism are the two ways that continental margins grow. And even if this could be inferred, it's still not big enough to be the main point of the passage.

(D) is incorrect because the first sentence of paragraph 4 states that the basic plate tectonic theory remains unchanged in the light of microplate tectonics; it's the *details* that are radically changed, not the basic theory.

2. E

This is an unusually worded detail question, but it does force us to focus on the details nonetheless. The question in each wrong choice is one that can be answered by the information in the passage, while the right answer is one that goes unanswered by the author. Let's check the choices.

(A) is covered in the first paragraph, which describes the growth of passive margins. There, the author says that passive margins grow, in part, through the accumulation of the carbonate skeletons of marine organisms.

(B) is the subject of the paragraph 3—the continental margin of the west coast of North America grew at first as a passive margin, and then as an active margin.

(C) is answered in the last sentence of paragraph 1: Miogeoclinal deposits are associated with passive margins and are "generally not associated with mountain building."

(D) We have to search a bit for the answer to the question posed in choice (D): Paragraph 1 suggests that the eastern edge of the South American plate is a passive margin, while the last sentence of the second paragraph says that the west coast of South America is an active margin.

(E) That leaves (E), which must be correct. In fact, if you had full confidence eliminating the other four choices, you could choose (E) without much fanfare and move on.

A 180 test taker has confidence in her work, and uses that confidence to save time whenever possible.

Indeed, the question in (E) cannot be answered by information contained in the passage. Microplate tectonics has revealed that much more crust was added to North America in the Mesozoic period than was added from volcanism and the accretion of sediments, but that doesn't tell us precisely how much crust the accretion of sediments accounts for in the grand scheme of things.

3. C

To answer this detail question, we focus on the third paragraph, since that's where the author mentions the Sierra Nevada mountains. The end of that paragraph states that the Sierra Nevada mountains "clearly originated as the roots of volcanoes similar to those of the Andes." This is correctly paraphrased in answer choice (C).

(A) There is no mention of terranes in reference to the Sierra Nevada Mountains.

(B) contradicts the author's statement that the Sierra Nevada Mountains originated as the roots of volcanoes, formed by the processes of active continental margins *after* the Paleozoic era.

(D) Miogeoclinal deposits are associated with passive continental margins, whereas the Sierra Nevada Mountains were formed while the west coast was an active margin.

(E) is wrong because the author states in the third paragraph that the Coast Ranges and the Sierra Nevada Mountains are "disparate features," formed by two different processes.

4. A

The Coast Ranges of California are introduced in paragraph 3 to provide an example of the variety of geologic features that the original plate-tectonic model could successfully explain: the Franciscan Rocks, formed by local subduction, and the granite rocks of the Sierra Nevada, formed by volcanic action. (A) therefore represents the best account of why this detail was mentioned.

(B) is wrong because the problems with the basic plate tectonic model are discussed in paragraph 4, a paragraph in which the California Coast Ranges are never mentioned.

A 180 test taker remains conscious of where in the passage certain ideas are presented, and uses that knowledge to help eliminate choices that deal with material far from the issue in question.

(C) is a distortion of the facts. We don't know if subduction processes are responsible for the *majority* of the west coast's geologic features—we're only told that they are responsible for some, such as the Coast Ranges.

(D) is wrong because the Coast Ranges were formed by local subduction processes, according to paragraph 3, not by the actions of passive margins.

(E) The concept of microplate tectonics was introduced to account for phenomena that the basic, or original, plate-tectonic model could not adequately explain. But the Coast Ranges are features that the basic model *can* account for, so (E) is incorrect.

5. C

The inadequacy of the plate tectonic model is introduced in the final paragraph of the passage. There we're told that genetically distinct pieces of the Earth's crust are found in the same area, a fact which the original plate tectonic model cannot explain. (C) gets at this issue.

(A) The original plate tectonic model can account for (A)—see the third and fourth paragraphs.

(B), (D), and (E) are true statements—see the first and second paragraphs—but none of these statements has a direct bearing on the issue of the inadequacy of the original plate tectonic model.

A 180 test taker is not tempted by a choice simply because it contains a true statement. It must, first and foremost, answer the question that was asked.

---

6. D

We're looking in this one for something that distinguishes passive from active margins. (D) correctly states a likely characteristic of passive margins which we hear nothing about in regards to active margins—carbonate deposits—as stated in the third sentence of the first paragraph.

(A) and (B) state characteristics more likely to be associated with active margins. In the first sentence of the second paragraph, the author states that active margins tend to grow much faster than passive ones. And the second to last sentence of that paragraph characterizes active margins as associated with mountain building, while the last sentence of paragraph 1 states that passive margins are "generally not associated with mountain building."

(C), (E) The aggregation of oceanic rocks (C) is something that microplate tectonics is involved with, as mentioned in the first sentence of the last paragraph, while (E) is also incorrect because it states a phenomenon associated with microplate tectonics, not with passive or active margins.

7. C

This final question asks you to identify the author's attitude toward the basic theory of plate tectonics. The passage as a whole suggests that the basic theory of plate tectonics is useful in that it adequately describes certain geological features, and even remains valid in its basic formulation in the light of the more advanced theory, microplate tectonics. However, by now we're certainly familiar with the author's beef with the basic model, as described in the final paragraph: It botches some of the details of the geologic history it attempts to explain, and it leaves other things (such as non-genetically related terranes) unexplained. All this points to a view that the basic plate tectonics theory is useful but not complete. Choice (C), "insufficient," therefore best captures the author's attitude toward the basic theory.

A 180 test taker attempts to gauge the author's tone early on, and is therefore prepared in advance for general "attitude" questions.

(A) The author never suggests that the basic theory of plate tectonics is outdated, just that it's incomplete. This is verified by the fact that the author believes the basic theory generally remains unchanged in the light of microplate tectonics. Such a thing would not likely be said about a theory the author considers "outdated."

(B) "Unassailable" means something that is incapable of being disputed or disproven, but the author clearly does think that there are minor problems with the basic theory of plate tectonics, so (B) is too strong to represent the author's attitude here.

(D) The author never suggests that the basic theory of plate tectonics is revolutionary. It's simply presented as a theory with some explanatory power, and some defects as well. If anything's revolutionary, it's the theory of microplate tectonics, since that theory calls certain details of the basic theory into question.

(E) Although the author thinks that the basic theory does not sufficiently explain certain phenomena, it is presented as a sound theory capable of explaining many features, not an unlikely theory, as (E) suggests.

What's Next?

Enough of science, you say? Good—let's move on. Maybe the more science-phobic among you will welcome with open arms the philosophical passages in the next chapter, while those adept at science who breezed through this chapter will be in for a rude awakening. That's the marvelous thing about the LSAT—there's something for everyone.

CHAPTER FOURTEEN

Philosopher's Corner

You probably think you've already seen some pretty dense material, so what's the deal with this special chapter entitled "Philosophers' Corner"? What's the difference between these passages and the ones, say, found in the "Just Plain Tough" category? Surely there's a certain amount of subjectivity in this kind of classification; the demarcation isn't fully clear-cut, and there's no doubt that these are all difficult passages.

What distinguishes the passages in this chapter, however, is the sheer level of abstraction inherent in their actual topics. Gerschenkron's and Hough's theories on the economic development of the former Soviet Union may be difficult to understand, but both the Soviet Union and its economic development are real, tangible things, so we can at least grasp in a real way the basic concepts the author is trying to describe. The same goes for "Illegal Constitution." The specific issues involved may be a bit thorny, but the Constitution and characters such as Madison are real, and familiar, and the basic idea of investigating the Constitution's legality is fairly understandable.

Not so with the passages in this chapter. Max Weber's perspective on objectivity, or the nondidactic, performative essence of virtue (the subjects of two of the upcoming passages), for example, occupy different territory entirely. These are themselves philosophical subjects, and not just complex, philosophical treatments of real-life, easy to grasp phenomena. As the author of the "Teaching Virtue" passage states: "Knowing what virtue is, is not the same as knowing what some kind of object is, because virtue is not an object." Precisely. And therein lies the difficulty of dealing with inherently philosophical material: They are based on abstract (to many, even obscure) concepts, not tangible objects like junk mail or the Soviet Union or the U.S. Constitution or even symbiotic stars. That's right; many find these to be even harder than science passages. Despite the technical terms, processes, and mass of details used to describe a star or a cell, these physical things are still easier for many to get their hands around than conceptual abstractions such as objectivity, virtue, or a theory of morality.

So buckle up for these final few. It may turn out to be a bumpy ride.

PASSAGE 9

Max Weber's work is traditionally viewed as supporting a strictly objective, or value-neutral, approach to investigating social science issues. In many respects, Weber does uphold the notion of
(5) scientific objectivity throughout his writings. If we look at both his writings and his academic philosophies more carefully, however, it becomes clear that Weber's perspective on objectivity is more complicated than the traditional
(10) interpretation would have us believe.

The term "objectivity" is used to denote that which lies outside of the framework of subjective perception or bias. It is traditionally defined as that which "exists as an object or fact,
(15) independent of the mind." Indeed, Weber does appear to believe in the concept of strict objectivity concerning questions of reality and truth. Weber postulates that there exists a true reality that is independent of individuals'
(20) viewpoints. This position is illustrated through his use of the concept of "ideal types." Ideal types are theoretical constructions that can be used to help the social scientist analyze, investigate, and uncover reality. If ideal types can help the
(25) scientist uncover true reality, then it stands to reason that "true reality" must itself exist.

In discussing our ability to investigate objective reality, however, Weber moves away from the notion of strict objectivity. While he
(30) postulates that an objective reality exists, he seems to believe that our knowledge of this reality cannot be totally objective. According to Weber, individuals can only know truths insofar as we share communal presuppositions about particular
(35) realms of knowledge. Our methods of investigating truths are limited to, and necessarily conditioned by, the value frameworks through which we approach issues. Thus individuals who investigate issues can generate only knowledge
(40) that is based upon assumptions and perspectives shared by the community of scholars within which they work. Knowledge may not be purely subjective, or influenced by individual bias, but it is only "objective" insofar as the scientific
(45) community upholds its presuppositions.

Weber goes even further afield from the traditional interpretation when discussing how individuals should use scientific knowledge to guide their actions. On this issue, Weber's stance
(50) approaches the purely subjective. He tells us clearly that each person should be free to choose how he or she acts upon the reality discovered by science. This position is put forth in his essay "Science as a Vocation," where Weber argues that
(55) teachers must avoid personally imposing their

own stances on their students, and must rather help students to account for the ultimate meaning of their own conduct. In Weber's view, a professor must sit back and allow his students to reach their
(60) own conclusions. When it comes to action, Weber believes that individuals must make their own decisions and that not even a teacher can assert the truth for another person.

1. Which one of the following best expresses the main idea of the passage?

   (A) Weber's theory on the topic of objectivity is more complicated than most other theories of objectivity.

   (B) Weber's views on objectivity are useful in supporting arguments against the notion of absolute truth.

   (C) Weber never clearly lays out his views on objectivity in his works.

   (D) Weber's views on the topic of objectivity are not as straightforward as is typically supposed.

   (E) Weber's views on objectivity are inconsistent and therefore cannot provide a reliable foundation for a belief in objective reality.

2. Based on the information in the passage, which one of the following statements would Weber most likely support?

   (A) Scientific knowledge about reality can never be completely free of subjective perceptions or biases.

   (B) The use of ideal types enables the scientist to perceive his or her own subjective biases concerning reality.

   (C) Teachers should refrain from imposing their personal views on students unless students are incapable of reaching their own conclusions.

   (D) The concept of objective reality is misleading because reality cannot exist apart from the value frameworks through which reality is perceived.

   (E) Ideal types are the only reliable method for investigating objective reality.

3. The primary purpose of the passage is to

 (A) resolve a debate over an author's theory
 (B) summarize the complexities of an author's view
 (C) reconcile two differing views of an author's works
 (D) argue against an author's perspective
 (E) present and test an author's hypothesis

4. According to the passage, which one of the following is true about Weber's views on how individuals should use scientific knowledge to guide their actions?

 (A) Individuals may choose their own courses of action freely unless they are unable to account for the ultimate meaning of their own conduct.
 (B) Individuals should distrust scientific knowledge when making decisions that will determine their personal actions.
 (C) Individuals should be encouraged to determine their own courses of action based upon discovered scientific truth.
 (D) If a teacher determines that a particular course of action would be most beneficial for a given student, he or she should direct the student toward this course of action.
 (E) Teachers should follow their students' leads in determining the most appropriate course of action for themselves.

5. Which one of the following best describes the organization of the passage?

 (A) An explanation is put forth and then rejected in favor of a second explanation.
 (B) An author's viewpoint is first criticized and then reclaimed for its redeeming values.
 (C) An argument is put forth and then negated by the presentation of conflicting evidence.
 (D) A hypothesis is advanced and then strengthened through empirical testing.
 (E) An interpretation of a view is presented and support for this interpretation is provided.

6. Which one of the following is mentioned in the passage as evidence for the assertion that knowledge of reality cannot be totally objective?

 (A) Scientific methods of investigation are always influenced by the subjective biases of the community of scholars within which the scientist operates.
 (B) Scientific methods of investigation are not legitimate unless they can be proven to be strictly objective.
 (C) Scientific investigations use ideal types, which at best help to approximate reality.
 (D) In order for truth to be objective, it must be independent of the mind of the investigating scientist.
 (E) The concept of objective reality is illusory.

7. The author presents the traditional interpretation of Weber's view of objectivity in the first paragraph primarily in order to

 (A) dismiss the relevance of all previous scholarship on Weber that does not accord with the author's line of reasoning
 (B) argue that the concept of objective reality has been historically misunderstood by social scientists
 (C) provide background for a contrasting interpretation of Weber's beliefs central to the argument that follows
 (D) show how critics think that Weber's value-neutral approach to the notion of objectivity is more complicated than is traditionally believed
 (E) illustrate the gist of a notion under attack that the author will subsequently attempt to vindicate

Passage 9: Weber on Objectivity

What Makes It Difficult

Here we have the aforementioned tract detailing Max Weber's view of objectivity. A definition of objectivity is given in the second paragraph, and we're told that Weber does buy into it as far as it applies to the notions of truth and reality. The somewhat vague concept of "ideal types" is presented as an example of Weber's sympathy with this doctrine, which just gives us something else to keep tabs on even though the real point is yet to come. And what's that point? It's the idea that Weber's support for objectivity wanes when a distinction is made between reality and our *knowledge* of reality. This kind of distinction may be common fare for philosophy majors, but for many others this is pretty deep stuff. The questions are long and complex, matching perfectly in this respect the tone and style of the passage. Let's, as always, break the passage down to see if we can make it a bit more user-friendly.

Key Points of the Passage

Purpose and Main Idea: The author's purpose is to make an argument regarding how Weber views the concept of objectivity and employs it in his writing. The main idea is that Weber does not believe in strict objectivity across-the-board, and that his views on objectivity are therefore more complex than they are traditionally portrayed.

Paragraph Structure: Paragraph 1 presents the "traditional" or conventional explanation of Weber's views: scholars normally see him as upholding a strict concept of objectivity in his work. Whenever we're presented with a traditional view in the opening paragraph, it's a good bet that the author will counter or refute that view in what's to follow.

A 180 test taker anticipates an opposing argument whenever a passage starts out with a "traditional" perspective.

This paragraph is no exception—sure enough, the author quickly counters the traditional interpretation by asserting that Weber's views are "more complicated" than the traditional view would have it.

Given this starting point, we might expect the following paragraphs to show us how and why Weber's views are complicated. This is exactly what happens. Paragraph 2 concedes that in certain respects, Weber does believe in the possibility of strict objectivity: we see it in his views on the nature of reality. When it comes to questions of truth, the author tells us, Weber does believe that a value-neutral reality exists.

In paragraph 3, however, the complexities of Weber's views are introduced. Here the author shows that Weber doesn't think our knowledge of reality can be totally objective. This is because knowledge is rooted in the assumptions and perspectives of those who investigate reality—thus, some subjective bias enters in.

Paragraph 4 shows that Weber deviates most from strict objectivity on questions concerning ethics. When people use knowledge to decide how to behave, the author contends, Weber thinks they should make their decisions subjectively, according to their own personal biases. So, as the passage progresses, so does Weber's deviation from the strict concept of objectivity that is "traditionally" ascribed to him.

Answers and Explanations

1. D   2. A   3. B   4. C   5. E   6. A   7. C

1. D

This question asks us for the main idea of the passage, and in this case the author presents an argument against a traditional view. Her opposing argument, or main idea, is laid out at the end of the first paragraph, where she tells us that Weber's views on objectivity are "more complicated than the traditional interpretation would have us believe." Choice (D) sums this up nicely.

(A) goes beyond the scope of the passage. Nowhere are other theories of objectivity discussed—the passage focuses only on Weber's views.

(B) contradicts what is stated in the passage. Paragraph 2 shows us that Weber upholds a strictly objective view concerning the nature of reality; he believes in the existence of absolute truth. It is in our attempt to *investigate* objective reality that Weber believes subjectivity creeps in.

(C), (E) Both of these choices are distortions of information in the passage. While the author argues that Weber's views on objectivity are complex, she never claims that these views are not clearly presented (C). Neither does she go so far as to claim that they are inconsistent (E).

> A 180 test taker relate all of the content in the passage back to the main idea, and is thus able to prephrase answers to main idea questions quickly and accurately.

2. A

It's difficult to prephrase an answer to such an open-ended inference question as this, so we must proceed to the choices to see which view can be most readily ascribed to Weber. Luckily, we don't have to look far: (A) presents a good summary of Weber's views on scientific knowledge as presented in paragraph 3. Here we learn that Weber believes that knowledge cannot be totally objective because it is influenced by the assumptions and perspectives of the particular scientific community involved in the investigation of reality.

(B) and (E) misrepresent Weber's use of "ideal types." Ideal types are presented in paragraph 2 as constructs that Weber believes can help scientists investigate reality, not their own biases regarding reality (B). And (E) goes way too far: Just because Weber believes that ideal types can be used to help the scientist investigate objective reality, that's far from saying that he believes this is "the *only* reliable method" possible.

> A 180 test taker is ever on the lookout for extreme-sounding words or phrases in answer choices. The word "only" commonly appears in wrong answer choices.

(C) In paragraph 4 we're told that Weber believes that teachers should refrain from imposing their views on students, *period*—regardless of how capable those students are.

(D) The fact that Weber believes that the *perception* of objective reality must be tinged by subjectivity doesn't mean that Weber finds the notion of objective reality itself "misleading"—on the contrary, paragraph 2 tells us that Weber *does* believe in the existence of strict objective reality.

3. B

Since this passage focuses only on Weber, the correct answer will indicate that one author's views are discussed. (B) throws in the key main idea word "complexities," describing the author's purpose succinctly.

(A), (C) It can be said that the author enters into a debate by countering the traditional view of Weber's scholarship, but that's not the same as "resolving" a debate. If (A) were the intended right answer, two independent views would have to be presented, with the author choosing one over the other. Similarly, she does not "reconcile" opposing perspectives (C)—she merely develops her own position regarding Weber's views.

(D) The author does not argue against Weber's perspective but rather describes it for the reader.

(E) The author presents Weber's views, but does not *test* them. Furthermore, Weber's views represent his position on objectivity, but they do not take the form of a formal hypothesis.

4. C

The phrase "according to the passage" here clues us in that we can expect the answer to draw on a specific detail from the passage. Which paragraph discusses how individuals should use knowledge to guide their actions? Exactly—paragraph 4. The phrase "free to choose how he or she acts upon the reality discovered by science" is the one that best captures the gist of Weber's position regarding the uses of scientific knowledge. Choice (C) stands out as the best paraphrase of this.

(A) distorts the author's meaning in the passage. Paragraph 4 tells us that teachers should help students account for the meaning of their own conduct. It does not tell us that students should be restricted from making decisions if they cannot account for the meaning of their conduct.

(B) According to paragraph 4, Weber believes that individuals should use scientific knowledge in making decisions about action, not that they should distrust it.

(D) On the contrary: We are told that Weber believed that teachers should not guide their students' actions, but should allow students to make their own decisions.

(E) also goes against the grain of the passage. "Weber believes that individuals must make their own decisions," which suggests that teachers should *not* follow the lead of their students but should also act on knowledge independently when determining their own course of action.

A 180 test taker is adept at spotting choices that contradict the ideas in the passage.

---

5. E

Next up we're asked for the passage structure, and hopefully your work on the passage to this point helped you prephrase an answer, or at least quickly eliminate choices that stray beyond your conception of the passage as a whole. We know that only one author's views (Weber's) are presented here, and that different aspects of these views are described in each paragraph. This fits with the gist of choice (E): The "interpretation" expands on the traditional position regarding Weber's view of objectivity, and the author certainly does support this interpretation throughout the passage with specific references to Weber's views and teachings.

(A), (B) The author spends her time in this passage developing Weber's views. She does not reject his views, as (A) indicates; nor does she first criticize these views, as (B) states.

(C) On the contrary: As we saw with choice (A), the author does not negate Weber's views. Instead, she supports them.

(D) This choice tries the same trick we saw in question 3. Again, no hypothesis is presented here and no testing is accomplished.

A 180 test taker is not tempted by terms such as "hypothesis" and "empirical testing" that sound impressive and official but don't apply to the passage at all.

---

6. A

The first step is to locate the assertion that "knowledge of reality cannot be totally objective." A quick review shows us that this point is raised in paragraph 3, where the author discusses scientific knowledge. This detail question asks for evidence specifically mentioned in the passage that supports the assertion in the stem, and again we return to the same idea that we've discussed previously: The interpretation of objective reality is biased by underlying assumptions. (A) describes this point made in paragraph 3 perfectly.

A 180 test taker knows that, even in difficult passages, at least a few questions are bound to cover similar material.

(B) reflects the opposite of what is stated in the passage. The author claims that Weber believes that methods of investigation can never be strictly objective, by their very nature.

(C) and (D) present ideas raised in the passage, but neither of these statements reflects evidence for the assertion in question. Ideal types are discussed in the passage, but only in paragraph 2. We're looking for evidence given in paragraph 3. The definition of "objective truth" is also raised in paragraph 2, but not as evidence for the point that knowledge can't be objective.

(E) once again plays off the distinction between objective reality and the *knowledge* of objective reality. Weber *does* believe in the concept of strict objectivity, so to say that objective reality is "illusory" goes against the grain of the passage, not to mention trying to posit it as evidence for something else in the passage.

A 180 test taker, when asked about specific details from the text, avoids choices formulated from information from other parts of the text.

---

7. C

Why does the author give us the "traditional" interpretation of Weber's view? To let us know which view she's reacting against—that is, to provide an introduction into her opposing interpretation of his views. Choice (C) describes this reason well.

(A) is an exaggeration. Although the author rejects the traditional view, it would be going too far to say that she "dismiss[es] the relevance of all previous scholarship" on Weber.

(B) again distorts the author's purpose. She does not argue that objectivity has been historically misunderstood in general, but rather that Weber's views on objectivity have been misunderstood.

(D) and (E) state the opposite of the author's reason for presenting the traditional view. She does not use it to develop critics' views of Weber, but rather her own interpretation. Neither does she attempt to vindicate the traditional view; on the contrary, she refutes it.

What's Next?

The writing in this one is fairly dense, but you won't find any relief from the wordiness and abstraction in the next passage, which follows nicely on the theme at the end of "Weber on Objectivity" concerning the ways in which individual actions can be guided. See what you can make of "Teaching Virtue."

THE NEXT READING COMPREHENSION
PASSAGE BEGINS ON THE FOLLOWING PAGE

PASSAGE 10

Virtue is not so much a matter of learning specific rules or principles or maxims as it is one of developing the knack of exercising one's capacity for right action. Since "virtue" can mean
(5) both "moral goodness" and "successful or excellent action," comments regarding the teaching of virtue must apply to both senses or uses of the term, narrow and broad. Both are matters of human action or activity and, as such,
(10) are taught nondidactically, performatively.

That virtue is taught (and learned) performatively has something to do with the ineluctably normative quality of human action or activity. Norms are ways of doing something,
(15) getting something done; these ways of acting are taught by doing and showing how to do. Being normative, however, human actions can go wrong. They can be done wrong, or be wrongly done. As Stanley Cavell wrote: "The most characteristic
(20) fact about actions is that they can—in various specific ways—go wrong, that they can be performed incorrectly. This is not, in any restricted sense, a moral assertion, though it points the moral of intelligent activity. And it is as
(25) true of describing as it is of calculating or of promising or plotting or warning or asserting or defining . . . These are actions which we perform, and our successful performance of them depends upon our adopting and following the ways in
(30) which the action in question is done, upon what is normative for it." Thus, in talking about virtue, we are talking about normative matters, matters taught and learned in terms of successful or unsuccessful human action. As such, we are
(35) speaking about the cultivation of human skills and practices, human ways of acting (or ways of acting humanly) in this world.

Whether virtue is narrowly or broadly understood, the teaching of virtue is the teaching
(40) of a skill within a practice or form of life, the training of a capacity, not the memorization or indoctrination of rules or guidelines. The latter may indeed play some part in teaching a skill within a practice, but it is not all, or even most, of
(45) what I understand the teaching of virtue to be. Virtue is embodied in action; accordingly, our knowledge of virtue is a kind of performative knowledge—both knowledge acquired through action and knowledge expressed or revealed in
(50) action, in performing a task. Our knowledge of virtue is not, then, a matter of *propositional* knowledge, but rather a matter of performative knowledge. This helps account for our relative inability to define or say what virtue is with any
(55) confidence or assurance. Knowing what virtue is,

is not the same as knowing what some kind of object is, because virtue is not an object. And since so much of Western thought uses our knowledge of objects as *the* paradigm of
(60) knowledge, any kind of knowledge that does not fit the model is apt to seem not quite or fully knowledge at all. In this respect, virtue is like language. Both are taught by example. Hence, an inability to articulate the meaning of virtue is not
(65) a sign of the lack of knowledge of virtue, contrary to Socrates (or Plato). Instead, it is a part of the grammar of virtue: it shows what kind of thing virtue is.

1. The primary purpose of the passage is to

   (A) urge that students consult teachers when pursuing knowledge
   (B) reveal different attitudes toward virtue in the history of Western thought
   (C) argue that most teachers approach the teaching of virtue incorrectly
   (D) insist on the value of cultural norms as guidelines for human behavior
   (E) argue that the teaching of virtue is best understood as the training of a capacity

2. According to the passage, which one of the following distinguishes the broad definition of virtue from the narrow definition?

   (A) The broad definition does not include physical activities.
   (B) The narrow definition was not recognized by Plato or Socrates.
   (C) The broad definition deals with cultural norms.
   (D) The broad definition involves the teaching of a skill.
   (E) The broad definition encompasses more than simple moral rectitude.

3. The author would be most likely to agree with which one of the following statements about norms?

   (A) They are derived from specific maxims that define different aspects of virtue.
   (B) Only by faithfully following behavioral norms can virtue be acquired.
   (C) Many norms are simply the correct way of performing a certain action.
   (D) They are the product of didactic teaching.
   (E) They do not evolve, but rather come into being spontaneously.

4. According to the passage, a person who is unable to define virtue

    (A) cannot successfully teach virtue to others
    (B) may impart knowledge of excellent action but not of moral goodness
    (C) can teach didactically but not performatively
    (D) cannot perform virtuous actions
    (E) may still have a knowledge of virtue

5. The author contends that teachers of virtue strive primarily to impart

    (A) skills
    (B) principles
    (C) maxims
    (D) moral goodness
    (E) definitions

6. The author would characterize the view that some human actions are non-normative as

    (A) profoundly mistaken
    (B) controversial and possibly untrue
    (C) reasonable and easily supported
    (D) ambiguous and misleading
    (E) logically persuasive

7. Which one of the following would serve as an example of the "*propositional* knowledge" referred to in lines 51–52?

    (A) experiments conducted on a trial and error basis
    (B) practicing virtue by imitating moral actions
    (C) learning a language in conversational classes
    (D) memorizing various philosophical definitions of virtue
    (E) advancing an argument based on insufficient evidence

Passage 10: Teaching Virtue

What Makes It Difficult

Abstract subject matter aside, the writing in this one is just plain difficult. Check out these terms and concepts: "nondidactically," "performatively," "ineluctably normative quality," "propositional knowledge." As if that's not bad enough, the author employs confusing word plays for what seems to be dramatic effect: "They (human actions) can be done wrong, or be wrongly done." Huh? Is there some subtle difference here we're supposed to pick up on? How about: " As such, we are speaking about . . . human ways of acting (or ways of acting humanly) in this world." If you need a further example of the high-minded complexity in this passage, note how the passage ends with a metaphor of an abstraction: "the grammar of virtue."

But really, how bad can it be? After all, the author is talking about learning how to be virtuous, which we can take to mean acting well in the world, to use her wording. By simplifying the material through paraphrasing, you have a much better shot at the questions. Here's how you may have understood the passage on your own terms.

Key Points of the Passage

Purpose and Main Idea: The author's purpose is to describe how virtue is taught. The main idea is that virtue is taught by doing—by example, by showing how to be virtuous—and not by abstract explanations of what virtue is.

Paragraph Structure: Paragraph 1 hits on the main point right at the end, noting that virtue is taught "nondidactically, performatively." For many, these terms are somewhat foreign, but not to worry; the rest of the passage essentially explains what this means.

> A 180 test taker rolls with the punches. He knows that everything needed to answer the questions must be found in the passage, and that if an obscure term or concept is introduced, the author must clarify it if a question is to test it.

As for the rest of the first paragraph, perhaps the most important concept, which ties in with the main point, is that according to the author, virtue has something to do with developing one's ability to act right.

In the long second paragraph, the author argues that human action is "normative." The detailed argument here is a lot less important than realizing what the author is doing: basically, expanding on the idea that virtue is taught "performatively." But to summarize briefly: The author says actions involve "norms," which are "ways of doing something" and are "taught by doing and showing how to do." All actions, the author says with an assist from Stanley Cavell, have this normative quality. So—getting back to virtue—virtue like anything else involves teaching by doing and showing.

Paragraph 3, equally lengthy and off-putting, expands on this same idea: The teaching of virtue is the teaching of a skill (a "way of doing something"), not "memorization or indoctrination of rules." At the end the author draws one more lesson from the central idea: Since virtue is taught and known through actions, being unable to define it doesn't mean you do not know what it is. The implication: If you recognize virtue and can act with virtue, then you know what virtue is.

> A 180 test taker recognizes when a seemingly complicated passage is simply made up of a number of densely written paragraphs harping on the same central point.

Answers and Explanations

1. E 2. E 3. C 4. E 5. A 6. A 7. D

1. E

The primary purpose question focuses right in on the "main idea." As expressed at the end of paragraph 1, this was that virtue is taught "nondidactically, performatively." In the rest of the passage, the author distinguishes between teaching of "rules or guidelines," "propositional knowledge," etc., and the kind of teaching he or she means: teaching "by doing and showing how to do" (paragraph 2), "matters taught and learned in terms of . . . action" (end of paragraph 2), "the teaching of a skill," the "training of a capacity" (paragraph 3). That last phrase is used in correct choice (E), but even if the phrase were not drawn from the passage, you should recognize it as a paraphrase of the recurring theme of the passage. Since the author basically does nothing in the passage except elaborate this one idea, (E) is the best choice.

(A) is an idea never expressed; the author's focus is on how to teach, not what students should do.

(B) tries to fool us with the tiny reference to Plato and Socrates at the very end; other than this, no "attitude toward virtue" besides the author's is ever mentioned.

(C) The idea in (C) is a possible inference—the author wouldn't care so much about how virtue should be taught if most teachers were doing a good job. But that's only an implication; the author never argues the point.

(D), finally, uses the word "norms" in one of its more common meanings—cultural norms—but not in the way the author uses it, to refer to "ways of doing something" and not to "rules or guidelines."

2. E

This question focuses on a subordinate point in paragraph 1. The author refers to virtue as meaning both "moral goodness" and "successful or excellent action," and then refers to these as the "narrow and broad" senses of the term. It's reasonable to assume that the author is keeping the terms in their original order—"narrow" refers to the first sense mentioned, "broad" to the second. Indeed, "successful or excellent action" can be seen as a broader, less specific meaning of "virtue" than "moral goodness." (E) rephrases "moral goodness" as "moral rectitude" and correctly states that the broad definition "encompasses more" than this.

(A) Physical activities are never mentioned, but if anything, they would be included, not excluded, under the broad definition.

(B) The single sentence about Plato and Socrates does not indicate whether they would have included or excluded either sense of "virtue."

(C) drags in "cultural norms" again; remember, to the author, "norms" are ways of doing things, and "cultural norms," in the familiar, everyday sense, are not mentioned in relation to either meaning of virtue.

A 180 test taker knows to keep everyday definitions at bay if the author has provided a more specific meaning for a word or concept.

(D) is definitely a true statement, but to the author, the narrow sense ("moral goodness") also involves the teaching of a skill, so this is not a distinction between the broad and narrow definitions.

3. C

This next question focuses squarely on the author's curious usage of "norms." As we've stressed already, for our author, norms are "ways of doing something, getting something done" (paragraph 2); this idea is paraphrased in (C).

In (A), "maxims" and "define" should have raised a red flag. Maxims are related to the dreaded "rules or guidelines" in paragraph 3, while "define" recalls the equally dreaded "propositional knowledge." In fact, the author talks about our inability to define what virtue is, so most of the wording in this choice should have clunked against your ear.

A 180 test taker can quickly recognize concepts that run counter to the author's central points.

(B) Behavioral norms are never mentioned.

(D) "Didactic teaching," like "maxims" and "define" in (A), should be a red flag. Sentence 2 of paragraph 2 says norms "are taught by doing and showing how to do"—not by didactic methods.

(E) is one of those "from absolutely nowhere" choices; nothing in the passage remotely suggests the idea of evolution versus spontaneity.

4. E

The challenge here is mainly locating the right material to work with; from there, the answer comes from a fairly simple paraphrase.

A 180 test taker is adept at assimilating the idea in the stem and then locating the relevant part of the passage that speaks to that idea.

The author's thoughts on the inability to define virtue appear in paragraph 3. If we add together the question stem and choice (E), we'd have a straightforward paraphrase of the sentence about Socrates, and it all stems from a point we've already discussed: the notion that being able to define or articulate what virtue is isn't a prerequisite for knowing it when you see or partake in it. It's stated very directly at the end of the passage: "An inability to articulate the meaning of virtue is not a sign of the lack of knowledge of virtue."

(A) The issue in (A) is not specifically mentioned; but since virtue is taught by "doing and showing how to do," probably someone who knew virtue but couldn't define it could teach it. At least, we can't say for sure that he or she couldn't teach it.

(B) makes a distinction the passage won't support. Whatever is true of the person who can't define virtue—whether he or she can or can't teach it—would presumably apply to teaching virtue in both senses, not just one.

(C) makes exactly the wrong distinction. Someone who can't define the subject matter can't teach didactically, where the main teaching method is to repeat definitions and explanations.

(D) is somewhat absurd, if you think about it—if this were true, only very learned philosophers could act virtuously.

5. A

It's right there in the first sentence of paragraph 3: "The teaching of virtue is the teaching of a skill . . . the training of a capacity." (A) is correct.

(B), (C), and (E) are all part of the "didactic" aspect of teaching. The author does admit, a little later in paragraph 3, that these "may indeed play some part in teaching a skill," but contends that this "is not all, or even most, of what I understand the teaching of virtue to be"; so they are not what teachers of virtue strive primarily to impart, as the question asks.

A 180 test taker considers every word of the question stem, understanding that even a single missed word can jeopardize her understanding of the question.

(D) is a misstatement: The author would say a teacher of virtue strives to teach moral goodness through imparting ways of doing, imparting skills. It also makes a false distinction; the teacher would strive to teach "excellent action" as much as "moral goodness."

6. A

Back to paragraph 2. The author refers to "the ineluctably [inevitably] normative quality of human action"; he or she states, "being normative . . . human actions can go wrong." And in the quote, Stanley Cavell includes a list of actions clearly meant to be as broad as possible, all of which are said to be normative. The author clearly views all human actions as normative, and hence would think the opposite view profoundly mistaken, choice (A).

Once you realize that the stem states the direct contrary of the author's view, (A) is easy to select, and the others easy to reject. (B) and (D) are critical of the idea in the stem, but not nearly critical enough; (C) and (E) are approving, and thus are wrong altogether.

7. D

Reading the context here, the key thing to realize is that the "propositional knowledge" discussed is contrasted with the author's main theme—the correct way to teach virtue. From this standpoint, we can rule out choices (A) through (C), since they all fit the author's definition of "performative knowledge": "knowledge acquired through action and knowledge expressed or revealed in action, through performing a task." Conducting experiments, imitating moral actions and learning a language are all ways of learning from actions—learning by example.

Choice (D), on the other hand, exemplifies the type of didactic learning the author contrasts with teaching virtue. We can infer then, that memorizing definitions of virtue is an example of "propositional knowledge."

(E) Advancing arguments without sufficient evidence may play on the word "proposition," but isn't supported in the passage at all.

What's Next?

Philosophical conjecture is not the sole province of professional philosophers or social scientists; literary stars often get into philosophizing mode as well. For example, some consider Fyodor Dostoyevsky to be not only one of Russia's premiere novelists, but also one of its foremost philosophers *and* psychologists. Another such multitalented thinker is Virginia Woolf, who is about to regale us with her philosophy of literary criticism, relying on the works of Dostoyevsky's contemporary (and sometimes rival) Ivan Turgenev for support.

THE NEXT READING COMPREHENSION
PASSAGE BEGINS ON THE FOLLOWING PAGE

PASSAGE 11

The critical essays of Virginia Woolf, when examined carefully, reveal a thematic and technical complexity that rivals her fiction. Although her fiction also focuses on the
(5)   problematical relationship between the reader's experience of the text and the original authorial presence, the problem of interpretation is more sharply visible in her criticism.

Some of her most rigorous essays suggest that
(10)   the personality of the author can be fixed if sufficient evidence can be amassed and if its logical implications are followed. In "The Novels of Turgenev," Woolf pursues the problem of interpretation by providing a detailed report of her
(15)   own response to Turgenev. She does this in order to make possible the question that leaps the gap between reader and text. That question—"what principles guided Turgenev?"—focuses on the fictional strategies that must have been in
(20)   operation in order to have produced her experience. Thus Woolf accounts for her experience of the novel by reconstructing Turgenev's method. But she pushes farther: the method must be a sign of a deeper informing
(25)   power, the mind of Turgenev itself. In other words, the gap between reader and writer may be eliminated in the reader's achievement of what Woolf calls the author's "perspective." This distance can be traversed by interpretation, Woolf
(30)   argues, because writers like Turgenev achieve a level of personality beneath the surface distinctions among individuals—a level at which all human beings are united. Her greatest examples of this impersonal power are Jane
(35)   Austen and Shakespeare. We are allowed by their art to make contact with what is most deeply personal, and therefore most widely human in them.

But one of the riches of Woolf's essays is that
(40)   they critique the very possibility of closing the gap between reader and writer. This critique takes the form of Woolf's awareness of the contemporary artist's self-consciousness, that is, the artist's entrapment in superficial, alienating
(45)   distinctions among people. Self-consciousness is the enemy of human contact and knowing. It is present, Woolf argues, in the anger of writers who increase our awareness of the division between he sexes, in writers too aware of their nationality, in
(50)   authors who can never write without class consciousness, and in realistic writers whose methods emphasize the external at the expense of the deeply human interior. There seem to be so many barriers on the road to the deepest level of
(55)   self that the journey is impossible. In fact, Woolf

asserts that it *is* impossible for the modern writer. In "How It Strikes a Contemporary," Woolf contrasts writers of the past—Chaucer is her most powerful example—who believed wholeheartedly
(60)   in an atemporal order verified by the entire culture, with modern writers who have lost this advantage. Woolf suggests that, if, for writer and reader, no way to a shared, universal level of experience is available, the very ground of the
(65)   interpretive enterprise is removed.

1. According to the passage, Woolf views a belief in an atemporal world order as

    (A) defining the literary customs of modern writers
    (B) being inadequate to the task of eliminating divisions in human society
    (C) having evolved from a belief in a temporal world order
    (D) supporting the values and priorities of modern culture
    (E) contributing to the distinctiveness of past literature

2. The author is mainly concerned with

    (A) revising an interpretation of Woolf's criticism
    (B) analyzing Woolf's interpretation of Turgenev
    (C) comparing Woolf's fiction to her criticism
    (D) examining a theme of Woolf's criticism
    (E) investigating a paradox in Woolf's criticism

3. According to the passage, Woolf believes that, compared to modern writers, writers of the past were

    (A) more interested in personal issues
    (B) more concerned with timeless themes
    (C) more self-absorbed
    (D) less impersonal
    (E) less objective

4. The passage implies that, in her essay "The Novels of Turgenev," Woolf assumes that

   (A) stable and defining qualities of an author's personality are discernible in his or her fiction
   (B) interpretation involves a compromise between the reader's perspective and the perspective of the author
   (C) a reader's experience of a novel's text is determined by a standard set of fictional principles
   (D) making contact with an author's mind requires the use of critical reasoning more than intuition
   (E) an author's achievement of the impersonal involves a renunciation of the personal in his or her fiction

5. The passage suggests that Woolf believes that self-consciousness among contemporary artists is

   (A) liberating for certain artists
   (B) a temporary deviation
   (C) a pervasive phenomenon
   (D) negligible in its effects
   (E) a hopeful sign

6. The passage refers to common themes of contemporary writers in the third paragraph in order to

   (A) exemplify a contemporary preoccupation with separateness
   (B) identify sources of contemporary cultural patterns
   (C) suggest parallels between past and present literature
   (D) refute the idea that self-consciousness is an affliction
   (E) point out a strong contemporary desire to experiment

7. The passage suggests that Woolf would be most likely to agree with which one of the following statements?

   (A) Literary works seldom reflect the period in which they were written.
   (B) Literary criticism should focus on the work rather than the artist.
   (C) Literary criticism should emphasize plot over structure.
   (D) Literary works are the product of an author's unique experiences.
   (E) Literary criticism seldom reveals the biases of the critic.

Passage 11: Woolf on Literary Interpretation

What Makes It Difficult

As in "Weber on Objectivity," we're presented with a description of an intellectual's theory on a relatively complex subject. This one deals with the possibility of bridging the gap between the minds of novelist and reader—pretty esoteric stuff. And it deals largely with abstractions such as perspective, interpretation, self-consciousness, and universal experience. As always, summarizing the purpose and main idea, and breaking it down into its structural elements, will help us handle the questions.

Key Points of the Passage

Purpose and Main Idea: The author's purpose is to discuss Virginia Woolf's philosophy regarding a reader's ability to "interpret" a writer. The main idea is that it's possible for readers to gain "perspective" on authors of previous periods because these writers capture a deep universal human experience in their work, but the gap between readers and modern writers is more difficult to traverse because these writers emphasize in their work that which separates people and do not provide a way "to a shared, universal level of experience."

Paragraph Structure: Paragraph 1 simply establishes the fact that Woolf is concerned in her critical essays with the problem of interpretation. We have to wait for the next paragraph for the author to get into what this really means.

Paragraph 2 outlines the argument Woolf makes in her essay "The Novels of Turgenev." She asserts that the central problem for the reader (or the critic) is understanding or *interpreting* Turgenev. As the passage explains it, Woolf believes that there are two stages in the interpretive process: first, understanding Turgenev's fictional strategies—his "method"; second (and more basic), gaining an understanding of Turgenev's mind and personality—his "perspective." Getting a deeper sense of the author's personality is a reader's fundamental goal, because it's at this level that essential human bonds can be established between author and reader. At the end of the paragraph the author generalizes: Woolf believes that Turgenev, Austen, and Shakespeare are great writers because their most personal concerns can be interpreted, understood—shared—by readers everywhere.

Paragraph 3 sets up a key contrast: Woolf argues in other essays (including "How It Strikes a Contemporary") that contemporary writers have abandoned the universal themes favored by past writers. According to Woolf, writers today are preoccupied with social differences and personal uniqueness—their own separateness as people. The result, according to Woolf, is the erecting of impenetrable barriers which jeopardize the traditional interpretive process.

Now, these ideas really aren't that tough. For instance, you probably already know about the universality of Shakespeare, Austen, etc. No surprise there. Woolf's argument about modern writers, their separateness and so on, is more provocative, perhaps even open to question, but it's not such a tough idea, either, if you keep your test-taking cool.

A 180 test taker uses his own knowledge to help him understand an author's ideas, but never goes so far as to replace the author's ideas with his own.

Answers and Explanations

1. E   2. D   3. B   4. A   5. C   6. A   7. D

1. E

The belief in an atemporal world order relates directly to the concern of past writers for universal themes. The point is made explicitly at the end of the passage. Writers of the past like Chaucer believed "wholeheartedly in an atemporal world order," which is something that distinguishes the work of past masters from contemporary writers. Thus it can be said that this belief contributes to the distinctiveness of past literature, choice (E).

All the wrong choices fly in the face of the passage:

(A) and (D) are nearly synonymous: They falsely suggest a link between belief in an atemporal order and *modern* writers. In paragraph 3, the author explicitly states that this is not the case.

(B) contradicts Woolf: She argues that the older, universal values were healing, and that we moderns are worse off for their absence from modern literature.

(C) A "temporal world order" is never explicitly defined, but we can assume that we're living in it now. We're never given a hint as to the precursor of the belief in an atemporal order.

> A 180 test taker is not fooled by concepts that sound familiar ("Temporal"? That's darn close to "atemporal," no?) but are found nowhere in the passage.

2. D

Next up is a straightforward main idea question. The whole passage, all three paragraphs, takes a look at one theme—the problem of interpreting an author—of some of Woolf's criticism. (D) states the author's concern in general terms.

(A) is out because of its verb. The author's not revising anything.

(B) focuses too narrowly on Woolf's Turgenev essay. Sure, this plays a large role in the passage, but it's there to support the larger issue of Woolf's general philosophy of interpretation.

> A 180 test taker understands the difference between an author's main concern and the vehicle through which he speaks to that concern.

(C) is plain wrong; in paragraph 1 the author makes a brief comparison of Woolf's criticism to her fiction, but it's by no means the author's main concern.

(E) doesn't work because the author never refers to any paradox in Woolf's work.

3. B

Another question focusing on the contrast between past and present writers. As is clear in both paragraph 2 and the passage's last couple of sentences, writers of the past were preoccupied with universal, timeless themes. Again, the wrong choices all contradict the passage. It's modern writers who focus on personal issues (A), are more self-absorbed (C), are less impersonal (D), and who are less objective (E).

4. A

This question is looking for an idea (an "assumption") that's clearly at work in Woolf's essay on Turgenev. We're therefore looking for an idea that's required in order for Woolf's discussion of Turgenev to make sense. (A) goes right to the heart of the passage: According to sentence 1 of paragraph 2, Woolf believes that, through a careful reading of the fictional work, a reader/critic can identify the personality of the author. (A) is a simple paraphrase of this idea. If, contrary to (A), the personality of a writer was *not* discernible from his or her fiction, Woolf would not be able to claim that "the personality of the author can be fixed" if only certain evidence were amassed and its implications observed.

> A 180 test taker uses techniques developed from any section of the test to help her answer questions. Assumption questions are more common in the Logical Reasoning sections, but a 180 test taker uses the skills developed in that section when one shows up elsewhere.

(B) Nowhere is it suggested that interpretation involves any "compromise" between reader and author.

(C) distorts things by suggesting that there is one "standard" set of principles at work in all fictional works.

(D) Nowhere is it suggested that intuition is less important than critical reasoning in fictional interpretation. In fact, getting a sense of an author's "perspective" or personality would seem to be a highly intuitive (and informed) process.

(E) distorts the generalization at the end of the paragraph: Woolf suggests that Turgenev achieves an impersonal quality as he reveals that part of himself with which his readers can identify. But he is *not* renouncing himself in doing so.

5. C

Here we're being asked about a key point of the last paragraph. We're told there that Woolf believes that self-consciousness—self-absorption—is rampant among today's artists. She is suggesting that it's a pervasive problem, really a blight. (C) gets the point.

As for the wrong choices, there's no talk of self-consciousness being "liberating" (A), "temporary" (B), unimportant (D), or a good thing (E). These choices ignore the intensity of Woolf's apprehension.

6. A

A question that asks why an author has done something we call a "logic" question, which, like most of these other questions, harks back to one of the key points in the passage. These typical contemporary themes are examples Woolf gives of the kinds of issues that today's writers are concerned with: issues of separateness, dividedness, or alienation. (A) is the choice that corresponds.

(B) may be the most tempting wrong choice, but it misses the point. It's illogical to think of the cited themes as "sources" of today's cultural patterns.

(C) and (D) are both inconsistent with the passage. The themes of contemporary writers are cited to show divisions, not parallels, between past and present writers. And the author cites these themes to illustrate how Woolf finds self-consciousness to be a barrier to literary interpretation, so *refuting* the idea that self-consciousness is a bad thing simply doesn't make sense in this context.

A 180 test taker expects to see some contradictory choices in passages in which ideas, people, or groups are compared and contrasted, knowing that many wrong choices play off these comparisons in illegitimate ways.

(E) The notion of experimentation is outside the scope of the discussion in the final paragraph, but if anything, we'd have to guess that contemporary horizons for writers are fairly restrictive, limited to issues of alienation and separateness. In any case, the contemporary themes cited aren't there to point toward an experimental vein in contemporary literature.

7. D
The last question is looking for the choice that's *consistent* with Woolf's ideas, and the winner is (D). Consider her essay on Turgenev. She believes that, even though his themes are universal, Turgenev's personality lies at the root of his novels. And Woolf would also apparently agree that contemporary fiction, bound by self-consciousness, is also the product of an author's special experiences.

(A) makes no sense. It's clearly not true of today's fiction, and Woolf never suggests that Turgenev's novels could have been written, say, in Shakespeare's time.

(B) contradicts Woolf: her critical method involves analysis of work and artist.

(C) Woolf is concerned with the "fictional strategies" and methods that must have been employed in order for her to experience a novel as she did. How this relates to plot and structure is unclear. Nowhere is it specified which of these elements is better represented in an author's methods and strategies, so we can't attribute this belief to Woolf.

(E) simply sounds unlikely and inconsistent with Woolf. The idea of a reader/critic establishing contact with an author clearly involves a personal, subjective response. If anything, it would seem that biases would be inevitable.

What's Next?

One more passage to go, and it's a whopper, for sure. What did you find to be the most difficult game in the Logic Games section? Perhaps "Video Editor" or "Plane Passengers"? Or maybe one of the process games such as "University Promotions" or "Children's Questions"? Well, many feel that this next passage is the Reading Comp equivalent of those, at least as far as brutality is concerned. It is (in our opinion) aptly titled: "Murphy's Law."

PASSAGE 12

If one always ought to act so as to produce the best possible circumstances, then morality is extremely demanding, perhaps overly so. No one could plausibly claim that at every moment of
(5) their lives they have acted with maximum efficiency to improve the condition of the world. Since it would seem strange to punish those intending to do good by sentencing them to an impossible task, some ethical philosophers have
(10) concluded that morality has an "overdemandingness" problem.

From an analytic perspective, the potential extreme demands of morality are not a "problem." A theory of morality is no less valid simply
(15) because it asks great sacrifices. In fact, it is difficult to imagine what kind of constraints could be put on our ethical projects. Shouldn't we reflect on our base prejudices, and not allow them to provide boundaries for our moral reasoning?
(20) Thus, it is tempting to simply dismiss the "overdemandingness" objection. However, in *Demands of Morality*, Liam Murphy takes this objection seriously.

Murphy does not tell us what set of "firm
(25) beliefs" we ought to have. Rather, he speaks to an audience of well-intentioned but unorganized moral agents, and tries to give them principles that represent their considered moral judgments. Murphy starts with an initial sense of right and
(30) wrong, but recognizes that it needs to be supplemented by reason where our intuitions are confused or conflicting. Perhaps Murphy is looking for the best interpretation of our convictions, the same way certain legal scholars
(35) try to find the best interpretation of the U.S. Constitution.

This approach has disadvantages. Primarily, Murphy's arguments, even if successful, do not provide the kind of motivating force for which
(40) moral philosophy has traditionally searched. His work assumes and argues in terms of an inner sense of morality, and his project seeks to deepen that sense. Of course, it is quite possible that the moral viewpoints of humans will not converge,
(45) and some humans have no moral sense at all. Thus, it is very easy for the moral skeptic to point out a lack of justification and ignore the entire work.

On the other hand, Murphy's choice of a
(50) starting point avoids many of the problems of moral philosophy. Justifying the content of moral principles and granting a motivating force to those principles is an extraordinary task. It would be unrealistic to expect all discussions of moral
(55) philosophy to derive such justifications. Projects

that attempt such a derivation have value, but they are hard pressed to produce logical consequences for everyday life. In the end, Murphy's strategy may have more practical effect than its more
(60) traditional counterparts, which do not seem any more likely to convince those that would reject Murphy's premises.

1. The passage is primarily concerned with

    (A) highlighting the disadvantages in adopting a philosophical approach
    (B) illustrating a philosophical debate by comparing two current theories
    (C) reconciling the differences between two schools of philosophical thought
    (D) reviewing scholarly opinions of an ethical problem and proposing a new solution
    (E) evaluating the merits of a model of ethical inquiry

2. The author suggests which one of the following regarding Murphy's philosophy?

    (A) The application of Murphy's philosophy to the situations of two different groups would help to solve the problems of one group but not of the other.
    (B) The application of Murphy's philosophy to the situations of two different groups could result in the derivation of two radically different moral principles.
    (C) The application of Murphy's philosophy to the situations of two different groups would be contingent on the two groups sharing the same fundamental beliefs.
    (D) The application of Murphy's philosophy to the situations of two different groups could reconcile any differences between the two groups.
    (E) The application of Murphy's philosophy to the situations of two different groups would not provide definitive recommendations for either group.

3. The passage implies that a moral principle derived from applying Murphy's philosophy to a particular group would be applicable to another group if

(A) the first group recommended the principle to the second group

(B) the moral viewpoints of the two groups do not converge

(C) the members of the second group have no firmly held beliefs

(D) the second group shares the same fundamental beliefs as the first group

(E) either group has no moral beliefs at all

4. According to the passage, the existence of individuals who entirely lack a moral sense has which one of the following consequences?

(A) It confirms the notion that moral principles should be derived from the considered judgments of individuals.

(B) It suggests a potential disadvantage of Murphy's philosophical approach.

(C) It supports Murphy's belief that reason is necessary in cases in which intuitions are conflicting or confused.

(D) It proves that more traditional approaches to ethical theorizing will have no more influence over the behavior of individuals than will Murphy's philosophical approach.

(E) It is a necessary consequence of the "overdemandingness" problem.

5. The passage suggests that Murphy would agree that the application of reason is necessary for forming moral principles when

(A) the beliefs of one group supersede the beliefs of another

(B) people's firmly held beliefs are conflicting or confused

(C) the belief system of a group conflicts with an overriding ethical principle

(D) individuals have no moral sense at all

(E) the demands of morality seem too extreme

6. A school board is debating whether or not to institute a dress code for the school's students. According to Murphy, which one of the following actions would constitute the best way to come to an ethical decision regarding the matter?

(A) consulting the fundamental beliefs of the board members

(B) analyzing the results of dress codes instituted at other schools

(C) surveying the students as to whether or not they would prefer a dress code

(D) determining whether or not a dress code has ever been instituted in the school's history

(E) determining the best interpretation of the guarantees found in the U.S. Constitution

7. The primary purpose of the last paragraph of the passage is to

(A) describing the method of determining the best interpretation of an individual's firmly-held beliefs

(B) explain the origin of the "overdemandingness" objection

(C) identify advantages associated with Murphy's approach to ethics

(D) reconcile two opposing schools of philosophical thought

(E) characterize Murphy's response to the "overdemandingness" objection

8. The passage suggests that the author would be most likely to agree with which one of the following statements?

(A) Arguing from a set of firmly-held beliefs is an important element of traditional moral philosophy.

(B) Philosophical works that attempt to discover a motivating force behind moral principles have no value.

(C) No one who lacks a moral sense can make a significant contribution to an ethical debate.

(D) Those who are not well-intentioned are unlikely to be influenced by traditional approaches to moral philosophy.

(E) The "overdemandingness" objection does not represent a serious problem for traditional moral philosophy.

Passage 12: Murphy's Law

What Makes It Difficult

Murphy's Law, in common parlance, states that whatever *can* happen, *will* happen, and is usually invoked in the context of an occurrence of particularly bad luck. Although the Murphy's Law of this passage—the principles of moral philosophy introduced by Liam Murphy—is not the same, there's no doubt that some LSAT test takers hit with a passage like this will feel that the more commonly known version of Murphy's Law has struck.

This one has it all: An abstract, esoteric topic. Complicated prose. A wavering pro and con structure ("This approach has disadvantages." "On the other hand . . . "). Eight tough questions, including four inference questions ("the passage suggests . . . ")—which are especially hard to handle when the material is so abstract—and a question that asks us to apply the premises of Murphy's theory to an external situation. A true killer, indeed. How did you fare recognizing the key points?

Key Points of the Passage

Purpose and Main Idea: The purpose of the passage is to assess the value of Murphy's views on morality. The main idea is that Murphy's argument may lack motivating force for those who don't have an inner sense of morality, but it also avoids having to justify the content of particular moral principles and is more practical than traditional views.

Paragraph Structure: Paragraph 1 introduces us to the "overdemandingness" problem in moral philosophy. If we define morality as requiring us to always act to produce the best circumstances, then morality may seem to be overly demanding; that is, it asks too much of people.

Paragraph 2 tells us that some people reject the idea that morality is overdemanding. The philosopher Liam Murphy, however, takes the "overdemandingness" problem seriously.

In paragraph 3, Murphy's philosophy is described. Murphy doesn't give people a set of firm beliefs or particular moral principles. Instead, he argues that each person should make moral decisions based first upon his or her own inner sense of right and wrong. If a person's inner sense of right and wrong is confused, the person can then use his or her reason to make the final decision.

Paragraph 4 lists the disadvantages of Murphy's view. The main disadvantage is that people who have no moral foundation aren't likely to get one through his approach.

Paragraph 5 then gives the advantages of Murphy's perspective. Murphy's view starts with the individual's own inner sense of morality, so it doesn't have to go through the difficult task of justifying specific moral principles. This view ends up being more practical than traditional approaches.

Answers and Explanations

1. E   2. B   3. D   4. B   5. B   6. A   7. C   8. D

1. E

This overall purpose question is a good one to prephrase based on our analysis above. The author's purpose is "to assess the value of Murphy's view." This answer is summed up well in choice (E), since the author is evaluating the merits of Murphy's model of ethical inquiry.

(A) is too narrow to qualify as the primary purpose. The author does discuss the disadvantages of Murphy's view, but only in one paragraph of the passage.

A 180 test taker knows that the answer to a primary purpose question must apply to the entire passage, not just one part.

(B), (C) Both of these choices are incorrect because they suggest that two views are addressed in the passage. Choice (B) suggests that two theories are discussed, while choice (C) suggests that two schools of thought are reviewed. In fact, only one view—Murphy's—is developed in the passage.

(D) The author does not pose a solution to an ethical problem.

2. B

Here we're asked to draw an inference, as is denoted by the word "suggests." This inference question is too broad to prephrase, so it's best to evaluate each answer choice, eliminating obviously incorrect choices. Each answer choice describes what might happen if Murphy's philosophy is applied to the situations of two different groups. Which outcome is more likely, based on the passage? We're told in paragraph 3 that Murphy's view starts with individuals' innate sense of right and wrong. We're also told in paragraph 4 that people's moral viewpoints might not converge. Thus, answer choice (B) is the most likely outcome: It's possible that the two groups could start with entirely different innate senses of right and wrong, and therefore come out with principles that radically differ.

In a case like this, it's also possible that the groups could come out with principles that were relatively similar. This doesn't negate answer (B), however. Depending on how similar the groups' starting views are, their principles *could* either be alike or very different.

(A) The passage gives us no reason to believe that this is the case. We're merely told that Murphy's approach requires all persons to start from their innate belief systems. If two groups were using the approach, it's possible that one group might come up with a resolution while the other did not—but there's no reason to believe that this necessarily *would* be the case.

(C) misrepresents the author's argument. Murphy's view could be applied to two different groups regardless of what views those groups held. Its outcome in each case, however, would depend on the group's particular beliefs. It is true that the outcomes would be similar only if the groups held similar views. But the philosophy itself could be applied to any groups, regardless of whether they shared the same beliefs.

(D) is beyond the scope of the author's argument. The author never discusses using Murphy's view to reconcile difference between groups. He merely describes how the view can be used to help individuals determine moral behavior.

(E) is a bit tricky. It's possible that Murphy's philosophy could be applied to two groups, and that neither group would use the philosophy effectively to determine a course of action for their group. This would be the case if both groups had no moral sense to begin with. This type of outcome is only possible, however—it's not certain. The wording of the answer choice is too definite—it states that the philosophy *would not* provide recommendations for either group—and we can't be sure of that.

A 180 test taker carefully scrutinizes the verbs in each answer choice, and knows that there's a significant difference between stating that something "would" happen and stating that something "could" happen.

---

3. D

This inference question deals with the same issue as the previous question, namely: What happens when you apply Murphy's philosophy to two different groups?

A 180 test taker is aware that LSAT Reading Comp questions aren't always unique; that is, that often one question will test the same concept as another question in the set. When this occurs, he uses his previous work to help answer the later question.

We know from question 2 that Murphy's philosophy can be applied to different groups, but that it would produce the same outcome for both only if both groups started with the same moral foundation. Another way of putting this is to say that two groups could apply Murphy's philosophy to their problems, but they would only come up with the same moral principles of action if they both started with the same beliefs. Therefore, a principle derived by one group would apply to another group only if the second group shared the same beliefs as the first. This notion is reflected in choice (D).

(A) is beyond the scope of the passage. Nowhere does the author discuss individuals sharing recommendations regarding Murphy's principles. The author tells us instead that principles are developed by first starting with individuals' own sense of right and wrong (as opposed to recommendations from others).

(B), (C), (E) On the contrary—each of these choices conflicts with the author's argument. If the moral viewpoints of the two groups did not converge, as (B) states, then the principle derived by one group might not apply to the other group at all. According to the passage, Murphy's view can be applied by starting with individuals' innate beliefs and then supplementing those beliefs with reason if the beliefs are conflicting. If people have no moral beliefs, it is difficult or impossible for them to develop principles through Murphy's view, since they have no innate belief system from which to start. Therefore, for (C), if the members of the second group had no firmly held beliefs, a principle developed using Murphy's view would be difficult to apply to them. Finally, if (E) were true, it would be difficult to even come up with the first group's principle—much less apply it to another group.

4. B

Here we are given a question that starts out with the words "according to the passage." That lets us know that we're being asked for specific detail from the passage. Where does the passage mention individuals who have no moral sense? In paragraph 4, where it tells us that individuals without moral beliefs would have no justification for using Murphy's system. This point describes one disadvantage of Murphy's approach, which is exactly what we're told in correct choice (B).

(A) On the contrary: The existence of individuals without moral beliefs provides one reason for refuting Murphy's views. These individuals might not follow Murphy's views at all.

(C) misrepresents the author's argument. The author does tell us that reason is necessary when people's beliefs conflict. But he tells us this in paragraph 3, as he's describing Murphy's approach. The issue of individuals without moral beliefs is not raised until the following paragraph, in the discussion of the philosophy's disadvantages.

(D) Again, this choice misrepresents the author's argument. The author does mention that traditional approaches might not be any more influential for some people than Murphy's approach would be. But he states this in paragraph 5, when discussing the advantages of Murphy's view. He doesn't raise the issue of people without moral beliefs to prove this point.

> A 180 test taker recognizes choices that attempt to slap together two separate parts of the passage, comparing these distinct elements in a way that the author doesn't.

(E) is beyond the scope of the argument. The author never discusses the consequences of the "overdemandingness" problem. He merely describes this problem for us.

5. B

This question asks us for an inference regarding Murphy's views (as distinct from the author's views), and "the application of reason" is the key term that should jump out at you from the stem.

> A 180 test taker focuses on "buzzwords" in the question stem—words or phrases that strongly suggest the place in the passage that the answer will likely reside.

Where is the issue of "reason" discussed? In paragraph 3 we're told that a person can use reason to determine moral principles if his or her fundamental beliefs are conflicting or confused. Choice (B) reflects this notion perfectly.

(A), (C) The issue of some beliefs superseding others is not discussed in the passage. Neither is the issue of a belief system conflicting with an ethical principle.

(D) conflicts with the ideas in the passage. An individual who had no moral sense would not be able to apply Murphy's philosophy because he would lack an innate sense of right and wrong.

(E) explains the meaning of the overdemandingness problem, discussed in paragraphs 1 and 2. Murphy's philosophy responds to this problem in general—but the problem itself doesn't explain when reason should be used.

6. A

This "application" question requires us to take information from the passage and apply it to a situation not presented in the passage. We know from paragraph 3 that the use of Murphy's philosophy requires two steps. First, the person or group starts with innate beliefs about right or wrong and then uses reason if necessary to derive moral principles. The first step for the school board, then, is reflected in (A): Members would have to determine their fundamental beliefs regarding the dress code issue.

A 180 test taker is comfortable with questions that require her to apply ideas from the passage to alternative scenarios not raised in the passage itself. As with any other question, she makes sure her answer fits within the scope of the author's argument and can be reasonably deduced from the text.

(B) and (D) are irrelevant to the application of Murphy's philosophy. The author never states that analysis of other situations or historical precedents is necessary for determining moral principles with Murphy's view.

(C) Since the school board members are deciding the policy, according to Murphy they would need to start with their own beliefs—not those of the students.

(E) misrepresents the author's argument. In paragraph 3, the author merely compares Murphy to legal scholars who interpret the Constitution. He doesn't imply that people using Murphy's view must actually consult the Constitution.

A 180 test taker knows not to take analogies, or parallelisms, literally, but rather understands them in the context in which they are presented.

---

7. C

Finally, another "gimme" (hey, we deserve at least one or two on such a tough passage, right?). What does the author discuss in paragraph 5? As we saw in our initial analysis of the passage, here's where the advantages of Murphy's theory shine through. A quick scan of the answer choices reveals correct choice (C).

(A) Murphy doesn't give us any means of determining the best interpretation of beliefs—at least not in what we're told here.

(B) The "overdemandingness" issue is discussed in paragraph 1. That's *really* far away from the stuff at the end.

(D) The author does not address two schools of thought. Notice how this very realization is used to eliminate choices (B) and (C) in question 1.

(E) This idea is addressed in paragraph 3, where Murphy's views are summarized.

8. D

Which one of the answer choices would Murphy be likely to agree with? Well, we know enough about him by now to answer a more specific question, but hey, we're not psychic, so we better go right to the choices:

(A) contradicts the passage: People who argue from firmly held beliefs would be following Murphy's approach, not a traditional approach.

(B) Again, contradictory: Paragraph 5 tells us that these sorts of works have value—they just aren't as practical as Murphy's approach.

(C) exaggerates the author's argument. In paragraph 4, we're told only that people who lack moral sense won't be able to apply the particular approach developed by Murphy. However, they might still have contributions to make to ethical debates. We can't be sure from the passage that they would not contribute anything.

(D) is the winner. In the last paragraph of the passage, the author tells us that people who reject Murphy's premises aren't likely to accept traditional views either. What kind of people would reject Murphy's views? Moral skeptics, or those who have no moral sense at all, according to paragraph 3. So (D) provides the best inference here.

(E) We cannot determine whether the author himself believes that "overdemandingness" is a serious problem for traditional philosophy. We're only told that some scholars think it's not a serious problem, and that Murphy does take it seriously. The author's tone in the passage implies that he sides with Murphy—but we don't have enough information to be sure. So this statement is either definitely incorrect or too poorly supported to evaluate. Either way, it must be ruled out.

A 180 test taker keeps all of the characters in a passage straight, and can always differentiate between the views of the author and those of the personalities the author sets out to describe.

A Special Note for International Students

In recent years, U.S. law schools have experienced an increase in inquiries from non-U.S. citizens, some of whom are already practicing lawyers in their own countries. This surge of interest in the U.S. legal system has been attributed to the spread of the global economy. When business people from outside the United States do business with Americans, they often find themselves doing business under the American legal system. Gaining insight into how the American legal system works is of great interest around the world.

This new international interest in the U.S. legal system is having an effect on law schools. Many schools have developed special programs to accommodate the needs of this special population of lawyers and students from around the globe. If you are an international student or lawyer interested in learning more about the American legal system, or if you are considering attending law school in the United States, Kaplan can help you explore your options.

Getting into a U.S. law school can be especially challenging for students from other countries. If you are not from the United States, but are considering attending law school in the United States, here is what you'll need to get started.

- If English is not your first language, you'll probably need to take the TOEFL (Test of English as a Foreign Language), or provide some other evidence that you are proficient in English. Most law schools require a minimum computer TOEFL score of 250 (600 on the paper-based TOEFL) or better.

- Depending on the program to which you are applying, you may also need to take the LSAT (Law School Admissions Test). All law schools in the United States require the LSAT for their J.D. programs. LL.M. programs usually do not require the LSAT. Kaplan will help you determine if you need to take the LSAT. If you must take the LSAT, Kaplan can help you prepare for it.

- Since admission to law school is quite competitive, you may want to select three or four programs and complete applications for each school.

- You should begin the process of applying to law schools or special legal studies programs at least eighteen months before the fall of the year you plan to start your studies. Most programs will have only September start dates.

- In addition, you will need to obtain an I-20 Certificate of Eligibility from the school you plan to attend if you intend to apply for an F-1 Student Visa to study in the United States.

KAPLAN INTERNATIONAL PROGRAMS

If you need more help with the complex process of law school admissions, assistance preparing for the LSAT or TOEFL, or help building your English language skills in general, you may be interested in Kaplan's programs for international students.

Kaplan International Programs were designed to help students and professionals from outside the United States meet their educational and career goals. At locations throughout the United States, international students take advantage of Kaplan's programs to help them improve their academic and conversational English skills, raise their scores on the TOEFL, LSAT, and other standardized exams, and gain admission to the schools of their choice. Our staff and instructors give international students the individualized attention they need to succeed. Here is a brief description of some of Kaplan's programs for international students:

General Intensive English

Kaplan's General Intensive English classes are designed to help you improve your skills in all areas of English and to increase your fluency in spoken and written English. Classes are available for beginning to advanced students, and the average class size is 12 students.

English for TOEFL and University Preparation

This course provides you with the skills you need to improve your TOEFL score and succeed in an American university or graduate program. It includes advanced reading, writing, listening, grammar and conversational English, plus university admissions counseling. You will also receive training for the TOEFL using Kaplan's exclusive computer-based practice materials.

LSAT Test-Preparation Course

The LSAT is a crucial admission criterion for law schools in the United States. A high score can help you stand out from other applicants. This course includes the skills you need to succeed on each section of the LSAT, as well as access to Kaplan's exclusive practice materials.

Legal English Communication Review Course

This program is for international legal professionals and law students. Lessons include: mastering pronunciation, building your legal vocabulary, and developing presentation and legal writing skills.

Other Kaplan Programs

Since 1938, more than 3 million students have come to Kaplan to advance their studies, prepare for entry to American universities, and further their careers. In addition to the above programs, Kaplan offers courses to prepare for the SAT, GMAT, GRE, MCAT, DAT, USMLE, NCLEX, and other standardized exams at locations throughout the United States.

APPLYING TO KAPLAN INTERNATIONAL PROGRAMS

To get more information, or to apply for admission to any of Kaplan's programs for international students and professionals, contact us at:

Kaplan International Programs
370 Seventh Avenue, Suite 306
New York, NY 10001 USA
Telephone: (917) 339-7591 Fax: (917) 339-7505
Email: world@kaplan.com
Web: www.studyusa.kaplan.com

Kaplan is authorized under federal law to enroll nonimmigrant alien students.

Kaplan is authorized to issue Form IAP-66 needed for a J-1 (Exchange Visitor) visa.

Kaplan is accredited by ACCET (Accrediting Council for Continuing Education and Training).

Test names are registered trademarks of their respective owners.

What LSAT* course did students at the top 25 law schools take?

527-8378

All Others

75%

1997 Bruskin-Goldring Research Study of students at the top 25 law schools who prepped for the LSAT using a course

Call today to enroll!

KAPLAN®

1-800-KAP-TEST
kaptest.com

*LSAT is a registered trademark of the Law School Admission Council.